Walking in Circles

Walking in Circles

The Black Struggle for School Reform

Barbara A. Sizemore

Foreword by Safisha L. Madhubuti
Afterword by Asa G. Hilliard III

THIRD WORLD PRESS
Chicago

Third World Press
Publishers since 1967

First Edition
Printed in the United States of America
Cover Designer: Keir Thirus
Typesetter and Interior Designer: Relana Johnson
Editor: Solomohn Ennis

Library of Congress Cataloging-in-Publication Data
Sizemore, Barbara A.
Walking in circles : the black struggle for school reform / Barbara A. Sizemore.
p. cm.
Includes bibliographical references and index.
ISBN-13: 978-0-88378-252-1 (alk. paper)
ISBN-10: 0-88378-252-9 (alk. paper)
ISBN-13: 978-0-88378-298-9 (alk. paper)
ISBN-10: 0-88378-298-7 (alk. paper)
1. African Americans—Education—United States. 2. Discrimination in education—United States. 3. African American educators. 4. Educational change—United States. I. Title.
LC2717.S59 2007
371.829'96073—dc22
2007040987

Contents

Contents

Contents

Foreword

Barbara Ann Sizemore stood as a giant in the forest. Everyone who knew her well or occasionally has vivid memories of a woman warrior who always entered the room to make sure that the rights and needs of peoples of African descent and the poorest among us, especially the children, were placed front and center. She had no fear, none. She was filled with deep compassion and an intellect of unprecedented capacity. In one sense, she could be considered a renaissance woman, a high priestess with the gift of second sight who mastered many intellective disciplines. Regardless of the topic, you could be assured that Barbara would bring significant knowledge and a distinct, well-informed point of view.

Barbara wrote this book in the last two years of her life. She had been diagnosed with cancer. The doctors were never able to locate its source. So Barbara knew that her years were marked, both because of her life status as an elder and because of the illness. But Barbara faced the challenge of cancer as she did all others throughout her life, without an ounce of fear. Early on when she was first diagnosed, I talked with Barbara about possible alternative medical routes to consider. Barbara was emphatic that she had lived a full and a good life and she was simply not afraid to die. As I watched her through the next year and a half, I learned so many lessons about courage, about the gift of eternity that the Creator makes possible, and to be thankful for each day.

This book is reminiscent of Mary McLeod Bethune's (1996) *Last Will and Testament*. Like Barbara, Mary Bethune fought for the rights of her people and understood the essential political capital that education made possible. Like Barbara, Mary Bethune realized that education is capital through which a people negotiate and navigate their place in the world. In her *Last Will and Testament*, Mrs. Bethune wrote:

> I leave you ... a responsibility to our young people. The world around us really
> belongs to youth for youth will take over its future management. Our children must
> never lose their zeal for building a better world. They must never be discouraged

from aspiring toward greatness, for they are to be the leaders of tomorrow. Nor must they forget that the masses of our people are still under-privileged, ill-housed, impoverished and victimized by discrimination. We have a powerful potential in our youth, and we must have the courage to change old ideas and practices so that we may direct their power toward good ends." (pp. 672–673)

Those tenets hold true as steadfastly today as much as they did fifty years ago when Mrs. Bethune wrote them. Mrs. Bethune wrote the testament because she had a vision of the future and what would be required for people of African descent to re-ascend the world stage. She understood that our history did not begin with the African Holocaust, but rather, as she said, that we are heirs to a great civilization. She understood that the values which allowed us to survive generations of enslavement and Jim Crow would continue to serve us in the new delicate waters of the Civil Rights Movement and its current legacy. The legacy of enslavement, of Jim Crow into which she was born, and the dilemmas of the post civil rights era are the inheritance with which Barbara Sizemore wrestled.

In many respects, this book chronicles not only Barbara's own personal and professional history, but equally important the book provides a critical analysis of the political forces that have shaped the course of African American education, indeed African American life over the last fifty years. Barbara's penchant for detail abounds in this book as well as her deep interest in history. In chapter 1, we learn details about the Laffoon family across generations leading to the birth of Barbara Ann Laffoon, known affectionately by family as Bobran. In recounting her early years as a child and adolescent growing up first in Terre Haute, Indiana and then moving to Evanston, Illinois, we see the spirit of the woman-to-be in the child: feisty, inquisitive, daring, and curious. These traits were both developed in the social contexts of her family and community and sustained in spite of them. It is clear from this early history that Barbara was a very complex human being.

I can remember Barbara recounting the stories of life at Northwestern University where she earned both an undergraduate degree in classical languages with an emphasis on Latin and much later in life a Master's Degree in Education. These stories were particularly compelling to me because I teach at Northwestern. Barbara told me that when she was a student there in the 1940s, Blacks could not live on campus. A dear friend of my mother, Leontyne Lemon, attended Northwestern a decade before Barbara tells the same story. Barbara had learned the difficult and tenuous paths of navigating integrated schools through her experiences at Evanston Township High School. Thus life at Northwestern at that time was not a surprise. Barbara played a leadership role in protesting Northwestern's segregation policy, much to the dismay of her mother. Barbara told me that her mother said she could stand on protest lines after she received her degree. Her mother's reaction captures the complexities of African American struggles: what price to pay to gain access to resources that represent future potential, psychologically understanding what that price means in terms of one's own personhood, and the ability to navigate across multiple spaces each requiring different norms, different demands for participation. My best friend, Kimya Moyo, also attended Northwestern University, but during the early 1970s. (She was among the handful of Black students at the university who took over the administration building to struggle for African American studies, increased Black enrollment and Black faculty.) One legacy of that struggle was the establishment of The Black House as it is affectionately known by Northwestern students, now officially the home for African American student affairs. On the wall is a picture of Kimya, then Saundra Malone, standing near the window of the administration building, and her father outside the window pleading for her to come out. Barbara had great insight in calling this book *Walking in Circles*. While Northwestern University has come a long way, some sixty years after Barbara graduated, the university for the last decade has had a standing university wide committee whose mission is to monitor and recommend policies to increase minority student enrollment and faculty recruitment. Despite its efforts, the African American student population has remained around 5 percent, and African American faculty between 2 and 3 percent. I use Northwestern as the example here not to berate the university. I have worked there for fifteen years and two of my children have graduated from the university. I clearly hold Northwestern University in high esteem as did Barbara. I choose it because Barbara and I both have intimate histories there.

As with other universities, the challenges at Northwestern are influenced by the broader set of political, economic and cultural issues in the society at large, problems which Barbara dedicated her entire life to battling. The biggest culprit is the dire state of K–12 public education for African American, Latino/a, American Indian, some Asian American groups and for youth from low income backgrounds generally. Lack of adequate housing, employment opportunities, social support services, and health care all conspire to create significant challenges for African American and other minority youth as well as youth from low income communities. However, Barbara knew from her own educational experiences in all Black segregated schools during the 1930s and 1940s that poverty in no way precludes the ability to learn. Barbara states emphatically throughout the book, and in every professional encounter I had with her that all children can learn when teachers have high expectations and have deep understanding of subject matter and how people learn. Barbara was the epitome herself of the master teacher. When she was a teacher at Dvorak elementary school on the west side of Chicago, she said that parents would say, "Mrs. Sizemore can teach a brick to read."

Besides serving as a critical documentary on key issues and events of the last fifty years, this is also the story of ordinary people, particularly educators about whom no media writes: from Mrs. Ella Mae Cunningham who taught Barbara as a young inexperienced teacher at Shoop Elementary School to Mrs. Thelma Gray who as one of the early principals under whom Barbara worked taught her fundamental lessons about school organization and leadership. These unnamed educators represent the kinds of liberating professionals that Michele Foster (1997) and Vanessa Siddle Walker (1996) document, many of whom in the South were displaced in the civil rights and post-civil rights era. They are the same educators whose voices continue to be unheard in current accountability reforms, but they are also a dying breed, difficult to find among those who teach the children of the poor in America's urban landscape. Barbara never looked at the world through rose-colored glasses. She understood clearly not only what teachers needed to know to teach all our children, but also how schools as organizations needed to go about supporting the joint learning of teachers and families.

Barbara was highly successful in doing what many who profess liberation have not done. She created institutional structures to bring her ideas into fruition and demonstrated empirically how to build institutions where youth with the greatest needs can flourish intellectually, emotionally, physically and socially. Her work in transforming schools in Pittsburgh, Washington, D.C. and Chicago is unprecedented, even in comparison to a number of large scale, highly funded major reform efforts in this country. And yet Barbara always had to fight to secure funding for her research and school intervention work. She was never funded at the level of other programs, many of which she critiques in the book, almost all of whose leadership are white scholars (with the exception of the Comer Project) (Comer, 1980). Whether such programs show significant achievement gains for Black, Brown and poor students generally, they continue to be funded and held up as the answer to the dilemmas of public education in the United States. Barbara attacks many of these alternatives for school, accountability and curriculum design in this book as she did in life. I know personally that when many of these very well intentioned scholars saw Barbara coming, they would turn in the opposite direction because they knew that on any playing field, Barbara would use well grounded data to raise very discomforting questions. There are many who will be very uncomfortable reading this book—white and Black, scholar and practitioner, politician and community activists—because Barbara never discriminated in whom she criticized. Her fundamental question was always:

> What is the evidence that this will result in significant increases in academic achievement for Black and Brown students, youth living in poverty, or youth with special needs?

Whether it was small schools, decentralization of schools, alternative certification of teachers, arguments against social promotion, school hiring policies, or university-based models for professional development, Barbara publicly deconstructed their arguments always with data. And sad to say, more often than not, the responses to Barbara's public attacks were not grounded in data driven counter-arguments, but rather personal attacks against her. This pattern followed Barbara from Chicago, to Pittsburgh, to Washington, D.C. and back to Chicago again. In our educated circles, we do not like direct attacks. We prefer to dance around one another, with polite round-abouts. Barbara did not.

Barbara offers in this book at least two lines of critique that get to the heart of the dilemmas that African Americans face. She provides very detailed analyses of the rise and demise of several Black organizations and of several prototypes of district reform and its consequent models of school transformation. Both venues offer a lens for understanding some of the fundamental challenges of the African American struggle for self-determination. Her analyses of the African Heritage Association and the National Association of Black School Educators (formerly the National Association of Black School Principals) are stunning and informative. She brings these analyses not as an outsider, but as one intimately involved with the early development of these institutions. The struggles over ideological clarity, in-house struggles over political direction, and the ever-persistent problem of insufficient funding come across loud and clear. These struggles are in no way restricted to these organizations, but are endemic to our efforts to build sustainable institutions that directly address the needs of our people. Her analyses of reform movements in Pittsburgh and Chicago (including her analysis of her experiences as superintendent of the Washington, D.C. school system from 1973 to 1975 in her first book *The Ruptured Diamond*), unearth the persistent contradictions and political struggles that undermine these efforts to transform our urban schools. We see so many instances in which excellence in achievement is neither rewarded nor acknowledged, while unending perks accrue to institutions and people who are politically connected; where new reforms are instituted despite the fact that there is no strong empirical base to support them, and as a consequence reforms come and go with little long term impact on the health of the system. Barbara's descriptions of both the evolution of these Black institutions and the system wide school reform efforts are ripe with very detailed information about people and events. Barbara's acumen as an archivist and historian are very evident here. As one who lives in Chicago, I was delighted to see Barbara name so many key players whom I remember from the 1960s and 1970s, most of whom would go unheralded without Barbara's meticulous record keeping.

Two issues repeated across the book have to do with decentralization versus centralization and with racism, the persistent elephant in the room. Barbara took an adamant position about the role of a strong principal in setting the tone, expectations, supports and routines for high expectations and rigorous but flexible teaching practices. That was the kind of principal Barbara was at Forrestville High School (where I first met Barbara), Dvorak Elementary School and later as the head of the Woodlawn Experimental District, an early Chicago experiment in decentralization and community based control of schools. Barbara consistently drew on the research base of scholars like Ronald Edmonds (1979) to demonstrate with empirical evidence the impact of this conception of school leadership. When the Chicago Public Schools moved to establish local school councils to provide administrative oversight and the power to hire and fire principals, Barbara argues vociferously that the lessons of the Oceanhill-Brownville district in New York, efforts in Pittsburgh, or even earlier efforts in Chicago itself were neither examined nor taken into account. As a consequence, Chicago was not able to sustain high levels of community involvement. Beyond that, Barbara raised difficult questions about who should make key professional decisions. Such questions are difficult because most parents do not have the knowledge base to make instructional decisions, but ironically in schools serving the Black, Brown and poor, neither do most teachers or principals. But it is not like we don't know how to teach all children to high standards. We have literally hundreds of examples of schools where these same children excel, many of them directly through the efforts of Barbara Ann Sizemore. There are many culprits contributing to the pervasive low levels of achievement in schools serving Black, Brown and poor children: inequitable funding, licensing standards for teaching, pre-service teacher training, professional development opportunities, basic skills orientation to instruction, inadequate facilities and access to technology. But the underlying question is why these culprits remain and why they are so pervasive.

Barbara's answer and the historical record shout loud and clear. Racism informs the underlying set of beliefs that are institutionalized in practice. Whether you examine the record in 1776, 1976, and 2006, you will continue to see unveiled, out in the open, assertions of Black inferiority. While a residential fellow at the Center for Advanced Studies in the Behavioral Sciences at Stanford University in 2004, I was walking in the Stanford campus bookstore in the sociology section. Lo and behold I see a book entitled *Race: The Reality of Human Difference* (Sarich & Miele, 2004). I examine the book and there before me is the master narrative unfolded again. And for our purposes, the claims are made on the basis of scientific research, just as it was in the 1600s, the 1700s, the 1800s, and the 1900s. It is perhaps Barbara's keen understanding of the impact of racism and her unwavering ability to see racism in its manifold manifestations, hidden in gentility and liberal advocations that made her such an annoyance to the educational reform community, to politicians, to professional interest groups, at the university, in the school building, in the school district, in the city, and state legislatures. But let me acknowledge there were many in these communities who understood Barbara's vision and who loved her. Paul Vallas, former head of the Chicago Public Schools and currently superintendent in Philadelphia; the staff of the School Academic Structure (SAS) which she founded at DePaul University and the many schools where Barbara worked in the trenches and actually improved the academic achievement of schools with long histories of under-achievement; her colleagues at NABSE (National Association of Black School Educators) who shared her vision for Black achievement; the parents and children, most of whom are now adults, who experienced her as a principal and a teacher who "could teach a brick to read"; those activist-scholars across disciplines who believe that excellent public education is a right of citizenship, so many of whom worked with Barbara in the struggle for Black self-determination. So many people have been touched by this woman's life.

When esteemed scholar Dr. Asa Hilliard heard of Barbara's death, he was traveling in Ghana, West Africa. He said he knew he had to leave immediately because he had to stand and bear witness at the Home Going ceremony for Barbara. My husband and I sat in the audience with Asa and hundreds of others who loved Barbara. I sat saddened by her death and fighting back tears until Ollie McLemore took the stage. Ollie McLemore is one of our premier educators, recognized by President William Clinton for her leadership, and a colleague of Barbara's at SAS. Ollie played a clip from Barbara's last public presentation, on a panel discussion about the education of Black youth in Chicago. The hosts were Chicago television news anchors Diann Burns and Warner Saunders. They asked Barbara a question, hoping she would give a short response. But Barbara went on and on. Diann and Warner looked at each other. Other members of the esteemed panel looked at each other. And finally all sat quiet and listened to the wisdom, the stark and brutal truths that the elder among them bestowed. I knew in that moment, Barbara lives. Here she is as powerful in death as she was when she walked amongst us. She lives in the feisty vision and commitments of her children. She lives in the work we are trying to do at the Betty Shabazz International Charter School where she was a member of the Board of Directors. And when I see the vision, the unwillingness to fail, the energy to do good in the world in the children in our school, I know that Barbara lives. Everyday now when I wrestle with a question of education or a question of principled struggle, I literally ask myself, what would Barbara say?

Barbara calls this book *Walking in Circles*. She knew first hand about walking in circles. When she first became the inaugural Dean of the School of Education at DePaul University, she moved to an apartment on Chicago's prestigious North Lake Shore Drive. One Sunday morning, she was in the basement doing her laundry. An older white woman came down and saw that Barbara was using all of the laundry machines. She looked at Barbara and said, "tell your employer that you are not to use all the laundry machines at one time. Other people have to use them as well." Barbara looked the elderly woman in the eye and brashly said, "I certainly will tell the President of DePaul University just what you said." In 2002, this took place. As Barbara sadly notes in the closing paragraph of the book, we continue to walk in circles, in part, because as a nation we have not faced the multi-horned monster of our historical legacy of racism; and as a people, African Americans have not assumed the fighting spirit that ancestors showed when after so-called emancipation in 1865 from the horrors of the African Holocaust of

Enslavement, the very first institutions they developed were schools (Anderson, 1988) to serve their interests as a people. This book will contribute much to helping our community wrestle with the dilemmas of *Walking in Circles* in the hope that we can together build the institutions necessary for our children's future.

Carol D. Lee (Safisha L. Madhubuti), Ph.D.
Professor, Northwestern University, School of Education and Social Policy; Chairman of the Board of Directors, Betty Shabazz International Charter Schools

Preface

A bias is a predisposition to believe something or think something or some way to the point in which one cannot believe or think in another way. Biases obstruct objectivity. Objectivity is the condition of emphasizing or expressing the nature of reality as it is, apart from personal feelings or prejudices. Scientists try to control or eliminate biases in pursuit of objectivity. My position is that objectivity, like perfection, is an ideal condition. Humans can approximate it, but cannot achieve it. Since I believe that all work is subjective because it is filtered through the prism of human experience and that experience creates bias.

My research is based on the following beliefs: (1) all children can learn; (2) race, poverty, gender, class, family configuration, crime or violence do not prevent students from learning what they are motivated and inspired to learn, especially when taught by superior (committed) teachers and parents; and (3) ordinary teachers can elevate and accelerate learning in children from the most disadvantaged backgrounds if those teachers know what they are teaching and understand how their learners process information and apply it. Throughout this book, I declare my biases and trace my experiences in education to illustrate how I came to have them and how they influence what I did on a daily basis in my various professional capacities. It is my hope that the revelations springing from the impact of these experiences will illuminate the readers' understanding of the work that I have done and its results. Although this book is not an autobiography, much of it is autobiographical. However, as a young person I did not keep diaries, nor do I have complete scripts for all of the conversations I have recorded here. Thus, the conversations are my and my family's recollections; as such, they are approximations of what took place.

Lastly, this book is not in strict chronological order; consequently, some causes are linked directly to their eventual effects, and not according to their respective time.

Acknowledgements

This book has been written, first, to satisfy the requests from Nancy Arnez, Haki Madhubuti, Geneva Smitherman and the many conference participants who have yearned for information about my studies of high achieving predominantly African American public schools serving students who live in low–income census zones characterized by crime and violence; and, second, to respond to the persistent prodding of Asa G. Hilliard III who was my mentor even though I am older than he is. This work is dedicated to the many principals who made these schools, namely: Sherwin Allen, Janet Bell, Doris Brevard, Sandra Givens, J. Jerome Harris, Regina Holley, Rollie Jones, Napoleon Lewis, Lawrence Nee, Melver Scott, Louise Smith, Hazel Steward, Louis Venson, and Vivian Williams.

I am indebted to Marjorie Branch, Margaret Harrigan, Phedonia Johnson, Ollie McLemore and the School Achievement Structure (SAS) coordinators for all the things they have taught me about school reform and bringing about change. This book would never have happened without the love, care and assistance of my daughter, Kymara Chase. And there would be no story about success in Chicago if it had not been for the courage, conviction and commitment of Paul Vallas, former chief executive officer of the Chicago Public Schools, who, knowing that all children can learn, believed that we must make it happen now. "Children First! No Excuses!"

In the highest regard, I am always indebted to my family for its sustaining inspiration: Kymara Chase, Kafi Chase, Lansing Edward Chase III, Furman G. Sizemore, Beatena Nance, Marimba Milliones, Momar Milliones, Aldwin E. Stewart, and my deceased parents Delila Mae Stewart, and Sylvester Laffoon.

Introduction

I was born a year-and-a-half before the Great Depression on December 17, 1927, in Chicago's Cook County Hospital, during Jim Crow. Being born during that period destined me, a Black American, to be in enrolled in a rigorous social course covering the finer points of racism.

I began working in the Chicago Public schools in 1947. During my lifetime I have been a teacher, principal, director and superintendent of schools. I have seen, with my own eyes, how the implementation of unconventional, advanced education models achieved substantial accomplishments in some of the poorest urban schools in the United States. Specifically, the model that was once practiced at Pittsburgh public schools: Beltzhoover, Madison, McKelvy, Vann, and Westwood. Regrettably, the betterment was short-lived (like it is so often, for so many, across the U.S. and abroad;) because, foundations, corporations, politicians, practitioners, groups and individuals who had other goals (particularly the preservation and expansion of white supremacy and its counterpart, the imputation of Black inferiority) sabotaged progress.

This book has taken twenty years to write mainly because I have procrastinated waiting for a success story to tell. Unfortunately, the successes went unheeded because they were anomalies which provided evidence for the falseness of white superiority and denied credibility to the imputation of Black inferiority therein. I was certain that the Pittsburgh Public Schools would replicate the major successes at Beltzhoover, Madison, McKelvy, Vann and Westwood. It did not. In fact, it destroyed them. The African American community in Pittsburgh lost its direction and failed to support the models created in those schools. They changed the nature of their struggle to the appointment of high black officials in the administration. When the heroic principals of those schools retired and disappeared, they returned to the practices which assured failure for predominantly Black schools.

There was absolutely no support for the story of effective schools. Plugging along since 1978 major efforts have been made to reveal and describe these schools to concerned people. But the foundations and corporations, the politicians and practitioners had another goal: the preservation and expansion of white supremacy and its counterpart, the imputation of Black inferiority.

Because I was a part of the glorious 1960s and 1970s, my belief that my country, the United States of America, could live up to its major goal, government of the people, by the people and for the people, was strong. After all, I had been born during Jim Crow, and I knew how it felt to be relegated to the back of the bus, the Colored Section of the movie house, to be denied the right to eat at F.W. Woolworth's stores or to try on certain clothes at a department store. I also learned during those years that strong coalitions were possible to redress past wrongs and that all white people were not bad. The real problem for Black people is that there are not enough white people who feel that way.

I realized that my struggle against white supremacy and the imputation of Black inferiority was a circular one when I became Dean of the School of Education. Forced with the choice between a highly experienced African American female with a five year old doctorate from the University of Chicago and a newly graduated white female recipient of the doctoral degree, the faculty recruitment committee chose the white female. They chose her because she was a close and intimate friend of another faculty member. So if you have no friends on a faculty, you will hardly be chosen. Since the faculty members are overwhelmingly white and since qualifications are secondary to friendship, white supremacy continues. Since these sessions are private, and rights to privacy can be invoked if information is sought, the process remains uninterrupted.

Lastly, as my life ends, I must encourage the freedom fighters who follow that any approach which fails to address white supremacy and its counterpart, the imputation of Black inferiority, will force you to walk in circles as I have done. Unless you want to wind up where you came in, seek strong confrontation to white supremacy at every opportunity and keep the glare on it.

Barbara A. Sizemore
January 13, 2003

CHAPTER 1

THE ROOTS OF MY BIASES

At earlier times in my life I may have written for somewhat personal reasons, but I now write for these five: (1) For the total, uncompromising Liberation of Black people. (2) For the creation of a just world-order where each and every person is able to reach his or her highest potential and in doing so not violate the cultural or human rights of his or her neighbors as we all strive to live and develop in an atmosphere of productive peace. (3) Writing is the most lasting and the major (yet limiting) form of communication that I have access to that reaches a good number of Black people. (4) Writing is a cleansing, dialectical, meditative and communicative process that helps keep me honest and committed to struggle, keeps me open minded and active among those I dearly care for, many of whom I do not have daily contact with. (5) I love my people and know the greatness we have in us and know that that greatness, at this time in our lives, must be continuously pushed and forced out of us if we are to survive and develop as a people. Writing is one of the enforcers that I use.

—Haki R. Madhubuti, *Enemies: The Clash of Races*

Section 1.1 Along Winding Route 41

My earliest memories are of traveling through Indiana and Chicago during that time and learning "what my place was." During World War II, my maternal grandmother, who always preferred to call us colored people, and I would often ride the Chicago and Eastern Illinois (C&EI) Railroad to Chicago, passing through towns like Danville, Hoopeston and Chicago Heights. My grandmother would pack chicken sandwiches, fruit and pie for me. One time, when I was around thirteen years old, my stepfather's best friend, Willard Waugh, accompanied me. He was a soldier, and he was a lot of fun. He made people laugh so much that we hardly knew we were Negroes on that trip.

Chicago was the great migration center for African Americans during the 1930s. I vividly remember the long drives from Terre Haute, Indiana to Chicago, along winding Route 41. Route 41 ran north from Terre Haute through many towns whose names I learned, but whose terrain I never visited: Clinton, Attica, Hammond, Gary and finally Chicago. Kentland was the midpoint time-wise, and we often stopped there at the NuJoy Restaurant to eat and go to the toilet because it was a Greyhound Bus stop. At places other than Greyhound Bus stops, having to go to the bathroom usually meant inconveniences. I never knew when my parents would say that they didn't serve Negroes at some Indiana rest stop. My father called it redneck, Indiana Redneck was a popular name for bigoted white folks. They were also called crackers and honkies. My parents never used honky.

An excerpt from *Indiana: A New Historical Guide*[1] says: "Terre Haute, French for "high land" is Indiana's ninth largest city and the seat of justice of Vigo County named after a Sardinian named Francis Vigo (pronounced Vee-go) who supplied George Rogers Clark with information, money and materials for use in ending British influence in the Northwest Territory." This extremely Eurocentric history of Terre Haute makes no mention of the free Blacks aggregated in the rural part of the County whose first deeds were registered in 1810, but it does mention in passing that this land originally belonged to the

Wea or Quiatenon Indians prior to its occupation and the construction of Fort Harrison in 1811.

Negroes settled in Vigo County, of which Terre Haute was the seat, in the early years of the nineteenth century. Free and emancipated, they came from North Carolina. The first Negro to live in Terre Haute was a slave, Armistead Stewart, and came in 1815 with his master Daniel Durham, a Quaker who brought other Negroes with him on return trips. Dixon Stewart, born in 1801 and manumitted from slavery in 1827 in Wake County, North Carolina, came to Vigo County in 1829 and acquired eighty acres of government land. Dixon married Lucinda Roberts, who was born in North Carolina in 1809, and they had four sons and four daughters: Elisha, Nancy, Mary, Joseph, Julia, Dixon Jr., Thomas and Sara. Jeremiah and Abel Anderson had 240 acres and the Roberts family acquired 280. This was virgin land from which trees had to be cleared and brush removed in order to farm it.

Section 1.2   Vigo County, Terre Haute (We're From Lost Creek)

In 1830, Negro migration to Lost Creek Township increased. By 1860, a large number of Negroes had settled in Terre Haute. By the time of his death, Dixon Stewart had acquired a total of 900 acres of land, which he divided among his eight children. One hundred acres went to each of his sons and seventy-five acres went to each of his daughters. By 1835, Vigo County Negro settlers had built a combined school and meeting house on Lost Creek Township land donated by Kinchen and Nancy Roberts.

Kinchen Roberts had emigrated from Virginia and owned 280 acres of land. The log building was located on the northwest corner of the Stop Ten Road and Fort Harrison Road. This structure was used as a general meeting place and for educational and religious services; Methodists and Hard Shell Baptists practiced the washing of the feet as Jesus demonstrated in John 13: 5–7, and they would meet there. Its first Methodist minister was William Paul Quinn; and John Alexander was the superintendent of the Sabbath School.

The 1850 census showed that forty-one Negroes owned land valued at $37,850.00 In January of 1850, Reverend Lewis Artis organized the Missionary Baptist Church, later called the Lost Creek Baptist Church. The first frame building was destroyed by fire in 1868, but it was rebuilt in 1869.[2]

Section 1.3 Paternal Ancestry

My paternal grandfather, William Laffoon, was born in Crofton, Kentucky, Christian County, on July 3, 1879. My paternal grandmother, Viola (Violet) Rudy Laffoon, was born in Providence, Kentucky, Webster County, on May 31, 1885. William and Viola married in 1898 and moved to Mt. Vernon, Indiana. They had three surviving children: Leefronia, born March 30, 1901, in Mt. Vernon, Indiana (Posey County); Herbert William, born December 26, 1903, and Sylvester Walter, both born in Terre Haute, Indiana. William and Viola's second child, Justine, died in infancy. My paternal great grandfather was George Washington Columbus Laffoon, and his father was said to be John Bledsoe Laffoon, a white man, who was also the father of Governor Ruby Laffoon, (governor of Kentucky 1931–1935).[3]

George W.C. Laffoon, also known as Lum, married Emerline Robinson. To this couple seven children were born: Beverly, William (my grandfather), Horace, Mary, Sallie, Birdie, and Georgia. When Emerline died, Lum married Sally Barker, and to them three children were born: Barker, Goldie and Augusta. Upon Sally Barker's death, Lum married Lottie Ramsey Bounds, and to them three more children were born: Ira, Vashti and Lum, Jr. My paternal great grandfather also had an out-of-wedlock child with Mattie Clark named Walter Clark.

My paternal grandmother, Viola Rudy, (Grandpa called her Violet,) was the youngest and sixth child born to Isaac and Charlotte Parker Rudy. Her oldest sister, Janie Rudy Ware Brown, raised her. William and Viola Laffoon moved to Terre Haute, Indiana in 1903. Initially, William and Viola had a couple's job as a chauffeur and maid in downtown Terre Haute. Later, William Laffoon opened a restaurant and was the first Black man to have a business on the main street, Wabash Avenue at Sixteenth Street. This restaurant made a good living for the Laffoons until the Great Depression of 1929. After his business folded my grandfather took odd jobs here and there. He later opened a barbershop and finally another restaurant, at Fourteenth Street and Crawford Avenue. The restaurant was very successful and many people patronized the spot, including local musicians who could often be found playing for dinner. He also built up a good clientele for the barbershop, and until 1940, it too was doing well.

Grandma Laffoon loved to cook. It was an art for her. She was the main chef in Grandpa's restaurants. I can remember sitting in her kitchen licking cake batter from bowls, and eating pies and hamburgers. My Grandmother could make a hamburger taste like roasted duck, her specialty and preferred delicacy. She also had a peculiar dialect and used strange words for common things; for example, a "banket" was called a "curb." When she became excited, she talked so fast that her speech took on a foreign language sound. People said she was a "Geechee," leading some to believe her family's roots were in South Carolina. My Uncle Herbert also sometimes sounded that way when he became upset and emotional.

Grandma Laffoon was very modest. I never saw her undressed. Even when I would get up early in the morning to catch her dressing, she would be standing there in her long white apron with her hair in a net. She was petite, never weighing more than 112 pounds. Grandpa, who was over six-feet tall, dwarfed her. They had a big brass bed—although it does not seem so big now that I have it. She would roll me around on that big feather bed and we would laugh and laugh. I loved her. Grandpa left my management to Grandma and she was ever present. I recall that one day Dr. John Wesley Lyda Sr., later to be my seventh-grade teacher and author of *The Negro in the History of Indiana*,[4] came in for a haircut. He had very little hair. I asked him why he came to the barbershop when he had no hair. I can hear Grandpa bellowing, "Violet! Violet! Come and get Bobran." Grandma came and got me, and although I was almost as big as her, she picked me up and carried me back to her kitchen.

She was always my friend and loved me unconditionally. She never said an unkind word about anybody or anything to me. She was stoic, bearing life's woes without complaint, silent, sturdy and strong. She was a black-skinned wry thin woman with a soft voice that wrapped around you, healing all wounds. Grandmother was also a very gentle woman, she never raised her voice. She was loyal, faithful, dependable and reliable. One day, she had forgotten that she was supposed to dress, but she had her pocketbook with her bus fare in it. When Grandma Laffoon was eighty-eight, Aunt Fronie (Leefronia) took her to live with her in Los Angeles, California.

Section 1.4 Maternal Ancestry

My maternal grandfather, Jesse James Alexander, was born on August 30, 1885. When Jesse was seven years old, his father died, leaving his mother with children ranging in ages from one to fourteen years. Both sides of the families came to her aid, but two years later Nancy died at the age of thirty-five. A year after their mother's death all of the children had settled with different aunts and uncles. At age eighteen, my grandfather's brother, James Turner, found himself on his own and became the first to migrate to Evanston, Illinois. Jesse was taken in by a strict aunt who was very demanding and harsh.

My maternal grandmother, Myrtle Mae Evans, was born on April 8, 1890, to Delila Evans from an alleged illicit union with a white doctor, named Creel or Creal, or his son. Delila's parents, were Margaret Rose Burnett Evans and Jesse Evans who had four children: Elizabeth, whom we called Aunt Lib, Delila and the twins Charlie and Maude. Much gossip was bandied around about these pretty ladies and Uncle Charlie. Nothing could be confirmed in spite of oral history and community gossip and the real truth was carried to the grave.

Myrtle Mae grew up in the household of her mother, her stepfather, Tazwell Howard, and her two half brothers, Murrell and Burrell, in Crawfordsville, Indiana. When she was fourteen she married Jesse James Alexander. They had fourteen children: Hortense; Delila; Nancy Madelyn; Elva Marguerite, who later changed her name to Evelyn; James Albert; Bonnie, who later changed her name to Helen Rosetta; and Orville Arthur. In addition, two sets of twins and one set of triplets died in infancy. Grandmother Alexander worked as a cook and maid for white people until she left Grandpa. The family folklore says that she worked at one time for Birch Bayh's grandparents in Rushville, Indiana. She was a great cook too. Nobody in this world could make better baked beans and meatloaf than Grandma!

In an unpublished paper prepared for family reunions, Alice Bethel, granddaughter of James Turner Alexander, brother to Jesse James Alexander, reports that James Alexander, is listed as a freed slave born in Virginia with family (no names were given) in the 1810 census of Mercer County, Danville, Kentucky. Bethel wrote: "By the 1820s, also living in Danville was Free Frank from Pulaski County, Kentucky, a successful businessman in his own right. Free Frank had a partner whose name was Free Zibe (Harrison). Undoubtedly, all three men knew of each other. It is thought, James Alexander operated a stable there." And Bethel noted:

In 1836, Daniel Alexander, son of James, married Pantha Harrison, daughter of Zibe. This marriage was witnessed by Zeba Harrison. The settlement in which they lived for most of their lives became a target for white segregationists. No legal action had been taken to protect them, even though complaints were filed.

The attacks were taking a toll on Pantha, mentally and physically. Daniel along with a few of his neighbors scouted for other territories outside of Mercer County, Kentucky. He finally settled in Washington County, Indiana, sent for his family and started anew. Daniel and Pantha show up in the 1850 and 1860 censuses. On the 1860 census a notation is made about Pantha as 'insane at intervals'. Daniel and Pantha bought 80 acres of land for $425 from William Lowery in Howard Township, Washington, County on Canton Road near Salem, Indiana where there existed a settlement of freed Blacks. On December 8, 1864, Daniel and Pantha sold their property back to William Lowery for $350 signing the bill of sale with an X. By 1870 there was not one Black living in Howard Township, Washington County due to the white organizations that had formed and restricted freed Blacks by dubious means after the Civil War.

Daniel and Pantha Alexander had eight children: Betsy, Martha, Nancy, Susan, Pantha D., Alfred Westly, Eliza, and John. Nancy, Susan, Eliza and John appear on the 1880 census for Otto Creek Township, Vigo County, Indiana. The dates and whereabouts of all others are unknown. John Thomas (JT) Alexander married Nancy Norton, the daughter of William and Elizabeth Norton, who established their roots in Otter Creek Township, Vigo County, Indiana in the 1840s, on December 13, 1878. John Alexander and Nancy Alexander had nine children, eight of whom survived to adulthood: James Turner, Luetta, Ella, Blanch, Jesse James, Eura, Stella and Agnes. An unnamed baby boy died in infancy. I knew only Uncle Turner and Aunt Stella.

Jesse James Alexander worked two jobs all of his adult life. Taylor et al. say in their book, *Indiana: A New Historical Guide*, that at the time Terre Haute "dreamed of being the Pittsburgh of the West," as Birmingham dreamed for the south, because of the coal which stood second to farm produce as the area's most valuable commodity by 1900." Grandpa worked in the coalmines from five o'clock in the morning until one o' clock in the afternoon. Afterward, he came home to work his farm until twilight, then he ate dinner and retired. He continued this grueling routine until coal mining declined in the 1930s, due to "an outgrowth of mechanized underground digging, the inception of strip mining and its shift to less depleted deposits in far southwest Indiana, coal company consolidations, competition from petroleum, electricity and cheap coal extracted in nonunion fields in Kentucky and West Virginia."[5]

Section 1.5   My Parents and Their Marriage

On December 17, 1927, I was received into two big cohesive families that were generally unaffectionate toward each other. I was the only child of Sylvester Walter Laffoon and Delila Mae Alexander Laffoon. My parents were ill matched, my father ever searching for new opportunities, and my mother perpetually struggling for stability. God was good to me, I got to know my parents, though not well.

My father, Sylvester Laffoon, was the youngest child of four children born to William and Viola Laffoon on February 14, 1905, in Terre Haute, Indiana. My mother, Delila Mae Alexander, was the second-oldest child of fourteen children born to Jesse James and Myrtle Mae Alexander. She was born on September 25, 1907, in Highland, a rural area now incorporated into Terre Haute.[6]

It was always interesting to me how my mother was the pillar of the family, but not held in the highest esteem. Mama gave in too much. She was too passive. She didn't like a fight, but she was always in the middle of one. Delila was a complex but compassionate mother. She was absolutely resolute about education. (Her child, grandchildren and great-grandchildren graduated from college.) She was always there when you needed her. She was family oriented and directed. Everything was done for family, nothing for herself. She was always saving for the rainy day, because of that she had very few sunny ones.

My father was a remarkable man. Being Black during Jim Crow was not easy. A Black man had been lynched in Terre Haute in 1909 when Sylvester, whom everyone called Sy, was four years old. Segregation, though not fiercely enforced on buses or in housing, was firmly enforced in movie houses, stores and restaurants.

Sy graduated from the integrated Wiley High School in June 1925, having distinguished himself as a football champion and a state track relay athlete. Daddy was a strong athlete, and his brother Herbert was a Wabash Valley All State Champion, the first in Indiana. The Black community held the Laffoon family in high esteem. He went on to Indiana State Teachers College (ISTC) and graduated from there in 1932 with a Bachelor's Degree in Physical Education.

When my father was a student at ISTC, his psychology professor was teaching the theory of the inferiority of the Negro. He maintained that the intelligence of the Negro was genetically low. Classmates and friends of my

9

father's, Campbell Upthegrove and John Wesley Lyda, Jr., told me I accompanied him to class when I was around five or six to take an intelligence test with several white children whose fathers were professors. Everyone testifies to the fact that I was precocious and bright. They said after the test was conducted I emerged with the highest score putting the professor's theory in jeopardy. He told me the Negroes in the class were elated, but all I wanted was some candy.

Because of the Depression and discrimination my father was never able to secure employment in the field for which he was trained. My father worked for his father and his brother until both businesses failed. Then, he began working at the Terre Haute Malleable, an iron factory. Many Blacks were hired there during those hard times.

My father was mercurial, extremely argumentative, and provocative, and he constantly challenged the white man's place for him. My mother, on the other hand, was secretive, pacifying and eager to please. Yet she was a dominant figure who was subordinate and passive, ambitious and aggressive. She was an obsessive worker, always busy, never idle—strange character traits for a woman who wanted to be cared for. She never liked to fight, even though she precipitated many, Mama always had to have her way.

My parents divorced on December 24, 1934. Their disunion was a bitter one. My custody was highly contested by my father, who seemed not to want their marriage to end. When I was awarded to my Mama, Daddy would come to see me frequently. My maternal grandmother did not approve of his visits, and I was often caught in the middle. Most often, I would only see my father when I visited my paternal grandparents.

That year, I moved into a house with six adults: Mama, Grandma, Aunt Helen, Uncle Orville, Uncle Jimmy and a college student, Elroy Johnson. Mama and Aunt Helen both took classes at ISTC. I remember always being taught something by someone who was practice teaching. A few months later, my cousin Buddy (whose name was Nathaniel Rice II, was born October 2, 1926, in Mt. Vernon, Indiana to Aunt Evelyn and Nathaniel Rice) came to live with us. He was in second-grade.

Section 1.6 Grandpa Jess, Grandma, and Their Children

When Grandpa Jess lost work at the mines, my grandfather did odd jobs and farmed. His was a tragic and unhappy life, common for a Black man at that time. Grandpa drank a lot. He was the kind of alcoholic who liked to fight when he was inebriated. It cost him his family, and resulted in my grandmother coming to stay in our home. My most vivid memory of my maternal grandfather was sad. He was standing in the front yard of our house at 720 South Thirteenth Street in Terre Haute one summer morning in 1935, very drunk and very loud, begging his family to come home. We all hid in the house until he went away. My mother, his daughter, cried all day. She loved him very much.

Grandma had favorites among her children. Hortense was loved the most because he was lost to her. All of her life Grandma fed hobos, strangers and anyone who came to the door hungry, because she prayed that people would do the same for her son if he showed up in such straits. She loved Orville the next best because he had a short leg. After Orville, Uncle Jimmy was the favorite, and she grieved over his death until she died. Aunt Helen was her best loved daughter, and Grandma fought her marriage to the end. The order of the others was relatively the same: Madelyn, Delila and Evelyn.

Hortense Alexander was headstrong with solid convictions to which he was strongly committed. He hated coal mining and was extremely protective of his sisters and my grandmother, whom Grandpa periodically would beat. At sixteen, he ran away from home to escape my grandfather's alcoholism and the drudgery of coal mining. No one knew where he was until 1961, when my grandmother fell sick with cancer. We found out he had fled to Duluth, Minnesota where he tried to disappear. Grandma absolutely loathed Grandpa, whom she blamed for the loss of contact with her beloved oldest child, Hortense. On January 28, 1943, Grandpa Jess wrote a letter to his daughter Delila, my mother. He said:

> i recived your box ok and also Madlyn can of tobaco and cards and Stella christmas cards and Turner and Jane card i am not feeling so well at this time i am not working now but i will haf to try to do something anyway mother should forget the dense feeling she has against me and Hortents because its better like it is because she can't make him recknise her unless he wants to because he has had more experince than both sides of generation and shuld know more and i think he does and i think and anybody should be proud of that don't you.

My grandfather, Jesse James Alexander, died in August 1945.

11

Section 1.7 The Death of My Father

On December 10, 1935, seven days before my eighth birthday my father was shot and killed by a policeman who alleged that he ran when the officer tried to arrest him for failure to pay child support. The entire family was traumatized by this event. My mother became hysterical and blamed herself for his death—for all of her remaining days, until the very end of her life.

When the white policeman killed my father, there was a big fight in the family. My uncle said that the policeman had been a football rival of the Laffoon brothers and had killed Daddy on purpose. But mama felt that the Laffoons held her responsible for Daddy's death and she never recovered from that imagined accusation and my grandma Alexander grew to hate my paternal grandparents for how my mama felt.

Mama developed paranoia after my father's death. She never completely trusted anybody again—not even her second husband, Aldwin Stewart, to whom she was devoted.

Section 1.8 The Barbershop and The Seal Coat

My mother sent Orville to barbering school in Indianapolis to learn how to cut hair after Uncle Jimmy died. He lived with us until he quit high school. Then Uncle Jimmy inherited my father's barbershop tools and equipment, which my mother got in the divorce settlement. Uncle Jimmy married Charlene Dickson, whom we called Aunt Bunny, and settled down to cut hair in the barbershop which he opened in the South End on College Avenue. Charlene and James had one son, James Albert, Jr., whom everybody called Little Jimmy. Nancy, now called Madelyn, lived in Evanston, with Uncle Herbert and their children, and Aunt Helen married Willis Wright from Washington County, Indiana and lived in Indianapolis. They had five children: Donald, David, Daniel, Delilah, and Dale.

Winter was very harsh in Terre Haute, Indiana, January 1936. The school was closed because there was not enough money to buy coal to heat it warm enough for students to be inside. On the day school closed I tried to carry home all of my books. Before I reached the corner of Thirteenth Street and College Avenue, a Black area known as "Baghdad," my hands were numb. I walked over to the barbershop instead, and Uncle Jimmy warmed up my hands with cold water. I thought that was so strange. Uncle Jimmy was a man whose understanding was couched in humor and concern. He told me that I didn't need to bring home all of my books on such a cold day. He said that he was sure they would have waited for me to come back to school for them when school reopened. I experienced another loss when he died in July 1936, from Lobar Pneumonia (for which there was no cure at that time), after contracting it in the local swimming hole called "The Gravel Pit."

When Uncle Jimmy died, Uncle Orville began to cut hair. Aunt Bunny didn't understand that the barbershop equipment was my mother's. So, when she didn't get anything from the barbershop by December of 1936, she stabbed my mother three times in the back. Mother had on a thick seal coat given to her by a former employer, Mrs. Tiedman, and this heavy coat saved her life. They took her to the hospital to stop the bleeding and she survived. That year I went to live with Aunt Helen, while my mother was recuperating. I attended school at Public School No. Eighty-seven, right down the street from Aunt Helen's house at 2435 Indianapolis Avenue in Indianapolis. I returned to Terre Haute in June of 1937. Aunt Bunny died that year from a ruptured appendix.

Section 1.9   Orville Arthur Alexander

Around 1939 my mother's baby brother, Orville, brought a girl home. Her name was Reva Sales and she was painfully shy. I couldn't blame her for not talking much because Grandma didn't cotton up much to dark-skinned Black people, even if they were pretty. Reva was dark skinned, and an orphan. She had grown-up in the orphans' home in Lost Creek. Still, Orville tried to make Grandma like her. It really didn't matter much I guess, because Orville and Reva were married the next year. They had two children: Orville, Jr. and Alyce.

Orville Jr. looked like his mother, but he was his father's color. Alyce looked like Aunt Evelyn, and she was Orville's color too. Grandma liked them. My grandma had a hard time with being Black. She looked just like a white woman and was often mistaken for white, much to her dismay. This ambivalence made her actions unpredictable. You never knew when she wanted you to be white or when she wanted you to be proud you were Black.

Section 1.10   Mr. and Mrs. Aldwin Stewart

Aldwin Stewart was my mother's eighth cousin. He was eight years younger than my mother when he married her and only twelve years older than me. Al and Mama moved to 2015 North Twentieth Street in the North End. I used to make the round-trip on my bicycle from Thirteenth and Crawford Streets to North Twentieth and Buckeye Street two times a week to see my mother. She worked as a domestic ten hours a day, six days a week, for a succession of white people from 1933 to 1936.

In 1936, my mother was hired by the Works Progress Administration (WPA) as a timekeeper for a sewing project, a job she held until 1939. She would bring home dresses for me and the next day I would wear them to school, only to find at least half of the girls in school in the same dress.

I was baptized on Easter Sunday in 1940. At that time, my mother was running the elevator at Herz Department Store part-time on weekends. She bought me a pair of new shoes for Easter Sunday. The clerk would not let me try the shoes on because Mama could only come around closing time, and he wanted to get home. When we got home we found two left shoes. I cried all the way back to the store. The man had been so mean that I just knew Mama couldn't get any redress. When we got there, my mother banged on the door until the janitor opened it. She told him her story, and he said that he couldn't help her. She asked him to call the manager. Fortunately for us, he was still there, and Mama got my shoes. I loved my Mama for that. She never would give up on anything. "Nothing beats a failure but a try," she always said.

In 1940, my mother and stepfather hired themselves out as a couple to a Lincoln car dealer from Barrington, Illinois. They served as chauffeur/butler and maid/cook to this family. One of the requirements was to travel with the dealer and his family during the winter and work in Vero Beach, Florida from November until April. Now, my parents had never been in the South. While driving there, they became separated from their employers in Georgia. The Georgia State Police stopped my father, demanded his license and spread-eagled him on the car. My mother became hysterical. Fortunately, the Lincoln car dealer came back for my parents and liberated them from the Georgia cop who told my father, "Remember, ni**er, you ain't in Chicago. We lynch ni**ers here! So you better keep close to your boss." Needless to say, my parents were scared.

Around Christmas, 1940, the Lincoln car dealer told my parents that they could no longer honor the agreement they had made regarding pay. The man said that his friends were greatly concerned about the amount of money the Lincoln dealer was paying my parents. His friends said that if their ni**ers found out that his ni**ers were getting that kind of money, they would all have to raise their ni**ers' pay. The car dealer apologized to my father. Since the week before a Black man had been lynched thirty miles away, my father agreed without argument. He also plotted his escape. He and my mother planned to take the Dixie Flyer home in three weeks from that Christmas. I vaguely remember receiving boxes of stuff from Florida prior to their arrival. Dixie left Florida at midnight. My father drove my mother to the train station and returned the car to the home, left the lights on in the servants' quarters as though they were home, and made his way through the Florida swamps to the station. He could not walk on the road, because a Black man's life was in peril there. At last he arrived and he and my mother came home.

Section 1.11   Cousin Buddy

Grandma was a tough disciplinarian. She gave out chores in the beginning of the day before we went to school. Mine were washing dishes, emptying the pan underneath the icebox, sweeping the kitchen, cleaning the stove and other kitchen furniture. Sometimes we had to kill chickens and pick off their feathers. She had a small garden, which we had to deworm. I hated the chores. I learned early that Grandma had a high respect for schoolwork. If she saw you idle, she would give you work to do. If you were reading a book, she would pass you by, so I got out of doing chores a lot. Buddy never learned this. He didn't like schoolwork.

One day I was reading when Grandma hollered for Buddy to come and do something. He was not in the house. She called and called, but no Buddy. Finally, she told me to go out and find him. I knew exactly where to look. He was playing checkers with the firemen in the firehouse at Thirteenth and Crawford Streets. I went inside and summoned him home. When we got home, Grandma was enraged. She was upset because he had not told her where he was going. She gave him a whipping I have never forgotten. On top of that punishment he was forbidden to go to the firehouse, which hurt Buddy more.

When Buddy was in sixth grade, Aunt Evelyn sent him to St. Benedict the Moor Boarding School in Milwaukee, Wisconsin. It was a grand place. Buddy made great friends there. It was all Black and very Catholic. Later, Buddy became a great athlete and earned the title of All City in Milwaukee, Wisconsin. I missed Buddy a lot. He was a loveable person, generous and kind.

He had absorbed most of Grandma's wrath which I now received. Grandma gave me his chores to do as well.

Buddy was a Catholic. I had never known a Catholic before. Once Buddy came back to Terre Haute to visit. He had to go the Catholic Church on the southeast corner of Thirteenth and Poplar. When he told me that he had to confess that he had eaten a hot dog on Good Friday. I thought that was preposterous. Anyway, we went to the church and had to go in the side door. I asked him why we couldn't go in the front door, and he replied that Negroes had to go in by the side door. I refused to accompany him. I told him I would rather go to church at Second Baptist Church on Fourteenth and Oak than to a church where I couldn't go in by the front door. I asked him why he was confessing something to a white person who wouldn't let him come in by the front door anyway. Buddy told me to go home, and went in by the side door by himself.

Buddy and I came together again when we both attended Evanston Township High School (ETHS). We got married at the same time, and our first children were born in the same year. He became an Evanston policeman in 1950 and served with distinction as a police firearm's expert until he retired in 1978. He also served in the United States Marines during World War II. Buddy was a great human being, a good son, husband, father and a great friend. I cherish all of my memories of him. He died on July 23, 1980.

Section 1.12   Aunt Fronie and Uncle Carson

My Aunt Fronie's first husband was a baseball player in the Negro League named Arthur Shelton. They weren't married long because, she said, "he was gone most of the time playing ball." She then married a second time to Carson Anderson, Sr. who was the father of my best friend, Barbara Lee Anderson (Teedie). Ours was a precious friendship, especially given that my aunt had run away with her father. Nevertheless, Teedie's mother, Mrs. Mary Eva Anderson, always treated me well.

Aunt Fronie (who later took in my paternal grandmother) and Uncle Carson had no children of their own. They lived a fabulous life working first in Detroit, then migrating to Los Angeles where they worked for famous movie stars like Robert Stack. They never stayed in one place. I thought their life very exciting by comparison. When I was in college, they moved back to Lost Creek, Indiana (outside of Terre Haute) and lived for a while on a farm. But, something happened between them, and Uncle Carson tried to have Aunt Fronie committed. Uncle Herbert interceded. I never learned what happened, but they got back together again and moved to Henderson, Kentucky in the 1970s. They lived there together until Uncle Carson died in 1992.

CHAPTER 2

THE DETAILS OF MY EDUCATION

Section 2.1 Barbara Ann Laffoon
In the Beginning There Was School

From the beginning I knew that Black people could learn if taught. I attended a segregated elementary school (kindergarten–eighth grade), named Booker T. Washington, and the Black teachers there were committed to teaching "Negroes." I always loved school and my teachers, although they all complained about my talking in school. My report cards from that time show that I received all As and Bs in my academic subjects, with Fs and Ds in deportment and conduct. I just could not stop talking. My first grade teacher was Myrtle Ann Smith. She was very good to me, except when I had trouble going to the bathroom.

My mother enrolled me in school three months before I was four because my godfather's sister, Cecilia Upthegrove, was the kindergarten teacher. I knew how to read when I went to school. My mother and father taught me to read, and I honestly do not remember not knowing how. My father also taught me French when I was in second-grade; sometimes, my teacher, Marie Kennedy, would practice her knowledge and further strengthen mine.

Jane Dabney Shackleford was my third grade teacher. She was the leader of the Girl Scout troop. I loved that troop. My maternal grandmother made meatloaf dinners to sell with baked beans, cole slaw, corn bread, and baked apple pies. Ms. Shackleford taught us to be proud we were Negroes. Ms. Shackleford wrote *The Child's Story of the Negro*,[1] which was the first book about Negroes for children in the United States. She was a persistent taskmaster. She believed that education was the Black man's savior, and she taught me: Knowledge is power. "What you don't know can kill you," she often said. Ms. Shackleford was quick with the switch. If you misbehaved she would give you some taps with this wiry slender tree limb. In spite of the many switch bruises I carried home, I did not learn to stop talking in class.

My teachers—Thomas Walden, Eva Belle Porter, Edith Hodge, and Edna Edwards—all nurtured my spirit while I was in my segregated elementary school. Our principal, Charles Hyte, encouraged us to advance ourselves and uplift the race. Ms. Porter taught me to love music and Ms. Edwards taught me how to make a dress. I still sew in the way that she taught me.

Our school often had assemblies to promote Negro history and Negroes' contributions to the United States of America. It was in the sessions led by Ms. Hodge, Ms. Porter, and Mr. Lyda that we learned about us. Because white supremacy demanded we occupy inferior spaces of deference—we were taught "Lift Every Voice and Sing"—the Negro national anthem. America's national anthem did not include us, so the Pledge of Allegiance was invalid and a lie. My Black teachers taught me to always do my best and to resist the notion that our race was primitive and inferior. They taught us an unbelievable work ethic, underlining determination and persistence. They strived for perfection and provided optimistic models for overcoming discrimination and Jim Crow.

Jack Parks was my sixth grade teacher. He taught me not to lie. I used to lie a lot. One day in class we were discussing World War I. He asked for some comments from students who had read the book. I told him that I could remember my mother telling me that she could hear the guns. He told me how interesting that was since the war was being fought in France. I felt so foolish. I never lied in his class again, although I did continue lying for some time after that. Mr. Parks also talked to parents a lot. This kept me straight. Trouble at school always meant trouble at home.

In seventh grade, my teacher was John Wesley Lyda, Sr. He was a brilliant man who had no idea how to manage adolescents. We took advantage of his kindness. However, he would give whippings if we got too "out-of-hand." Because he knew a great deal about the Negro and he wrote the book *The History of the Negro in Indiana*,[2] I learned a lot from him.

My best friend during seventh and eighth grade was Edith Higgins. She had shiny long thick Black hair and looked like an Indian person. She had four sisters and two brothers, and they all lived near Second Baptist Church. Edith was better behaved than I was, and this had an effect on me. I started acting more like Edith in school. I know my teachers thanked God.

My eighth grade teacher, Marguerite Taylor, taught us Algebra long before we went to ninth-grade at the integrated Sarah Scott Junior High School. I can hear her now, telling us to learn all we could from her because white teachers would not always care whether we learned or not. She motivated us to make good grades. In fact, if I failed a test, she behaved as though I had done something to her personally. When I made a C instead of an A on her work, her furrowed brows would meet over her straight nose while her black eyes bored into me with the question, "How could you do this to me?" We students were extensions of our teachers. If we failed, they failed. In us they saw themselves. "You must be better than white folks," Ms. Taylor cautioned me one day after I submitted some sloppy work to her. "It is not enough to be as good. You must be so good that it becomes impossible to say otherwise." From her I learned to do my very best.

When I entered the ninth grade at the integrated school, my white teachers were impressed with my achievements. Yet I was not placed in the highest achieving class, which was all white. My mother protested that the work I was being given was too easy, and finally, I was placed in the third highest achieving class. I made mostly As at this school. From there I went to Wiley High School, from which my mother and father had graduated. My father and uncle were outstanding athletes in football and played on several winning teams, and my family members were remembered as hardworking students. When I entered Mrs. Grace Arnold's English class, she shot a fierce look at me from over her round wire eyeglasses.

"What is your name?" she asked me.

"Barbara Ann Laffoon," I whispered.

"What did you say?" she asked again. "Speak Up!"

I repeated my name.

"Who is your father?" She continued her questioning.

"Sylvester Laffoon," I answered.

"And what is your mother's name?"

"Delila Mae Alexander-Laffoon."

"You can make two grades in this class, Miss Laffoon," she resumed. "A or F."

And without another word, she began questioning the next student.

The white teachers did not cut me slack. They knew I could do the rigorous curriculum there, and they demanded the best I had to offer. Thankfully, my teachers at Booker T. Washington laid a good foundation. I was already determined to do my best. This determination helped me overcome the racism I later encountered at Evanston Township High School (1943–1944) and at Northwestern University (1944–1947).

Section 2.2   Going Higher in Education

I was first in my class at Wiley High School and the president of the Honors Society of this integrated school. Terre Haute was a strange place with regard to segregation. Negroes were segregated in elementary school, but not in high school. Because my mother lived in Evanston, she made an arrangement for me to attend Evanston Township High School (ETHS) for my senior year, although I graduated from Wiley on January 21, 1944.

When I arrived at ETHS, I was placed in an average achieving class. Uncle Herbert William Laffoon, Sr. insisted that ETHS test me for higher placement in English. Exasperated by the principal's obstinacy, he yelled, "There are no dumb Laffoons! Can you get that through your head?" Principal Francis Bacon was so astonished, that he placed me in a class with a teacher who proved to be my nemesis.

Many ETHS teachers seemed to resent the fact that I was an honors student and number one in my class. My senior English teacher openly discriminated against me, giving me harder assignments than others. While my peers in the class were asked to recite John Milton's sonnet, "On His Blindness," I was given twenty-two lines from the "Canterbury Tales" in Old English. In the end, I was in the highest achieving senior English class and the second highest achieving class in Problems of Democracy.

The teachers worked hard to prevent me from being the best student in the class. In my Problems of Democracy class, no one received a "1" which was the highest grade given. My teachers were determined I would not receive the highest grade in her class and the award from the Women's Civic Club that was given to such students. But by that time, my parents had so schooled me in resisting white supremacy that they could not break my spirit, nor quell my motivation.

I made many friends at ETHS. My cousin, Georgia Williams nee Laffoon, was only fifteen years old when she graduated from ETHS. I remember when we were range captains in Mr. Nuckols's homeroom. There were at least thirty rows of ten seats in that room. At the back of each row was the range captain who was responsible for keeping records of attendance and the sale of war stamps and bonds. When Georgia (we called her Jo) and I were assigned to this homeroom, there were no Negro range captains. When Uncle Herbert, Jo's father, discovered this, he stormed up to the school and told the Principal Bacon, that he wanted this to change. Mr. Nuckols appointed Jo and me as range captains the next week. Now this was a job that I didn't want, and I was really angry with my uncle. I learned a lot about war bonds I tell you that.

Uncle Herbert was a model for the best in American manhood. He was a devoted father and husband, a talented athlete and businessman, industrious worker and inspirational leader. He never shrank from his responsibilities as a citizen and a Black man. Always fighting racism, whether in the public schools, or in athletics, or in the workplace, he stood tall for freedom, equality and justice, and was the first Negro parent to serve as an advisor to Dr. Lloyd Michael, district superintendent of No. 202 and principal of ETHS during the 1960s.

I started taking classes at Northwestern University (NU) March of 1944 during the spring quarter. My mother worked for a dentist who was the chairman of the Northwestern Alumni Association. Mother begged him to intercede on my behalf for a scholarship to Northwestern. Because I was good in languages; he told Mama to have me take the examination for the scholarships in Latin and the Classics.

This was my forte. God had given me the gift of learning Latin quickly. When I entered ninth grade at Sarah Scott Junior High School in Terre Haute, Indiana, my teacher, Minna Rappaport, asked my mother who had been teaching me Latin? Truly, no one had. It was a gift, like having the potential to be the world's greatest chariot driver when the world had stopped using chariots. Anyway, I made a high score on the test and did get a scholarship. My mother's love and persistence was once again rewarded.

At Northwestern I made friends easily with Beverlee Stams, Gwendolyn Braithwaite, Yvonne Braithwaite, Patricia Sizemore (cousin to Furman Sizemore.) At that time, Negroes could not live on Northwestern's campus. I was told that Bernie Jefferson was the only Negro who had lived in Pearson Hall and that was because he was an All-American. Out-of-town Negro female students lived at Ms. Gray's home, this was the Negro family who kept Northwestern students. Out-of-town Negro male students stayed at the Negro YMCA on Emerson Street, across from the house that my parents lived in when they first came to Evanston.

There were very few Negro men at Northwestern, due to the war and discrimination. But there were a lot of white sailors taking classes there. As a result of boredom, a lot of time was spent on the struggle for racial equality. We had a big march in 1945 and a protest in 1946. The president, Franklyn Bliss Snyder, told our parents that we would lose our scholarships if we did not stop. I can see my mother walking up the street now. Although the silhouette resembled her, I was so certain that it was not hers. After all, my mother never learned to drive, and she worked at the Great Lakes Naval Training Station in Great Lakes, Illinois. So, when my mother jerked me out of the protest line and snatched away my sign, I was surprised as well as humiliated. By that time I had been elected as president of Quibblers and was considered extremely militant and aggressive. Jewish mothers came. After all, Northwestern had a quota on them, too. In fact, although the Jews had a house on campus, it was isolated and entirely separate from the other houses in the quadrangle. I don't know what my Jewish friends' mothers said to them, but they were inactive too for the rest of that year. Luckily, the end of our term was quickly approaching and we graduated from NU on March 28, 1947.

CHAPTER 3

MAKING A LIVING

Section 3.1 Finding a Job and Ella Mae Cunningham

Immediately after graduation, I sought employment. Northwestern University would not place its Negro students in white schools, not even ETHS, which I had attended, and The Evanston papers were advertising jobs as "For Whites Only" and "Only Whites Need Apply." So, I began teaching in the Chicago Public Schools (CPS).

I wanted to be a French translator in the United Nations, but I didn't know how to get into that employment network, and my parents had made it clear that I had to start working immediately upon graduation. My first assignment was to replace an ill Latin teacher who was on leave from Wendell Phillips High School, where I had completed my student teaching. When she returned, I was sent as a substitute teacher to the John D. Shoop Elementary School in Morgan Park.

I was first assigned to a second grade classroom. The children spent the day throwing erasers and objects at each other. I could not get them to stay in their seats. They would not listen to what I was telling them. The entire day was a disaster. When I went home that evening, I told my parents that I was not cut out for school teaching. My stepfather very calmly indicated that he would help me get my old job back at Montgomery Ward, a local department store. This I definitely did not want to do.

I prayed for God to help me and my prayers were answered in the person of Ella Mae Cunningham, the school's adjustment teacher. The adjustment teacher was the person who tested children referred to her for special help. Mrs. Cunningham came into my room the very next day and introduced herself to me. "You seem like a pretty smart girl to me," she said. "Do you want to teach school?"

"Yes," I answered. Pictures of working at Montgomery Ward loomed before me. "But I don't seem to know how to hold the students' attention."

"Do you want me to help you?" she asked.

"Yes," I blurted out. "Please help me."

27

From that day on, my life was never the same. Mrs. Cunningham taught me how to diagnose students' needs, provide activities for them, and make the materials necessary for these activities. Although I didn't know it at the time, I was learning how to teach children with mild learning disabilities how to read, write and understand mathematics. She also taught me how to circumvent white supremacy and how to give the Negro children pride in themselves, their lives, culture and history.

Section 3.2   Furman Edward Sizemore

When we (me, Aldwin Stewart, and mama) moved to Evanston in 1943, we moved next door to the Sizemore family. That summer I met Furman Edward Sizemore. Even though I was only fifteen years old, I knew that I was going to marry him. During those times, scores of young Black men were going to war. Furman was drafted as soon as he graduated from ETHS at age eighteen in 1944. He went into the U.S. Navy from Great Lakes, Illinois, to California, to Saipan, and then to Okinawa. He was gone eighteen months. I wrote a letter to him everyday he was gone.

When the war was over, the men came home. It was the same world to us, but for them it was different. They had definitely grown up. The shy boy that left for the war in 1944 returned a mature man in 1946—and with a lot of baggage. Stories about the racism among the officers and in the U.S. Navy filled my life. Disappointment at finding residues of racism still abounding was apparent. The one good thing was the G.I. Bill. Furman Edward Sizemore used his to enroll in the Worsham Mortuary College. To earn a living, while he studied he worked for the U.S. Post Office.

We were married on June 28, 1947. We lived at 1105 Emerson Street in Evanston, Illinois with Furman's mother, Mrs. Lillian Garrett Sizemore; his sister, Barbara Sizemore Griffin; and her son, Roy John, whom we called Sonny Boy. On September 17, 1948, our daughter, Kymara Madeleine, was born. She was a beautiful baby and was a complete and utter joy to her paternal grandmother. Mrs. Sizemore took great care of "Kimmy-poo."

Section 3.3   John D. Shoop and Jantena E. Jensen

During the time I used for my maternity leave (1948–1949) I returned to Northwestern University for a Master's degree in Elementary Education.

28

Mrs. Cunningham had convinced me that I could make a good schoolteacher just like she was. She was my model, and most of what I learned about teaching Black children, I learned from her.

In 1950, Furman and I purchased a house. At that time, I did not drive, plus we could only afford one car, so we purchased a two-bedroom Georgian at 9115 South Perry in Chicago near my place of employment at Shoop School in Morgan Park on 112th Street. This was not a good decision for our marriage. Furman had to spend entirely too much time driving back and forth, and his friends and family were all in Evanston. He had to be at work at 5:00 A.M., and this meant rising at 3:00 A.M. His school, work, and training for becoming an embalmer and funeral director schedule was strenuous—his time at home became less and less, and so did our time together.

Because I had graduated from NU, I was ineligible for employment as a fully assigned and certified teacher in the Chicago Public Schools. Only graduates of Chicago Teachers College were accepted. Not until 1950 were the examinations opened to all. I took the exam in 1950, and received my assignment as a full-fledged teacher the following year at Shoop. I loved Shoop School until Jantena E. Jensen came to be the principal. She did not like me, nor did I like her.

I was told that she was from Texas and had the idea that Black people were not patriotic enough. To insure our education in these matters, she arranged for us to march through the school corridors each morning for our opening exercises. We would march around whatever floor our classrooms were located on singing the "Star Spangled Banner" to drums and bugles. When we arrived back at our classroom, we would say the "Pledge of Allegiance" to the Flag in unison and then commence classes. This exercise took anywhere from fifteen to twenty minutes. I had forty-one sixth graders who could not read, and I figured they could not afford this luxury. Therefore, I did not participate after the first week. Ms. Jensen summoned me to a conference during which I was told to comply or be charged with insubordination. I refused. She filed an insubordination charge against me, and I, in turn, filed a grievance. I won the grievance because Board Rules dictate only five minutes for the opening exercises. From then on, I was on her short list.

Ms. Jensen assigned me to teach the Educable Mentally Handicapped (EMH) students during the 1952–1953 school year. Teachers kept referring normal students to it, and I complained to the principal. I argued that many of the children, though not all, placed in EMH from our school were not mentally retarded. They had lived in the South, where the school year was shorter because of the cotton planting season, that is, if they went to school at all. I produced statistics showing the disparities in school funding. Many Chicagoans are Mississippi migrants or relatives of these migrants, and at that time Mississippi was the most truculent state in the union on race conditions. Sharecropping had reduced Black people to peons immersed in debt from which they were rarely able to extricate themselves. I angrily defended these students who had not been taught.

Ms. Jensen snapped back at me one day. "Well if you don't want them in EMH, then teach them how to read yourself." I conferred with Mrs. Cunningham about this reaction and she said, "That's exactly what we'll do." She diagnosed seven children who had been referred and targeted the skills they needed to master. Then she directed me to find activities and exercises that would stress these skills. She guided me to storerooms where supplementary materials were kept and we searched together through boxes and boxes of old textbooks. I sat up all night once, cutting up old books into short reading segments with questions at the end. I prepared reading flashcards of words from the Dolch Lists. I made posters and pictures of hard-to-learn words and word sounds for those youngsters who spoke with strong Mississippi dialects. One year, three of them came home with me every Saturday for further work. Eventually, one of these students we saved from EMH went on to graduate from the University of Michigan.

Many teachers, chief among whom were Minnie Wallace, Beatrice Dixon, Grace Pannell, Evelyn Jackson, Marcella Pradd and Victoria Reske, contributed everything from books, paper, pencils, and even clothes. Once, one of my students was arrested wearing a shirt donated by Victoria Reske's husband and emblazoned with his name. The next day, she was surprised at a visit from the police. It was she who convinced the police that this mildly mentally retarded student was a victim of misunderstanding the policeman's directives.

In 1952, someone wrote a letter to the Committee on UnAmerican Affairs, reporting that I was teaching Communism in the public schools. I never knew who it was, but I strongly suspected Ms. Jensen. I was investigated for two years. Every member of my family was investigated. A cousin outside of Uniontown, Kentucky wrote to my grandmother: "Dear Violet, Tell Bobran to stop. The revenooers [revenuers] was here and almost found our still." I knew

I had to leave Shoop, but I dreaded doing so. Mrs. Cunningham was my guardian angel, a great teacher, and an ideal teaching model, and she had become a dear friend by this time. Leaving Shoop was a significant turning point in my life, so I took a leave of absence and went to Europe.

Section 3.4   Going to Europe

My neighbor was Ann Douglass Fook, eldest daughter of the renowned Marjorie Stewart Joyner, inventor, civic worker, and manager of Madame C.J. Walker's School of Beauty in Chicago, and founder of the nation's largest Black beauticians sorority. She planned a trip to Europe for the sorority from April 10, 1954, through May 17, 1954. My aunt Evelyn was a licensed beautician and a member of the sorority and she was taking the trip and invited me to join her. Having been a classical language and French student, I was intrigued by the itinerary, which included LeHavre, Paris, Lausanne, Milano, Firenze, Roma, Genoa, Nice, Monte Carlo, Cannes and London.

The most exhilarating experience was had stateside, when we met with Mary McLeod Bethune, the founder of Bethune-Cookman College in Daytona Beach, Florida and good friend of Marjorie Stewart Joyner, who served on the college's Board of Trustees. She was present at the sailing to bid us farewell and a safe journey. She also prayed with us and gave us one of her visionary speeches. It was so thrilling to be with this woman whose courage and strength was so well known, for she had been the first Black woman to head a government agency under President Franklin Roosevelt. Though she was never able to convince him to press for anti-lynching legislation, she never ceased trying.

While traveling through Europe, the first important finding for me was the absence of overt racism in the countries we visited. Accustomed as we were to continuous and constant denigration, we were blinded to the covert conditions. We were accepted everywhere as important Americans, not unimportant Negroes. We found self-exiled Americans everywhere living "free."

It took me four days to get my ear in France. We lived at Eleven Rue de Lyon near the train station, and I would carry on conversations with the people who lived nearby. But when they responded, I had a hard time understanding. Finally, one day on the metro, I overheard two women talking about their personal affairs and I understood. It was such an overwhelming realization that I could actually understand another language when spoken by native speakers.

The sights of the Roman ruins, the Coliseum, the art in Firenze and Milan—all were expected. After all, I had read about them for ten years. We attended a Roman wedding, however, and I was not prepared for the seven-course dinner. In one course, we were served a banana. Luckily, I did not eat mine until I observed that the Italians were eating theirs with a knife and fork. Thank God they did not see me eating mine monkey-style. I probably would have set a stereotype there of the watermelon-eating Negro in the U.S. (let it be known that I do like watermelon).

All over Italy, the people were generous, courteous and kind. The French Riviera was probably the most open society we visited, and, strangely, there, we were probably perceived more as Americans. After the continental visits, London seemed staid and still ravaged by World War II.

I returned to the United States, more determined than ever to be a first-class citizen. I also returned to a militant six-year-old, who told me that I could never go anywhere again without her. Since 1954, she has visited: Mexico; every island in the Caribbean (except Barbados and Grenada); London; Paris; Egypt; Senegal; Ghana; South Africa; China; Zimbabwe; Nigeria; Kenya; Tanzania; and Botswana.

Section 3.5   Gillespie and Mrs. Gray

September 1954, I transferred to Frank L. Gillespie Elementary School at 9301 South State Street, right around the corner from my house. I enrolled my daughter in kindergarten there. Thelma E. Gray, the principal, was dedicated to her profession, committed to her students, and in charge of her school. She had high expectations for both teachers and students. Gillespie School was a segregated school. She assigned me to teach Reading and English to the seventh and eighth grades in a departmentalized program. Each teacher had weekly goals and lesson plans that were to be submitted to the principal for approval every Friday. She returned them on Monday. Mrs. Gray was in charge of discipline. She demanded that she be informed of any deviant behavior, especially when chronic violators or known "troublemakers" were involved.

One day one of my students told me that another of my students had brought a gun to school to shoot Mrs. Gray. I was upset, especially since I didn't know what to do. The rule was to send the student to the principal.

But how could I do this? The student was planning to shoot the principal. I called him to my desk and asked him to go into the hall with me to discuss a problem I was having. He did.

"Did you bring a gun to school today?"

"Yeah."

"Whose gun is it?"

"My uncle's."

"Does he know that you have brought his gun to school?" I realized immediately how stupid the question was.

"Naw."

"Why did you bring it here?" I asked, stalling for time, trying to decide what to do next.

"I was going to use it to make Mrs. Gray give me back my hat because she took it yesterday and said she wasn't   going to give it back because I done wore it too many times after she done told me not to."

"Well, I can't let you do that. Do you want to give me the gun or do you want me to call the police?"

"I'll give you the gun if you get my hat."

"We can't make that kind of a deal. Do you have your uncle's telephone number?"

"He at home…where I live at."

"Well, give me the gun and I'll call him and tell him to come up here and get it."

"Naw, thas alright. I'll take the gun home at noon when I go home to eat."

By this time, beads of sweat had popped out on my forehead. My hands were clammy and my knees felt weak. I could hear that my class was talking and bordering on disorder, but I felt compelled to get the gun. "Look," I began again, "You can't sit in this classroom with a gun in your desk. I'll have to call the police if you don't hand it over." He finally gave me the gun. Immediately, I called his uncle and asked him to meet his nephew at the school at noon. When he came, I gave him his nephew and the gun.

My principal was furious with me. She told me that I had not only violated school rules, but the law as well. She discussed the case with the full faculty so that no one would ever entertain such a thought again. By the time she had finished, I wished I had sent the student down to her with the gun.

"What kind of values are you teaching your students?" she railed at me.

"These Negro boys cannot flout the law like this. That's why so many of them are down there at Twenty-sixth and California (Cook County Jail). We must teach them to have more self-respect, to get a good education, and to obey the rules. Not to do so may kill them."

"But I was afraid he would kill you," I replied.

"My life is not the central issue here," she continued.

"Let me take care of that problem. The students' lives are our major responsibility here. Your student has to understand that he cannot disobey the rules here without a consequence, whatever that is. Everyone must have something to die for. If you and I don't make a difference in the lives of these Negro students, who do you think will care enough to do so? What lesson have we taught this boy? That he can get away with bringing a gun to school to threaten someone or to let him do something that he shouldn't do?"

She glared at me as though she expected an answer, and after a moment, threw up her arms, sighed and walked away. In my despondency, little did I realize how much this lesson would help me when I became principal of Forrestville High School in 1965, where there were four warring gangs. Mrs. Gray taught me the value of organization. If you want to reach a goal, you must design and implement activities that will take you to it. I still use her examples to illustrate this point. "If you are going downtown (Chicago), you don't get on a bus headed toward Gary (Indiana)," she would often say.

She was the very first principal who cared whether or not my Black students performed well on standardized tests. If my class performed poorly, she wanted to know what I planned to do about it. She would review these plans and comment on them. She would help procure the equipment, supplies, and materials necessary for implementation. She was supportive but demanding; pleasant but rigorous; kind but firm;intelligent and curious. Mrs. Gray was always teaching and always learning. Not everyone liked her. In fact, I was not her fan for a year.

In 1956, I was assigned a class of Spanish-speaking students from Puerto Rico who had moved into the Frank Lowden Public Housing on Ninety-fifth Street. My job was to teach them how to read, write and speak English. It was an impossible task. They could not understand me, nor could I them. Eventually, I began to study Spanish on my own and with help from Berlitz records.

Early in my tenure, I realized how mistreated some of these students were. I had students who had finished the ninth grade in Puerto Rico, very intelligent and good academic students assigned to the seventh grade merely because they could not speak English. I reported this to Mrs. Gray and asked her to transfer these students to high school and to seek tutors for them in English. She was one of the first principals to request bilingual services for these students. For Thelma E. Gray students came first. She wanted the best for them, and she always gave them her best. She tolerated no poor performances, either by students or teachers. She was a great taskmaster and a good principal.

Section 3.6 Educating Kymara Madeline Sizemore

When my daughter was in kindergarten, she came home late from school one day, for which she was punished. She kept insisting that the teacher had put her in a closet and forgot about her because she had not done something that the teacher asked her to do. She told me over and over again that she could not hear the teacher. So insistent was she that I went to observe the class and determine for myself the seat of the trouble. Sure enough, I could not hear the teacher from where I was sitting. I spoke to the teacher about my concerns, and she proceeded to discuss Kymara's learning problems. Since she was so unconcerned about her own presentations, I went to the principal, who immediately discussed the situation with her. This was important to me because the teacher was a veteran teacher whose seniority provided union protection.

During first grade, Kymara was having trouble learning to read. Because she was such an obedient, sweet little girl, I took her to the University of Chicago to be examined. The experts there diagnosed her problem as auditory-perception. They gave me exercises for her to pursue, but told me the problem could not be corrected, and that she would have to compensate for this loss. She would have to memorize a lot of things using graphics, acronyms, and other aids. To be sure she understood how she would have to learn, I was told to go through certain exercises with her everyday. Some of them were fun. We used to create rhymes, which was one of the activities. Kymara and I used to race for the bus singing, "Greenie the Bus, Greenie the Bus. Greenie the Bus is gonna pass by us!"

The University of Chicago experts gave me instructions for her teachers. From that time on I had to select teachers who would follow these instructions. Kymara went to St. Edmond's Episcopal Elementary School for second and third grades. In the fourth grade I brought her to Drew, where she attended for fifth-grade as well. She was a quick learner and we covered a lot of ground each day. She eventually compensated for her handicap, and by seventh-grade, she could read on grade level. But she never did learn to spell, and she had difficulty sounding out some syllables for several years.

Kymara graduated from ETHS and matriculated at Arkansas AM&N College in Pine Bluff, Arkansas. Her white counselor at ETHS would not recommend her for college, but Dorothy Littlejohn Maggett, the Black counselor, helped her get into Arkansas AM& N. From 1962 to 1966, the Civil Rights Movement in the South had captured the energies of Black college students. Arkansas AM&N was no exception. However, the president did all he could to keep his school out of these activities. When I was invited to speak at the college during the fall of 1964, I did not know of his opposition. Consequently, when I was barred from speaking to the students, it was news.

By that time my daughter was a school leader who was opposed to the restrictions generally accepted by students who attended Black colleges. She hated the curfews for women especially, and disobeyed these rules several times. Letters from the dean appraising us of her activities were not uncommon. Finally, when she was a senior, she secured off-campus housing. While the restrictions were released, she began having ideological differences with her major professor.

One of Kymara's assignments was a term paper in partial fulfillment of a course titled Elizabethan Drama, a required course for drama majors. Her topic was "A Look at Elizabethan Drama and Black Drama as Ethnic Studies." Kymara argued persuasively that Elizabethan Drama was as ethnocentric as Black Drama and failed to achieve the four goals and objectives for the Black college. Her teacher's response was: "I dig your thing, but it ain't in the bag of this course." Enraged, Kymara vowed to quit school. Since she was a graduating senior, we could hardly let that happen. Grudgingly she wrote a critique of Faustus, which earned her a D. This happened at a Black college! It was an important lesson for the both of us, and the case was discussed in the *Notre Dame Journal of Education*.[1]

Kim graduated in 1970, she has a doctorate in Educational Leadership from Roosevelt University. If I had not been Kymara's mother, she likely would have languished in special education programs throughout her academic life.

Section 3.7 Peter Flemister

In 1957, my sister-in-law, Ruth Sizemore Flemister, and her little boy Peter, came to live with us. Ruth was a licensed obstetrical practical nurse (OPN) at Providence Hospital in Chicago. Peter was gifted and was in the second grade then.

After Peter had become a successful corporation lawyer, I talked with him about his school life. Race had always had an effect, he told me, regardless of the racial makeup of the student body. "[W]ith one exception in my school life," he said, "the faculty was always overwhelmingly white. Color had an effect on the predominantly Black student populations. Class and gender had effects, but to a much lesser extent than race or color. Race had an effect because, although I went to school in the middle of the Civil Rights Era, racial issues were rarely, if ever, discussed during my elementary school years and the first two years of high school. Indeed they were avoided as being too controversial and political."

Peter recalled trying to raise racial issues in his U.S. history class and economics class in high school. His teachers, both male and white, as well as Jewish and Christian, told him that he could not bring up such disruptive topics in class. He wanted to talk about the continuing existence of slavery in the United States after July 4, 1776, and the existence of discrimination after the Civil War in his history class. He wanted to talk about the dire economic state of Blacks, as a result of slavery and discrimination in his economic class. There were always brotherhood assemblies at the high school due to the frequently racially-motivated mass fights between Blacks and whites.

The principal told the students that they had to learn to go to school together in peace. This could be achieved by avoiding the discussion of racial topics. He also repeatedly told them that when fights are confined to members of one race or the other it is merely a fight, but that interracial fights were riots with bad consequences. The statement was true since the police always arrested the Blacks, but never the whites, even when the Blacks were the victims.

Peter recounted that the magnet school Blacks were always terrorized at Lindblom High School by the local Black street gang that attended the school as a general high school, as opposed to the college prep school, which Peter attended, with its selective admission policy requiring passage of an entrance examination. He said, "We were from all over the city, south of Twelfth Street, and of many social classes, but overwhelmingly middle-class, in contrast to the local Blacks who were not. The local white gang, however, could not touch us, or the Satan Lovers would defend and protect us."

In his appraisal of his school life, Peter thought that Charles Richard Drew Elementary School was an oasis and his very best experience, ever, in school where his race, and race in general, were positive factors. He said, "From the man the school was named after, to the administration and faculty, this was heaven! This experience positively colored my educational experiences." Peter attended Drew from second through fourth grade. I was his third grade teacher. Peter was so completely superior in his work that I recommended him for a double promotion, which the principal approved. Peter was a very sensitive, as well as an intelligent student who was curious about the world and often asked very difficult questions. I encouraged him to do so and helped him to pursue routes for the accumulation and creation of knowledge.

Peter attended Hookway Elementary School from fifth through eighth grade. He endured some of the same teachers Kim had endured. At Hookway and at Lindblom High School, he had a few teachers who were either ineffective, or incompetent, or uncaring, and sometimes all three. These teachers were both Black and white, male and female. Some Blacks, especially younger ones, wanted to be his buddy. He had teachers who were placed in classes they were unqualified to teach. Peter also endured Harriett Mull at Hookway, in the eighth grade, students complained that she had personal hygiene problems and wore only two dresses all year. And although Peter was one of the best students in her class, she would repeatedly refuse to accept his papers and homework, dismissing them with "let them remain in your notebook to ripen." Once again, his mother and I complained to the principal about this terrible teacher.

In high school, the whites were assumed to know all of the answers and were recognized in class by white faculty. Peter and other Blacks were ignored and had to prove themselves. Once his high school physics teacher realized that Peter understood and could do the work, he had no more problems. Indeed, the teacher tried to get Peter a position at Argonne Lab, but he had no way of getting there and needed to work after school and on weekends.

Other instructors were harder to convince and remained staunch in their dismissal of Peter's abilities. Once, Peter took a course on algae that required a review of the literature and also required writing weekly papers. He kept getting Cs on these papers, which was a very new experience for Peter.

Exasperated, he copied the paper of a white classmate verbatim. When the papers came back, Peter had his usual C, and the white student got an A. Peter confronted the professor, a white male, and went to the head of the department, also a white male. He never had another problem with that teacher, and got an A in the course.

Peter continued to experience problems, however, with other faculty members. His advisor in the biology department had to sign off on his course selections. He was a Hindu Indian who thought Peter was too dumb to be a biology major. He would not approve of Peter taking too many upper-class "hard" biology courses at one time. And he would not let him take his embryology class at all. Peter had to get another department head to sign off on his course selections.

In spite of all of the racism Peter endured from teachers in elementary and high school, he considered peer pressure to be a serious problem. Peer pressure from fellow Black males "to stop being a brain, and to f**k school, miss class and don't do the work" was a big problem his first year in high school. The peer pressure from other Black students to not even try to academically excel, and the physical fear of street violence breaking out in the high school were far worst experiences. The random nature of what could happen to you from violence was a major distraction. And a culture of failure was bad, period.[2]

College and, to a lesser extent, law school, lacked the support mechanisms from faculty and staff to deal with Black students' needs. Peter felt that conditions got better over time, but for many it was too late. Once in college, Peter talked extensively about the race issue. The turmoil of the 60s made race an issue in college and law school. It was always discussed. The white supremacist stereotype of Black men had switched from shiftless, stupid, sex crazed ni**er do-wells, to ignorant, angry, criminal, drug and sex crazed, violent ni**er do-wells. The Black students had to organize and take action as a group because, though their numbers were increasing and times were changing, they were still relatively very few.

There were fifty Black law students in Peter's class, of whom ten would finish. At every level, Black faculty took an interest in and tried to help Peter. There were also a few white faculty members who took an interest in Peter's education and tried to help him, especially in the sciences and in English. But at all levels, among Blacks and whites, Peter's color had an effect. Among some dark-skinned Blacks, he was that yellow ni**er, or white boy, and was treated with some hostility because they thought he saw himself as better than them. Some whites had no idea what he was. When told, they treated Peter differently than they treated more visibly Black people. Overall, as a Black male in college, Peter was often stereotyped as a violent, ghetto-bred animal, regardless of his background.

Section 3.8   Charles Richard Drew Elementary and Byron C. Minor

The Charles Richard Drew Elementary School opened in 1957 to relieve the overcrowding at Gillespie. I was part of a mandatory transfer and was assigned to teach third grade. My principal, Byron C. Minor, was a Black man and became my mentor for the principalship. He had two mottos: (1) if it ain't broke, don't fix it; and (2) if it don't work, fix it, or try something else. By the time I arrived at Drew, I knew that Black children could excel. What I needed to understand better was exactly what activities would work best with the slowest learners.

During the 1960–1961 school year, I requested a class consisting of the children that other teachers did not want to teach. Every year, Mr. Minor placed students in classes according to reading achievement test scores. However, on occasion he would split up discipline problems so that no teacher would have too many in one class. Every year teacher's would gather in the teachers lounge and complain about those problems. I was now asking for them.

Mr. Minor asked, "Do you realize that your class will probably be mostly boys?" his blue eyes twinkling. I hadn't realized that, but after a thought, I said, "I want it anyhow. I must learn how to better teach those students whom we have discarded as lost and unsalvageable."

My class of thirty-five consisted of twenty-eight boys. Half of the students were two years behind in reading or performing at the first grade level. They were in grades second, third and fourth. To help them I used the Cunningham Plan, which instructs: (1) diagnose needs, skill mastery and skill deficiency; (2) target those skills which need attention; (3) select activities which will provide and strengthen these skills; (4) test repeatedly for mastery; (5) provide abundant opportunities for practice; (6) provide immediate feedback; (7) provide supplementary materials for home practice; (8) provide rewards to students who make progress; and (9) give many opportunities for learning about Negro life, culture and history.

Except for one student, each member of my class progressed ten months or more in reading during that school year. Some students advanced twenty months. Most of these students were girls. I kept this group for two years, and in the second year they made tremendous progress.

Section 3.9 Furman Garrett Sizemore

On April 12, 1958, my second child, Furman Garrett Sizemore, was born. When he was born, I had to have an occipital rotation because he was coming out face first. All of his life Furman has been curious about things, questioning and exploring everything. Furman entered Chatham-Avalon Nursery School on Seventy-ninth Street near State when he was four. He attended Jane A. Neil for kindergarten and first grade.

In second grade, his teacher put him under the desk for misbehaving and left him there for the whole morning. He fell asleep, and she forgot he was there. After that, I transferred him to a Negro private school, the Howalton Day School at Forty-seventh and State Street. This was the first of many transfers my young son would have to make during his lifetime.

Furman attended Howalton Day School for seventh and eighth grade, De La Salle Institute in Chicago and Woodrow Wilson Senior High School in D.C., the district high school. It was located in northwest Washington and had a sizeable white student body. Furman ran into trouble during his sophomore year in geometry, during his junior year in trigonometry and finally as a senior with Dr. Maguire, the senior English teacher.

For some reason, the geometry teacher never found a way to communicate with Furman, and he could not seem to please her. In trigonometry the teacher was Korean, and her accent made it hard for him to understand. I could barely make out her English, myself. But Maguire had a cultural or racial problem with Furman. It all happened over her senior term paper assignment.

Maguire told the students to write about an English author. Furman chose Chinua Achebe, an African colonial who writes in English. His paper was brilliant. But Dr. Maguire rejected it, because Achebe was not "English" English. She made Furman choose another author. The second choice was Alistair Maclean. To me, this was white supremacy at its best. I began to wonder why my children had problems only when they manifested moments of brilliance. What was indeed going on here? Yet I simultaneously stifled these thoughts, attributing them to the proud parent syndrome that afflicts most parents.

Section 3.10 Anton Dvorak, My First Principalship

Mr. Minor encouraged me to take and pass the Chicago Public School's principal examination in 1961, and in January 1963, I was assigned to the principalship of the new Anton Dvorak Elementary School at 3615 West Sixteenth Street on Chicago's notorious west side. This part of Chicago was then called the port of entry for Mississippi migrants. This is also the section in which Martin Luther King, Jr. chose to locate his residence during his sojourn in the city. Sixteenth Street was called the "Street of Dreams" by local residents because of the volume of heroin sold on it in the 1960s. Most integrationists saw my new racially isolated school as a disaster about to happen and told me that my children didn't have a snowball's chance in hell for success.

The school opened on April 8, 1963. It was a K–sixth, all Black, which is what we were calling ourselves then, non-graded elementary school of 1,263 students, approximately 60 percent of whom were born in Mississippi. These children had been attending school on double shift from September of 1962 to April of 1963. Some came to school at 8:00 A.M. and left at noon; others came at noon and left at 4:00 P.M. They shared books, materials, seats, supplies and sometimes teachers. The new school was structured to relieve overcrowding.

There were forty-two teachers: 65 percent were first-year assignments, 66 percent Black, 30 percent Jewish and 4 percent other whites. Georgia R. Williams; my double cousin Jo, the counselor; Mary J. Faust, the nurse; Gladys Berry, the librarian; and Clara K. Holton, the assistant principal were all Black. Clara K. Holton profoundly changed the direction of my professional life. She introduced me to the non-graded school.

The non-graded school concept operated from the premise that grouping children as learners by ages and grades, and then passing them in lockstep fashion from grade to grade because of age, was dysfunctional, since such grouping and promotion neither accounted for nor accommodated human incommensurability.

CPS called it Continuous Development. Students aged six and up were placed in teaching groups according to a constellation of ten factors. Teaching groups were called lanes and were lettered instead of numbered. There were actually three grades: kindergarten, primary and intermediate. There were two divisions, which were all male, each taught by a male teacher. Students were placed, by achievement in reading, in four lanes: A, B, C, D. This placement was determined by stanines. In a normal curve of distribution, such as reading test scores, there are nine stanines, with stanines one, two and three representing low achievement levels; four, five and six, representing average achievement levels; and seven, eight and nine, representing high achievement levels. Students at or beyond stanine level seven were placed in Lane A; stanines five and six in Lane B, and so on. Their ages ranged from six to eleven in the intermediate block/grade.

The reading and mathematics curriculum consisted of skills sequentially ordered in a hierarchy from simple to complex. Students progressed according to maturation and readiness and were exposed to knowledge through activities, tested to ascertain mastery, and given a new group of exercises when warranted. Students weren't penalized for not learning, but were given another chance to learn with a new set of experiences.

Of the schools in District Ten of the Chicago Public Schools, Dvorak ranked at the twentieth percentile in reading achievement in 1963. By 1964, it had risen. There were 184 students enrolled in kindergarten in October 1963. Of the 184 students, only forty-two (23 percent) were ready to read. Of the 205 students enrolled in kindergarten one year later, ninety-seven students (47 percent) were ready to read according to the Metropolitan Readiness Test administered in 1964.

students' skill mastery needs were diagnosed and taught by direct instruction. Phonics was an important part of reading instruction in both the kindergarten and the primary grades. Staff development was continuous. The faculty even provided in-service for other schools. We ran a tight ship and produced great students.

I tried to have a meeting with Martin Luther King, Jr. to discuss the students' achievement at Dvorak, but I never was able to do this. I did speak with Jesse Jackson. But, by that time, (1963–1965), the Civil Rights movement wanted enforcement of the Supreme Court's Decision in *Brown v. Board of Education*, which was ten years old. Chicago's schools were more segregated than ever. But the leaders of the Civil Rights Movement were sold on mixing up the races in the classrooms and Benjamin C. Willis, the superintendent of the Chicago Public Schools, was opposed to this and he became their target.

Consequently, I could not get anyone to take me seriously when I argued that Black students could excel, even in a segregated setting, if the teachers and the principal believed that they could and taught them to do so. I even argued about this issue with Ron Edmonds during those years. At that time, he agreed with the Movement. But the failure of integration to occur with all deliberate speed convinced him otherwise. The major problem with *Brown v. Board of Education* was the necessary assumption that anything all Black is no good. This was a reinforcement of Black inferiority and white supremacy. Many Chicagoans called me a traitor because of this, and accused me of defending Superintendent Willis and referred to me as Aunt JeBarbara.

Section 3.11   Too Busy for Love

Because both my husband and I worked full time and were away from home for long hours, we divorced in 1964. We had grown far apart (mostly due to my ambitions and pursuits.) To make matters worse, Kymara was sixteen and my son was six. This is all I will say about this matter.

CHAPTER 4

BEING A SCHOOL LEADER

In order to understand what is happening to Africans as a people, and especially what is happening to Africans in education, we must begin at the beginning and describe the entire story. The whole story reveals patterns. These patterns, not details, give us the essence of what is happening. To fail to perceive the pattern is to raise one's susceptibility to the seductiveness of attractive, but false, issues. Jean Piaget calls this capacity in young children "conservation," that is, being able to see the changes in form may not mean that there are changes in substance. There have been many changes in the form of educating Africans in America, but few changes in the substance.

—Asa G. Hilliard III, Ph.D.
SBA: The Reawakening of the African Mind

Section 4.1 Separation in an Integrated School

From the time she was five years old, Kymara took ballet lessons at the Chicago Conservatory of Music. So, in 1964 she applied for entry into Esande, the honors dance group at ETHS. To my surprise, she was denied. Not believing that the candidates who were accepted were better than my daughter, I went to observe them at practice. I was outraged at what I saw. Several of the accepted dancers were just plain clumsy, leaping across the stage with the grace of untrained baby elephants. I went directly to the principal, Dr. Lloyd Michael, and protested the school's decision. He promised an investigation, but for me he took too long to carry out his promise.

I then contacted Bennett Johnson, an Evanston community activist, and later president of the Evanston NAACP, for help and sent out over 300 letters to Black parents asking them to attend a meeting at Foster Field regarding the exclusion of Black students from extra-curricular activities and performing groups in Evanston. My mother said she would go with me because she was sure no one would show up to the meeting. We were astonished to find an overflow crowd at Foster Field.

Apparently, many other Black students with real talents had been excluded from drama, choirs, bands, and the orchestra. We selected Bennett Johnson as our spokesman and set up a meeting with Dr. Michael. At that meeting the teachers blamed the administration and vice versa. Teachers said that the administration advised them not to put Black students in lead roles or in the performing arts groups because the white people in Evanston would not like it. Though the administration was in denial, the outcome was the inclusion of Black students in these groups.

Section 4.2 Forrestville High, My Second Principalship

When the principalship for the Forrestville High School was advertised, friends advised me not to apply. The school was located in the center and converging boundaries of four warring gangs: The Blackstone Rangers, the youngest group, the East Side Disciples, the War Lords and the aging Four Treys. Drexel Avenue was the war zone line between the Blackstone Rangers and the East Side Disciples. Students could not come across Drexel Avenue to attend Forrestville without a fight. Sometimes guns were used and people were shot.

Forrestville started with a freshman class and was a grow-a-year high school. When I was assigned there as principal in September 1965, there were 1,159 students in ninth and tenth grades. The assistant principal who had been running the high school then was Anderson Thompson. He proved to be the next important person in my professional life. It was he who taught me how to be a high school principal in a time of turmoil and tension. Many teachers were full-time basis substitutes. Most people did not want to come into the area to teach. Several teachers were vocal dissidents opposed to racially isolated Black schools.

The Forrestville faculty was approximately 70 percent Black and 30 percent white. The administration, however, was entirely Black: Anderson Thompson, Frank Allen, William Hunter, Beverly Daniels and myself. Teachers immediately, upon my appointment, divided into two ideological camps: (1) those who believed that Blacks could be educated in a segregated setting and who wanted the new high school to be located in the Black community; and (2) those who wanted the new high school built in an area conducive to integration, and who believed that it was impossible to have an excellent education in a segregated high school. I took a position with the first category. It was war from the start.

The protest teachers considered me an Aunt Jemima, encouraged students to challenge the administration and, knowingly, incited the gang leaders to war. In the spring of 1966 the Council of Coordinating Community Organizations (CCCO), under the leadership of Al Raby, picketed the high school and recruited teachers as members.

In spite of these troubles, Anderson Thompson gave me some strong points on high school organization. Although he is a historian by training, his intuition for social dynamics of organizations is enormous. I told him that I entered the girls washroom one day and found some students smoking. When I told them to stop, they reminded me that my washroom was in my office. When I complained about this lack of respect he told me, "The biggest weapon teenagers have is anonymity." In five days I learned 900 names. After that, Mr. Thompson urged me to identify the leaders of all the organizations in and out of school. Whenever there was trouble we called these student leaders in to talk. Most of our students had trouble. At one time, over 60 percent of our male students were either on probation or had been incarcerated. Thompson's process was to identify students needs, to win them over to his side by meeting those needs, to take a strong stand with the students when it met their needs, to defend his position and never to act as though he was afraid.

In two weeks, I knew the Forrestville student leaders. Interestingly, we found that certain gangs dominated the teams. Thompson suggested we meet with these leaders. From this meeting we learned that a gang war was imminent, involving a majority of our male students. Two days after the meeting, two gangs declared war and members of one of them shot into the school from a passing car. Luckily, no one was hurt. Students who lived at Forty-second and Oakenwald in a huge twenty-seven story public housing project with large apartments of four bedrooms, could not come to school at all. Crossing Drexel meant death. We appealed for two uniformed juvenile officers to be assigned to the school. CCCO teachers criticized this recommendation, calling for the school to be closed. Grievances were sent to the Chicago Teachers Union in October of 1966. During that time James Redmond became the superintendent of schools. After a great deal of negotiation, begging and pleading, we were assigned two officers.[1]

The first step enacted was disarmament. Weapons were taken from students and removed from school premises. The second step was an improvement in self-esteem. In the midst of this turmoil, self-image building assemblies called the "Men of Forrestville" were held each month for all male students and faculty, and "Women of Forrestville" for all female students and faculty. These programs produced the Magnificent Seven, a group of young male student orators who represented Fredrick Douglass; Martin Luther King, Jr.; W. E. B. Du Bois; Booker T. Washington; Malcolm X; Marcus Garvey; and Adam Clayton Powell. These students performed throughout the city, state, and nation. Social science and history teachers were given an African American centered curriculum to teach, starting with the Forrestville community and extending into the universe. And the division periods, sometimes called homerooms, were lengthened to establish a school family for our students. The third step was tackling the low achievement of many students. For example, those who were four years behind in reading were placed in English classes for reading.

In response, English teachers grieved to the union, protesting that they were not reading teachers. In November, teachers refused to do lunchroom duty, declaring the area unsafe for teachers. All administrators were assigned duty. There were four lunch periods from 10:20 A.M. to 1:00 P.M. I supervised the last lunch. For the rest of the term, CCCO teachers resisted any administrative attempts to improve the quality of education at Forrestville. Finally, unsatisfactory ratings were sent for twelve teachers charging them with insubordination and failure to exercise assigned duties. Since ten of them were substitutes, these were transferred out. New teachers were assigned to Forrestville the next term.

When I left Forrestville in 1967, it was on the brink of improving student achievement. I learned the hard way that Black academic achievement can occur only when there is an orderly climate conducive to learning, and where there is a principal convinced that Black students can learn, and where there is a consensus about the priority of achievement among the faculty. Forrestville produced the only Black National Merit Scholar in 1968 in the Chicago area, Carolyn Haynes, who went on to graduate from the University of Chicago.

Section 4.3 The Center for Inner-City Studies, Northeastern Illinois University

In 1965, Dr. Donald H. Smith, then assistant professor of speech at Chicago Teachers College-North (CTC-N) and later assistant professor at Northeastern Illinois University, together with urban anthropologist Stanley Newman, submitted a proposal to the U.S. Office of Education under the Experienced Teacher Fellowship Program, which resulted in the Center for Inner City Studies (CICS). According to Gerald Butler (A Case Study in Urban Teacher Education: The Center for Inner City Studies: 1966–1971)[2] CICS was one of the first institutions in the United States to dedicate itself to the preparation of teachers for service in the inner city ghetto areas. The program trained experienced teachers from all over America to be more effective with inner city youth. I became an adjunct faculty member of this program, as did Anderson Thompson, under the urging of Dr. Smith.

CICS had its legitimate base in the traditional academic center, but it was a radical departure from the general academic framework. In Northeastern Illinois University's "Center for Inner City Studies Report 1972–1973" it states that the primary concern of this organization was the "human condition in the inner city." It further explains that "the accepted categories of academic speculation are generally considered too limited and remote from the total life experience to produce the insights and ideas that would promote the relevant changes in human relations as they are determined by the real needs of inner city communities."

Gerald Butler commented that CICS's impetus was a letter from U.S. Congressman William L. Dawson, First District of Illinois (1943–1970), to Dr. Jerome Sachs, academic dean at Chicago Teachers College–North (CTC-N), outlining a preschool educational and activity program for four and five-year-old children who lived in the poorer precincts of the city. Faculty and administrators at Chicago Teachers College–South (CTC-S), however, felt that this was an infringement on their territory. The inhabitants of this predominantly Black neighborhood resented CTC-S for being a school that was predominantly White. Although Dr. Sachs responded favorably to it, Dawson's proposal was set aside.

In his book, *Climbin' Up the Mountain Children: The Journey of an African American Educator*,[3] Donald H. Smith notes: "I believed it was important to locate the program in the heart of the Black community, rather than at the college which was located in an all-white neighborhood. After a lot of exploration I came up on an ideal site." That ideal site was the Abraham Lincoln Center, a place with which Smith was familiar. He had attended its library as a little boy while living in the Ida B. Wells Housing Project. After a meeting with Mayor Richard J. Daley, Sr., Smith was able to get the building leased to the college.

During the spring of 1965, William Itkin, professor of psychology at CTC-N, submitted a proposal to the United States Office of Education (USOE) for funding of a National Defense Education Act (NDEA) institute for teachers of the disadvantaged. At that time, he was director of the college's Master's Degree Program for Teachers of the Culturally Disadvantaged. Itkin and Smith engaged a number of education people, of whom I was one, to present at this institute. Although the federal government did not fund it, Itkin and Smith managed to secure funding from acting dean, Robert Goldberg. Itkin was unable to devote sufficient time to the endeavor and most of the work fell on Smith, who became the college's catalyst for these ideas. Eventually, Smith and Newman secured funding for CICS and it opened on September 8, 1966.

Butler and other informants described Smith as highly regarded and dedicated to the advancement of Black people and other minorities. He had little difficulty assembling a group of six people of like mind. I was a member of this group, but without a doubt, Donald H. Smith was the brilliant visionary in this operation. Smith was so committed that he forfeited his position as assistant professor of speech when his faculty demanded that he give all of his professional energies to his duties on the main campus or resign. He resigned.

Between 1969 and 1970, five long-range programs were developed at CICS. The ExTFP, a program in which experienced teachers who wanted preparation for teaching in the inner city were recruited for a master's degree in education, was funded for three years. According to Butler, the program was structured around four principles: improvement of communication between teachers and students through mutual respect for language patterns; respect for ethnic minorities through knowledge and appreciation of their histories and cultures; empathy toward students through an awareness of, and respect for divergent lifestyles; and awareness of the individual worth of each student, combating the self-fulfilling prophesy syndrome. Confrontation of racism was a technique frequently used to carry out these principles. Students wrote to the USOE regarding their negative perception of this practice, complaining about the perceived lack of traditional course work usually given in graduate programs; emphasis by faculty on students attitudinal change; and a lack of rapport between faculty and fellows. The students asked that Smith be removed. Smith offers some insight into this in his book:

> In the midst of a tumultuous civil rights movement students and faculty
> were being obliged to examine their racist tendencies and ethnic stereotypes. The
> information we helped students to gather that first year proved so traumatic for
> some that a delegation of students met secretly with the college president and
> asked for my removal as director. (Smith, 2002)

He remained for another cycle and left at the end of the 1967–1968 school year when the faculty turned him down for promotion to full professor, but not until CICS had been evaluated and recognized by the faculty Senate as a permanent academic department. This testifies to the kind of leader Don was. He later said of this experience, "It was with pain that I left my beloved Center and my beloved Chicago." Sonja Stone was named acting director and chair of the Department of Inner City Studies and Dr. Arnez was selected to be director of ExTFP.

The Prospective Teachers Fellowship Program (PTFP) was funded in April 1967, before Dr. Smith's departure from CICS, for a period of five years. The unique feature of the PTFP was its emphasis on language development. Its recruits were college graduates who aspired to be teachers, and it offered a master's degree in education in inner city studies. Elise Tucker and Dr. Nancy L. Arnez co-directed this program. Arnez, Smith and Tucker created the

Alternative Teacher Training Program long before those who now claim precedence.

Several programs were initiated through CICS under the dynamic leadership of Dr. Arnez. The Extended Day Program offered course work leading to a Master's Degree in Education for students who worked during the day. To accommodate these students' work schedules, classes were held late in the afternoon and early in the evening. The Career Opportunities Program (COP) and the Cultural Linguistic Follow-Through Model were both developed and implemented under Arnez's tenure. COP was designed to provide an opportunity for low-income people to enter the teaching profession and was sponsored by USOE. Teacher's aides enrolled in the courses at CICS while they still served in local schools. The first class began on July 1, 1970, with 116 participants. CICS also produced a national model for Follow-Through with its Cultural Linguistic Follow-Through Program developed by Dr. Arnez, Martha Bass, Renee Edmonds, Clara K. Holton and Edythe Stanford Williams and implemented in Chicago, Illinois; Akron, Ohio; Compton, California; and Topeka, Kansas during the 1969–1971 school years. The model was designed to improve the education of children in kindergarten through third grade. This model included the Ethno-Linguistic Oral Language Technique, which was a framework for inclusion of the language of the child's culture in the content of the curriculum. The technique provided a means of utilizing, as a bridge to academic tasks, the rich background of stimulating experiences from community resources familiar to the child.

An outgrowth of CICS, initiated by Sonja Stone, was the Communiversity, which was a forum of Black intellectuals seeking and creating knowledge. It was the Communiversity that expanded my intellectual horizons. There were many courses and workshops on capitalism, enslavement, and Jim Crow, as well as African history, life and culture. There I was introduced to the works of men and women I had not known: John Henrick Clarke, Josef ben Jochannon, George Padmore, Zora Neale Hurston, Toni Cade Bambara, Sonia Sanchez, Haki Madhubuti and Mari Evans. The Communiversity was an important part of CICS and its legacy. I entertained many of these visiting lecturers at my home on Chicago's south side. So the Communiversity was not only an important part of CICS and its legacy, but it also impacted my personal life as well.

Donald H. Smith brought many faculty people together who later influenced my thinking about African and African American education: Nancy L. Arnez, who also wrote a book about my superintendency, and Sonja Stone, who introduced me to creative strategies for teaching. Moreover, Smith introduced me to consulting, which I have done for all of these nearly forty years. I also met Ruth Jones Farmer, now Swinson, from USOE and Arthur Thomas from Model Cities in Dayton, Ohio. Thomas later became the highly regarded president of Central State University in Xenia, Ohio. At CICS I also met Charles Smith of the Rockefeller Foundation, who later saved my professional life after I was fired from the D.C. superintendency.

Dr. Arnez was a very impressive intellectual leader with a vision for African American education and a mission to which she was devoted. She was also an accomplished poet. CICS grew under Dr. Arnez, adding many programs, including cultural events, such as "Rapsodi in Black" by Sonja Stone, a West Side youth school, the Career Opportunities Project with the Woodlawn Experimental School District and adult activities. After Smith's departure, the faculty adopted a sexist view regarding the participation of female faculty. I was very much opposed to this direction, as was Dr. Arnez, but the female faculty failed to articulate any effective protest. By 1972 I had separated myself from CICS.

I was gone from Chicago for twenty years (1972–1992). When I returned, searching for partners to work in the Chicago Public Schools, I found that CICS was somewhat indifferent. They were still training teachers, but, their emphasis was now on Africa and African culture under the leadership of Jacob Carruthers and Donn Bailey. I did some work with Anderson Thompson in several Chicago Public Schools for them, but I was never able to engage CICS in any of our school reform activities. In 1969, Donald H. Smith and Nancy Levi Arnez wrote in the *Journal of Teacher Education*:[4]

> The central thesis of this article is that the key to improved instruction for
> educationally deprived children is improved training for their teachers. Ideally,
> this should commence during the undergraduate years, but even then, there will
> still remain a tremendous job of retraining teachers already in service. (Smith and
> Arnez, 1969)

They outlined their philosophy of educating African American and minority children who were poor in public schools. In a 2002 article titled, "High Performance in High Poverty Schools: 90/90/90 and Beyond," Douglas B. Reeves,[5] president of the Center for Performance Assessment and on the faculty of several programs sponsored by the Harvard Graduate School of Education, reiterates the same observation. He noted: "The 90/90/90

54

research and the other evidence offered in this article falls far short of perfection. It does, however, contribute to the larger body of evidence, which, in its totality, suggests useful strategies for high poverty schools." Smith and Arnez saw the way to solve the achievement gap in 1969, and the permanence of CICS serves as Donald H. Smith's legacy to Chicago, his hometown.

In 1999, Carol Adams, then Director of CICS, submitted proposals to the CEO of Chicago Public Schools for a principals training institute. And in 2003, Conrad Worrill, then Acting Director of CICS, hired Grace Dawson as a faculty member to train principals. Dr. Grace Dawson had been the principal of Beethoven Elementary School located at Twenty-five West Forty-seventh Street and in the center of the Robert R. Taylor Homes. The Taylor Homes are a public housing project stretching for miles down Chicago's State Street. When she failed her eighth graders, Arnez, Smith and I protested by writing a letter against her nomination for the 1989 Ida B. Wells Risk Takers Award. This award was given annually by the National Alliance of Black School Educators (NABSE). But in spite of our protest, she received the award.

After my return to Chicago, I realized that she had done so to dramatize the terrible inequities present in the distribution of resources among the Chicago public schools. Vallas later adopted her policy of retention, although I do not think retention, social promotion or referral to special education eliminates the causes of school failure. Those causes all stem from the regular education program.

Dawson went on to lay the foundation for Beethoven to be an effective school where a larger percentage of students there reached or exceeded the national norm in reading and mathematics on the Iowa Test of Basic Skills than students in similar schools. She also organized a Saturday school in her church for tutoring these children and providing experiences that would elevate and accelerate achievement. By 2002, under a succession of highly competent principals (former teachers under Dawson—among who were Lula Ford and Frances Oden), 45.9 percent of Beethoven's students reached or exceeded the national norm in reading on the Basic Skills test, and 54.9 percent reached or exceeded the national norm in mathematics. Dawson also served as Instructional Supervisor and Coordinator for the School Achievement Structure at DePaul University, mentoring principals of low achieving schools upon her retirement from CPS. She has contributed much to Chicago Public Schools and strengthened CICS's connection with school reform.

Section 4.4 Director of Woodlawn Experimental School Project (The WESP Years)

Hedged in by the Black community, the University of Chicago was always in some kind of discussion about moving out of Chicago or containing the Black community. I entered the doctoral program there in 1962, but was never serious about completing it. At the time, the school of education at the University of Chicago had some distinguished professors: Roald Campbell, Luvern Cunningham, Franklin Seaberry Chase, Allison Davis and Donald Erickson. Later, Edgar Epps and Diane Slaughter-Defoe would join the faculty. Chase, Cunningham, Davis, Epps, Erickson, Paul E. Peterson, and Diane Slaughter-Defoe played important roles in my intellectual development from 1965 to 1970.

Bernard Charles Watson 'Bernie'[6] was an intellectual giant from little Gary, Indiana. He completed the doctoral program at U of C in two years, while I took fifteen. In his book, *Negro Colored Black: Chasing the American Dream*, he said of U of C: "I entered the program in 1965; I intended to be out of there with my degree in 1967. Of course, everybody thought I was deranged when I said this—nobody finished a doctorate from U of C in that time—so I didn't mention it again." Later, Bernie would serve as deputy superintendent of schools in Philadelphia, vice president for academic administration at Temple University and president of the William Penn Foundation.

By 1969, Black Power was in vogue. Community control was the implementation of this ideology. Community control was a form of decentralization. Throughout the struggle for equal educational opportunity there have been cycles of desegregation and decentralization but never an effective assault on white supremacy and its consort, Black inferiority. Negro was out and Black was in, even though there was a growing preference for African culture, as illustrated by afros and such terms as "Africentered." Of course, this last term had to wait another ten years to pass into popular use.

I was studying at the University of Chicago for my doctorate (1967–1969) when I was chosen to be the director of the Woodlawn Experimental Schools Project (WESP) District, a Title Three Elementary and Secondary Education Act (ESEA) government-funded program under Public Law 89–10. WESP was established by the University of Chicago in collaboration with the Chicago Board of Education and The Woodlawn Organization (TWO) to improve the quality of education in three Black schools: Wadsworth Elementary, Wadsworth Upper Grade Center and Hyde Park High School in East

Woodlawn, the home of the Blackstone Rangers in District Fourteen of the CPS. At the time, East Woodlawn was the home of the Blackstone Rangers and was otherwise known as District fourteen of the CPS.

By this time, Black people in Chicago had given up on integration. While few noted the problem, most were still confusing segregation with racism or the belief in Black inferiority and white superiority. A new site in the community had been selected for Martin Luther King, Jr. Senior High School to replace the old Forrestville, assuring its racial isolation. The new high school had been planned by the faculty and administration of Forrestville and the specification sheets lay on my living room floor for six months.

Martin Luther King Jr. Senior High School was planned to be the premier performing arts high school of Chicago. The school was built around its two theaters, following Shakespeare's notion that the world is a stage and all of us are its actors. Every single occupation related to performing arts was represented in the curriculum, from using graphic arts to designing the playbills to constructing the sets and making the costumes. There was a ballet studio, an Olympic-sized gym, a television studio and a radio station. After serving as its director for three years, I left Chicago in 1972, and somehow the school was allowed to disintegrate. CPS built another performing arts high school outside of the community.

Although Superintendent Willis had been deposed, Chicago's schools were very much segregated; and those that were predominately Black were low achieving, except for a few bright spots where students were mostly middle class. WESP developed from a proposal for a Research and Development Center in Urban Education planned by the Committee on Urban Education (COUE) of the University of Chicago in 1965 and 1966.

WESP was governed by the Woodlawn Community Board (WCB), which originally consisted of seven members from each of the collaborating organizations: TWO, the University of Chicago, and the CPS. Later the university relinquished three seats to TWO. WESP consisted of three components: (1) the in-school, or the instructional, component controlled by the CPS; (2) the research component controlled by the University of Chicago; and (3) the community component controlled by TWO. The project had a director and a deputy director, Julius B. DeNye.

The in-school component consisted of an associate director in charge of that component, Clara K. Holton, two program officers in charge of each school, and consultants. The associate director in charge of in-school and the associate director in charge of the community supervised the forty-five community teachers. Theoretically, the principals and faculty of the three schools were part of the in-school component that provided in-service, curriculum supervision and new programs to the schools. The community component consisted of an associate director, Anthony Gibbs, two community organizers, twenty-five community agents and forty-five community teachers.

TWO was a strong and militant community organization that had been created by the vision of four Woodlawn pastors and through the efforts of the Industrial Areas Foundation directed by Saul Alinsky in the early 1960s. It was an organization of civic, religious, business and other community groups that had pledged themselves in a cooperative venture to work together for the improvement and the enrichment of life in modern urban society. Its basic aim was to take the initiative in developing adequate standards and values for community living by generating and maintaining community power.

Voting membership in TWO was by organization, each of which selected five delegates and two alternates to represent it at the delegates meeting, which was held at least once a month. However, in his testimony at the U.S. Senate's hearing investigating the Youth Demonstration Project in 1968, TWO president, Reverend Arthur Brazier, said that the basic unit of membership and participation in TWO was the Block Club. At that time, TWO had approximately ninety block clubs and neighborhood associations and eight standing committees, of which the schools committee was one. The thirty community agent slots and sixty community teacher positions provided by WESP considerably strengthened TWO. Although these positions dwindled as funding failed to keep up with fiscal needs, these people organized more than twenty-five parent councils and managed to send 100 to 200 people to the Woodlawn Community Board's monthly meetings.

Woodlawn is the community contiguous to the University of Chicago to the South. The Woodlawn Community Board (WCB) emanated from a letter written by the Reverend Arthur Brazier to Dr. Roald Campbell, chairman of the COUE. Reverend Brazier criticized the planning procedures and indicated that TWO did not support the use of Woodlawn as a research laboratory by the University of Chicago. Brazier deplored the university's failure to involve TWO in planning the research and development center it wanted to establish in Woodlawn. The Woodlawn Community Council was designed to resolve this conflict. When CPS joined the council, the name was changed to Woodlawn Community Board to avoid confusion with the District fourteen Council of the CPS.

The WCB was to set policy for WESP, but this policy was subject to veto by the CPS Board of Education. The problems around teachers' evaluations provide an example. For me, teacher and principal evaluation formed the crux of the Black student achievement. At both Dvorak and Forrestville, I had learned that many teachers will not teach Black students unless taught how to do so and then made to do it. Consequently, it seemed imperative to me that the WCB have control over principal and teacher evaluation. Friction between Anna Kolheim, the Black principal of Hyde Park High School, and her teachers started early in 1969. Grievances were lodged against the efficiency marks given by the principal, who was a "new" principal in the sense that she was giving marks to that faculty for the first time.

According to CPS Board rules, a new principal "shall give an efficiency grade to those teachers who are on their probationary period. He shall not grade other regularly certificated teachers whose work is satisfactory or better until he has served in that school at least five months." Additionally, the new principal was not bound by marks given by the previous administrator. In her reply to two of the teachers' grievances, the high school principal indicated that she had not visited the teachers' classrooms, nor held conferences. And in her statement before the union representative, the principal said she "assumed" that the classroom teaching was satisfactory.

Teachers were assigned to summer schools if they had excellent marks and qualifications, and promotions demanded superior or excellent ratings. The principal had been asked by the WCB to make her criteria known to the teachers; but I really wanted to change the procedures for teacher evaluation to fit the CAPTS (Community, Administrators, Parents, Teachers and Students) decision-making model, which had been designed by both the in-school and community components and around which a consensus had been developed in WESP.

CAPTS demanded that each group form and meet regularly to report to the WCB on its findings and deliberations. The vehicles for the operational functioning of CAPTS were: (1) the parent councils; (2) the Wadsworth Senate; and (3) the Hyde Park High School Senate. The community agents mobilized parents to form councils. The two Senates were to be established by the two principals in WESP. Neither ever materialized.

During the 1969–1970 school year, the high school principal described her criteria for the next teachers evaluation (May 15, 1970). To be satisfactory, a teacher must do everything a teacher should do, such as prepare lessons, execute plans, arrive on time, meet classes on time, obey school rules and regulations. To be excellent, in addition to meeting the criteria for a satisfactory mark, a teacher must sponsor a club, contribute something to the community through outside efforts, and go beyond the call of duty. To be superior, in addition to meeting the criteria for satisfactory and excellent marks, a teacher must make a contribution to the literature of, or contribute something of worth to, the discipline and the profession.

Some teachers felt that the actual teaching job itself had diminished in value in the face of the new criteria, and they protested to the WCB. To provide teachers with the time to design their own criteria and evaluation process, WCB ordered the principal to give all teachers a superior mark for that term, to be changed, if necessary, according to criteria approved by the teachers and agreed upon by the principal in the CAPTS process. The high school principal complied with the WCB order but refused to sign her name, arguing that she was caught in a bind and forced to obey CPS rules when and if they differed from WCB's.

Edna C. Hickey, director of personnel at CPS, sent a copy of the following letter to me as director of WESP and to the WCB:

> Dear Mrs. Kolheim:
>
> The principal's signature must appear on the rating
> form. Please return your Efficiency Report
> (T.Per.104, Revised 1970) with the individual rating
> of each teacher indicated and signed by you.
> One copy is to be sent to Dr. Donald Blyth, District
> Superintendent, and one copy is to be retained by
> you.
>
> Sincerely,
> Edna C. Hickey
> Director
> Bureau of Teacher Personnel

On March 31, 1970, I held conferences with the teachers who had lodged grievances against the lowering of their efficiency marks by Anna Kolheim in May of 1969. Two of the teachers reported activities such as club sponsorships and involvement in community and related projects conducted during the 1968-1969 school year. These activities seemed to meet the criteria outlined by the high school principal for excellent teaching marks for that school year, and the lowering of the teachers' grades did appear to be arbitrary and capricious. Attempts to get an explanation from the high school principal proved fruitless and teacher morale began to disintegrate. "The problem facing the WESP staff was that it did not have the clear authority to implement a strategy of intervention, which could test this hypothesis: If you want to increase academic achievement, you have first to change the system so that those most immediately affected by the educational process have power to influence that process," noted John Hall Fish,[7] a member of TWO, in *Black Power/White Control*.

Hiring Anna Kolheim, to fill the position of high school principal in WESP had been my idea. I cannot blame anyone else for it. When Reverend Brazier consulted me about the person for the job, she was my first choice. In fact, both officers in TWO and the area superintendent brought their perceptions of her stubbornness and willfulness to my attention. The area superintendent told Reverend Brazier that because of her past attitudes she was not only low on the list, but was unacceptable. Reverend Brazier supported my preference and she was appointed. So in this case I chose my own nemesis.

But I truly saw these characteristics as positive. Several friends who knew people working with her said that she was a person willing to fight the system, a person with courage, stamina, intelligence, industry and commitment. I knew a principal had to have plenty of heart, stamina, and guts. What I did not know was that Anna Kolheim's commitment was to herself, and that, in effect, when I became her superior I was the system she would fight. This, too, was a valuable lesson which I had to experience. A lesson that I experienced again, later in my career in the District of Columbia, before I learned it.

The WESP in-school component, after much involvement in Hyde Park, supported the teachers' efforts to solve this problem. What I learned from this struggle was that the WCB had no power to change CPS Board rules. The principal did indeed have the ability to thwart anything WCB wanted to do and could disregard the project director's orders. John Hall Fish noted in *Black Power/White Control* that the authority relationship between WESP and school personnel was at best ambiguous. During the last years of the project, the high school principal did not attend the WESP meetings, nor those of the final evaluation committee. It was at this point, one year before the project ended, that I knew the road ahead would be rocky and unproductive.

Conditions at Hyde Park High School went from bad to worse. WESP staff meetings were consumed in arbitrating difficulties between the community component and the principal on one side and the Hyde Park program officer, Joseph Montgomery, and me on the other. In June, 1970, teachers demanded better security in the school and criticized the administration for not taking sufficient action in the face of escalating conflict between the two major gangs, the Blackstone Rangers and the East Side Disciples. In his book *Black Power/ White Control*, John Hall Fish wrote:

> In 1966, the Rangers, a small neighborhood gang since the late 1950s, were locked in combat with a rival gang, the East Side Disciples, which shared the Woodlawn turf. Attack, retaliation and escalation continued throughout the winter and spring of 1966. Partly for protection and survival and partly out of zeal, the Rangers entered into intense organizational activity, recruiting youth not only in Woodlawn but in neighboring communities and even distant parts of the city. The core leadership began talking about the Ranger Nation, a confederation of Ranger units. (Fish, 1973)

By 1970, the Ranger Nation was called the Blackstone Nation and could summon over 1000 members at short notice. John Hall Fish also commented that the Nation posed a threat to Woodlawn and to TWO since these youth were "products of the school system, welfare system, unemployment situation, police strategies and poverty" and that "what TWO had done and what TWO meant had not touched them."

A group of teachers mobilized by the WESP high school program officer sat in the deputy superintendent's office seeking help, since they had decided that WESP and WCB were incapable of any action. TWO and the associate director in charge of the community component had never trusted the teachers at the high school and resented this implication of impotence. This action moved TWO into the principal's camp.

In October 1970, students protested a rule governing student conduct, and the necessity for implementing the senate became paramount. In March 1971, students angry about the unimplemented senate decisions around Black History Month, protested against the administration's disapproval of a Black Student Union cultural assembly. Teachers boycotted the senate meeting that was called because they felt the administration had blocked senate actions concerned with security matters. The administration stated that some motions previously adopted were in violation of CPS Board rules. Students claimed that these arguments should have been presented by the administration up front.

On April 5, students were joined by several teachers in a boycott of boycotted classes at Hyde Park High School. The area superintendent placed the principal on a five-week sick leave. The faculty and students began to develop a collaborative relationship with the new acting principal, Spurgeon Gaskins. But on May 20, the WCB voted to return the principal to the school. There was actually nothing else they could do. CPS had no place to put her. WESP was running out of money, and there was no possibility that it could be refunded, especially with the controversies so widely publicized. Students and teachers were so outraged by her return that they went on strike. The high school was removed from my jurisdiction, and students and faculty were arrested. Five teachers were transferred, and WESP joined Ocean-Hill Brownsville as a tragic failure.

The student unrest was too much for CPS, in the face of the many activities of the Blackstone Nation. However, Anthony Gibbs had many contacts with the Nation, and several of their war counselors were alleged to have been community agents. In the spring of 1971, near the close of the program, community agent Frances Cain was distraught because the Nation was attempting to recruit her son, Vincent, who was determined not to join. Vincent was thirteen years old, very stubborn and proud. He claimed that he wasn't going to let anybody bully him. During this time executions were ordinary and the police seemed not to care. At the same time, someone produced a forged advertisement from the Ku Klux Klan offering to sell guns to the Blackstone Nation in support of the good work they were doing killing "ni**ers." Frances asked me to take Vincent to live with me for a while. So in June 1971, Vincent Cain came to live with me and my family. Vincent attended Howalton Day School with Furman for seventh and eighth grade, Metro High School in Chicago and Woodrow Wilson Senior High School in D.C. He graduated from Wilson in June, 1975, and attended Morgan State University in Baltimore, Maryland for two years.

Three factors impeded progress in WESP: (1) the WCB did not have the power to enforce its policies or to hire and fire school personnel; (2) the WESP staff did not have the authority to assign, transfer or evaluate school personnel; and (3) as a consequence of this impotence, the project was used as a patronage program. It soon became obvious to me that there was no future for me in the CPS. The fracas over Hyde Park High School and WESP, and my role in advising the high school leaders of the boycott, had strengthened my reputation as a radical troublemaker among the CPS leadership. WESP taught me the impotence of poor people's chronic need to use schools to fulfill patronage and personal agendas.

The community component became a patronage organization. Because the WCB did not have the power to evaluate the CPS personnel, the in-school component was emasculated and stripped of any power, making the community component the power base. Unable to affect instruction or student achievement, it operated in the only realm possible, job creation and employment. TWO had no choice but to use its community component to organize community power against the CPS. It could not, through WCB, make the CPS recognize its decisions. While Local School Councils created in 1988 by the state legislature can hire, evaluate and fire the principal, they had no control whatsoever over the evaluation of teachers, nor their hiring or firing, nor could they in any way maintain a high quality of instruction in their schools.

Even though the high school dominated the WCB's agenda, it was not the sole problem in WESP. The performance of the deputy director was unsatisfactory. He would not do his work, and he was often late for appointments. More aggravating, he would approve expenditures of money without the project director's knowledge. As participants began to understand the futility of the operation, it was almost impossible to get serious work done. When the high school principal made it clear that she could stop anything from happening, other personnel decided to get the most they could get for as little effort as it took. Personnel started looking for jobs. Work in WESP remained undone. Ultimately, student achievement suffered.

Student achievement, the real target of the expenditure of the federal dollars, was almost forgotten in the conflict between the community, the teachers and the high school principal. Student achievement proved to be mixed. As expected, gains occurred in the area where there was the most teacher consensus: Wadsworth Elementary School.

In 1966, only 29.3 percent of first grade students were ready to read according to the Metropolitan Readiness Test. In 1969, the first year of WESP, 39.1 percent were ready; in 1970, 61.9 percent were ready, and in 1971, 66 percent were ready, due largely to the leadership provided by Clara K. Holton, Renee Edmonds and Ethyl Holmes. For the third grade, the mean score in reading before WESP was 2.920. After WESP, it was 3.108, where the result of the "T" test was significant. The "T" test is a statistical test that determines whether or not two populations are sufficiently dissimilar enough that one could say that one does not belong to the same population. In the case of Woodlawn Experimental Schools Project, students engaged in WESP from 1968–1971 were compared to those who were not.

The evaluation of student achievement was executed by psychologist James Savage and nuclear engineer Warrren Miller, both from Northwestern University and hired to conduct the outside evaluation in determining the extent to which WESP accomplished its stated objectives regarding the academic performance of the students in the district, through the completion date of the project in June of 1971. The questions which the evaluators tried to answer were: (1) Is there a significant increase in mean scores of each subtest of the Metropolitan Achievement Test and the Davis Reading Test under WESP? (2) Do students' scores vary as a function of quartile rank? (3) Do students in the lower grades show greater relative improvement than students in the upper grades?

As expected, the younger the student, the better the performance. On average, post-WESP first graders achieved higher reading scores than pre-WESP first graders. Statistical analyses were conducted to determine whether the observed differences could have occurred by chance. WESP experiences appeared to be the most important variable. In terms of the mean subtest scores by quartiles for the reading test, the first graders in the lowest quartile showed the greatest percentage gain of the post-WESP first graders when compared to the pre-WESP first graders in the same quartile. The students in the third quartile showed the next highest percentage gain. Thus, there appeared to be a strong tendency for the students in the bottom half of the distribution of students to show the most beneficial effects from their WESP experiences, as they are mirrored in reading test scores. However, post-WESP students in the first and second quartiles showed non-significant percentage decreases when compared to their pre-WESP counterparts.

In June 1971, to bring me in line, I was assigned to Government Funded Programs under the supervision of James Moffatt, with whom I was never able to work out a satisfactory relationship. We first fought over the pictures hanging in my office space of Malcolm X, Angela Davis and Martin Luther King, Jr. I was ordered to remove them from my walls. I refused on the grounds of discrimination. Immediately, Richard Tygielski, my straw boss, began hounding me for their removal, although my white coworkers had pictures of their ethnic heroes and heroines on their walls, and many Catholics had crosses hanging over their desks with other religious artifacts. However, on February 29, 1972, Richard Tygielski sent a bulletin to everyone in the unit saying:

I would appreciate your taking whatever steps are necessary with members of your staff to assure that the physical surroundings of the Department of Government Funded Programs are businesslike in nature. I am sure you will agree with me that personal pictures, check lists, calendars, etc, taped or stapled to the outer walls of the office do not create a businesslike tone for the general public. I appreciate your assistance in this matter.

This order hardly made me popular in my unit.

Although Mr. Moffatt reminded me daily that he was the only person who had been willing to hire me after the WESP fiasco, I seemed to be at odds with him on almost everything. We rarely agreed on procedures, processes or routines. The explosion came when he tried to involve me in his attempt to eliminate William Jones, then director of the Bureau of Dropout Prevention.

On July 14, 1972, I wrote my second letter to Mr. Manford Byrd, Deputy Superintendent of Schools for CPS, regarding the discrimination against Black directors in the Government Funded Programs unit. Mr. Moffatt had invited me to a meeting where his intent was to reprimand Mr. Jones and use me as a witness. I refused to be so used, and Mr. Moffatt indicated his intent to cite me for insubordination. I stormed out of the office and wrote my letter. I never received a response from Mr. Byrd; and Mr. Jones, with whom I have a common nephew, kept his position. In fact, his wife, Nina Flemister Jones, was promoted to director of personnel after Edna C. Hickey retired.

By this time I was in deep, deep trouble. I requested to be placed back in the field in a principalship, if possible. Isaac and Jessie Huey, whose son had been clubbed to death in Cicero in 1968, while searching for employment, mobilized a parent and community group to draft me as district superintendent, but Mr. Byrd would not be moved. So, I left CPS in December of 1972. Much later, James Moffatt was convicted of child molestation and sent to prison.

Section 4.5   Organizations; African Heritage Studies Association

While I was director of the Woodlawn Experimental School District in Chicago (1969–1972), I joined the African Heritage Studies Association (AHSA). In AHSA, I developed a closer relationship with Molefi Asante, John Henrik Clarke, Gerterlyn O. Dozier, Leonard Jeffries, Maulana Karenga, Charshee C.L. McIntyre, Acklyn Lynch, James Turner, Ronald Walters, and Barbara Wheeler, and strengthened my bond with Nancy Arnez and Sonja Stone.

AHSA was founded as a protest group to the African Studies Association. John Henrik Clarke, our greatly renowned and highly-regarded Africanist and a professor in the Department of Black and Puerto Rican Studies at Hunter College, City University of New York, described AHSA as an association of scholars of African descent, "dedicated to the preservation, interpretation and academic presentation of the historical and cultural heritage of African peoples, both on the ancestral soil of Africa and in the Diaspora in the Americas and throughout the world." Clarke, the accepted heartbeat of AHSA, wrote that the 1969 revolt against white scholars in Montreal was primarily over the search for the definition of, and direction for, an ideology for African studies. He further noted, "We dreamed some big dreams that day and we promised to make them into realities." Clarke mentioned six great aims: education, international Black students, domestic Black students, Black scholars, Black schools and Black communities.

Under the educational program, AHSA was to reconstruct African history and cultural studies programs along Afrocentric lines in order to effect a union of international Black scholars, to act as a clearing house of African program information, to present papers at seminars and symposia where any aspect of African life and culture were discussed, and to relate, interpret and disseminate African materials for all levels of Black education.

Under the international program, the objective was to reach African countries in order to facilitate greater communication and interaction between Africans in Africa and Africans in the Americas, to assume leadership in the orientation of African students to America and the orientation of African Americans in Africa, and to establish an Information Committee on African and American relations whose function would be to research and disseminate membership information on all aspects of American relations with respect to African people.

The objective of the domestic program was to relate to those organizations that were predominately involved in, and influenced the education of, Black people, to solicit their influence and affluence in the promotion of Black Studies and in the execution of AHSA programs and projects, to arouse social consciousness and awareness of these groups, and to encourage their financial contribution to Black schools with programs involving the study of African people. For the Black student and scholar programs, the objective was to encourage and support students who wished to major in the study of African people, to encourage Black students to relate to the study and heritage of African people, to acquire the ranges of skills for the production and development of African people, to encourage Black attendance and participation, including the reading of papers at meetings dealing with the study of African life and history so that the American perspective is represented, and to ask all Black students and scholars to rally around AHSA in order to build it up as the sturdy organization for the reconstruction of our history and culture. To achieve the aim of the Black community program of the AHSA agenda, the objective was to seek to aid Black scholars who needed financial support for their community projects or academic research and to edit a newsletter or journal, through which AHSA activities would be known.

AHSA limps along on its last legs, never having achieved its aims and objectives as an organization, although individual members's pursuits were fruitful. According to Gerterlyn O. Dozier, adjunct professor at Bernard Baruch College and Fordham University, and former treasurer of AHSA, the organization's funding relied on the university departments of the members involved. The universities funded travel and other expenses for members to attend AHSA conferences. When the universities denied these requests, funding of organizational projects and programs became problematic.

AHSA never dealt adequately with raising funds. Dozier further notes that the resources for organizational maintenance came primarily from City College of New York, Cornell University, and Queens City College under Clarke's leadership. She states that members were concerned about getting tenure and "how they were going to look to organizations [that] were going to fund them." As an example of the type of organization helping with tenure, she cited the National Council of Political Economists, then led by William Nelson (head of the Black Studies Department at Ohio State University), Shelby Smith (a former professor of Political Science at Atlanta University) and Ronald Walters.

And because AHSA had so many distinguished scholars, there were many arguments over ideology and procedure. Clarke had hard feelings towards Maulana Karenga and constantly referred to his position on the deference of women as an obstacle to progress. While Clarke's criticism was just at a previous time, Karenga was attempting to make adjustments in his viewpoints, for which Clarke gave him no credit. In addition, AHSA had a sexist quality regardless of Karenga.

In the early days of AHSA, women, especially Dozier, McIntyre and Wheeler, did most of the work while the men occupied the ceremonial positions of leadership. While Arnez and I protested vehemently, Dozier, McIntyre and Wheeler took more moderate positions. Haki Madhubuti was

68

the only male who supported Arnez and me. Eventually, McIntyre became the first president.

Clarke also charged Acklyn Lynch, a professor at the University of Maryland and a brilliant political scientist from Trinidad, with malfeasance and drove him from the organization, even though the charges were never proved or believed by other members of the AHSA. Barbara Wheeler, a former professor of Black Studies at City College of New York and chair of Black Studies at Keane College in New Jersey, struggled valiantly to clear Lynch's name, but to no avail. No one wanted to challenge our revered patriarch.

Tilden LeMelle, James Turner and Ronald Walters were the mediators attempting to keep these extremely talented and vocal men together for the good of the organization, but their work was overwhelmingly difficult. Turner was a brilliant intellectual who was, at the same time, soft-spoken and calm, yet fully committed to the progress of Africans and African Americans, both organizationally and individually. Not one given to petty actions, he tried to solve problems and eliminate confusion within AHSA. In fact, if it were not for Turner and the support of the Africana Studies and Research Center at Cornell, AHSA would have disappeared long ago. Turner was the only person to offer me a job after I was fired in 1973.

Walters was more of the professorial problem solver, while Clark and ben-Jochannon were word warriors. Walters had a gift for analyzing Black political affairs and writing about them so that anybody could understand them. Although Walters worked for African and African American issues, his interests in African American affairs seemed paramount. Ronald Walters and Acklyn Lynch were the prime movers in my political campaign for a seat on the D.C. City Council in July 1977. I never got to know Tilden LeMelle well. He was very low-profile.

According to Maulana Karenga, at Charlotte "Charsee" Lawrence McIntyre's inaugural presidential address in 1989 titled, "Agenda for AHSA: 21st Century" she listed several organizations in which AHSA members played a founding role, including: TransAfrica (a lobby group for African interests), the National Council for Black Studies, the National Association of Black Educators, the Association for the Study of Classical African Civilizations, and the National Congress of Black Faculty. McIntyre also cited several on-going projects to which AHSA was committed to: (1) Focusing on transnational and international African world interests and cooperative relations among scholars throughout the African world as outlined in Locksley Edmondson's 1985 memo 'Redefining the Role of AHSA; (2) strengthening and expanding the

AHSA student commission to mentor and support young scholars; (3) publishing projects to aid Africana Studies Scholars in publishing their work and producing regular organization literature; (4) sustaining and expanding the AHSA newsletter; and (5) building a Pan-African research institute dedicated to the pursuit of truth and the reaffirmation of African heritage. As members participated in founding of these new organizations their participation in AHSA waned. Fewer and fewer members attended conferences and officers were bereft of support.

Charsee Lawrence McIntyre was a tireless advocate for John Henrik Clarke. McIntyre was Professor of Humanities at the State University of New York at the time. When Clarke lost his sight, it was Charsee who collected money to purchase a reading machine for him. She was convinced that AHSA's primary mission was to promote his work, philosophy and ideology. As a result, she was unable to deal with the real problems that AHSA had. In spite of this shortcoming, there was no one more devoted to the aims and the objectives of the organization, nor anyone more energetic in the promotion of African and African American causes.

However, Charsee struggled with the Afrocentric concept because she was proud of both her Black heritage and her Native American heritage. She consistently pointed out that both her Native American and African ancestries were enslaved people and often insisted that she had a problem with a theory that denied who she really was. Later members began to see this conflict again when students with both Black and white parents entered. The question arose: in order to be African, did one need to deny their white parent? Did AHSA, or any organization, have a right to make such demands?

At an AHSA conference at Wayne State University in Detroit, Haki Madhubuti, Distinguished Professor of English at Chicago State University, attended the conference with his students, some of whom were white. This became a controversial position with AHSA,when advocates for an all–Black conference protested, Turner immediately reminded them that they depended on the largesse of white universities "where a lot of white students attended" for travel and expense funds.

McIntyre's presidency consistently reflected this resiliency and forethought. For instance, a student group was formed with the purpose of developing them into future leaders of Black Studies. Many from this group did enroll in Black Studies Departments, and several completed the requirements for a doctoral degree. Even when she became afflicted with Lupus, she carried on as though she was the same highly charged and effective person. I stayed in the organization because of Charsee. She was a very influential person in my life, and I still mourn her untimely death.

In the middle of the disintegration of AHSA, Leonard Jeffries, former president of the AHSA; founding director of the Association for the Study of Classical African Civilizations (ASCAC); and chair of the Department of Black Studies at City College of New York, gave a speech on July 20, 1991, at the Empire State Black Arts and Cultural Festival in Albany, New York. According to the *New York Post*, Jeffries asserted that "rich Jews" controlled the Black slave trade and that Hollywood was the site of the Jewish-dominated conspiracy to systematically denigrate Blacks. I read Jeffries's speech and all of his citations, which were mainly by Jewish authors, and was very disturbed at this attack on academic freedom. Yet, as disturbed as I was by this, Dozier, McIntyre and Wheeler were consumed by it. They fought against Jeffries's accusers, but lost. He maintained his full professorship, but lost the chair.

Whatever the reasons, Leonard Jeffries continued to be the target of Jewish wrath, especially after the "New York Curriculum of Inclusion" (NYCI) was published. Upon Donald H. Smith's suggestion, Jeffries had been recommended to work on the NYCI at Bernard Baruch City College and became the consultant to the African American group. But, NYCI became the target of Diane Ravitch, Nathan Glazer and Arthur Schlesinger, who rejected Jeffries's contributions after the Albany Speech. Smith notes that:

> On the very day that the advisory committee met to report to Dr. Thomas Sobol, [New York] State Commissioner of Education, Ravitch was already being quoted in John Leo's column in *U.S. News & World Report*, condemning the report…[and naming it] "A Curriculum of Inclusion," [that was] anti-western, its writers and commission non-scholarly, and its purpose as "feel good" curriculum without substance.

Although Smith and others gave support to Jeffries, he was overwhelmed by such big and well-financed guns.

Arnez tends to judge these controversies as contributing causes for the decline of the AHSA, less important is the officer's lack of attention to the dwindling membership and the independent funding. She was in charge of membership for several years and said that AHSA declared that it had 300 members long after that number had declined, and the leaders made no special plans for recruitment. Because many of the AHSA founders and leaders were also heads of Black (African and African American) Studies departments and programs, AHSA competed with the National Council of Black Studies for members, students, time and resources.

Turner and Jeffries were among the very first heads of such departments, Turner at Cornell and Jeffries at San Diego State University. As the leaders split their interests and time with new organizations, AHSA's program became one of rhetoric, rather than action. But this was foreseeable, as AHSA never had a permanent base, said Dozier. Each time there was an election there was a different membership present. Influential members who could have drawn others into the organization left, such as Herschelle Challenor, board chair of the National Summit on Africa, director of the African Diplomatic Outreach Program, and holder of several positions with the United Nation's Educational, Scientific and Cultural Organization (UNESCO) and Willard Johnson, professor of Political Science at the Massachusetts Institute of Technology.

This lack of attention to recruitment and retention of members reduced the organization's financial capability. W. Ofuatey-Kodjoe (former president of AHSA), Jeffries, and Turner provided many resources through their individual departments at Queens City College, City College of New York and Cornell. Charshee McIntyre financed many projects from her own resources. This is certainly no way to operate an organization. As for the student commissions originally projected by McIntyre when she was president, some members financed their participation from their universities and others from their own resources.

For myself, I became more interested in the National Alliance of Black School Educators (NABSE) and less involved in Pan-African pursuits. My entire agenda revolved around African American education; therefore, my participation in AHSA became less. Those whose interests concerned Pan-African and nationalist issues, however, left because of the prominence of the restrictive atmosphere and the constant bickering over small ideas and irreconcilable conflicts.

Section 4.6   The Chase Family

Kymara Sizemore married Lansing E. Chase II in December 1968, and on May 25, 1970, while I was in the midst of this confusion, my grandson Lansing E. Chase III was born in Jefferson County Hospital in Pine Bluff, Arkansas while they were both in their final year at Arkansas AM & N College. Unknown to us he had an allergy to milk that kept him crying almost twenty-four hours a day, exhausting everybody who cared for him. Nearly a year went by before

72

he was properly diagnosed and put on the right diet. After graduation in 1971, his father began working in the research component for WESP.

On August 5, 1972, my granddaughter, Kafi Nicole Chase, was born at Lying In Hospital at the University of Chicago. She weighed eight pounds and filled up the basket. She was a quiet, happy baby. This was a good thing considering that her brother was the opposite. How unlucky for me that I was about to leave town when this little bundle of joy entered my life. My daughter and grandchildren stayed in Chicago with my parents while I went to the Capitol to meet more challenges. I have many regrets about leaving my daughter alone to take care of two small children, and, if I had to live my life over again, knowing what I know now, I don't think I would do it. On the other hand, it is probably better for her that I did. She developed a strong spirit, a sound educational background and managed to see her children successful college graduates.

When my grandson Lanse was in kindergarten at the King Magnet School in Evanston (School District Sixty-five), he had an interesting experience. One day I was visiting the school. When I entered his room, he was standing on top of the piano in his Superman suit. With arms spread out, he jumped to the floor and came running to me. I asked his teacher what he was doing, and she responded, "I am a Piaget teacher." Now another student was trying to catch the fish in the fishbowl with his hands, and two or three others were running around the room. I told her that I thought she should teach the students who were present since Piaget was not there. Fortunately, for Lanse, his mother was a teacher.

At Evanston Township High School, Lanse had this geometry teacher who seemed incompetent. During the 1985–1986 school year I served on the North Central Accreditation Association's team under the leadership of Gordon Cawelti. I observed Lanse's teacher. Surprisingly, most of the students in this teacher's regular geometry class were Black. During my observation, I noticed that four male students were playing cards at the rear of the classroom. Another male student called out, "Hey, Mack, I need to see my counselor. Write me a pass." Other students called him by this nickname, and each time he would respond with some answer. Twice he gave students passes to leave the room. Hardly any teaching occurred, and when it did, some student conducted the activity. When I reported my observations, no one seemed to be aware of this problem. Finally, I asked who was responsible for monitoring teaching and evaluating teachers. The department chair did not seem to be functioning in mathematics. Later, when we met with the mathematics teachers, I inquired into the high percentage of failures among Black students. The teachers unanimously agreed that these failures were due to poor attendance, but when the superintendent provided the attendance statistics, this answer proved to be false. When asked to worry over this enigma, they fell back on blaming the parents, poverty and the community.

My granddaughter, Kafi Chase, was in Honors English and Math classes at ETHS (1986–1990). Normally, she was the only African American student in these classes. Most of her problems came about in Honors English. She began to feel extremely uncomfortable with some of the reading material. Sophomore Honors English reading material included Richard Wright's *Native Son* and *Black Boy* and Shakespeare with an elderly white male teacher named Mr. Workman.

With no background given, and with no knowledge of the atrocities of enslavement, lynching, discrimination and segregation, nor any information about the more recent Civil Rights Movement, she did not become comfortable in that class until they received a student teacher from Northwestern University. This young, white girl introduced the class to African American authored short stories and poetry from her course text, *Being and Becoming*, which Kafi was later assigned at Florida A&M University for freshman English. Her presence generated Kafi's participation in class, and she began reading the material before class and meeting with the other Black honors students before and after their separate classes.

Kafi greatly complained about the feelings of inferiority generated by her ETHS freshman U.S. history class when the teacher informed her predominately African American class that following the Great Depression, FDR, and WWII they were going to study the Holocaust for the next week. When the class realized that meant they were going to skip the Civil Rights Movement completely, they were shocked to find that Martin L. King, Jr. would be discarded also. The entire class objected, arguing that the Holocaust was German history not U.S. history, while the Civil Rights Movement, enslavement and Jim Crow were solidly American. Kafi felt like her history had been relegated to an inferior symbolic universe. Their objections led to the discovery that ETHS had elected to place the Illinois state requirement to study the Holocaust in the required freshman U.S. history class. This made the majority of the African American class fully understand their exclusion.

This struggle for the inclusion of the Civil Rights Movement into U.S. history led to the creation of United Brothers and Sisters (UBS) on campus, in which Kafi took a leadership role. A group of African American students came together to write a newsletter to expose the covert racism that still lingered at ETHS within the curriculum and policies. There were three or four editions of the newsletter, as well as discussion sessions and events. A group of African American male students put together a cotillion for the African American students in ETHS. The rich white students had invitation-only cotillions for years.

My granddaughter was in honors English for two years, but signed herself out of it without her mother's consent because the curriculum neglected the contributions of African Americans, and the teachers would not change it. Instead, she worked on the *Amandla*, a newspaper devoted to African American history, life and culture. My daughter Kymara went through a similar situation at ETHS when she fought against tracking there in 1990, but she was confronted with six system lawyers when she tried to take the matter to court.

Section 4.7 American Association of School Administrators and The National Alliance of Black School Educators

Probably the best discussion of the trials and tribulations of Black school superintendents is still in Hugh J. Scott's *The Black Superintendent: Messiah or Scapegoat?*[8] He says:

> The survival and success of black superintendents is greatly dependent on their ability to demonstrate conclusive evidence of professionalism in the discharge of their duties and responsibilities and to effect appropriate linkages with black-directed endeavors to resolve the problems and needs of Black Americans in a racist society. (Scott, 1980)

When I left the Chicago Public Schools in December of 1972, I joined the staff of the American Association of School Administrators (AASA) as Associate Secretary. One of my assignments was to act as liaison to the newly formed National Association of Black School Superintendents (NABSS).

Dr. Charles D. Moody, Sr. secured funding for and called the first meeting of the nation's Black school superintendents to complete his dissertation on the emergence of Black superintendents and to hold a first meeting of all Black school superintendents. This meeting was held in Chicago in 1970 and was funded by the Metropolitan Applied Research Center (MARC) in New York City. MARC was headed by Dr. Kenneth Clark, famed for his role in *Brown v.*

Board of Education.[9] Meeting again in 1971 in Miami, they formed the NABSS and became self-supportive. The NABSS's purpose was "to provide an organizational means through which the problems of relevance in education as applied to the Black ethnic minority in the United States could be adequately and systematically addressed."[10]

It's functions were to eliminate and rectify the effects of racism in education; to raise the academic achievement level of all students; to place emphasis on that type of learning that built positive and realistic self concepts among Black students; to establish and promote the degree of awareness, professional expertise and commitment among Black educators necessary to enhancing and contributing to the efforts of other educators and community persons; to provide an avenue for recruiting qualified school personnel; to offer specialized training to prospective chief school officers via the development of courses for personnel through cooperative programs with institutions of higher education and school systems; to seek to cultivate resource personnel equipped to assist the Black educator in dealing with special problems; to meet and share ideas, proven programs and guaranteed techniques for demonstrating that Black youth can achieve irrespective of socioeconomic conditions; to provide resources and intelligence banks for Black school educators on proven educational programs; to exchange information of methods for obtaining funds from federal, state and private source; to support educational programs in the schools; and to develop positions on key educational issues that affect the education of students.[11]

Scott states that almost from the beginning NABSS was approached to allow entry to educators other than superintendents. So a meeting was held in April of 1973. I attended this meeting for AASA. To maintain the integrity of the superintendency, the group formed six commissions for the new organization: superintendents, general administrators, local school administrators, and higher education supervisors and directors. Since that time, other commissions have formed. There are now ten: Affiliate Council Commission, District Admission, Governance in Education, Higher Education, Instructional and Instructional Support, Local School Administration, Program Development, Research and Evaluation, Retired Educators, Special Administration and Superintendents. Each affiliate council has members, although they may or may not be national members. For several years, Nancy L. Arnez struggled to persuade the members to make all affiliate members national members, but she was unsuccessful in her efforts. After many years of fruitless attempts, she finally left the national organization. NABSE has continuously worked toward its goal without adequate personnel or funding under various leadership. In 1975, after my public firing from the D.C. superintendency, I offered to serve as Executive Director of NABSE, but nothing ever came of it.

At the 1983 annual convention the NABSE President, Dr. Donald H. Smith, announced the appointment of the Task Force on Black and Cultural Excellence. The Task Force met in Atlanta and in Newark. In addition, members of the Task Force did independent research during the course of the year. Asa G. Hilliard III and I were co-chairs, at least that is what I thought. In reality, President Smith saw Hilliard as chair and me as co-chair.

In 1984, the Task Force[12] issued its "Saving the African American Child" statement (SAAC). It was a bold statement of expectations, high standards and accountability, released before these types of things became standard operating procedures for public school responses.[13] And it was another indication of Smith's vision and leadership. As important, the report articulated the principles of equity, academic and cultural excellence and their relationship to resources. I wrote large sections of this report and sent them to Hilliard, who consolidated all contributions, a testimonial to the insight and deep thinking of Hilliard.

Criterion performance goals were set for African Americans: algebra in the sixth grade, calculus by the twelfth; an understanding of the workings of the American economic and other economic systems; an understanding of and the ability to discuss the workings of the American political system; the ability to write computer programs in one or more languages; an understanding of and the ability to discuss African American perspectives on standard historical topics commonly taught in schools; an ability to write a term research paper demonstrating the ability to use common English, appropriate documentation of ideas and appropriate presentation of ideas; speaking, reading and writing knowledge of at least one foreign language (and the acquisition of competence in an African language should be available as an option) and; the receipt of a passing grade in a course equivalent to chemistry (this assumes that the common practice is to require appropriate course work in biological and physical sciences as a prerequisite); ability to type, care for children, exhibit work habits and develop employability; ability to tell the general story of African and African American people from earliest times to the present; the demonstration of critical thinking and creativity; and the acquisition of a systemic approach to problem solving and the demonstration of an understanding of the scientific method.[14] SAAC defines the discipline and outlines an approach to it. It states:

> We see discipline as the students' ability and the will to do what needs doing for
> as long as it needs doing and to learn from the results. Classroom control is not
> the major task of teaching, but a necessary function of teaching. Most approaches
> to school discipline focus on the wrong things. Educators and parents tend to have
> false conceptions of what causes undisciplined behavior, and thus, do the wrong
> things with the best of intentions. Teaching alternate behavior should be the aim
> of discipline, rather than simply punishing bad behavior. Punishment, as opposed
> to discipline, is most destructive and useless as a deterrent; unlike punishment,
> discipline should be predicated on the premise that a school is a place
> of learning, and that discipline, in a constructive sense, provides educators with
> an opportunity to help students to change their behavior toward more positive
> ends.[15]

Working with Hilliard was a door opened for me by Donald H. Smith, and I will always be grateful for this relationship. Although Hilliard and I wrote SAAC together for the Task Force on Black Academic and Cultural Excellence, he was the greater intellect without a doubt. In spite of this, I felt disappointed when Don wrote (in *Climbin' Up the Mountain Children*) that the report was written by Hilliard.[16]

In the Cleveland conference of 1984, where the report was to be revealed by the two "co-chairs," Don commented that:

> Many of the organizational representatives spoke beyond their allotted time, and
> I was told by the management of the hotel that if we didn't stop the program
> immediately, the room could not be prepared in time for the luncheon. I made the
> difficult decision to ask Dr. Sizemore if she would forego giving her address. She
> answered angrily that she absolutely refused not to speak. And she did speak,
> eloquently as usual, and though the luncheon was delayed, we managed. But the
> relationship between Barbara and me was never the same. It was the beginning of
> the unraveling of a close friendship. Shortly after the conference, Barbara sent me
> a letter that almost caught fire in my hands. She accused me of being sexist and
> made a number of other hurtful remarks. To this date, I never responded to the
> letter. But almost twenty years later, I am still stunned by the charge of being a
> sexist.[17] (Smith, 2002)

In my defense, Don had many opportunities to cut short the presentations of the previous speakers. He could have asked Hilliard to shorten his talk, for instance. He could have done many other things, rather than ask me to forego the presentation I had spent much time preparing. Another thing frustrated me: how could he not have known that I wrote a good part of the report? I agree that I may have been too sensitive about the matter, but by that time, I had done a lot of writing about the issues under review in the report. In 1973, I wrote an article, "Sexism and the Black Male" that caused great consternation at the time and is still often quoted in gender literature.[18]

The article clearly showed that sexism exists as a result of conscious decisions and expectations. I felt that Don's decision to choose me to stop, rather than any of the numerous men there, was such an occasion, regardless of his past behavior, however benign previously. I am grateful to Donald H. Smith for the opportunity to serve on the Task Force, to help implement the great ideas that he generated, and to work with Hilliard. No one has ever given me the opportunity to write a curriculum for African American students, to participate in the development and implementation of one of the first teacher training programs in America geared toward the needs of African American students, or to work with geniuses, as Donald H. Smith has done. Fortunately, I did not change my feelings about him. I thought then, as I think now, that he is one of the most visionary educational leaders in America.

Shortly after Task Force I, Task Forces II and III followed, but no dynamic national thrust made a difference in the elimination of the achievement gap. The President and Congress continued to bless school choice and comprehensive school reform models approved by the New American Schools, in spite of the protestations of Stanley Progrow and Hilliard.

The NABSE Demonstration Schools/Communities Initiative was an outgrowth of the work of the NABSE board of directors' Task Force I and II to establish criteria for identifying schools that had proven successful in educating students of African descent. "Saving the African American Child" and the Blue Print for Action were the documents that preceded the current work of Task Force III. The Blue Print for Action emerged from a meeting sponsored by the honorable Augustus F. Hawkins, U.S. Congressman from California and held on February 26, 1986. The Blue Print was an action plan with implementation activities for parents and families, students, teachers, support services, providers, paraprofessionals, administrators, policymakers, higher education, community and business and religious communities. If NABSE had operationalized this blueprint through the affiliates, as opposed to operationalizing it through Diana Daniels of Indianapolis, profound changes could have occurred in predominantly Black school systems. Both the Blue Print and the SAAC were based on the effective school's model researched by Ronald R. Edmonds. Although J. Jerome Harris and Donald Clark tried to institutionalize the Edmonds Institute through NABSE, it did not happen and they, themselves, had to sponsor it and keep it going.

Task Force II,[19] under the leadership of Jay Cummings, selected schools that were high-achieving and honored their leadership at the NABSE annual conference. It's initiative plan stated:

> To be recommended by Task Force III and approved by the NABSE Board, the schools were required to demonstrate significant progress in the following areas: effective leadership, mission statement, maximum performance expectations, cultural excellence, relevant and effective curriculum, monitoring and reporting student progress, safe and positive climate, active parent and community participation, and civic responsibility and participation.[20]

In my opinion, NABSE strayed from its mission over the years, and in 1998, I gave a speech at the national convention about these problems. I had been invited to give the Houghton Mifflin Breakfast Speech, which was a big event on the conference's calendar. Because I felt that the issues I wanted to raise needed consensus and support, I did something that I rarely do, I shared my comments with the officers of the organization prior to presenting them.

Houghton Mifflin immediately contacted me because they had been informed that my speech would wreak havoc on the organization. Their representative, although a generally supportive person, asked me to change my presentation. I agreed and presented it in my scholar's session instead. But here was the problem as I saw it: members were not attending meetings at national conferences. Since the national organization was governed by the chairs of the commissions, this reduced the number of members making decisions to a number that represented only a few people. The annual meeting was the only contact with the organization for many members.

At the time, NABSE had more than 100 affiliates doing business in the name of NABSE, but not all of the affiliate members were national members. My recommendation was the strengthening of the affiliate and the abandonment of the commissions. In my opinion, the disadvantages of the commission outweighed its advantages. It met only once a year; members did not attend these meetings. A person could be elected chair and serve on the Executive Board with only ten members or less. Its action agenda was difficult to coordinate. It had no recruitment capability, a limited communication capacity and a minimal budget. Affiliates, however, could change this condition. Commissions could not. The fate of the organization, therefore, rested ultimately in the hands of a few who rarely met.

In addition, the president had to maintain his or her full- time job while serving, leaving most of the national organization's public relations and presentations to the executive director. As with other African American organizations and institutions, there is a basic unwillingness on the part of the people to fund their own interests. NABSE was no different. At the constitutional convention held in D.C. from July 27 to July 29, 2001, affiliates voted down the recommended requirement that all members be national members. In addition, all commissions remained on the executive board, with six regional representatives for the 100 affiliates. So in effect, no change occurred. Like many organizations before it, NABSE is ineffective in bringing about change in the condition of African American children because it has no money and it is governed by a few who have their own vested interests to meet.

To show how much the organization has disintegrated, there has been a recent dispute as to whether or not Charles Moody Sr. is the founder. This after all of his hard work in bringing about the superintendents whose organization led to NABSE! Currently there are three founding members, present at the first meeting, who want to be considered the founders. This request came after the death of several founding members. Yet, according to Christella Moody, Charles Townsel, the second president of NABSE, was the first person to refer to Charles Moody as the founder. In 1974, Townsel gave Moody a plaque that named him founder. Moody still has the plaque on his wall. It should be noted, not many people have the vision to create institutions. Charles Moody is one of those rare people who has it. Yet, these petty interests and conflicts occupied the organization.

The energy of the organization is consumed in this kind of pernicious and trivial activity, even at the highest levels. Therefore, the organization is unable to achieve Charles Moody's visions and goals. The membership is still absent from the decision-making. The organization is still poorly funded. The president is still not occupied full time with the organization's business. The organization is a service organization without clout, not even in the Democratic Party. On July 29, 2003, there was no plan to protest the exclusion of African Americans from leadership in the big cities where we are concentrated. Outsiders with little school experience and minimal education

81

now capture those posts as appointees of the mayors or state takeover committees. And other problems prevail. NABSE has a non–functional research arm that produces little research. It begs for money to fund its own affairs.

Having been a fully participating member of NABSE, I saw my work with and for this organization as an integral part of my struggle for school reform. I have been a member of many organizations. Some have disappeared. Others are dysfunctional. Even the most venerable, the NAACP and the Urban League, are not fully-funded by African and African American people, nor can they stand up against strong groups opposed to African and African American development. Presidents can ignore them, if their agenda and goals are too aggressive. However, when I came into this world, my grandparents told me that the real problem Black people had was a lack of unity around purpose and direction, and that there are too many churches and too many organizations.

Section 4.8 D.C. Public Schools, D.C. Board of Education, and the Superintendency

When I accepted the job of superintendent of the D.C. Public Schools (DCPS) in 1973, I still thought that community control or decentralization was the means to elevate student achievement. This was my bias. For me, that was the only reason why we should pursue it. I knew that some people were obsessed with job security and their own self-aggrandizement. I knew that they would do nothing to elevate student achievement, which would jeopardize that goal. My immediate need was to find a way to decentralize quickly and in a way that would not be threatening to the teachers and principals. They had to know that I was on their side even though I advocated sharing control with parents. Surprisingly, the Washington Teachers Union supported community control. That should have been a clue to the state of the Capitol.

I thought the seven D.C. Board of Education (DCBOE) members who selected me were committed to community control. While they were, indeed, it was not my vision. One member, Charles Casselle, the son of a distinguished African American architect, and a renowned architect himself, as well as a civic leader, saw my main role as being the person who fired employees against whom he had a grudge. I was to take his word on the matter since I was new. Another member, Hilda Howland M. Mason, a respected civil rights leader, wanted community control, but she saw the central board as the agent of the community and the vehicle for control. Two members, Marion Barry and James Coates, were considering other political roles to play in D.C. politics using the DCBOE as a vaulting pole to these positions. However, Barry was committed to the privatization of many school programs. Another, Delores Pryde, voted for me, but really wanted someone from inside the system for the position. Only Mattie Taylor and Bardyl Tirana really were persuaded by my ideas about the elevation of student achievement.

Raymond Kemp, Albert Rosenfield and Martha Swaim, all white, argued that I was short on administrative experience and voted no. In actuality, they believed I was a Black militant out to force whites to go to school with Blacks by universal busing. Rosenfield later changed his mind. Swaim wanted administrators fired yesterday, like Casselle. Evie M. Washington was opposed to anything Marion Barry was for; therefore, when he voted for me, she abstained. I never knew the origin of her animosity towards him. So by 1974, the only member of the DCBOE who had selected me was Hilda Howland M. Mason, who eventually became my worst adversary.

By 1975, the D.C. School Board had changed membership. Virginia Morris replaced Delores Pryde; Julius Hobson replaced James Coates; Barbara Lett Simmons replaced Charles Cassell; Therman E. Evans replaced Bardyle Tirana; Bettie G. Benjamin replaced Mattie Taylore; John Warren replaced Martha Swain; Elizabeth Kane replaced Marion Barry; Carol Schwartz replaced Albert A. Rosenfield; and William Treanor replaced Evie Washington. Benjamin, Evans, Simmons and Warren supported me. Opposed to me were Hobson, Mason and Morris and the four Whites: Kane, Kemp, Schwartz and Treanor. Of the board that fired me: Morris was president and Hobson vice-president, both are Black.

The DCBOE works under severe constraints because D.C. is a colony. The people do not govern themselves. While they elect officials, these officials have delegated powers that can be withdrawn at the pleasure of the President or Congress. For instance, the Subcommittee on Appropriations for the D.C. in the House of Representatives, and another in the Senate, can both veto line items in the school board's budget, even though the Congress does not contribute any money to the school's budget—other than the federal funds which are given to all other school districts in the nation.

I didn't fully understand the implications of these restrictions at first. I only knew that my board members had conflicting objectives. I searched for a way out of my dilemma. Mistakenly, I thought I had the administrative fiat to decentralize, because I thought there was a consensus among board members about decentralization, and because Congress had made it apparent to the board that it would not increase funding to support it. It had to be done with the funds available.

I tried to gather as many public school resources as possible to implement PACTS, which was the old CAPTS model used at WESP, as the centerpiece of the decentralization plan. But I ran smack into the intent of several DCBOE members to funnel public school funds into their pet private enterprises. Furthermore, I thought the board members would accept structures declared by fiat as long as they were temporary and could be vetoed by them. I couldn't have been more mistaken.

On July 1, 1974, I decentralized the D.C. school system by creating six regions and appointing six interim regional superintendents. Board members were angrier about the appointments than they were about the decentralization. I used positions that were already funded to create the regional superintendents positions. Therefore, I closed the assistant superintendent positions and reopened three of them as regional superintendents. The incumbents remained: Gilbert Diggs, Dorothy Johnson and William Rice. One of the incumbents, Vincent Reed, was placed in a new position, assistant superintendent in charge of state affairs.

Three new appointees were temporarily chosen: Margaret Labat, Preston Gary Freeman and Napoleon Lewis. Half of the board members had expected me to fire Johnson, Diggs, Rice and Reed when I was hired. In fact, so heated did the DCBOE controversy become that Margaret Labat was never paid for her work as a regional superintendent, yet, promotions of high school principals had generally come about through Reed's recommendations. In addition, Floretta McKenzie was chosen to be my deputy superintendent. She and Reed had a long standing feud as a result of differences that had developed during Hugh Scott's tenure, or so I was told. McKenzie and Kenneth Haskins, my vice superintendent who was torn between his friendship with me and his friendship with Mason, both resigned by September of 1974.

By July 1, 1974, the war over resources existed not only between the superintendent and the board, but also between the two bureaucratic lines: management and instruction. Because D.C. is a colony, Congress and the local government make decisions through an influential network of powerful people in business. This alliance with the business community, specifically the *Washington Post*, local government and Congress contributed greatly to the defeat of my ideas in the D.C. Public Schools. My ignorance of the political workings of a colony did not help either, even though I had substantial support among the people whose children attended the D.C. Public Schools. (On July 17, 1977, I ran for city council at large against Hilda Howland M. Mason and lost to her by approximately 600 votes. Total, I received around 10,000 votes. At that time I was sorely disappointed. But now, I thank God I did not win.)

Although I was able to outline an ambitious instructional program to elevate student achievement in the "Superintendent's 120-Day Report" in 1974, we were never able to attack it with all of our energies. Too much time was spent on warring over power and resources. The Ellington School for Performing Arts was created overcoming much opposition. The Ballou School of Science and Mathematics was created, but undermined by the creation of the Banneker Academic High School. Nothing was done to replicate the high achievement models operationalized at the Mildred Green, LaSalle and Bunker Hill elementary schools.

The decentralization of the D.C. Public Schools contributed more evidence that jobs, power and influence replace student achievement as the primary goal of boards of education, community control groups and local school councils. The patronage model overwhelms the achievement model in implementation. D.C. convinced me that educating Black students can never just happen. It is considered subversive activity, an activity that seeks to undermine or destroy the privileged positions of whites, males and the wealthy in our nation. Consequently, those who try to elevate the achievement of Black students in the public schools are often penalized, suppressed or unrecognized in this society.[21] Those who fail to elevate achievement are rewarded.

I am partly to blame for my firing by the D.C. Board of Education on October 9, 1975, at 4:00 P.M. Hobson, Kane, Kemp, Mason, Morris, Schwartz, and Treanor charged me with seventeen points of inefficiency, nine of which dealt with management issues. The first administrative judge, Herman Benn, ruled that the board had not properly preferred the charges and transmitted them to me. The board promptly fired him and hired another, Herbert O. Reid, also Mason's personal lawyer.

Herbert O. Reid had been an important figure in the cases that culminated in *Brown v. Board of Education.* I trusted him implicitly, but it was not long before he showed me that his only goal was to get rid of me as quickly and quietly as possible. Reid ruled that four chares were not sustained by the evidence produced at the hearing. With the reports before him, he ruled that I had failed to comply with the board's directives to submit status reports on expenditures, to provide responses to the board's inquiries about a financial plan, to provide quarterly finance reports, and to fail to provide quarterly personnel reports.[22]

Finally, my lawyer told me that the case had already been decided and that nothing we said or he did would make a difference. He urged me to settle. My good friend and attorney, Audrey McCutcheon, encouraged me to settle. My daughter, in disgust with my obstinacy, went to Africa. It was difficult for me to come to terms with the reality that there really was no justice as far as the law was concerned if justice was fairness as John Rawls claimed.[23] Still, another important lesson was learned here: All Black people are not good and right, and all white people are not bad and wrong. In this imperfect world, self-interest is a better determinant of behavior than color.

For two years, I could not find employment in public school administration. I had committed the ultimate sin, fighting the school board. The D.C. Board of Education effectively blackballed me in my profession. I helped them a lot by being strident in my dissent and harsh in my criticism. I had no grace. Now I must confess that my own ignorance of colonial operations and the significance of powerlessness made me tremendously naive and unnecessarily vulnerable. In addition, my intransigence in the face of these conditions violated the pretense of power vainly exhibited by the board of education members to whom it was important. Many people tried to help me, but I was confident that I was right. I admit my foolishness. But it wasn't fatal.[24]

Section 4.9　The University of Pittsburgh and The Coleman Study

During the summer of 1977, Margaret Milliones of Pittsburgh, Pennsylvania called me to tell me that there was an open position at the University of Pittsburgh in Black Studies, and that I should apply. At last, in September 1977, after losing the election for city council, I was hired by Curtis Porter, the department's director, to teach in the Department of Black Community Research and Education at the University of Pittsburgh.

When I arrived in Pittsburgh on August 22, 1977, an abundance of evidence had accrued to convince me that Black students could learn, if taught. My experiences affirmed: (1) the principal must believe that Black students could learn and have expectations for their achievement; (2) the principal must create an environment safe for and conducive to learning and routines must be established to solve discipline problems; (3) the principal must develop a consensus around high achievement as a high priority goal in the school and assessment, placement, pacing and instructional routines must be implemented to attain the goal; (4) students' needs and strengths must be assessed, learning standards and goals set, and activities highly structured to achieve them; (5) direct instruction must be used to teach basic skills; (6) phonics must be taught orally to bidialectical and bilingual students; (7) African American life, history and culture must be incorporated into the curriculum both in content and methodology to curtail the imputation of Black inferiority; (8) students' progress must be monitored and measured regularly; (9) teachers' performances must be monitored and evaluated regularly; (10) professional development must be provided for teachers who need it to implement the routines required to execute the above; (11) teachers must be supported with mentoring, resources, supplies and equipment; (12) parents must be informed about and included in decisions made regarding their children's education; (13) African Americans are perpetually bombarded with conditions that make them feel inferior: discrimination, prejudice and humiliation, teachers must be aware of this; (14) African Americans devote much energy to overcoming racism, energy that could be used for intellectual, economic, artistic and spiritual development; (15) the constraints of racism limit the effectiveness of African American organizations and institutions because of the need to fight white supremacy without aggravating its supporters who could take one's means of livelihood or one's life; (16) neither laws, nor the state, will protect African Americans, who are judged guilty until proven innocent.

Unfortunately, most scholars studied African American student achievement from a pathological model. These studies often began with a litany of characteristics describing the students' poor performance, poverty, race, family dysfunction and community disorganization, and recommendations were generally directed toward changing the students, their parents or their communities. Seldom were recommendations made toward changing the school or teachers or administrators.

Since 1966, educators have used James S. Coleman's "Coleman Study" as their theoretical framework for Black education. The formal name for the study is "Equality of Educational Opportunity,"[25] and it was commissioned by the U.S. Congress in response to Section 402 of the Civil Rights Act of 1964. It found that "the great majority of American children attend schools that are largely segregated," and that "among minority groups, Negroes are by far the most segregated." However, taking all groups, "white children are the most segregated." The Coleman report also found that "schools are remarkably similar in the way they relate to the achievement of their pupils when the socioeconomic background of the students is taken into account." It is known that these factors are statistically controlled. However, it appears that differences between schools account for only a small fraction of differences in pupil achievement.

The Coleman report generated the thesis that schools could not impact family background. Not regarded were caveats throughout the report that conflicted with this thesis. For example, the Coleman report found that "schools do differ, however, in their relation to the various racial and ethnic groups. The average white student's achievement seems to be less affected by the strength or weakness of his school's facilities, curriculums and teachers, than is the average pupil's." To put it another way, the achievement of minority pupils depended more on the schools they attended than did the achievement of the majority pupil. The inference might then be made that improving the school of the minority student would help to increase his or her chances at achievement.

I was definitely in search for a new paradigm.

CHAPTER 5

THE SEARCH FOR A NEW PARADIGM

Section 5.1 A Look at What Is and What Isn't

My history reflects the roots of my biases. Experience and education both have convinced me that schools can change if the actors inside it are committed to high achievement as a high priority and are willing to work together to achieve that end.

Although there have always been schools in which African American and poor students have demonstrated high achievement, as measured by standardized test scores, each instance has been the exception and not the rule.[1] This is supported by a body of well-documented evidence that reveals the massive underachievement of African American students in the United States' public school system.[2]

Throughout the years, communities of scholars have accepted five theories, and their resultant paradigms, to explain this phenomenon: (1) African Americans are genetically inferior in intelligence;[3] (2) African Americans are culturally deprived, or their cultural conflicts prevent learning;[4] (3) African Americans' families, homes and community environments are deficient, indifferent, non-stimulating and immoral;[5] (4) the school and/or school system is inefficient, underfunded and ineffective;[6] and (5) the larger social order, through its value system, dictates a racial caste/class system that perpetuates itself throughout the schools.[7]

From 1877 through 1954, segregation was considered the primary contributing factor to underachievement, and because of the segregation problem in national society, since the late 1940s the larger social paradigm has occupied center stage.[8]

During the 1960s, a multitude of attempts to make desegregation work ended in failure and, in so doing, advanced counter mental intelligence, social class, school effects and parental involvement programs.[9]

During the 1970s and 1980s, due to the work of Ronald R. Edmonds and his use of the school effects paradigm to challenge the social class paradigm championed by Coleman, during the 1970s and 1980s more and more schools with poor African American students scoring on standardized tests at or above national norms in reading and mathematics were discovered.[10] These high achieving, predominantly African American schools became an abashing anomaly, frequently embarrassing school officials who could not explain why such a large number of other predominantly African American schools were underachieving. This anomaly posed serious challenges to paradigms one and two as well.[11]

Races of people possess distinctive characteristics that define and determine their respective cultures. Hope Landrine and Elizabeth A. Klonoff argue the following:

> Race is any ethnic group that has been socially defined as such on the basis of any arbitrary, culturally relative, and culturally specific physical and/or ancestral criteria. Races are created from ethnic groups by applying and institutionalizing said criteria, if, and only if, racial constructions are needed to justify the enslavement, exploitation, expulsion, or abuse of one ethnic group by another. Races are created only when initial conditions of ethnic-group differences in power exist.[12]

Therefore, racism is defined here as the belief that one's race is superior.[13] Although establishing equal status and the redress of prior deprivation were the goals of desegregation, and despite emerging from research accumulated around the social order's cause-belief theory, desegregation did little to impact the very social order it was intended to change.

Generally, desegregation stressed: (1) 80/20 white majorities; (2) one-way bussing for African Americans only; (3) closing schools with predominantly African American enrollment; (4) ability grouping of African Americans through diagnostic testing; (5) increased remedial and compensatory programs for African Americans; (6) additional special education teachers and staff, primarily for the mentally retarded and socially and emotionally disturbed; (7) the firing or demotion of African American staff; and (8) exit testing for students and entrance testing for teachers. Some theorists view these practices as errors in desegregation and policy making that grew out of the belief that segregation, and not racism, is the evil.[14]

The political struggles surrounding desegregation and decentralization greatly obstructed substantial efforts to eliminate the underachievement of African American and poor students. Research has revealed the following after effects: (1) racially isolated schools remained, even after school districts desegregated; (2) many metropolitan urban areas housing a large population of African Americans had not yet desegregated (as of 2004, fifty years after the

Brown decision); (3) whites fled a host of desegregated public school districts, and in many cases student enrollment became predominantly African American; (4) a number of districts had re-segregated by 1999; (5) elevating student achievement in desegregated schools was often as difficult as in their segregated counterparts; (6) methods used to lure whites back to the systems from which they fled often included re-segregating schools, as in the case of magnet schools; and (7) the side effects of inadequate desegregation further institutionalized racism in the public schools.[15]

Some African Americans became impatient with desegregation's slow progress and its failure to improve the quality of education in their neighborhood schools. Consequently, in the late 50s and early 60s, many African Americans pressed for community control, contending that they could ensure a better education for their children by developing policy for the institutions that were failing to properly educate their children. A highly-respected body of research documents the community control struggle control and its effect on student achievement.[16]

After reaching its peak in the late 1960s, the community control movement began to lose momentum and impact, largely because of the controversy over New York City's Ocean-Hill Brownsville community control experiment and the 1968 New York City teacher strike that resulted when the community district board attempted to fire nineteen teachers. Although several cities continued to experiment with decentralization after 1968, the power to develop policy as envisioned by the initiators of the movement rarely materialized.

In some instances, these later attempts delegated central office powers to area and district officials; in others, the central office shared some of its control with the local boards. For the most part, however, decentralized units could not negotiate with the unions, nor could they hire and fire staff.[17] Just as board members tried to control the selection of local community participants and fought against decentralization in Washington D.C. and New York City, patronage dominated the community control process throughout the rest of the United States. Regardless of the fact that decentralization did not noticeably improve student performance in predominantly poor schools, it still attracts many whom believe it to be a viable paradigm, capable of solving the problem of mass underachievement.

The Chicago Public Schools appears to have learned little from research documenting the failure of decentralization, and even less from its own experience with the Woodlawn Experimental Schools Project (WESP) mentioned earlier in the previous chapter. This is especially evident in the system's school reform efforts.

In December of 1988, Illinois passed school reform legislation intended to improve student achievement and provide greater teacher and administrator accountability.[18] This legislation had four major effects: (1) it stripped principals of tenure by restricting them to a renewable four-year performance contract; (2) it required that each of CPS's more than 500 schools institute a Local School Council (LSC)—a site-based governing body comprised of the principal, two teachers elected by the school's staff, seven parents and one community representative elected by the school's parents. The principal is provided with uncontested LSC membership for the length of the contract (or until the principal resigns or is removed from the position) teachers, parents and the community representative serve two-year terms; (3) it shifted the power to hire and fire principals from the CPS Board of Education to the LSCs; and (4) it invested the LSCs with the fiscal authority to decide how their schools' discretionary funds (federal and state monies) were spent. In reality, the LSCs control only 15 percent of the schools' total budget.

While most schools located in stable neighborhoods operated well, a number of schools experienced great turmoil and upheaval as the result of LSC members manipulating discretionary funds to meet their own needs and agendas, even when it meant damaging teachers' and principals' careers. In one school, the LSC reduced the teaching force (funded by discretionary funds) to hire non-teaching staff, known in Chicago as career service employees. In another, an LSC advised its African American principal that he could not use discretionary funds to hire a white assistant principal, and should he try, the LSC would not approve funding for the position. The bottom line was that a certain LSC member wanted the principal to hire someone he recommended. It is not uncommon for principals to be removed when they do not bow to the wills of such members. Another factor contributing to principal vulnerability is the advantage given to teachers under the 1988 Illinois school law. While teachers retained their tenure rights, principals lost theirs. Teachers also have two seats on the LSC and are represented by the American Federation of Teachers (AFT).

CPS has never allotted enough funds to provide LSC members with adequate policy making training, leaving members susceptible to using the patronage model, especially in low-income census zones, where unemployment is high.[19] Paul E. Peterson, author of *The Politics of School Reform: 1870–1940*,[20] says that in the past corruption within the decentralized, ward-based, patronage-focused, lay-controlled school boards led to replacing them with centralized, city-wide, professionally-directed, reform-oriented boards.[21]

People who remember WESP and still espouse it as a model for school reform maintain that it will take the Chicago Public Schools' present reform model ten years to elevate student achievement. In the meantime, large numbers of children will be educationally damaged, having been sacrificed on Chicago's political altars. It is not necessary to wait that long, however, to evaluate the damage brought on by this present reform model. One simply has to look at what it has already done to Chicago's African Americans.

It seems that the real purpose behind the school reform legislation was to transfer power from the central office to the communities. However, the lack of unity among African Americans regarding a plan to recapture leadership lost prevented the use of this power when the former African American mayor, Harold Washington, died. Divided over who to choose as a successor to Mayor Washington, African Americans lacked the unity necessary for the execution of a plan to recapture the mayoral office. We have yet to recover from this defeat.

James S. Coleman[22] found the public schools did not impact student achievement as much as family background; although the study also observed that the achievement of minority students, as opposed to the achievement of majority students, was primarily related to the schools they attended. This basic refusal to study why African American students react to certain phenomena differently than whites is a paradox of school reform research. In the name of equity, many options have been chosen to solve the problem. Each failed miserably because there is no close fit between the finding and the reality.

The Nixon presidency, influenced by Daniel P. Moynihan's[24] idea of benign neglect and the school of scholars who followed Coleman's social class paradigm, projected the notion that "school reform was wasted on the poor since only massive intervention in their lives would ameliorate the intrinsic difficulties from which they suffered." Literature declaring the ineffectiveness and inefficiency of inner city public schools proliferated before and during Nixon's White House years, and was met by three oppositional streams: (1) African Americans' quest for community control and quality education; (2) social scientists' effective schools research; and (3) the AFT's idea of what creates an effective school.[25]

The union's notion was based on its belief that schools could become more effective if teachers were given more time to spend on instruction and allowed to make more decisions regarding their work conditions.[26] The union's more effective schools idea and the push for quality education by African Americans simultaneously dominated school reform thinking in northern communities throughout the 1960s. However, both fell to the background when social scientists started producing a growing body of effective school data in the 1970s. It was also during the 1970s that researchers sought to discover which elements enabled a school to teach poor students effectively.

Following Ronald Edmonds's lead,[27] George Weber,[28] William B. Brookover et al.,[29] reported that effective urban schools shared many common characteristics. Their studies confirmed that African American students and poor students could and would master basic skills. They also found that effective schools used direct instruction methods and strategies and that they had principals who functioned as instructional leaders. Weber's study especially emphasized the principals' "strong leadership" by showing them as instrumental in setting the tone of the school, deciding instructional strategies, and organizing and distributing school resources.[30] Edmonds found that one of the most tangible and indispensable characteristics of effective schools are "strong administrative leadership, without which the disparate elements of good schools" can be "neither brought together, nor kept together."[31]

Brookover and Larry Lezotte found that the principal in a certain declining school was very much "public relations" oriented and made a very strong effort to project a favorable image of the school. The principal considered his school to be effective, praised his staff for being cooperative without providing significant supervision, and played a minor role in directing instructional activities. No priority was given to student achievement in reading, mathematics and other basic skills; and teachers tended to "run their own show" and do whatever they wanted in their classrooms.[32]

Brookover and Lezotte summarized the consequences of this kind of leadership: (1) there are no achievement goals set and there is no evaluation of the level of mastery in mathematics and reading; (2) there is a general rejection of any accountability for student achievement; (3) the level of achievement is determined by non-school factors associated with the children and their parents and the home environment; the teachers, thus, have very low expectations and they assume no responsibility for successful teaching of mathematics and reading.[33]

In the New York State Office of Education Performance Review Study, Edmonds[34] reported on two New York inner city public schools, both of which

96

served an analogous poor public population. One was high-achieving and the other law was low-achieving. The differences in these schools were measured by: (1) administrative behavior, policies and procedures; (2) management, instructional routines and standard operating practices; (3) teachers' attitudes regarding student learning ability; (4) teacher expectations regarding student performance; (5) the amount of time spent on instructional activities; and 6) the degree and quality of assistance given to teachers by principals.[35]

Brookover and Lezotte reported similar observations and listed definitive differences between improving and declining schools: (1) improving schools put more emphasis on reading and mathematics goals; (2) staff in improving schools tend to believe that all students can learn, and teachers in declining schools project the belief that students' abilities are low and that they cannot master learning objectives; (3) teachers in improving schools hold higher long-range expectations for their students, and teachers in declining schools assume their students will not finish high school or go to college; (4) staff in improving schools take responsibility for teaching basic reading and mathematics skills, and teachers in declining schools tend to hold students' parents responsible for this foundational training; (5) improving schools spend more time on basic skills; (6) principals in improving schools actively assume the role of instructional leader and display a take-charge assertiveness, while principals in declining schools tend to be more permissive and emphasize informal and collegial relationships with teachers and staff; (7) teachers in improving schools are generally less satisfied than teachers in declining schools; (8) although improving schools exhibit a higher level of parent-initiated involvement, overall parent involvement is less than in declining schools; and (9) improving schools do not rely on paraprofessional staff and regular teachers in selecting students for placement in compensatory education programs; declining schools, on the other hand, rely heavily on teacher recommendation to fill such programs and use greater numbers of staff to teach reading.[36]

Findings by Bruce R. Joyce, Richard H. Hersh and Michael McKibbin listed a number of effective school attributes according to two categories: (1) social organization: clear academic and social behavior goals, order and discipline, high expectations, teacher efficacy, pervasive caring, public rewards and incentives, academic leadership and community; (2) curriculum and instruction: high academic learning time, frequent monitoring of student progress, organized and coherent curriculum, variety of teaching strategies and opportunities for student responsibility.[37]

Similarly, Donald E. MacKenzie[38] found three dimensions of effective schooling identified by research, and listed core and facilitating elements under each: (1) Leadership: a positive overall climate and atmosphere, goal–focused activities aligned with objectives that are clear, relevant and attainable, teacher-directed classroom management and decision making, and staff training to increase instructional effectiveness. Facilitating elements: shared consensus on values and goals, long-range planning and coordination, stability and continuity of key staff and district-level support for school improvement. (2) Efficacy: high and positive achievement expectations with a constant press for excellence, visible rewards for academic excellence and growth, cooperative activity and group interaction in the classroom, total staff involvement with school improvement, autonomy and flexibility to implement adaptive practices, appropriate levels of difficulty for learning tasks and teacher empathy, rapport and personal interaction with students. Facilitating elements: emphasis on homework and study, positive accountability, acceptance of responsibility for learning outcomes, strategies to avoid non-promotion of students, de-emphasis of strict ability grouping and interaction with more accomplished peers. (3) Efficiency: effective use of instructional time, amount of intensity of engagement in school learning, orderly and disciplined school and classroom environments, continuous diagnosis, evaluation and feedback, well-structured classroom activities and emphasis on higher order skills. Facilitating elements: opportunities for individualized work and number and variety of learning opportunities.[39]

In conclusion, MacKenzie stated that "all the new studies agree that schooling is a complex and continuous, multifaceted process that is always conditioned by the history and circumstances of its evolution." Consequently, no single element of school effectiveness can be considered in isolation from all of the others, or from the total situation in which it is found.

Edmonds's research showed that effective schools shared a common climate in which "all" personnel had to be instructionally effective for "all" students.[40] He posited that effective schools for African Americans and the poor shared a climate conducive to learning by being orderly without being rigid, quiet, without being oppressive and expecting "all" children to learn. Edmonds also found that effective schools essentially developed learning goals for all their students and some means of measuring goal achievement. He concluded his review with the following:

> Whether or not we will ever effectively teach the children of the poor is probably
> far more a matter of politics than of social science and that is as it should be. It

seems to me therefore that what is left of this discussion are three declarative statements. We can whenever, and wherever we choose, successfully teach all children whose schooling is of interest to us. We already know more than we need in order to do this. Whether we do it most finally depends on how we feel about the fact that we haven't so far.

To be sure, Edmonds's conclusion implies that his educational question has a political answer. The public school is a part of a vast political system where groups with vested interests—parents, administrators, general citizens, politicians, teachers and students—war over scarce resources. Often, their cause-effect beliefs do not match and are irreconcilable, just as with scholars and their paradigms.

Section 5.2 The Teacher Paradigm

Generally speaking, teachers seem to believe that they are essential catalysts for student achievement and "that teacher leadership stands at the center of this benign and desirable activity." In spite of this belief, many are "terribly uncertain about their ability to achieve their goal of education for every child." This means then that teachers expect some children not to learn, and accept the possibility that they will not be able to educate them. This lowers academic standards by militating against the need to set and maintain high expectations for every child.[41]

Studies that observe and report teacher-related phenomena often produce contradictory results. Some studies show them as conservative, individualistic and oriented toward the present. Other studies suggest that they are anything but individualistic and that students shape teachers' expectations, behaviors, work orientations and performances.

For example, Brookover et al., observed between teachers and students reciprocal exchanges and commitments, that occurred around instruction and learning.[42] These exchanges and commitments were the results of mutual expectations and satisfactory performances between both teacher and student, and student and teacher. It was these expectations and resulting actions that formed "fixed" teacher beliefs about student potential and performance, and that generated climate, standards and requirements.

This challenges Dan C. Lortie's[43] conception of the singular, highly individualistic, strongly independent and autonomous teacher who is not influenced by the dialectic of her students' social and cultural characteristics and responses to them. Brookover et al., argued that no such "untouched" teacher prevails, due to the fact that teachers react to and are influenced by the students they encounter, the shared values they hold with other teachers regarding school and students, and the schools' social systems.[44]

This is especially true when low achievement occurs in upper-class schools because teachers treat everyone as being educable to the genius level and create open systems where high expectations characterize all instructional delivery. Unlike poorly performing schools where entire groups of students are written off as uneducable, no one in upper-class schools is written off. In Brookover et al., "teacher behavior is clearly anchored to the school's social system to which the teacher belongs and is strongly influenced by the social, cultural and structural characteristics of these discrete school settings." Lortie's claim that universal teacher behavior is grounded in strong isolation, individualism and increasing conservative independence is not supported by the premises of Brookover et al. However, there may be an answer to this seeming contradiction.

Teachers are affected as much by their schools' organizational structure as by their students. Successful schools and programs seem to be characterized by specific and clearly stated curricular goals. Routines established to meet these goals differ from routines in schools that do not have clear curricular goals. Therefore, Brookover et al. could be referring to the former condition and Lortie to the latter.

Teachers, unless deterred from doing so, organize learning in ways that are compatible with their work imperatives, subjects and idiographic needs. The work of Sara L. Lightfoot and Jean J. Carew interfaced with that of Lortie's in emphasizing that teachers tend to make school-related decisions based on their own life experiences, rather than looking to any body of knowledge or body of information, and acting upon an understanding of students' needs and experiences.[45] Lightfoot and Carew also saw teacher behavior, preferences and selective biases, which would not be supported by Brookover et al. That study's premise predicts that something in schools produced these consistent praises, rewards and punishments of students.

Eleanor B. Leacock[46] suggests that the praises, rewards and punishments that students received from teachers were based on the secrets teachers passed on to each other while recording students' grades.[47] The image that becomes associated with a student as the result of this "sharing" determines how the student will be treated by teachers, both in the present and in the future.

Lortie, Lightfoot and Carew's findings, then, are not entirely compatible with Brookover et al. or Leacock's findings. One interpretation of this incompatibility is the effect of a school's structure on teacher behavior. In schools where teachers set goals individually, Lortie, Lightfoot and Carew may be correct. Where goals are set in other ways, they may be incorrect.

Lortie claims that basic teaching techniques have been extremely slow to change and the organization of teachers' tasks has undergone limited modification since colonial times.[48] In his study, the beliefs and preferences expressed by his subjects suggested individualistic teachers who wanted more elbow room to practice teaching, but for whom the nature of that teaching had not come under review. He also found that teachers prefer classroom tasks over organizational tasks, and classroom claims over organizational initiation.[49] This preference increases the possibility of the displacement of organizational goals by personal goals.

However, Pamela Bullard and Barbara O. Taylor argue that effective schools provided for teacher leadership opportunities. They believe that "the more involved teachers are in the operation of the school, the climate of their environment and the instructional decisions affecting their classrooms, the more committed they will be to the task before them.[50]" Essential to this achievement is time for professional development, planning and preparation.

In his analysis of perceived teacher autonomy, Jerry Leiter[51] observed that the factors which explained teachers' perceptions of their autonomy were directly affected by the level of competition among school actors over the choice of school goals or directions. He suggested that a high level of control and effective coordination was needed to generate consensus around school goals. Coordination, according to Leiter, was particularly important to counteract the tendency for teachers to pursue their own private goals, and also necessary to the elimination of individual behavior, which proved counterproductive to achieving collective ends.

Leiter identified two factors that led teachers to pursue private, instead of collective goals: (1) teachers lack the professional training and socialization needed to assure their dedication to a common set of goals and operating procedures; and (2) the pursuit of individual goals is supported by the schools' physical arrangement, and classrooms where teachers pursue their objectives behind closed doors.[52]

Section 5.3   John U. Ogbu, Susan Goldsmith, and Parents

Two factors often prescribe a certain condition of communication between parents and teachers. John U. Ogbu described the relationship between parents and teachers in his study as patron-client relationship in which teachers saw instruction as rendered service which helped raise the status of the children they taught. He also related that teachers expected parents to reciprocate by demonstrating the kind of gratitude, interest and cooperation that satisfied criteria established by the teachers.[53] This patron-client relationship made meaningful communication difficult, especially when parents maintained that teacher's services were rewarded solely by salary, fringe benefits and other forms of compensation. Although they acknowledged the teachers' services, parents did not accept the obligations placed on them by the teachers.

Ogbu saw teachers as representatives of the dominant power group and parents as members of a powerless minority.[54] In this unequal partnership, teachers defined parents and their participation in the teacher-parent interaction, and parents played the role of a client to escape being blamed for what they saw as the teachers' responsibility.

Ogbu concluded that subordinate minorities continue to have a high proportion of school failures because the factors that produced this adaptation still exist: (1) inequality of educational rewards and the continuance of subordinate minorities to regard their "struggle for equality" as a priority over hard work at school; (2) the fact that folk and scientific definitions of subordinate minorities is that of being inferior to whites, both in school and occupational placement, and remains an important element in today's American culture; and (3) schools have not changed their treatment of subordinate minorities, because their actions are determined by the ideas and policies of the dominant group.[55]

Lortie tended to support Ogbu's claims in his description of continuity in teaching, and he is not optimistic about change. He said:

> We should learn more about the mechanisms school boards and administrators use in deflecting pressures they do not welcome. There are indications that large school systems sometimes use new approaches in showplace schools while resisting their widespread adoption. This tactic can "cool off" enthusiasts until their ardor has waned. Another device is to change the rhetoric of school practice while leaving the substance intact; some school systems proclaim commitment

to "team teaching" when in fact they are merely taking public notice of voluntary patterns of cooperation which have existed among teachers for some time. Where resistance cannot be overcome, we can expect that research development efforts will falter as support is withdrawn. One might hypothesize that the movement toward change will have to be erratic, not linear. The forces of change and resistance will probably interact contrapuntally.[56]

Lortie confirmed, through his expectation, the impact of the values of the larger social order on the social system of public schools.

In a later study, Ogbu developed a thesis to account for the effect of such values on the educational outcomes of African American youth. He stated, the "lower school performance and lower educational attainment are functionally adaptive to minorities' ascribed inferior social and occupational positions in adult life."[57] As the study showed, "Blacks do not occupy inferior social and occupational positions in American society because they lack the educational qualifications for desirable ones; rather, the exclusion of Blacks from the more desirable social and occupational positions is because of their caste like status and is the major source of their academic retardation."[58]

Ogbu's study showed how American society rewards African Americans and whites who hold the same educational qualifications differently, and names this differential reward system as the prime contributor to the difference between the two groups in their reading performance.[59] He exposed the subtle ways public school systems reinforce inferior education for African Americans and superior education for whites: (1) the patron-client relationship, which prevents a mutual understanding of children's academic problems and what to do about them, since in this arrangement, the parents's views are not important; (2) the system of teacher evaluations of children's classroom performances, which prevents children from learning how their efforts are related to the rewards system of marks, thereby inhibiting their acquisition of good work and study habits; (3) the use of misclassification, testing, and ability grouping; (4) biased textbooks and curriculum; (5) a clinical definition of African Americans' academic problems arising from the belief held by school personnel that these problems are the result of the nation and condition of African American families and neighborhoods; and (6) a socialization mechanism which develops the personal qualities of dependence, compliance and manipulation in African American students and those of independence, initiative, industriousness and individualistic competitiveness in whites.[60]

Characteristics of teachers in the public school system seem ominous for

African American students. Ogbu's description of the system and its macro-environment bids foreboding as well. Attempts at changing the macro-environment through desegregation and decentralization have not been rewarding; and any research on this problem should seriously consider Lortie's assessment, as well as Ogbu's diagnosis.

Ogbu has subsequently changed his analysis of the causes of the achievement gap between African American and white students. He now claims that his findings of a study of Shaker Height's public schools show that it wasn't socioeconomics, school funding or racism that accounted for the students' poor academic performance; it was their own attitudes and those of their parents.[61] Ogbu did report that teachers treated Black and white students differently in 110 of the classes he observed. Strangely, he did not attribute this to racism: "Yes, there was a problem of low teacher expectation of Black students," he explained, according to Susan Goldsmith,[62] author of "Rich Black and Flunking", "but you have to ask why. Week after week the kids don't turn in their homework. What do you expect teachers to do?" He seemed more willing to blame the students than the teachers. It was unclear how he knew whether the teachers' low expectations caused the students not to hand in work, or whether the students' failure to submit homework caused the teachers to have low expectations. This seemed similar to the Brookover et al., argument of reciprocity.

Ogbu's claims generated a great deal of expected controversy. While he joins the ranks of researchers like John H. McWhorter[63] and Shelby Steele,[64] in finding that the cause of racism is in Black people themselves, Ogbu seems uncomfortable in that company. Goldsmith noted that Ogbu:

> [T]reads carefully when he talks about his work and reiterates repeatedly in his writing and in person that he is not excusing the system. First of all, he concedes that there are historic socioeconomic explanations to account for some
> Black academic disengagement. Historically, there has been a weak link between academic success and upward mobility for African Americans. Blacks traditionally saw big leaps in social mobility only during times of national crises such as war— or during shortages or immigrant labor. "If those are the points where they move," Ogbu adds, "it's not a kind of experience that allows a group to plan their educational future."[65]

In an *Education Week* article, Karla Scoon Reid describes Ogbu's study and notes that he is careful to point out that racism and the legacy of racism still shape the attitudes and the perceptions that African Americans have about education. "The school district" Ogbu argues "bears responsibility in addressing any barriers that negatively affect Black student achievement." He further noted that, "despite the challenges, Black families can take steps to help their children succeed."[66]

Many studies have found that African American parents's expectations differed from those of their white counterparts. Carole E. Joffe, for example, found that African Americans: (1) first and foremost, want an academic curriculum—the actual teaching of basic language and mathematic skills—because they do not want their children socialized into the role of "student;" (2) place great emphasis on academic instruction; (3) believe, unlike whites, that it was appropriate or preschoolers to be taught how to read in nursery school; (4) have an "anguished relationship" with the public schools because these institutions have consistently failed to teach their children basic skills, and fear that schools will undermine their child–rearing values; (5) hold a social image of their children as students that conforms with the traditionally structured classroom; and (6) while feeling uneasy about surrendering parental authority to professionals, support firm disciplinary policies, sometimes including corporal punishment.[67]

Jerome Taylor found that the aspirations African American parents held for their children fell into six categories: "(1) interpersonal skills; (2) learning orientation; (3) self-confidence; (4) self-persistence; (5) self-esteem and; (6) self-reliance."[68] Taylor's observational strategy focused on the extent to which a child was inquisitive, innovative, and linguistically competent, concluding that a child was on the way toward demonstrating a basic learning orientation to the degree that curiosity, inventiveness and receptive, expressive competencies were reflected in everyday behavior.

Section 5.4 Segregation, Desegregation and Effective Schools

It is possible for public schools to be both effective and efficient in elevating achievement among the African American poor. Chester I. Barnard's definition of efficient and effective achievement can be useful in understanding this end. These definitions are used to avoid the controversy surrounding the use of the term "effective schools," as present in various research. He notes:

When a specific end is attained, we shall say that the action is 'effective.' When unsought consequences of the action are more important than the attainment of the desired end and are dissatisfactory [yet] effective action, we shall say [this] is 'inefficient.' When the unsought consequences are unimportant or trivial, the action is "efficient."[69]

In the Sizemore, Carlos A. Brossard and Birney Harrigan study of high-achieving, predominantly African American schools, the attainment of national or local norms on standardized tests in reading and mathematics was what labeled a school effective.[70] If the routines achieved this end, they were considered functional and effective. If the practices which occurred in the implementation of these routines had unsought consequences that were trivial, a school was judged efficient, in 1985 the specific desired end of an effective school was the elimination of the achievement gap between white and African American students.

Education, which is defined for the purpose of the study as the acquisition of knowledge, information, skills and experience, was seen as consisting of three elements: (1) being trained, or learning how to do, something; (2) being socialized, or knowing when to use what one has learned; and (3) discovering why something is learned.

Although the 1970–1980 study of high-achieving, predominantly African American schools used standardized test scores to judge a school effective, it was fully understood that since quality education necessarily includes socialization and enlightenment the attainment of national or local norms was merely a training function. Standardized test scores were used as the criterion because of the chronic failure of most school systems to service African American poor clients and teach them how to read and compute.

Looking back to 1980, the schools identified as effective in the study I did with Brossard and Harrigan might not have met all the criteria evident in the effective schools literature of the day. For example, Edmonds's definition of an effective school did not consistently interface with our study's definition.[71] Our study identified effective schools as those which performed at or above grade level on standardized tests; this criterion, however, was not always used by Edmonds. His definition of an effective school was linked more with schools that had success rates comparable or equal to the performance of middle-class schools in their respective districts. In other words, to be considered effective under Edmonds's definition, schools had to produce the same success rates, regardless of students' social class.

Using Edmonds's criteria, schools during the 1970s in New York City with low socioeconomic status (SES) were considered improving if 50 to 61 percent of their students scored at or above grade level the performance level reached by students in the city's middle-class schools. Theoretically, if 85 percent of all middle-class students scored at or above grade level on achievement tests, schools serving the poor would be considered effective only if they could equal the same percentage.

By definition, the test norms placed 50 percent of the tested population above grade level and 50 percent below. Traditionally, a school was defined as an effective school if 50 percent of its students scored above grade level. By using performance standards derived from middle-class schools' achievement tests to label a school effective, Edmonds superseded the commonly held norm of 50 percent above and below. These class standards required poor schools to perform as well as middle-class schools. For purposes of discriminate analysis, Edmonds classified a school as effective if it scored above the 75th percentile in mean verbal achievement for the designated subgroup of pupils, ineffective if it scored below the 25th percentile.[72]

Although both Ronald Edmonds and John Frederiksen placed effective schools in one category, "general," they used two categories to classify ineffective schools: (1) "general" for schools producing effects, "regardless" of race and class; and (2) "discriminatory" for those producing effects "because" of race and class.

Yet, the logical counterpart of discriminatory effective schools was omitted. It is obvious that this category of schools, which had race and class sensitivities and performed "because" of race and class compositions, was discriminatory. Neither, Edmonds nor Frederiksen were looking for the schools found in the Sizemore, Brossard and Harrigan study—schools that performed well for African American students.

Differences in definitions, as exemplified when comparing the research of Sizemore, Brossard and Harrigan with that of Edmonds and Frederiksen, is not the only inconsistency that is found when examining effective school research. In discussing effective schools research with me, Brossard identified several others: (1) the measures of effectiveness are unreliable and invalid because they focus only on standardized test results and overlook other school goals; (2) the contrasting group designs provide little information about the causal relationship among variables; and (3) the penchant for describing the global characteristics of a school and ignoring important variations in school organizations and outcomes.[73]

Brian Rowan, Steven T. Brossart and David C. Dwyer[74] noted in "Research on Effective Schools" that organizational effectiveness is a multidimensional construct and that devoting scarce resources to improvement in one domain may lead to decreased effectiveness in other domains. The Sizemore, Brossard and Dwyer study's definition of effectiveness and efficiency, however, provided for the assessment of the outcomes of such tradeoffs. If the unsought consequences are more important than the desired end, and the unsought consequences are unsatisfactory, effective action is inefficient. Hence, the Rowan, Brossart and Dwyer definition of effective action is important: "...a useful way to formulate a multidimensional view of school effectiveness would be to develop 'grounded' definitions that reflect practitioners's subjective understanding of this term."[75] Perhaps research designs will improve if the definition of terms is more concise.

Rowan et al., criticize the use of contrast group designs that provide little information about the size of relationships between specific school–level variables and school effectiveness. They argue that researchers are uncertain about which specific features of school organization and climate most influence student achievement and recommend that future researchers consider longitudinal data, perhaps from the "turnaround" schools that are becoming more and less successful recently.

Rowan et al., also maintain that data collected on expectations for performance and attributions of leadership change over time. They further state: "...in quantitative studies, researchers should use some form of cross-lagged correlation design to disentangle issues of causal ordering in longitudinal data or estimate parameters using techniques that can estimate nonrecursive causal modes...." They seek another causal model for improving research procedures.

Finally, Rowan et al., believe that effective school research concentrates on global descriptions of school organization and outcome, failing to explain how school organization affects the processes of teaching and learning that have proximal effects on student achievement. In their view, the analysis of school effectiveness should begin by looking at classrooms.

In another study, Rowan argues that effective school researchers consider the symbolism attached to the research findings often more important and salient to policy debates than a systematic analysis of the findings' instrumental value. Rowan writes:

What is distinctive about "effective schools" research, in contrast to much past scientific work, is that it has taken a shamanistic approach to the problems of schooling. It has not fanned the flames of discontent and uncertainty like previous scholarly work, but instead has held out hope that the pervasive ills of modern urban schooling can be cured.[76]

Because Rowan does not clearly state his bias, the reader is left wondering whether or not he believes these ills can be cured. He does, however, continue building his argument with three definite characteristics of shamanism that he says are used in effective schools research: (1) the big success story, which claims that a school has solved all of the ills suffered by the United States' educational system; (2) divining the unknown by use of outliers—a system of categorizing a school as effective which relies on an analysis of residuals, which will always demonstrate that schools differ in achievement, even after controlling for socioeconomic conditions; and (3) using psychometric techniques to match test items with local objectives for the purpose of aligning achievement testing with the curriculum and testing systems of local schools.[77]

While Rowan et al., provide good criticism and make sound recommendations for correcting the pitfalls of effective schools research, it is unclear what they are recommending. Their bias is that nothing can help the millions of African American students, many of whom attend the most miserable schools in the nation; and they continue their defense of poverty paradigms that no longer explain why middle-class African Americans have failed to close the academic achievement gap.

Nevertheless, they do issue a definite warning that could give direction to those of us still interested in improving the segregated school system; namely, that it has yet to be proven that the relationships identified through past effective schools research are applicable to all types of schools. In light of this warning, African American schools should be studied separately from other schools. The No Child Left Behind (NCLB) legislation, designed to close the gap between America's minority students and their white middle-to-upper-class counterparts, calls for scientifically-based instruction. Methods of instruction should be studied in schools which are predominantly African American and predominantly low-income, using census zone data. If it works in these schools, then it will be useful.

S.C. Purkey and M.S. Smith's 1983 critical review found effective schools literature weak in that it presented narrow, simplistic recipes for school improvement, derived from non-experimental data. They simultaneously admitted that theory and common sense supported many of these findings.

Their comprehensive approach differed from other reviewers because they: (1) were more skeptical; (2) used a wider net when examining outlier studies, case studies, evaluations and studies of programs and theories of organization; and (3) were concerned with both process and content.[78]

Purkey and Smith complained that reviews assume that effective schools can be differentiated from ineffective schools, while at the same time failing to provide consensus on salient characteristics. They also pointed out how reviews did not address the changes a school needs to make to become effective, "suggesting either that the reviewers are not sure what to recommend or that they think specific recommendations are not necessary.[79]"

Regarding to outlier studies, Purkey and Smith found: (1) the regression analysis of school mean achievement scores is usually employed, controlling student body socioeconomic factors; (2) an "unexpected" mean achievement score based on the regression equation is calculated for each school, after which the "residual" for each school is found by subtracting a school's "unexpected" score from its actual achievement level; (3) researchers select the most positive and negative residual scores and label the schools they represent as unusually effective or ineffective; and (4) the characteristics of effective and ineffective schools are assessed to determine why schools are labeled as such.

Purkey and Smith argued that outlier studies exhibit the following weaknesses: (1) narrow and relatively small samples used for intensive study, which increase the occurrence of chance events; (2) errors in identification of outlier schools due to the failure to partial out the effects of social class and home background; (3) aggregating achievement data at the school level, which may mask differences in the achievement of different subgroups; (4) inappropriate comparisons between positive and negative outliers, rather than average schools; and (5) the use of subjective criteria for categorizing as effective a school that serves the poor, even though it is considerably lower in achievement than middle-class suburban schools.

In their general critique, Purkey and Smith maintain that effective schools research suffers major flaws: (1) a dearth of longitudinal studies showing that what has positive effects in one setting produces the same effects in other settings; (2) the history of educational reform demonstrates structural and procedural characteristics of schools, which mitigates top-down change; and (3) there is a weak linkage between administration levels and the relatively autonomous classroom, making notions of effectiveness dependent on strong and dogmatic administrative leadership difficult.[80]

In an endeavor to improve the quality of effective school research, Purkey and Smith offer a paradigm for studying school improvement and determining school culture that links content with process. Content, as they define it, refers to organizational structures, roles, norms, and values, instructional techniques and curriculum content; process, refers to the nature and style of political and social relationships and the flow of information within the school. This paradigm assumes that "changing schools requires changing people, as well as school organization and norms. Without ignoring the need for leadership, it also assumes that consensus among school staff is more powerful than overt control. They do warn, however, that consensus carries the potential of acting as a buffer that could prevent the school from being critically examined or the implementation of a proposed change.

It is clear that Purkey and Smith directed their school culture proposal model against "the assumptions of the recipe model, particularly its bureaucratic and static conception of schools," and believe that consensus is key to school improvement.[81] Along with favoring the notion that the consensus building process is key to improving schools, they offer two sets of variables for researchers to use when describing effective schools: (1) organizational structure—school site management, instructional leadership, staff stability, curriculum articulation and organization, school-wide staff development, parental involvement and support, school-wide recognition of academic success, maximized learning time, and district support; and (2) process—collaborative planning and collegial relationships, sense of community, clear goals and high expectations, order and discipline.[82]

By emphasizing consensus, Purkey and Smith are reluctant to accept the strong administrative leadership that is universal to most effective schools research. They state:

> A forceful principal or other administrator would be an advantage, but leadership could also come from a 'critical mass' of teachers or a few influential teachers with sufficient energy and vision. At the very least, the school administration must support, however passively, the change process. Active hostility seems likely to prevent leadership from arising from any other groups within the school.[83]

However, Purkey and Smith have little to offer regarding routines that speak to a racist faculty that is determined to protect or promote a belief that a particular minority group is inferior. What they have stated concerning the high–achieving African American school is also limited:

> The high achieving Black school emphasized discipline over achievement, without de-emphasizing achievement; the high achieving white school stressed achievement over discipline. The role of the principal differed in the two types of schools, and instructional grouping practices also varied. These variations suggest, as Brookover et al. (1979) pointed out, that there is no single combination of variables that will produce an effective school. Finally, the mean score of the Black school was considerably below both that of the white school and the state as a whole. While the effective Black school may have narrowed the gap, the gap remained.[84]

Hence, their findings suggest that predominantly African American schools may require a different mix of variables than white schools to close the gap.

Regarding the removal of teachers, Purkey and Smith stated, "[We] vehemently oppose policies designed to force people who are not demonstrably incompetent out of teaching."[85] By taking this stance, they failed to answer the most relevant questions in the minds of minority parents: If students do not learn in a teacher's class, is the teacher competent?

In addition to offering a new paradigm for effective schools research, Purkey and Smith provided an agenda for research in the future: (1) longitudinal studies; (2) fuller investigations of the process by which schools increase, decrease or maintain effectiveness; (3) clearer descriptions of the actual implementation of school improvement programs; and (4) clearer descriptions of the intermediate steps of "goal specification" and "problem diagnosis."[86]

The reader of this research is left without knowledge, however, of the biases of the writers. It is somewhat apparent that they don't believe that teachers, administrators and public school actors can change African American schools enough to eliminate the achievement gap. Also unclear is whether or not they think the parents, the students or the society can change.

We have made little progress toward our objectives of equality for African Americans in public schools. If our intent was to level the playing field, eliminate the achievement gap and abolish white supremacy—and its counterpart, the imputation of Black inferiority—we have failed. Public schools are re-segregating, and public policy, supported and encouraged by the U.S. Supreme Court, has abandoned any semblance of response to the 1954 *Brown v. Board* decision.

Gary Orfield, the country's most prominent social scientist in defense of desegregation, argues that "metropolitan-wide desegregation, rather than the fragmented plan ordered by the Court in Detroit (*Milliken v. Bradley*), has been the most successful and stable...."[87] As examples, he cites Charlotte-Mecklenburg-Wilmington County, North Carolina; Clark County, Nevada; Indianapolis, Indiana; Nashville-Davidson County, Tennessee; Jefferson County, Kentucky; Broward, Duval, Orlando and Palm Beach counties in Florida; and the cities of Tampa and St. Petersburg. His central thesis is that unequal performance is actually rooted in the social and educational isolation of city students and not in the administration of the city schools. Orfield wrote: "[T]he failure of desegregation policies such as busing and metropolitan desegregation are due to the Courts limitation of solutions to single districts, except in extraordinary conditions."

While Orfield grudgingly admits a relationship between white flight and desegregation and states that low-income minority children have little or no access to schools and teachers that most successfully prepare students for college, he fails to find those sufficient reasons for pursuing means to help the children stuck in isolated low-achieving schools. He does recommend changes in housing policy and strategies for eradicating isolation in this area, but Orfield is not interested in effective schools' strategies.

In an essay titled "Living and Learning: Linking Housing and Education" John A. Powell argues that there is an irrefutable link between housing and education. The two sides of the problem are clearly aired in this treatment. He quotes Thurgood Marshall: "Our nation, I fear, will be ill-served by the court's refusal to remedy separate and unequal education, for unless our children begin to learn together,[88] there is little hope that our people will ever learn to live together." He counters with a quote from Clarence Thomas, who argues, "It never ceases to amaze me that the courts are so willing to assume that anything that is predominately Black must be inferior." This is the crux of the problem.

Brown v. Topeka was argued within the context of segregation, rather than racism or the belief that whiteness was superior and must be supreme. The text of the court order reads in part that "segregation of white and colored children in public schools has a detrimental effect upon the colored children. The impact is greater when it has the sanction of the law: for the policy of separating the races is usually interpreted as denoting the inferiority of the Negro group." The Court acknowledged that this implied inferiority of Black children did in fact affect learning behavior among this group; it further determined/concluded that learning among Black children when segregated that assumes their inferiority is sanctioned by law can be retarded.

113

However, the language of the ruling allowed the justices to see the imputed inferiority of the Black person, but not the imputed superiority of whites. Consequently, approaches that eliminated white privilege and supremacy-manifest in the use of friendship and kinship as prerequisites for the distribution of resources and the impact of these resources accumulated as a result of African slave labor were not considered.

The justices concluded that in the field of public education, the doctrine of "separate but equal" has no place. "Separate educational facilities are inherently unequal." Inherent means existing in someone or something as a permanent and inseparable element, quality or attribute, innate. According to this doctrine, separation inferred inherent inferiority for Black students, but did not acknowledge that this also inferred inherent superiority for whites.[89]

Powell does discuss the relationship between integration and assimilation. His notion of integration, however, doesn't discuss the dislodgement of white supremacy. He said, segregation persists on multiple levels. We must therefore develop multiple strategies for breaking down segregation in our society. These approaches must be organized around the principles of participation and democracy. Focusing on the desegregation of schools alone cannot produce lasting results and ultimately does not integrate society or increase and enhance participation in our democracy. This is the path we followed with busing. The answer lies substantially in linking education and housing policies.[90]

Powell clearly sees that the assimilation model is one of racial supremacy, but does not recognize his integration model as one. Clearly, no integration model can exist with white supremacy intact. And any strategies for rectification of the condition will require some surrender of privileges and advantages which accrue because one is white. Powell makes these observations about this strategy:

> A true integration model challenges racial hierarchy and the need to be colorless or white. Such a model entails a redistribution of resources and opportunities, as well as a shift in ideology. Additionally, a real problem with the idea of assimilation is the assumption that whites have not been affected by growing up in a racialized society. Although whites may be injured differently by assimilation, they are harmed nonetheless. An inclusive approach cannot simply fit individuals into existing norms and structures; it must transform those structures to accommodate all individuals and groups. Put another way, a true model of integration recognizes that whites do not occupy a neutral position and does not seek to place people of color in the same position.[91]

While Powell acknowledges these facts, he does not explain why it should work against Black people to live in Black neighborhoods; but it does not work against white people to live in white neighborhoods. It is this imputation of white superiority and supremacy that requires adjustment. Segregation is the symptom of white supremacy, not vice versa. Powell made a reference to Norfolk, Virginia as an example of a trend in communities that have abandoned integration efforts in favor of a narrow focus on improving achievement. He gives data that shows that Black students' academic achievement has declined since the return to a segregated neighborhood school system.[92]

Yet, Douglas B. Reeves reviewed research in high poverty schools that had also demonstrated high academic performance.[93] He used the term 90/90/90 to describe them because of the students attending these schools, 90 percent were low income, 90 percent were minority students, and 90 percent were high achieving. He examined accountability reports of each of the schools in Norfolk and conducted numerous site visits and interviews during 2002–2003. He found that schools with the greatest gains were not demographically similar, as they included high poverty and low poverty student populations. The financial support, staffing patterns, union agreements and central office support systems were similar in all schools.

Reeves concluded that the keys to improved academic achievement are the professional practices of teachers and leaders, not the economic, ethnic or linguistic characteristics of the students. He reports that Simpson provided "compelling evidence that the practices of the 90/90/90 schools could be applied in a diverse urban environment with similar results."[94]   The work of Reeves and Simpson joins a large body of effective schools research confirming their findings.

I have reviewed much twenty-year-old data on effective schools since this research influenced me in testing my values, beliefs, hypothesis and theories. Not much change appears in the criticism of this research throughout the 1990s and the twenty-first century, although "Charles Teddlie and Sam Stringfield did conduct a ten-year study of Louisiana schools and found that to become effective requires the mustering of political will, as well as new knowledge and skills," as Janet Crispeels noted.[95]

Yet, while teachers' unions have finally gotten the researchers to bend toward their demand for teacher leadership, nothing appears about their commensurate accountability. In other words, do teachers want to make decisions, but still think principals should be fired if those decisions are wrong?

I have yet to find a 90/90/90 school where a principal is not the instructional leader. The buck has to stop somewhere and someone must be responsible for discipline.

In their 1990 review of effective schools' practices, Daniel U. Levine and Lawrence W. Lezotte[96] stated that the more effective schools movement had gone through five phases: identification, description, guideline development, school improvement approaches, and the larger organizational context of school districts, state organizations and agencies.[97] Six years later, Levine and Levine noted criticism very similar to that produced in the 1980s. Definitions of school effectiveness varied. Most research on effective schools was still correctional. Methodological problems still plagued efforts. Levine and Levine observed:

> Schools identified as effective in a given subject during a given year might not be effective on other measures or the same measure in subsequent years. Statistical control for students' social class and family background frequently had not been adequate to attribute high achievement to school characteristics. General characteristics of effective schools did not provide teachers and pupils with much specific guidance about what they should do in the schools. Most of the research had been concerned with inner-city schools.[98]

This debate over the effective schools model continued into the twenty-first century. M. Donald Thomas and William L. Bainbridge[99] argued the facts and fallacies about effective schools in the May 2001 issue of *Phi Delta Kappan*. They listed four obvious fallacies: (1) all children can learn at the same level with the same curriculum and in the same amount of time; (2) the principal is the sole instructional leader; (3) standards are set on the basis of exceptions; and (4) uniform standards should be set for all children.

Thomas and Bainbridge are unclear as to just whose students will not meet these standards, but there is a strong inference that they are talking about minority and poor children. They said:

> Although it is difficult to accept, and even more difficult to admit, children in the United States do not have equal opportunities to learn, nor do they have equal opportunities to succeed. In time, with enough effort and money and solid social policies, the achievement gaps between the advantaged and the disadvantaged can narrow. Until then, however, it is unfair to treat all children and all schools "equally" by setting standards that are not equitable.[100]

Thus, Thomas and Bainbridge recommended schools, in a rather pointblank manner, with lower standards for the poor. For example, if all children are expected to walk or talk at a certain age, then only the affluent children are expect to read at a certain age. This may go over big with folks who read the *Phi Delta Kappan*, but I don't know too many poor people who would appreciate this point of view.

Thomas and Bainbridge blatantly recommended schools with lower standards and expectations for poor children out of "fear that they may be used to deny differential financial support for those who come to school with environmental disadvantages." In January 2002, Phi Delta Kappa published a special section on effective schools. In it, Barbara O. Taylor responded to Thomas and Bainbridge's suggestions. She stated:

> The National Alliance for Effective Schools (NAES) and those who have developed the effective schools process and conducted decades of effective schools research have never subscribed to the five fallacies that Thomas and Bainbridge list. The extensive body of work that has descended directly from the research of Ronald Edmonds, Wilbur Brookover, Larry Lezotte, John Frederickson, George Weber, Mathew Miles, Daniel Levine and Eugene Eubands, and many others is now referred to as Effective Schools Research and is the applied research currently used by trainers and consultants who are members of the NAES.[101]

Taylor lists seven correlates of effective schools: (1) clearly stated and focused school mission; (2) safe and orderly climate for learning; (3) high expectations for students, teachers and administrators; (4) opportunity to learn and student time-on-task; (5) instructional leadership by all administrators and staff members; (6) frequent monitoring of student progress; and (7) positive home/school relations.[102]

In the same January 2002 issue of *Phi Delta Kappan*, Judith K. March and Karen H. Peters[103] discuss a six-district demonstration project that is an example of curricular development in the long history of the effective schools movement. Experienced effective schools researchers at the Center for Educational Leadership Services at Kent State University developed the instructional design process (IDP) to help school districts restructure the delivery and assessment of classroom instruction and to monitor the impact of these changes on student performance.

Between 1997 and 2000, IDP was piloted in two urban, two suburban, and two rural Ohio school districts whose boards of education had passed resolutions adopting the effective schools process. During this three-year demonstration project, teams of teachers and administrators in each of the six districts took a number of actions. March and Peters stated:

> Between the onset and the conclusion of the project, the percentage of students passing the Ohio Proficiency Tests (OPT) increased in thirty-six of forty subtests at grades fourth and sixth. At the conclusion of the project, the percentage of students who passed the OPT in districts chosen by the Ohio Department of Education as "comparable" was below that of the IDP districts in two-thirds of the forty subtests.[104]

Instead of desegregation and effective schools theories competing in an either/or paradigm, both should be considered for solving this dilemma. Desegregation policies should be pursued that do not require African Americans to be victims in order to benefit. For example, I simply refused to send my own children to schools where they were not wanted, where tracks were being created for them, and where one way busing was the means. In cases where whites do not want to be near African Americans, effective schools should be created and maintained in their neighborhoods.

In 2003, Ward Connerly continued his struggle to eliminate what he called racial preference. However, his fight was not against white supremacy, but Black advancement. He did not protest the continued support for white privilege or advantage, prominent in legacy, friendship policies and kinship policies. Instead, he protested against affirmative action policies. He seeks to stop the collection of racial data in order to outlaw affirmative action, which was narrowly upheld in *Grutter v. Bollinger* (2003), where the U.S. Supreme Court ruled that the "University of Michigan's efforts to maintain a 'critical mass' of minority students did not amount to using an illegal quota. In the undergraduate case, *Gratz v. Bollinger* (2003), the court ruled that racial preferences could be used in admissions, but it said that the University of Michigan's current mechanical approach is not narrowly tailored to achieve the goal of a diverse student body."[105]

If the attempt to outlaw the collection of racial data, white supremacy can escalate in its present subtle and extra-legal forms: legacy, kinship, friendship, and the accumulated advantages generated by slavery, American apartheid and tradition. African Americans and other "pariah" groups will be locked in an inferior position and status. And since no data will be available, no one can mobilize for change or prove racial preference for whites.

In both Chicago and Pittsburgh, desegregation proved to be a challenge. Neither city has been successful in its attempts. Both cities are still segregated, although size dictates severity. Pittsburgh did not start its desegregation efforts until 1980; Chicago is still trying, having been notified by the Court that it may be time to terminate the present decree demanding desegregation.

The 1990s reinvigorated the effective schools model under the name of accountability and the Comprehensive School Reform Demonstration Models. Texas led the way, with its state assessment mode. Illinois soon followed. By 2002, the federal government had embraced the concepts in the No Child Left Behind (NCLB) laws. NCLB mandated accountability and annual testing, highly qualified teachers who were certified and competent, monitoring, safety and security, school choice, parental involvement and notification and scientifically researched programs.

In Massachusetts and Illinois, anti-testing groups formed. They challenged the use of tests to determine school performance and failure. And although no parent in his or her right mind would willfully send his or her child to a school where most of the children failed the tests, these mostly white and middle-class groups persevered, arguing against testing for Black and poor children in Chicago.

Decentralization did not play as important a part in school reform in Pittsburgh as it did in Washington, D.C., New York City, and Chicago. However, during the 1990s and into the twenty-first century, when big-city mayors were given control of the school systems, or they were remanded to the states in takeovers, recentralization occurred. Thus, a national threat continued, relative to desegregation and decentralization.

During that time, a return to the Coleman thesis started. Neither in Pittsburgh nor in Chicago did this rouse the African American community to mobilize for any struggle against the causes of the achievement gap: white supremacy and the unequal distribution of resources which it required. As for the five factors generally discussed as causes of the achievement gap: genetic inferiority still lurked in the corners in books like *The Bell Curve*,[106] but was denied educational credibility; cultural deprivation reasserted its theory through the work of Ogbu; the Coleman thesis dominated revisionist theory; The No Child Left Behind laws reinforced Edmonds's effective schools model (though it captured fewer and fewer academic supporters); and the larger society became more and more exempt as national plans for desegregation and decentralization were diminished. Once again society was giving up on African Americans, precisely because real solutions require the surrender of white supremacy.

Alexander Family: Madeline, Delila, Hortense, Helen, Evelyn, Orville, 1917

Grandmother Viola Laffoon, 1918

Sylvester and Herbert Laffoon

Herbert and Sylvester Laffoon at Old Wiley High School, 1922

Horace and Ethel Laffoon

Delila

Barbara Ann Laffoon, 1928

"Grandpapa and Me" Sylvester and Barbara Ann Laffoon, 1928

Eighth Grade Graduation

Barbara Ann Sizemore,
Ninth Grade Graduation,
1941

Barbara Ann
Laffoon, 1941

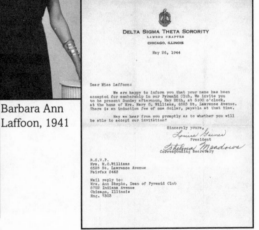

Northwestern Scholarship Letter,
1944

Delta Sigma Theta Acceptance
Letter, 1944

Barbara Ann Laffoon on
steps at Northwestern,
1946

Barbara Ann Sizemore,
1946

Northwestern Graduation
Picture, 1947

Helen, Evelyn, Madeline, Delila, Orville

Barbara Sizemore

Barbara Sizemore, 1971

Christmas, 1971

Barbara Sizemore, Washington, D.C., 1973

Barbara Ann Sizemore, 1971

Barbara Ann Laffoon,
"The Young Professional"

Barbara Ann Sizemore with family at Club DeLisa

Furman Edward Sizemore

Barbara Sizemore, 1952

Bachelor Benedict Picnic Social Club, (L-R)
Madeline Laffoon, Al Stewart, Delila May
Alexander, Herbert Laffoon, Barbara Ann,
Herbert Laffoon, Jr., D. Wright (cousin),
Kymara Chase (baby), 1949

Alexander Family: Myrtle Mae, Helen,
Barbara Sizemore, 1962

Seventy-fifth Birthday Party at DePaul, 2002

Home in Evanston

"Three Generations" (L-R) Kymara Chase, Barbara Sizemore, Kafi Chase

Class that passed the Principal's Examination

Principal's Certificate, 1961

Barbara Sizemore, Forestville High School's Principal's Office

Superintendent Inauguration with
Marion Barry and Grandson, D.C., 1974

Barbara Sizemore, Washington, D.C.,
1973

Barbara Sizemore and Grandma Laffoon,
1976

Barbara Sizemore and family

School Achievement Structure Collage

Barbara Sizemore, Women's Day,
Macedonia Church, Pittsburgh
1991

CHAPTER 6

THE PITTSBURGH ADMINISTRATION

If we can finally succeed in translating the idea of leadership into that of service, we may soon find it possible to lift the Negro to a higher level. Under leadership we have come into the ghetto; by service within the ranks we may work our way out of it. Under leadership we have been constrained to do the biddings of others; by service we may work out a program in the light of our own circumstances. Under leadership we have become poverty-stricken; by service we may teach the masses how to earn a living honestly. Under leadership we have been made to despise our own possibilities and to develop into parasites; by service we may prove sufficient unto the task of self-development and contribute our part to modern culture.

—Carter G. Woodson, *The Mis-Education of the Negro*

Section 6.1 Reform and Decentralization

During the 1980s national reform efforts sought to correct the exclusionary effects of African American segregation such as racially isolated schools, mono–cultural curricula and low standards of achievement. Reform of education had a long history in Pittsburgh, Pennsylvania. By and large the greater struggle had been for desegregation by open enrollment, magnet schools and, finally busing. At the end of this conflict, school improvement became the focus of endeavors such as teacher professionalism, parental involvement, multicultural education and school site management. This interest in school site management represented a cyclical turn toward decentralization.[1]

Decentralization is often seen as a necessary condition for social, economic and political development and for improving the efficiency with which demands for locally provided goods and services are met. Yet, centralization is frequently considered the best way to deliver services once decisions are made. What we find in a review of the literature is a repeating cycle of centralization and decentralization to solve problems. My article "Centralization and Decentralization" highlights this point. This is noted:

> Many think that decentralization strengthens accountability because
> it provides a training ground for citizen participation and political leadership. Still, studies have shown low turnouts, which may be an effect of class and education in local elections. Moreover, some scholars argue that local government, just as central government, is equally capable of restraining individual freedom in pursuit of collective action and that it is narrow and sectarian, allowing a local majority to subvert the will of the national majority, as in the case of African American apartheid in the South before 1960.[2]

Some think decentralization preserves the status quo when it reinforces the goals of the dominant groups, emphasizes material equality as a prerequisite for political equality and directs community activism to the control of the central government through the receipt of grants for perpetuating existing patterns of state intervention.[3] In spite of these caveats, decentralization is a popular recurring reform.[4]

Decentralization has generally demonstrated two approaches: administrative and political. Political decentralization—the devolution of significant policy-making powers to citizens through sub-communities or neighborhood committees—enjoyed its heyday during the 1960s with reorganized community control. This type of decentralization grew out of the Black Power Movement. The thirty-two community school districts of New York City are an outcome of decentralization. Administrative decentralization is the delegation of substantial authority and discretion to area and service delivery unit administrators, an example of which can be found in Washington D.C.'s Anacostia Community Schools. In Pittsburgh, favored methods have been open meetings, the election of African Americans to the school board, the creation of a community relations division, and an increase in public meetings where the community and parents can speak to the school board. School site management is another form of administrative decentralization; that is, it is the placement of new powers in the hands of the principal, parents and teachers.[5] This type of decentralization was carried to its maximum limit in Chicago during the 1990s.

However, reform for African Americans started in Pittsburgh in 1818 and has been continuous ever since. This reform effort has passed through four phases: (1) the fight for entry or to be accepted as students in the public schools; (2) the fight to work in the public schools or to have access to jobs; (3) the struggle for equity or the contest for desegregation and equal treatment inside the public schools and; (4) the struggle for excellence or a high quality of education. This chapter will discuss the reform efforts around equity and excellence, which began around 1959 in Pittsburgh and continued into the 1990s.[6] On February 24, 1959, the Pittsburgh Board of Education's Committee of Education received a series of recommendations from the Urban League of Pittsburgh. The recommendations dealt with the need for equal educational opportunities in order to allow each child to develop his full potential, intellectual and otherwise. The committee also indicated that it shared the same concern of the Urban League in assessing the handicaps to successful educational programs in depressed areas. The Pittsburgh Board of Education (PBE) resolved to recommend the appointment of committee members at the administrative level to the superintendent. These committee members would work with the Urban League to select an area in which a pilot improvement program might be undertaken that would be designed to meet the peculiar problems of such areas. Further, this action was taken to combat the PBE's seeming indifference to segregation in the schools and its arrogance regarding the deprivation of opportunities for African American children.

On May 20, 1958, the PBE issued a Committee of Education report, which recommended that pupils limited in mental ability and/or achievement be retained eight years in the first six grades and that such pupils be retained four years in grades seventh, eighth and ninth. It also recommended that pupils in grades ninth through twelfth be promoted on the basis of satisfactory accomplishment in individual subjects and that diplomas from a comprehensive high school be given only for a quality point average of 1.50. Certificates of attendance were to be issued to all others.[7]

The tensions arising from these recommendations brought Richard F. Jones to the PBE as the second African American director (1959–1971). His immense talents were utilized as chairman of the Business Committee and as one of the Board's vice presidents. He was an energetic man with strongly held beliefs and great integrity, and he served on the PBE with courage and commitment during a most difficult period of unrest.

Richard Jones was always a strong advocate for racial integration within the school system.[8] He was a cum laude University of Pittsburgh Law School graduate and had a prosperous legal practice with Homer S. Brown, who was the first African American member of the PBE from 1943 to 1950. Because of Brown's seniority and ability, he rose to a position of considerable influence, serving as chairman of the Judiciary General Committee. Once he presided over the House, and twice he was selected as the Most Outstanding Legislator by newspaper reporters covering the legislature. His powerful expertise on constitutional law led him to be a lower chamber authority in this field, and colleagues unanimously acclaimed his ameliorative abilities.

In 1937, Brown steered an amendment through the legislature to the McGinnis Bill, also known as the Pennsylvania Labor Relations Act. His amendment denied the McGinnis Bill's benefits to any union that discriminated in its membership. The Bill passed the House unanimously, and in January 1938 it also passed a compromise committee, paving the way for the Fair Employment Practices Act (FEPA) that Brown would introduce to the General Assembly in 1945.[9] Brown was later called the "Father of the Fair Employment Practices Commission" (FEPC), a commission created in Pennsylvania on October 27, 1955, and served as the original head of the Pennsylvania Human Relations Commission (PHRC), which monitors desegregation of public schools in Pennsylvania.

Pittsburgh had a vigorous discrimination policy against African American teachers from 1867 to 1937. Many people who were discriminated against during this time were still living in 1990. In 1935, Brown exposed the PBE's policy when he sparked the formation of a special legislative committee, of which he was a member, to investigate discriminatory hiring practices in the Pittsburgh Public School system. At the time, of the 3,000 teachers in the Pittsburgh Public School System (PPS), none were African American.

The chief investigator of this committee was Richard Jones. During this investigation the attitude of the Board president, Marcus Aaron, became evident. Aaron felt that there were more important things to do than getting African Americans jobs. After much publicity, and further investigation, Lawrence Peeler was hired to teach music at the Vann Elementary School in 1937, and during Brown's tenure the hiring of African American teachers began. By 1954, 2,577 African American teachers were hired.[10]

During the next two decades, from the 1960s to the 1980s, both the NAACP and the Urban League became more militant and aggressive in their demands for desegregation, equal educational opportunity and the inclusion of African American history and culture in the curricula of the PPS. And, both did much to shape the nature of the reform measures that followed. As a result, African American membership on the PBE increased. At one time, of fifteen PBE members, five were African Americans.

Behind this increasing militancy, the Ford Foundation allocated $493,620.00 (from 1960 to 1963) to the PPS to improve education in Pittsburgh's gray areas. Five elementary schools: Letsche, McKelver, Miller, Vann and Weil, clustered together in the Hill District, were chosen for the initial team teaching project. During the 1960s the PBE initiated many of these new programs, which included team teaching, advanced placement, the hiring of scholars, and occupational and vocational training (OVT). These great high schools were also directed toward reversing the exodus of the white middle class from the city.

Yet, as African American community leaders noted in 1966, there were few signs of reversing the exodus, and there was growing impatience[11]. Reverend LeRoy Patrick, pastor of Bethesda Presbyterian Church in the Homewood-Brushton area and chairman of the local NAACP Education Committee, charged that the team teaching projects in the Hill District and in Homewood-Brushton—the two areas where African American concentration was greatest—failed to demonstrate significant results. The NAACP, then led by Byrd Brown, the lawyer and son of Homer S. Brown, renewed its struggle...this time for desegregation as a means to quality education.[12]

In 1966, unlike other urban areas with sizable African American communities, Pittsburgh hadn't experienced any major legal suits or any race riots. The cause of this was unstated, but an outside observer labeled Pittsburgh's African American community as quiescent, apathetic and "Uncle Tomish".[13] This apathy came to an end in the late 1960s, even though the team teaching project was extended to include elementary schools in the Homewood-Brushton area such as Herron Hill Junior High School and Fifth Avenue Junior-Senior High School.

Open enrollment was the technique used by the PBE to deal with the de facto segregation of its schools. On February 26, 1963, the PBE approved a resolution to provide unrestricted transfers where space and educational programs permitted, and under such regulations as the superintendent could describe, in order to achieve a more even distribution of students by race and in relation to total school facilities. Moreover, the PBE stated its desire to maintain a basic neighborhood school policy, while at the same time allowing school choice. Both the Urban League and the NAACP dismissed this as a false attempt to deal with the massive problem of underachievement at segregated schools of the PPS.[14]

However, on October 22, 1963, a special committee gathered by the PBE and the superintendent were evaluating the new pupil assignment policy and studying ways to alleviate circumstances of segregation. The PBE authorized the superintendent to arrange meetings for the PBE and the administration with community members and public and private agency representatives interested in racial relations in order to advise with school authorities about suggestions and seek counsel for the reduction of de facto segregation. This delay in action aggravated an already tense atmosphere.[15]

In 1966, Reverend Patrick was calling for compulsory busing to guarantee that every public school would approach the citywide Black-white ratio. Board policy, which permitted parents whose children were in schools that were below the citywide ratio to voluntarily transfer their children to another school, was unacceptable. According to Reverend Patrick, Board efforts to upgrade segregated schools were futile because of this policy.[16]

Section 6.2   African Americans and The Pittsburgh Board of Education

During the turmoil of the 1960s, many African Americans were appointed to the PBE as another decentralization approach. Among them was Gladys McNairy who served as a board member from 1964 until 1976 and became the first African American president appointed to the PBE (1971–1976). She used her considerable talent and energy to develop the growth and modernization of education programs, to rejuvenate the physical plant and to increase the constructive involvement of parents and community. She had a high regard for integration and considered it the major unsolved issue confronting urban education. She was consistent in her attempt to redress the prior deprivations faced by African American children in schools, having been a part of a committee which addressed the PBE with particular reference to the superintendent's recommendation of a new principal for Herron Hill Junior High School in June of 1964 (prior to her appointment to the PBE). At the time, McNairy was a past president of the Pittsburgh City PTA Council. A longtime city activist, she had always been in the forefront of the struggle for civil, social and political rights for the African American in Pittsburgh.[17]

McNairy was also a member of the PBE Committee on Racial Equality, which gave final review to the staff's summary statement on racial integration. This summary was a statement of beliefs, practices and procedures on integration to be considered for adoption by the PBE after the NAACP's study of racial attitudes in forty-seven schools was presented to the PBE by Dr. Paul N. Geisel of the University of Pittsburgh. It was her committee that received integration improvement recommendations for PPS from the Urban League, the NAACP and the YWCA.

McNairy was on the side of Reverend Patrick and Byrd Brown when they sought to be heard before the PBE on the problem of integration and the summer school program on May 24, 1966. However, they were denied. It was to her committee that the motion for the creation of a special department to handle community school relations was sent. This department was headed by a person of the rank of assistant superintendent and was finally occupied by the first African American Assistant Superintendent, John Brewer.[18]

In spite of the advancement of African Americans in the school system and the presence of four African Americans on the school board, anger and aggravation increased. Activists agitated against the school board when the details of the great high school concept became available in 1967 as Superintendent Sidney P. Marland's plan for integration.[19] (The Great High School Concept was a proposal to build five large new high schools in which pupils who were segregated at that point in time would be desegregated into by reassignment.) African American leaders complained that the improved educational opportunity prophesized for the Great High Schools would be of little consequence as long as African American children attended inferior elementary schools. However, the plan was rejected by the Pennsylvania Human Relations Commission, and the proposal was dropped on June 29, 1970, because of escalating costs.

The assassination of Martin Luther King, Jr. on April 4, 1968, touched off a week–long riot in the city. It was termed the worst civil disturbance since the railroad riots of 1877.[20] In studying this event, the mayor's Special Task Force found that no programs were geared toward immediate or massive response to the chronic and overwhelming needs of ghetto residents, both white and nonwhite. These findings reflected adversely on the Great High School plan, and Byrd Brown's speech at the May 1968 NAACP dinner that exemplified the increasingly militant approach to this segregated school policy among African Americans. He ripped apart the PBE's policies for permitting the curricula and teachers to distort the cultural heritage of African Americans.[21]

On May 16, 1968, a special open hearing of the Committee of the Whole, along with the Racial Equality Committee, was held to accommodate the requests of citizens from the SouthWest Area Community Action Program. They demanded the following:

(1) Hold board meetings in the evenings to accommodate working parents.
(2) Two regular meetings should be held each month that would rotate between school districts.
(3) The public should be allowed to participate during a portion of the meetings.
(4) PBE's agency would be published one week prior to Board meetings using all media.
(5) Abolish the gag rule and reinstate Section 126 of the Board rules permitting the public to speak and be heard at Board meetings.
(6) Create a response system to deal with community problems.
(7) Make school buildings available for community use.
(8) Deal firmly with school personnel guilty of abuse to children through bigoted remarks. Persons found guilty should be immediately relieved of their positions, regardless of tenure.
(9) Take direct and immediate action to see that African Americans and their contributions are included in the curriculum.

(10) Set up student advisory committees for students elected by the student body.

(11) Postpone laying the foundations of the Great High Schools until the problem of poverty is addressed.

(12) Make available a report on the overall citywide average, school by school, grade by grade, on the Metropolitan Achievement Tests (MAT).

(13) Permit citizen's representatives of the community to participate in the selection of texts.

(14) Eliminate the fifth grade social studies text, *Changing New World.*

(15) Abolish corporeal punishment.

(16) Begin the immediate implementation of humanistically-oriented programs to develop self-discipline and a respect for the rights of other students.

(17) Delineate the responsibilities of the superintendent and the secretary of the PBE so that it is understood that the same person cannot be both.

(18) Report all business discussed in committee meetings to the full board at the next business meeting.[22]

On June 4, 1968, a concerned citizens group led by William "Bouie" Haden of the Homewood-Brushton based Black United Movement for Progress staged a mock trial of the PBE. Charges were brought against the PBE, and in the eyes of the concerned citizens it was guilty as charged. They gave the Board an ultimatum of citizen demands, including those above, and said that if they were not met by September of that year they would organize a mass transfer of students from ghetto schools to white schools. To reinforce their demands citizens picketed the private homes of board members, including those of the Black board members. And, in 1969, several white board members left the Board.[23]

During these years organizations formed to reflect a growing desire for greater community or neighborhood control of schools. Maxine Aaron, PBE member from 1948 to 1969 and PBE president from 1966 to 1969, deplored the concept of neighborhood control, deeming it a divisive action that led to greater separation of the races. (Her reign as president continued the nearly fifty years of PBE Aaron dominance. Her father-in-law, Marcus Aaron, served on the PBE from 1911 to 1947 and was the president for twenty years from 1922 to 1942.)[24] Yet, the PBE provided for more community input by having an open meeting one week prior to its regularly scheduled meeting. The militancy of the African American community around the lack of PBE responsiveness to citizens gave impetus to the reform movement around the structure of the PBE.

Thus, the Pittsburgh Council on Public Education was formed in July of 1968, which was a private citizen's organization working in coordination with Chatham College whose concern was with improving Pittsburgh's public schools. It appointed a select committee to study the PBE. Appointed to this committee was neighborhood leader Carolyn Howe, Majority Leader K. Leroy Irvis, and State Representative Majority Leader J. Warren Watson. The work begun by this committee during this time culminated in the elected PBE.[25]

Section 6.3   The African American Education
Association

In the summer of 1968, the African American Education Association (AAEA) was formed and elected Louis A. Venson as its president. The Association attempted to organize a tutoring program for college bound African American students and to organize fundraisers for scholarships. During 1969, the organization's board of directors, under the leadership of William Fisher, principal of Taylor Allderdice High School, arranged a meeting with then Superintendent Louis Kishkunas. One of their goals was to demand a redress of certain concerns regarding programs for gifted African American children, the promotion of African Americans to principalships, and other matters.

Venson recalls that at least twenty-three administrators showed up at Bill Fisher's house. And according to Venson, Fisher began the discussion by stating that the group was not there to discuss Black issues, but rather, they were there to discuss educational issues in general, to which Venson strenuously objected by remarking that everybody in attendance was Black except Kishkunas. He also noted that Fisher was visibly upset, and he told Venson to sit down and shut up and that they were not there to discuss racism in the Pittsburgh Public Schools. Emboldened by the Fisher's reprimand, Kishkunas called Venson a Black racist. Venson returned the compliment and called Kishkunas a white racist. The superintendent jumped to his feet, took off his coat and verbally challenged Venson to a fight. Venson gladly began to oblige when Brashear High School Principal Robert Niklos and Westinghouse High School Principal Ted Vassar jumped him and pushed Venson into the kitchen and locked the door. After the meeting was over the superintendent, who had dined sufficiently on food provided by the group, left the meeting with this comment, "I will be glad to meet with this group again, particularly if you are serving good food." With Kishkunas gone, Venson was released from the kitchen. Upon entering the room, the embarrassed Black principals verbally attacked him. The issues discussed were class size, lunch programs, budgets and other matters unrelated to the achievement gap, dropout rates and ineffective teachers. Kishkunas was given fifteen days to respond.

Kishkunas's response was not to promote any administrator who joined or belonged to AAEA. And, after that encounter the organization failed.[26] This was the only attempt made by a group of African American educators to address the hard core problem of unequal opportunity in education to the PPS. Ten years later, when PBE members Jake Milliones and Reverend Elmer Williams would try to meet with African American administrators, this experience would overwhelm their efforts.

Venson remained a principal with a chance for promotion, a lost option. To his credit, he went on to build a high-achieving elementary school and continued to provide leadership to the African American community, whose administrators had been immobilized by fear of non-promotion. He was also the only school administrator who dared to be a vocal part of the Equity Coalition that was formed around the desegregation plan formulated in 1981, and he served on the elected school board from 1993 to 1997.[27]

Section 6.4   The Pennsylvania Human Relations Committee

As mentioned previously, the Pennsylvania Human Relations Commission (PHRC) was assigned the task of desegregating public schools in Pittsburgh. It asked the PBE to submit a plan that would correct the problem of racial imbalance in the PPS by March 1968. The PBE submitted a plan to PHRC in July 1969, but it was not acceptable, and a formal complaint was made against the PPS by the PHRC. Subsequent to a three-day hearing in March 1971,which was held before the members of the PHRC, a final order was entered by PHRC. It required the PPS to submit a plan that eliminated student racial imbalance in the schools and also corrected the concentration of professional and non-professional African American staff in limited numbers in schools.[28] The school district submitted a reorganization plan to the PHRC in an attempt to comply with the amended final desegregation order from September 1971, but the plan was not acceptable to PHRC. On January 13, 1977, the Commonwealth Court ordered the PBE to prepare and submit a definitive plan to correct racial imbalance in the schools to the PHRC by July of 1977. On January 26, 1977, the PBE adopted a resolution to engage the law firm of Goehring, Rutter and Boehm to appeal the Commonwealth Court order against the advice of their solicitor, an African American named Justin Johnson, who eventually resigned as the PBE solicitor when his advice was ignored.[29]

A review petition was filed with the Pennsylvania Supreme Court. A document prepared by the staff titled "PPS System-Wide Open Enrollment Plan" (dated May 10, 1977), was submitted to the PBE and the public. A copy was sent to the PHRC on May 13, 1977, but the plan had not been formally adopted by the PBE.[30] In August of 1978, an opinion and order of the Supreme Court upheld the PHRC's right to require a plan to correct racial imbalance in the schools, but it also remanded the case back to the Commonwealth Court for adjustment of the timetable for compliance.

Meanwhile, the President of the PBE announced the members of the Magnet School Advisory Committee. The committee was to submit a report with recommendations for the types and locations of such programs by February of 1979. The school district filed a request to present testimony to assist the Commonwealth Court in establishing a new timetable. An opinion and order for the Commonwealth Court was then filed, requiring the school district to submit a plan to correct racial balance on or before July 1, 1979.[31]

The Magnet School Advisory Committee submitted its report to the PBE in February of 1979. The staff submitted a plan to the PBE utilizing some recommendations of the Advisory Committee, and the PBE adopted a set of general guidelines for desegregation. The PBE accepted the magnet school desegregation plan on March 21, 1979, however, the implementation of special subject centers was delayed until September 1980.

In April 1979, the board assigned attendance areas for students displaced by total magnet schools. In June 1979, the board and committee agreed to make Project Pass voluntary. Project Pass provided a separate classroom experience for students scoring substantially below the norms in reading and mathematics on the standardized tests. African American board member Jake Milliones had opposed this measure, indicating that it would increase segregation and would be 70 percent African American when opened. Despite his admonitions and objections the plan was carried by both the board and the committee, and his predictions came true in the first class. Meanwhile,

PHRC rejected the Pittsburgh Desegregation Plan on June 30, 1979.

In August 1979, the PHRC officially communicated their rejection of the proposed plan to the PBE and enclosed some suggested alternatives for the PPS. The receipt of the letter determined that the school district had until November 7, 1979, to submit another plan. In October 1979, the staff presented two desegregation models to the board based on a Five-Three-Four grade organization. Each of the models had two options: with pairing, and without pairing, for grades K–fifth grade. On November 5, the school district requested another ninety-day extension, this time set for February 4, 1980, in order to present a desegregation plan to the PHRC. And, on November 15, new board members submitted a letter of intent to the PHRC to desegregate the PPS.

By this time, the new board members had changed the character of the PBE. In December 1979 the school board passed a resolution stating its commitment to the Five-Three-Four grade organization and its intent to submit an outline of a desegregation plan to the PHRC by January 31, 1980. The PHRC gave the board until March 14, 1980, to submit a plan. The board met with staff to discuss desegregation models based on desegregating the schools, utilizing a Five-Three-Four grade configuration within each geographic division of the city and on the closing of schools, the redrawing of attendance areas, the pairing of some elementary schools and satellite zoning. In January 1980, the PBE organized the 100-member Community Advisory Committee to assist in the development of a desegregation plan.

Out of the Community Advisory Committee came the Equity Coalition, led by Sala Udin (who later became a city councilman) and Jerome Taylor (a professor at the University of Pittsburgh). The Equity Coalition (EC) was a group of African American leaders of community organizations and members of the Advisory Committee interested in a more equitable plan for the African American community. The EC charged that under the school board's plan, the Black community bore a disproportionate burden for integrating previously white schools. This burden was extended to Black students, who had been displaced by school closings and were sent to other all-Black schools, causing further segregation. The Equity Model that was prepared by this coalition paired forty-four elementary schools and two high schools.

However, the PBE ignored the suggestions and recommendations of both groups and designed its own plan, which integrated the middle schools and left the high schools and elementary schools segregated. The plan was supported by a majority of the PBE but vetoed by the minority, including African

American members Jake Milliones and James J. Robinson. The vote was five–four, with France Vitti and David Engel, both white, voting with Milliones and Robinson against the plan.

Although the plan was rejected by the PHRC, and the court supported their decision, in 1982 PHRC conducted negotiations with the PBE and a modified version of the plan was approved.[32] The modified version left five segregated elementary schools and two segregated high schools. The prolonged struggle also left a bitter taste in the mouths of the participants, which was intensified by the side struggles over quality education in certain schools. But it is important to point out that the character of the elected school board impacted the pace for desegregation.

Section 6.5   The PBE and the Millioneses

The PBE plan became clearer to the African American community from the Herron Hill Junior High School experience. Its plan, as revealed in the construction of John Brashear High School on the Southside (a white district) that was kept opened and after Fifth Avenue High School in the Hill District (a Black district) was closed, was to abandon the African American schools and keep the schools open in white communities in order to stem the white exodus from Pittsburgh. Parents and community representatives in the Hill District, led by Margaret Milliones (wife of Jake Milliones), and Delores Southers, protested this intent and struggled for the renovation and retention of Herron Hill Junior High School.

During the early seventies, the reform movement increased, and overtures were made for an elected school board. Allegheny County Court of Common Pleas Judge Ralph H. Smith proposed a plan to his colleagues in December 1971 that would permit only judges from Pittsburgh to participate in the selection of Board of Education members. Because only eight of the thirty-five judges were city residents, board selection would be in the hands of a few. The Smith Plan became a legislative bill in February 1972, and was introduced by State Representatives Errol B. Davis and K. Leroy Irvis. Opposition to an elected school board formed around past history, which showed an elective system resulting in graft, corruption and politics.[33]

Particularly prolonging this struggle was the division of African Americans around the desegregation issue on the PBE. John Conley and John Cundieff tended to oppose McNairy and Patrick. In fact, in 1972 Conley proposed an approved anti-busing amendment. On behalf of the PBE he stated: "We are resolved that it is the position of the PBE that we do not endorse the concept of forced busing for racial balance purposes and that we direct staff not to include the elements of forced busing solely for racial balance purposes in their reorganization plan."[34] This difference of ideology was marked by Conley's opposition to McNairy's third attempt at the board presidency. Conley supported Helen Miscimarra (an arch foe of racial desegregation and the appointment of African American administrators) in her bid against McNairy for the board head in 1973.

On the other hand, after Conley had left the board in 1975, Cundieff nominated Patrick in his tight race for the school head post. Patrick was elected on the fifth ballot (after a tie vote for four ballots) with Joseph Pois, who was supported by Helen Miscimarra. McNairy's highest priority was instructional improvement in the educational programs.[35] She thought that desegregation was the first necessity in that formula. Affirmative action, while of the utmost importance, had to serve that end. She was interested in improved performances from African American educators and consistently urged them to improve. On the other hand, Conley was more interested in affirmative action and the restoration of corporal punishment.[36] This difference was to later manifest itself on the elected school board when Conley would oppose Jake Milliones.

The Pittsburgh community divided on the issue of the elected school board. However, the home rule charter that became effective January 1, 1976, provided for a nine-member school board of directors elected from nine school districts. In the 1976 elections, Margaret Milliones and John Conley were the African Americans elected to serve on the PBE. Since 1976, there has never been more than three African Americans on the elected board at one time and only one African American board President, Jake Milliones, who served five years as president. It is this board president who turned the next important reform milestone toward accountability and the evaluation of school programs, personnel and systems for the improvement of the equality of education for all children including African American children.[37]

Since he was appointed to the board to replace his deceased wife, Margaret, Jake Milliones struggled for accountability among all staff, both African American and white. The racist practices of previous boards had concentrated African American personnel in African American majority schools and programs. Hence, these personnel were bearing the brunt of accountability approaches.[38]

Yet, there were several administrators whose performances were striking and outstanding in the face of adverse criticism, the absence of central office support and sometimes the support of the African American community. Among these outstanding people were: Doris Brevard, Vann Elementary School Principal from 1969 to 1996, Lawrence Nee, McKelvy Principal from 1981 to 1988, Vivian Williams, Madison Elementary School Principal from 1981 to 1999, Louis A. Venson, Beltzhoover Elementary School Principal from 1968 to 1981, Henry Stephens of the Miller School (which was the lowest achieving elementary school in Pittsburgh in 1979 and the sixth in the achievement of African Americans in 1988) and Janet Bell, Westwood Elementary Principal from 1981 to 1990, where the African American students exceeded the white norms in the PPS.

The Milliones presidency from 1978 to 1989 provided leadership to the tide that had been turned from desegregation to quality education, accountability and evaluation with the 1979 elections of James J. Robinson, David Engel and Frances Vitti to the PBE. During the Milliones Presidency more attention was given to high-achieving African American schools. More diagnostic and prescription testing occurred. More emphasis on learning was given, and more attention to the performance of administrators was considered.[39]

However, Mary Jane Jacobs, a white conservative woman, occupied a seat on the board that could have been won by the African American community if there had not been so much apathy. Milliones persuaded James J. Robinson, pastor of Bidwell Presbyterian Church, to run for that seat, he won and served from 1979 to 1983. With this victory Milliones was no longer alone on the PBE. However, Conley remained a problem.

When it became clear that John Conley was not going to vote with Milliones and Robinson in what they perceived to be the best interests of African American students, Milliones began to publicize the voting patterns of his adversary. Milliones reported to the media and in public meetings that Conley voted in favor of the city's desegregation plan and also voted for renewing the district's open enrollment policy, both of which Milliones opposed. Moreover, Milliones voted to hire Richard C. Wallace, Jr. as superintendent, and Conley cast the lone vote against it. Because Milliones saw Conley as part of the five-member conservative voting majority, he vigorously campaigned against him.

However, the six African American ward chairmen of the Democratic Party supported Conley. Consequently, Milliones was advised to "go easy" on Conley by Dock Fielder, the African American head of the city's thirty-two ward chairmen, or, he was warned, someone would run against him. When Conley came up for re-election, Milliones failed to heed this advice and persuaded Elmer Williams, pastor of the Sixth Mt. Zion Baptist Church, to run against Conley. Energetically and enthusiastically Milliones campaigned for Williams. However, at the time the ward chairmen supported Ernestine Parks, a retired schoolteacher and civic leader, against Milliones.[40] Both Milliones and Reverend Williams won the election; and Williams unified the African American vote on the PBE.

With five votes now available, Milliones, Robinson, Williams, and Frances Vitti, a liberal white woman who had served for several years as an official of the citywide PTA, and David Engel, a liberal professor of education at the University of Pittsburgh, a new day was declared for the PBE. For the very first time, a majority was in favor of equity, excellence and a more comprehensive desegregation plan for the PPS than the one that it had previously adopted.

It soon became clear that David Engel had plans for the board presidency, and he changed his position on some issues in return for the support of conservative members. In 1979, Milliones ran for the presidency of the PBE against Elinor Langer, the daughter of Maxine G. Aaron and the granddaughter of Marcus Aaron. He lost by a vote of five to four. Elinor Langer served on the PBE for two terms. When she asked not to be considered for a third term, Engel decided to run, he was elected president in December 1981, defeating Milliones by a five–four vote, and served two terms.[41]

Section 6.6   The Barbara and Jake Milliones Family

I married Jake Milliones on September 29, 1979, and nurtured four lovely children with him: Beatena, DuBois, Momar and Marimba. They all attended Schenley High School Teacher Center (SHSTC,) Madison Elementary and Milliones Middle School (formerly Herron Hill Junior High). Each school tracked their students, and the tracks were segregated. With a few exceptions, the children were penalized for pursuing the study of Africans or African Americans. For example, my second daughter, Beatena, had a senior class advisor who tried to censor her graduation speech on the Declaration of Independence and its application to African Americans.

With the exception of the youngest child, the children were all in the Scholars Programs for the Gifted. Because they were often more informed about African and African American studies than the teachers, the children

144

were always in disputes with teachers over facts. These teachers mainly wanted to suppress discussions about these topics, considering them divisive in an integrated school. Very few teachers were extremely caring and/or had high expectations for my children. The result was that, although avid readers, they were not enthusiastic about schoolwork. Nor did they think it important to please their teachers.

As indicated by intelligence tests taken in kindergarten, DuBois, was the most gifted of my children. In second grade he had read the reading textbook by the second week of school. When I asked the teacher to give him other work, she balked. I referred the case to the principal, who was unable to make this tenured teacher comply. Around the second month, DuBois was well into poor behavior, about which the teacher complained. It was the third month of school before this teacher developed accelerated work for DuBois. Throughout school the work was never challenging for him; and, in spite of the fact that he was in the Scholars Program, teachers never developed a curriculum that met his needs. Because he was such an avid reader, he learned to fake learning in his classes; and because he was so articulate, teachers were completely fooled.

When she was in kindergarten, Marimba, was not in the gifted program because we were not pleased with it at the time. Today she says that racism affected her learning experience more than gender, color or class. She always found herself in a struggle to encourage the acknowledgement of Black life and culture throughout her school life. This behavior was most evident in high school. Both her middle school and elementary schools were predominantly Black, so it seemed that there was more of a general understanding that Blackness just is, that is, excluding her third grade experience, which will be outlined further. Her high school experience was saturated with situations that were manipulated and controlled by both race and class. These circumstances ranged from segregating low-income Black students from the rest of the school, to ignoring Black History Month, to placing better teachers with the students who likely needed them least. All of these activities occurred in the Schenley High School Teachers Center, where retraining of PPS teachers was in place.

In third grade, Marimba was asked to do a Black History Month project on a Black individual whom she felt to be significant. She chose Ludwig Von Beethoven. Her teacher informed her that she was unable to write about him because he was not Black. Marimba disagreed and came home very frustrated. She asked me for the book that had Beethoven in it as Black. We had a meeting with the teacher, J.A. Rogers's book in tow, and after this she did her report on Beethoven.

One year SHSTC did not celebrate Black History Month. Marimba, recalling this year, told me: "I can remember clearly that February started on a Thursday or Friday, so I reasoned for the first couple of days that they are trying to get ready for the next week, since there are only a couple of school days left this week. They'll start fresh on Monday. However, that Monday and the start of the first full week of February they started the Word of the Month [program]. I remember the word was "collate." That was the first word, put up just in time for Black History Month. I could not understand for the life of me why that space was not occupied for the celebration and recognition of Black culture and life. After all, it was not as if we had heavy integration of such topics in our every day curriculum. At any rate, there was no mention of anything about Black History, right up until I implemented my own program."

Truly Marimba has always had strong leadership skills. So in a fit of frustration, she decided to type up her own Black history lesson of the day for every day in February. Each lesson highlighted one prominent figure and the definition of an African word. The first hero was Nat Turner and the first word was ankh. Marimba discretely plastered these letters all around the school. She also decided to talk about this omission at the public school board meeting. It did not take long for the school's administration to let her know that she could not post literature on the school's walls without permission from the Activities Director. Afterwards, the administration hurriedly organized a Black History Month observation.

But, thereafter Marimba's experiences in SHSTC spiraled downward. She felt that there was flagrant segregation at the school and began talking about it at community group meetings. At SHSTC most Black low-income students were placed in the Classics program. This program emphasized the basic skills and was housed in the school's basement. Marimba was outraged that other students called the students in this program the "basement kids" and that their academic path was predetermined. She felt her education was good, but these students could not feel that way being labeled the way they were. With the exception of her trigonometry and chemistry teachers, Marimba praised her teachers until her junior year at the school.

Her junior year in high school was very emotional and trying. She was a cheerleader, the class president and a member of the softball team. During that time she was boisterous and opinionated. She always wanted to keep people informed of what she thought was important and how she thought things should be. In essence, she was a young leader who needed a little balance—maybe a mentor would have helped. From her high school years, she can remember very clearly feeling as though she was being singled out for unwarranted attention by the administration, especially the Activities Director.

To be fair, she always had trouble keeping her mouth closed, which eventually resulted in her getting unsatisfactory marks in citizenship. As a cheerleader she knew that one could not get more than two unsatisfactory marks, but she got three. Consequently, she was excluded from the squad for a term. She did understand this action, because she knew the Cheerleaders Constitution, which outlined their rules and regulations. However, she was extremely agitated when the rules were also applied to the office of class president. Such rules had never been applied before, and Marimba felt that they were changed specifically for her expulsion. She completely lost faith and trust in her teachers when the Activities Director's daughter was elected class president in an uncontested election. For Marimba, favoring one's own daughter and changing the rules so that she could win was not only irresponsible, but also unethical.

Important to an understanding of my children's school experiences, however, was the fact that their father was president of the school board and a clinical psychologist; and, equally important was that I was a Black Studies professor at the time, and that both of us were faculty at the University of Pittsburgh and were very involved in their education.

Section 6.7 The Milliones Presidency

In 1983, Milliones won the presidency with votes from Reverend Williams, the swing voter Evelyn Neiser, two newcomers to the PBE: Barbara Burns (who won Robinson's seat when he declined to run again) and Edwin Grinberg (who captured Elinor Langer's seat when she vacated) and his own vote. In his 1983 presidency, Milliones waged a crusade for three goals: (1) An improvement in the quality of education in all of the schools in the PPS; (2) the narrowing of the achievement gap between African American and white students and; (3) an improvement in the evaluation process for administrators, teachers and staff employees of the PPS.[42]

Next, the external review showed a racial achievement gap that existed between African American and white students' test scores. Progress was made, reducing this gap between 1979 and 1984, but since that time there had been little change in reading and language. In mathematics the gap had widened by five points after 1984. The team then found that high levels of suspensions and undue emphasis on rote learning tasks in detention and in-school suspension programs were narrow and punitive, and the commitment to discipline issues was unevenly implemented.

In 1986, the PBE reviewed and revised its priorities, setting four major areas as improvement goals: achievement, fiscal responsibility, student discipline, and sustaining and improving district initiatives. In 1988, an external review of the PPS was commissioned by the PBE to evaluate their efforts. This team presented many significant findings. They found that standardized test scores reported by the PPS in reading, mathematics and language had shown major gains in PPS's students' achievements. Yet, they also found that these gains may have reached a plateau, because the district's main instructional program was so focused on basic skills that higher order thinking was relatively neglected, and the energy that motivated program implementation needed renewal, and the achievement tests used to assess the gains were limited measures of student achievement.[43]

In addition, while the team saw a positive approach to staff evaluation in the unique relationship between and among the board, the superintendent and the teachers' union, a negative tone appeared to them to characterize the PBE's relationship with the district's principals and administrators. They particularly noted an air of "mistrust and uncertainty that is inconsistent with the constructive programs and support that have been the foundation of the district's accomplishments."

And last, the team viewed the district's efforts to hold students mixed. The data collected showed that as enrollment decline ended dropouts and suspensions remained problems. Their major recommendations focused on: (1) the development of "a more comprehensive program, one that includes higher order cognition, and affective, social and cultural components that engage and support the multiracial, multicultural urban community it serves"; (2) making closing the achievement gap a priority of the board, the superintendent and the district staff, especially instructional team leaders and cabinets, which are the district's promising approaches to strengthening school site and shared decision-making; (3) a continuation of the funding and encouragement of staff development programs that enhance the skills of district staff members as they undertake new and more complex efforts to improve instruction in Pittsburgh; (4) the development of a comprehensive discipline program like the achievement program proposed above and; (5) the collaboration of the PBE and the central administration to work with school principals in a manner like that used with the teachers' union, using a positive approach such as the PRISM program, which would allow all four groups to work together to move the district to yet a higher level than has been achieved.

Their recommendations aside, the PPS always had model schools that had accomplished the elusive goal of equal achievement between white and African American students. For instance, Madison received a new principal in 1981. This new principal decided to emulate the routines at Vann, which was near to it. In two years Madison had surpassed Vann in achievement, becoming the highest-achieving elementary school in Pittsburgh that year.[44] The former principal of Madison was assigned to Westwood, which she turned around from a low-achieving school to a high-achieving one. And Beltzhoover was integrated in 1980.

In 1981, the PBE set ten priorities under two broad headings: school improvement and cost effective management. This occurred when Richard C. Wallace was superintendent. As a result of these priorities the superintendent designed many new standard operating procedures for the PPS. Among the most important was the Pittsburgh Research-Based Instructional Supervisory Model (or PRISM), the Monitoring Achievement in Pittsburgh (MAP) testing system, the School Improvement Program (SIP), and the establishment of teacher's centers and various magnet programs.

Based on the Madeline Hunter Supervisory Model, PRISM is a staff development effort designed to improve the instructional leadership of administrators. In turn, the Madeline Hunter Supervisory Model was created to improve the instructional leadership of administrators, the effectiveness of teachers and the learning of students. This model included the four elements of: effective instruction, the lesson design for effective instruction, supervisory skills for instructional growth and adult learning theory for effective inservice. PRISM was initiated in Pittsburgh during the 1981–1982 school year.

The Monitoring Achievement in Pittsburgh (or MAP) plan is a pre-post instructional testing system designed to increase student achievement in basic skills. The core of the MAP project is the diagnostic testing program. In the MAP plan all teachers of involved subject areas teach the same basic objectives at each level. A standardized criterion referenced testing program helps the teachers to determine the progress of their students in learning these objectives.

The School Improvement Program (or SIP) was designed to develop and test school improvement strategies in seven low-achieving schools. The long-range goal was to disseminate effective school improvement strategies that were developed in this project to schools in the district. Begun in 1981, the time line for the project was three to five years. Louis Venson was Director of SIP I from 1981 to 1989.

The SHSTC was established in 1982 to provide nine weeks of staff development for all secondary teachers in the PPS, and the Brookline Elementary School Teacher Center (BESTC) was established in 1984 to do the same for elementary school teachers. Finally, there were various magnet programs established in elementary, middle and secondary schools. All of these goals won the support of Milliones's hard line opponents: Helen Miscimarra and Jean Fink, for instance, both of whom had fought him "tooth and nail" on the desegregation issue. They saw these goals useful in attracting white students back into the PPS.

In December 1989, a new majority took over the PBE and a totally different cast of characters assumed the policy-making responsibilities for the reform effort. As this happened, several serious circumstances prevailed. The Milliones majority's goal for effective evaluation of school personnel was never achieved, although much progress had been made. Principals' evaluation of the staff had never been adequate in the PPS. Also, the deputy superintendent evaluated the secondary schools' principals and the assistant superintendent evaluated the middle and elementary schools' principals. The latter could not possibly execute this task with the small staff at her disposal. In fact, only a few people in the PPS have been able to elevate the achievement of African American students enough to eliminate the gap between them and the white students. To make matters worse, these few are generally held in low-esteem by central office personnel.

To illustrate this point, the principals in SIP did not report to Venson, their director. Supervisory teams were implemented to help the assistant and deputy superintendents with their supervisory tasks. Yet, some of the people assigned to these teams lacked credibility and competence. They had never demonstrated the ability to accelerate African American achievement. They had never, as the external review team stated, made "the instructional cabinets accountable for closing the racial achievement gap or reducing the numbers of suspensions at their schools as a specific role central to the priorities of the districts." They also recommended that for "them to become effective leaders, staff development will be necessary."[45]

Little change occurred in the Eurocentric curriculum that dominated the PPS, in spite of thirty years of reform effort in that direction. While African

American board members urged that multicultural curricula be implemented and that textbook changes reflect the PBE priority, it did little to affect these changes. And although teachers in the high-achieving schools were conscious of the ethnic background, history and culture of their students, this was not true system-wide. In general, teachers had so little knowledge of African American life, history and culture that they could not supplement the regular textbooks and workbooks. For example, when questioned about a unit on space exploration that used only white astronauts, a sixth grade teacher said she did not know if there were any Black astronauts. Another said he simply forgot about them.

In 1988, at the lowest achieving elementary schools in Pittsburgh, the teachers insisted that they could not narrow the achievement gap because their students were so poor, their students' parents too indifferent and uncaring, and their students' communities were too heavily wracked with drugs and other social disorders to do so. They simply refused to believe what was happening before their own eyes at Miller, Madison and Vann, where the children from public housing projects with the same problems and conditions were learning at or above the norms based on the test results from the Iowa Tests of Basic Skills.

And to resist the efforts of SIP, they solicited the help of the union to defy its requirements. In another low achieving SIP school the principal refused to mark incompetent teachers unsatisfactory, even when his supervisors so advised, because he did not want to have any more trouble with the union teachers. What's more, the SIP Director did not have the authority to rate him unsatisfactory.

Although the external review team noted that the pilot programs in the system were supplementary in nature, and therefore insufficient to close the gap, even if fully implemented throughout the district, it did not suggest that the system use the models already available or that they attach schools to that teaching model and let those who know how to do this teach others. Instead, the PPS had the BESTC, where the scores for African American students were seriously below the white norms in the system for reading and mathematics. Nor did the external review team observe that the staff development models in both teaching centers failed to include a research component that could have determined whether or not what they taught teachers actually helped them to elevate and accelerate achievement.[46]

Milliones's emphasis on competence and excellence was lost in the next decade because of the tendency for 1989 school board candidates to lean toward patronage instead of academic models for making policy. Three candidates vied for Milliones's seat when he ran for the city council. They were all committeemen in the Hill District's Democratic Party organization and had been supported by the ward chairman who expected to have some influence over people in the Hill's public schools. Without an emphasis on competence and excellence, PPS administrators and teachers once again considered it acceptable to permit low-achieving predominantly African American schools. The cyclical return to centralization then recurred.

On June 26, 1990, Richard C. Wallace, Pittsburgh's Superintendent of Schools, terminated the School Improvement Program (SIP I) and proposed SIP II, using six principals of schools where African American students were high–achieving to each mentor one administrative practitioner. The director of SIP I, Louise Brennen (1992–1997), had placed pressure on the superintendent and the assistant superintendent for the authority to evaluate the principals whom he monitored and had protested the addition of programs to SIP I without an increase in resources. In general, Wallace ignored these requests and Brennen seldom marked poorly performing principals unsatisfactory.

In 1990, the superintendent had to submit some cuts in the budget to avoid a tax increase. Finding a spot where there would be little or no conflict, and where you could get five votes, was a persistent problem. The logical places for such cuts were the Teacher Centers. While the superintendent did propose to cut eight staff positions at the Schenley High School Teacher Center, it really should have been closed, as should have been Brookline and Greenway. At no time had the superintendent or the director of research shown how the Teacher Centers' results impacted student achievement. It seemed a straight-up boondoggle to many African Americans, a nine-week vacation supported by the taxpayers, who also paid for a substitute teacher for each teacher attending the centers. But to cut the Teacher Centers meant the superintendent had to take on the Pittsburgh Federation of Teachers (PFT) and their militant president, Al Fondy.

In addition to these cuts, there were small schools with 100 students or so. These could have been closed and sold. But if this approach had been taken, these parents would have mobilized to replace their school board members. So the superintendent decided to make his cuts at the expense of African Americans. He closed the Community Education Activity Centers (CEAC), which operated in schools in low-income census zones and provided academic reinforcement, cultural activities and tutoring under the SIP I provisions.

Costs reductions were negligible because the six principals in SIP II received no extra help, and only $1,300.00 extra in pay, for training three administrators and maintaining high achievement in their own schools. And as predicted by board member Ron Suber, the principals refused the first SIP II proposal and negotiated eleven demands.

On August 15, 1990, the following memorandum of understanding between the six principals, Richard C. Wallace and Louise Brennen was issued: (1) that the title Principal/Mentor be changed to Principal/Coach; (2) that each Principal/Coach be able to provide input into the selection of his/her trainee whether from the ranks of teachers or supervisors except that the latter must agree to the administrative practitioner pay schedule, which could require a reduction in pay; (3) that additional clerical personnel be assigned to the SIP II in the form of one full-time clerk or typist to be housed at the school of the Coordinating Principal/Coach; (4) that all Principal/Coaches and each school assigned to SIP II be provided with the necessary computer hardware and software; (5) that a collaborative network be established between SIP II and divisional directors in the content areas to provide instructional support for the schools assigned to the program; (6) that final selection of the schools for SIP II will be made collaboratively by the Principal/Coaches, the Superintendent and the Deputy Superintendent; (7) that the Superintendent, the Deputy Superintendent and the Principal/Coaches meet at least monthly; (8) that all participants be held accountable for reaching specific performance criteria established for each school; (9) that each Principal/Coach be actively involved in the collection and dissemination of formative data for summative evaluation of SIP II Principals. (Where a Principal/Coach and a SIP II principal were unable to carry out an effective plan for improvement, the six Principal/Coaches would collaboratively develop a plan. If improvement still did not occur, it would become the responsibility of the appropriate Deputy Superintendent to insure improved performance of the SIP II principal in keeping with the previously established criteria and to evaluate accordingly); (10) that the 1990–1991 school year be considered as a developmental year, with the practitioner program beginning in September 1990 and work with the SIP II schools beginning with the second semester in 1991 and; (11) that each Principal/Coach be granted a stipend of $5,000.00 in recognition of his or her new and multiple administrative responsibilities.

The six principals were Janet Bell, Doris Brevard, James Chapas, Lawrence Nee, Louis Venson and Vivian Williams. It remained unclear just how they would secure the supervisory help they needed by way of a collaborative arrangement and maintain their high-achieving schools without a competent assistant principal. If supervisors were expected to accept a reduction in salary to serve as administrative practitioners, what did that say about the district's commitment to find the best administrators? Further, because SIP II was designed to save money and not to elevate and accelerate student achievement, it was set up to fail. It was terminated by Louise Brennen in 1992 when she reorganized the school system and appointed three area directors, only one of whom (Janet Bell) had created a high-achieving predominantly African American school.

In 1990, Wanda Henderson, the chairperson of the Title One Parents Group at PPS, and Tamanika Howze, community activist and parent, formed The Advocates for African American Students. This group made statements to the PBE in support of equity and excellence in the PPS for African American students. I, myself, made a statement on May 20, 1991, regarding the dispute between Valerie McDonald, an African American board member representing Homewood who wanted to recruit for new personnel from within the system, and Superintendent Richard C. Wallace, who wanted to search outside. My position was to do both. However, a bigger concern for me was the achievement gap in the Teacher Centers between Blacks and whites.

As late as 1991, these problems still existed. For instance, at a meeting of the Advocates on September 14, 1991, Ron Suber made the following observations: (1) there had been a change of attitude at the Board; (2) the district was having budget problems; (3) it seemed as though African Americans could just be overlooked by the Board; (4) the Board was indifferent to the recognized identified leader of the Advocates; (5) suber was running for president of the school board because the conditions in PPS schools were that bad and; (6) that African American schools were not getting fair treatment in terms of equipment and physical changes.

Present at this meeting was Linda Bryant, Wanda Henderson, Regina Holley, Tamanika Howze, Huberta Jackson-Lowman, Ronald Lawrence, Valerie McDonald, Andre Perry and Louis A. Venson. The issues discussed were student achievement, the California Achievement Test scores, the achievement gap, parental support for the Advocates, monitoring of schools, parental and community mobilization, problem solving, school reform, school restructuring, Afrocentric curriculums, and teacher recognition. The Advocates continued to bring their issues before the Board of Education, formed committees and worked hard on these issues.

But while the Advocates brought charges against the school board (in

1992) when it hired Louise Brennen as superintendent, rather than the more highly qualified Loretta Webb, an African American, after they lost in court they were never able to mobilize the African American community to advance the cause of African American students. And shortly after, I left to become dean of the School of Education at Chicago's DePaul University. This was also after my divorce from Jake Milliones in 1992, who died on January 2, 1993.

Section 6.8 Beltzhoover, Madison, and Vann

In 1979, while I was at the University of Pittsburgh, the National Institute of Education (NIE) under Grant application No. 9–001721 funded a study I was conducting from 1979 to 1985 of three high-achieving predominantly African American public schools in Pittsburgh: Beltzhoover, Madison and Vann. Assisting me in this study were Carlos A. Brossard and Birney Harrigan, both from the University of Pittsburgh. The following information summarizes the report's findings, which were filed in January of 1983 under the title "An Abashing Anomaly: The High Achieving Predominantly Black Elementary School."[47] Our conclusion was that "the high achieving Black school is an abashing anomaly in any public school system and not the result of ordinary organizational routines. In fact, it forces the system to explain the existence of low achieving Black schools and raises questions about standard operating procedures and policies which allow such schools to operate."

The NIE funded this study for the school year of 1979 to 1980 in order to investigate the organizational factors important to producing a quality education in three predominantly Black and poor elementary schools, all three from kindergarten through fifth grade, in the PPS system. Of the twenty-one elementary schools that were 70 percent or more Black, only five were high-achieving. This was reflected by reading and mathematics scores on the Metropolitan Achievement Tests (MAT) that exceeded or reached the national and/or city norms received by more than a majority of the students in the school (at least 51 percent). However, students were not tested in kindergarten. Therefore, there were five grade-equivalent mean scores for each school in reading, and five for grade-equivalent mean scores for each in mathematics or ten for each school year.

Over the five-year period beginning with the school year from 1975 to 1976, and ending with the school year from 1979 to 1980, and out of fifty possible grade-equivalent mean scores, one of the three schools scored forty-six; the second, thirty-one; and the third, twenty-three. This means that the first school achieved a grade-equivalent mean score at or above the national and/or city norm, forty-six times out of the fifty possibilities. The lowest achieving of the three predominantly Black elementary schools in the PPS achieved twenty-three grade-equivalent mean scores at or above the national and/or city norms out of the fifty. And during the study year, the second school achieved a grade-equivalent mean score at or above the national and/or city norms in ten out of ten possible grade-equivalent mean scores. This school was indeed an abashing anomaly.

Of these three study schools, the outcome in two, Beltzhoover and Vann, was high achievement and high growth in both reading and mathematics. In the third school, Madison, the outcome was high achievement and high growth in mathematics, but low achievement and high growth in reading. However, by 1985, Madison had outstripped both Beltzhoover and Vann.

Non–participant observation was the primary technique used and was supplemented by the study of documents, materials, records and reports. These techniques were used to examine the routines, scenarios and processes of the school through the lens of Graham T. Allison's Organizational Process Model (OPM), which emphasized organizational output and is used to discern the behaviors the organizational components exhibit in the implementation process, specifically in terms of outputs delivered in routines, scenarios and processes. A routine is a series of repetitive activities that are related to a goal, such as high achievement in reading. A scenario is a series of routines. A process is a series of scenarios. This model permitted the study of organizational routines, scenarios and processes, which produced the output of high achievement and this puzzling occurrence with ethnography.

Each school in this study represented a general style of life for the culture exhibited by the actors in the environment. Ethnography is the task of describing these cultures and is most exemplified by the knowledge the school actors used to generate and interpret their social behavior, not only from the investigators' points of view, but also from the school actors' points of view. Semi-structured interviews were conducted with teachers to determine goal consensus and also conducted with parents to discover their opinions about their school's achievement. This data was cross-checked with observations.

The study attempted to answer two questions: (1) what organizational factors produced high achievement in reading and mathematics in three predominantly Black elementary schools, as reflected by the attainment of scores on standardized tests at or above the national and/or city norms by a majority of the student body of the school?; and (2) what were the differences between the study schools, if any? These two questions produced some hypotheses as to the nature of this anomaly, which will be discussed further. We hypothesized that these anomalies were set in motion by the following organizational factors:

(1) The recruitment and selection of a moderately authoritative principal who believed that poor Black students could and would learn.

(2) The willingness of this principal to risk differing with the system's norm of low achievement for poor Black schools. In other words, he or she dared to be different in order to create the anomaly.

(3) The mobilization of consensus among school and community actors around high achievement as the highest priority and goal.

(4) The generating of a climate of high expectations for student achievement conducive to teaching and learning.

(5) The choice of functional routines, scenarios and processes for the achievement of this highest priority.

(6) The willingness to disagree with superior officers around the choices of these routines and their implementation.

Further, we found that the organizational output depends on the routines, scenarios and processes in place at the time and that the following items seemed to be the most important in maintaining the anomaly of a high-achieving predominantly Black elementary school:

(1) The assumption of responsibility for all student discipline, attendance and parental conflict through the publication of processes to be followed when violations, infractions or confrontations occurred and prompt enforcement of the same with selective sanctions. (Discipline)

(2) The rigorous supervision of teacher and staff performance and daily visitations of classrooms and programs. (Monitoring)

(3) The consistent monitoring of students' reading and mathematics skill mastery process. (Measuring)

(4) The use of staff and teacher expertise, skills, information and knowledge to conduct problem–directed searches for the resolution of school concerns and dilemmas. (Decision-making)

(5) The involvement of parents in some participatory and meaningful way in the school's program. (Decision-making)

(6) The prompt evaluation of teacher and staff performances and the

provision of assistance, help and in–service where necessary; however, this includes the rating of performances as unsatisfactory where warranted and the persuasion of such teachers to transfer in spite of central office resistance. (Evaluation and Professional Development)

(7) The establishment of the school's office as the central by communicating routines that control information and coordinate school activities. (Monitoring)

(8) The implementation of a horizontal organization based on some kind of reading skill mastery grouping, which is determined by criterion-referenced tests with no more than three reading groups per class, within which arrangement grouping and regrouping for mathematics is permitted; therefore, teachers assignments are dictated by teacher expertise, with a particular kind of learner rather than on teacher desire. And self-contained classrooms are modified by some kind of non-grading and team teaching is the norm. [Further, a reading clinician provides support for the diagnosis of student problems related to pacing and progress and classroom structures are high, but moderated by affection and consideration.] (Instruction, Pacing, Placement)

(9) The expansion of the school day by using prep. This includes Essential Staff Education Practice (ESEP), special subject, social studies and science periods for tutoring and small group instruction for students who need reinforcement. It also includes remediation and an increase in student attendance patterns. (Decision-making, Instruction, Pacing)

(10) The demand for the use of materials that prove functional for elevating achievement when such are not approved by the Board of Education, especially in the areas of phonics, Black history, culture and literature, mathematics and word problems. (Instruction, Decision-making)

(11) The denial of student placement in Educable Mentally Retarded (EMR) divisions, unless all strategies for regular learning occur and have been exhausted. (Placement, Instruction)

(12) The refusal to accept system-wide programs which consume administration and supervision time normally given to the regular program. (Decision-making, Instruction)

For many, these findings probably seem simple and direct; they may wonder why principals would have to take a risk to create a high-achieving school and why they would have to disagree with superiors in order to acquire functional materials and establish functional routines. Some of these differences result from a principal's tactics used in teacher union contracts. Others result from the system's belief in the inferiority of Black people and the inability of these students to learn in the regular school program.

Historically and commonly, the decision-making in school systems has been, and continues to be, hierarchical. Education Boards set policy and superintendents determine programs and directives. Lower administrative echelons are informed and held accountable for implementation. In general, teachers are involved in this through their unions or educational associations, and parents and students are excluded from this decision-making process.

For all intents and purposes, the community control movement resulted from such exclusion when Black parents saw principals and teachers as the key personnel in the educational performance of their children. They wanted to hold these personnel accountable. Consequently, they sought the power to fire and hire them. The teachers' unions won this battle in New York City's Ocean-Hill Brownsville. But the need for the decentralization of authority remained, especially for schools serving poor Black populations.[48]

Two principals in this study reflected this need and sought to fill it by exerting their own hierarchical independence: Doris Brevard, Vann Elementary School Principal; and Louis A. Venson, Beltzhoover Elementary School Principal. Both were loosely coupled with central office and had decided that they would make the decisions about how their schools operated.[49] Within the constraints of the administrative structure of the PPS, they were willing to take the risk of non-promotion and censure.

In effect, they decentralized the PPS by flattening the decision-making base and usurping some administrative prerogatives reserved for their superiors. In exchange for the loyalty and support of their teachers, these principals assumed the responsibility for student discipline and parental conflict, and they made attempts to share their influence and power with parents and teachers who worked with them for the goal of high student achievement, thereby generating consensus.

The routines they implemented profoundly affected the curriculum designed by the Board of Public Education (BPE). For example, they used materials rejected by the BPE, because their own materials proved most effective with their Black students. They used teaching positions for functions no longer approved by the BPE, because these functions were needed to elevate achievement for their students. They encouraged parents to protest system practices and policies perceived by them as unfair and/or unjust. They emphasized flexible time sequences, permitting teachers to use special subject, prep, ESEP, social studies and science periods for reinforcement and re-teaching in defiance of BPE rules and union contracts. They discouraged teachers from dumping poor Black slow learners in EMR classes until they were certain that such a placement was educationally sound. These principals also evaluated their teachers, after strictly monitoring their performances based on student achievement, growth and progress. When teachers failed to improve, the principals urged them to transfer, or they received an unsatisfactory rating. Because of the loyalty, solidarity and consensus among the other teachers, unsatisfactory teachers generally chose to leave.

Hierarchical independence was exhibited by both of these principals in the highest-achieving study schools. This suggests that principals need more decentralized authority in decision-making over curriculum, which is defined as everything that is taught, how it is taught and how this is all managed and administered in a school. However, all principals do not have the same dedication, commitment, skills, knowledge or courage as these two principals. And since no two schools are alike, no one management style will fit all cases or applies equally to every situation.

For example, the PPS superintendent implemented a research-based supervisory model in the school year of 1981–1982. After training in the model, this program required the principal to make three teacher visits per week, to make an anecdotal record of each visit and to subsequently hold a conference with the teacher in order to improve instruction. Moreover, each principal had to implement the model's training program, which required teaching the model guidelines to the faculty. These guidelines concerned lesson planning, classroom management and lesson presentation. Teachers were to demonstrate the model to the principal after the training. Certainly some principals needed this training, but such a model hardly seems right for one study school where the teachers had been working together for sixteen years, especially one in which the principal knew each teacher well and where the achievement scores of a majority of the students had exceeded or reached the national and/or city norms for at least seven years. If the model had been research-based, it should have emerged from the data provided by these exceptional school actors. Here is a principal who has been making daily visitations, now told to reduce that allocated time down to three visits per week. Here are teachers who are experts in classroom management, lesson planning and presentation, forced to consume their time with a model that may be less effective than what they are already doing.

While the performances of principals should be improved and evaluated on a more consistent basis (using student achievement as one important criterion), more study must be made of the individual school units to determine what kind of help these leaders need. Where the principal exhibits sharp skills and expertise in the elevation of achievement, especially with hard-to-reach populations, more decision-making authority should be given to them around curriculum, teacher recruitment and assignment, teacher evaluation and transfer, and parental involvement and participation. In addition, these principals need to be directly involved in goal setting and planning for other similar schools and should be involved in the determination of the horizontal and vertical organizations. A mutuality of effort among parents, administrators, community, teachers and students is absolutely necessary to set, and subsequently achieve, educational goals in a coherent and orderly fashion. Therefore, every support should be given to principals seeking to build this kind of consensus in their school communities. Once these principals and schools are identified, research units could be placed in them to observe, study and analyze the routines, scenarios and processes employed to elevate achievement and improve instruction. Ultimately, this would produce a real research-based supervisory model.

For example, the PPS superintendent implemented a mathematics monitoring achievement program during the school year from 1981 to 1982. Students were pre-tested and post-tested on prearranged skills. Between testing, teachers were instructed to teach the designated skills. (Although, such a program had been in effect at two study schools for several years). In addition, a Teachers Corp's project, stressing learning mathematics skills, was conducted at a third school. Yet, when the PPS superintendent's new program began, these schools were involved in it on the most elementary level, as though their programs had never existed. Moreover, during the dispute over phonics among school board members in 1982–1983, little attention was given the success of one study school with its phonics program. And when pilot schools were chosen, their history was ignored. These observations seem to point toward a tendency to hide the high-achieving Black schools, to ignore their contributions to teaching and learning, and to pretend that they simply do not exist. To admit their presence is too embarrassing for the PPS and would be an open admission that the decision to improve the quality of instruction for Black students is a political decision and not an educational one. But the fact is that much is already known about how to elevate achievement in the poor and Black learner. The problem is that the commitment to do so may not be there. Unless this commitment is accepted, the imputation of Black inferiority will continue, and low achievement will remain the norm in Black schools.

Perhaps the political effect of the 1982 State Human Relations Commission's amendments to the Pittsburgh City Desegregation Plan that called for the improvement of instruction at the remaining segregated Black schools will hasten a change in the present attitude toward these exceptionally high-achieving schools. Somehow, sometime and somewhere better efforts must be made by school systems to recruit and hire teachers and principals who believe that poor and Black students can and will learn.

Unless school actors have high expectations for students, their potentials will not be reached. As a matter of fact, teachers who do not believe that their students can and will learn, stop teaching them. Goal displacement occurs and discipline or growth replaces achievement as desired ends. Principals and teachers who believe that the students can and will learn look at system practices and policies for answers when achievement does not occur, rather than projecting these failures on the victims, the students and/or their parents. Since the principal must mobilize consensus among the school actors and maintain high expectations, he/she should have more say about who comes into teaching and certainly who stays there. School board members and central office administrators should not bargain away these principals' prerogatives with teachers' unions.

Every school has two kinds of organization: (1) the horizontal, which is the plan for placing children in groups for the reception of instruction, and (2) the vertical, which is concerned with moving the students from entry to exit. There are several ways to group students horizontally. One way is the age–graded structure wherein children are placed into grades according to age. Another is placement according to homogeneous achievement, as reflected by standardized achievement tests or according to ability, as shown by intelligence tests; this practice is called tracking or streaming. A third way is to place students according to individual need by skill mastery or deficiency. A fourth way is to place them by random selection. In the schools in this study students were placed in grades according to age and skill mastery in reading, as reflected by the Ginn 360 or Ginn 720 Level Tests. By this method, students were tracked into the Elementary Scholars Program (ESP) and EMR.

Teachers in these high-achieving schools did not use the norm referenced standardized tests for teaching. Rather, they used the criterion referenced tests provided by the Ginn and Lippincott series in reading and the Heath series in mathematics. Hence, they did not judge their students' growth in achievement by the standardized tests. They insisted on the mastery of procedural knowledge (learning skills such as how to read, write, and compute) as well as on propositional knowledge (learning information such as knowledge about the earth). The emphasis, however, was on procedural knowledge.

Looking at the data collected, there did not seem to be a high correlation between the achievement of students in the basal reader and the scores on the standardized tests. In other words, the criterion referenced reading level and unit tests reflected not the mastery of the specified skills, but the success of a student at a certain level, and, they did not necessarily predict what the grade equivalent score would be on the standardized test in reading. From this information it is not clear that whether what the standardized test publisher says should be taught in a grade matches the grade equivalent on the standardized tests. Students who have strong skill mastery records, however, do make higher scores. Teachers believe this is due to reinforcement, repetition and re-teaching.

Moreover, grouping for reading is an instruction fundamental when handling the extensive human variation that occurs among students in learning. This grouping also seems to facilitate the learning of mathematics, because the only school to use this routine managed to lift 81 percent of its student body to or above the national and/or city norms. Since every human being is different, and since it is fiscally impossible to hire a tutor for each student, small and large grouping practices should be planned for in-school schedules.

Another routine utilized to account for human variation in learning, and implemented in these schools, is the inter-room transfer of students whose reading groups are unavailable in their own grade placement. This is a form of the non-grading concept. It is evident that teachers try to modify the scheduling of students to account for the phenomenon of human difference in growth and achievement. What teachers in these three schools try to do is to create multi-modal, multilevel groupings for more effective instruction. Here, modes concern styles of learning and levels refer to skill placement. What's more, greater scheduling flexibility is attained through the use of team teaching, which was practiced in all three schools to some extent. In this routine teachers who specialized in certain areas or subjects could teach several groups of students. These teachers worked together as a team and shared information, knowledge and skills. This practice was exceedingly beneficial in the second grade at one school and in mathematics in the departmental group. Attempts at another school were less fruitful. Nevertheless, the practice of departmentalization needs more investigation. Its restriction on the manipulation of class time and usage precludes the expansion of the school schedule to accommodate slow learners. On the other hand, it permits the utilization of teacher subject matter expertise at a time when the elementary school curriculum expands (grades forth and fifth). The advantages and disadvantages need to be examined and weighted in some future research.

In any event, schools servicing poor and Black students should provide a horizontal organization that allows for large and small groupings. According to education author David Olson, "Knowledge is defined in terms of statements and propositions and is communicable by definition."[50] While knowledge may be represented in abstract symbolic forms such as sentences—which because of their symbolic structure can be conveyed through the mass media—skills cannot. Small grouping will be necessary for teaching skills that are private and that are located primarily in the motor system. The horizontal organization in all three schools failed to provide enough of these opportunities. Hence, teachers and principals were forced to create them. This they did by extending the student-day past dismissal, by denial of attendance in special subject classes, by using teacher prep time, ESEP and lunch periods, by sending students who failed to perform to the principal for extended work time and by monitoring student attendance.

Another point to make is that teachers were tightly coupled with the principal in a mutual and reciprocal relationship at Beltzhoover and Vann. They made important decisions in their classrooms around teacher use of expertise, student placement and progress, curriculum interventions, such as the use of Lippincott readers, and the administration of Ginn Level Tests to incoming transfer students. These teachers took certain risks by violating their union contract and by usurping parental rights. However, it was their very dependence on the principals for support in negotiating problems arising from these actions that encouraged them to take the risks in the first place. The tendency of the principals to rely on teachers as resources for problem solving in the school gave them status and made them an integral part of the administrative and supervision process, further tightening the coupling.

Language (words), music (notes) art (images) and mathematics (numbers) are all symbol systems. Yet, hierarchical skills are organized in reading and mathematics, but not in music and art, because standardized tests are not given in these subjects. This is an unfortunate problem in the study schools. Teachers, in general, do not have enough time to meet the needs of students on slower learning cycles. They must steal time from vocal and instrumental music, art, drama, poetry, dance, social studies, science, library and physical education periods. Many regret this practice, but see no alternative. Even though during the school year principals and teachers managed to produce very professional programs and plays such as *The Wiz, Grease* and *Barnum*, in general teachers are pushed to consider special subjects, social studies and science less important than reading and mathematics. Black and poor students need school experience in these special subjects; and some means of providing more time in terms of a longer school day should be studied for schools servicing Black and poor students, even though it will cost more money.

It's also clear from the research available that spending equal amounts of money on children does not provide an equality of opportunity. Some pupils begin their schooling with more physical disabilities (and less psychological preparations) for adjusting to formal education procedures. If we expect school results to provide equal opportunities in later life, then greater schooling resources should be given to those who begin with disadvantages.

Consequently, from an educational point of view, equalization would require bringing all schools up to a standard, rather than depriving any school of the resources necessary for providing an adequate educational program for the students attending. It further means that the education of some students would require spending more in order to provide them equal educational opportunity.

Special education classes represent a tracking mechanism for students who have special needs that cannot be met in the regular classroom. Consequently, these services must be provided in another setting. Unfortunately, in two of the study schools (Madison and Vann) these students were isolated from the main student body, and mainstreaming them depended on teacher ingenuity and persistence. We need to re-think the conceptualization of special education. These services need to be synthesized with the needs of students, rather than the needs of the system (i.e. removing a discipline case from a room). Any child, or every child for that matter, may need special education at one time or another, such as tutoring for a student having difficulty with geometry. More flexible horizontal organization will create more chances for dealing with these kinds of needs, and special education practices need to be planned accordingly.

One such way that this can be achieved is by using better diagnostic testing. Better diagnostic testing is required to be certain that students need special education. Reliance on intelligence tests channel many deprived and disadvantaged youngsters into these programs when they really do not belong there. Yet, the failure to diagnose early leads to further failure and frustration for students and teachers alike. Another way is to return education counselors to the schools. The return of a position like a reading clinician could work toward the achievement of this end. More counseling and guidance personnel at the elementary school level could help redirect school policy in special education referral systems also.

All three schools displayed pictures of Black men and Black women who had made major contributions to American life, i.e., Martin Luther King, Jr., Harriet Tubman, Mary McLeod Bethune, George Washington Carver and Fredrick Douglass. In addition, two schools (Beltzhoover and Vann) stressed the importance of the study of Black history, literature and culture in everyday lessons and work materials. Black picture alphabets hung on the walls, and pictures of Black and white girls and boys on illustrated posters and bulletin boards. Library books about Black people and Black life were also abundant; and Black music and Black art were taught. In essence, Black culture and Black life surrounded students, making them aware of the importance of both in their education.

Most Black students fail to reach, much less exceed, the national and/or city norms in reading and mathematics on the standardized achievement tests. Certainly, learning to master reading and mathematics skills is not all of what constitutes quality education. Yet, quality education, whatever it is, cannot be attained unless students can read, write and compute. A school must first meet these prerequisites, and with hope they will achieve this in the early grades. However, it is important to point out that scores on standardized achievement tests do not necessarily reflect a quality education when they are at or above the norms. And, it is equally important to point out that, despite this, most parents and educators judge schools and educational opportunities by them.

While we commonly believe that norm-referenced tests are culturally biased and based on Eurocentric norms, we found predominantly Black elementary schools where a majority of the students were scoring at or above these norms. We wanted to know why and how this anomaly occurred. We also felt that because the number system is less dependent on language and cultural effects, students in these schools would and did score higher in mathematics than in reading. However, some teachers felt that the mathematics scores were not true scores because the standardized test used did not include word problems. Also, teachers in the three study schools did not use the standardized tests for instructional purposes.

Although there was a mini-testing experiment in the public schools to improve test-taking skills during the study year, very few of the study school teachers participated. Instead, these teachers used the criterion-referenced level and unit reading tests for determining their students' placement, pacing and progress. Group assignments in class rosters were determined by these tests, as was promotion. For mathematics, the textbook chapter tests provided the same information. In the kindergarten classes, teachers had extensive lists of skills that had to be mastered before the reading series could begin. But even the use of criterion-referenced tests did not completely erase the effects of Eurocentric testing biases. To combat the heavy cultural bias of the reading texts, teachers in the study schools relied on repetition, reinforcement, re-teaching, and rote and drill to overcome this disability.

Where concepts were too difficult or alien, teachers simply increased the amount of time spent teaching them. In two schools (Beltzhoover and Vann) a variety of activities had been accumulated for each skill so that any student could repeat any activity several times in order to achieve mastery. There was a firm belief among the teachers of the highest achieving schools that a strong phonics background and word attack/analysis skill foundation was essential for poor and Black students (whose language was primarily Black English) and that a reading series that provided these skills was vital. However, these skills could not always be gained from the schools' textbooks. In fact, one twenty-year veteran acknowledged having served on several reading textbook committees where teachers were urged by central office personnel to choose texts other than those the teachers wanted because of certain benefits offered the school district by the publisher.

Teachers generally kept lesson plans and taught their lessons as outlined in the teachers' guide to the reading and mathematics series. Students were taken through all skills, whether or not mastery had been attained. Very little pretesting occurred to determine whether or not level or unit skipping should be permitted. In the two highest achieving schools (Beltzhoover and Vann), special treatment was given to advanced readers. For instance, in Vann a special series was used; and in Beltzhoover a variety of enrichment supplementary materials was used. In both of these schools, more instructional time was given to the slow learners. In one school, Vann, there was also an Early Learning Skills division for the placement of kindergarten students who had failed to sufficiently master skills well enough to begin the formal first grade. Only in one school, Beltzhoover, was there an enrichment program for advanced mathematics students.

Scheduling of reading and mathematics classes posed a problem for the Title One remediation teachers. In two schools, reading was usually taught in the morning, and mathematics was usually taught in the afternoon. In one, Vann, this was not the case, as there was departmentalization. Under such a schedule in schools (where the Title One program is a half-day in the morning), students often missed their regular reading and were forced to make it up during special subject times. Only at one school was there a close relationship between the Title One curriculum and the regular reading program. In this school, the Title One teacher also served as an ex-officio reading clinician that diagnosed students and assessed level and unit placements of transfer students. However, the same problem occurred in Title One mathematics.

Interestingly, at Beltzhoover and Vann the assignment of teachers to accelerated achievement level classes was rotated among the teachers in that particular grade from year to year. However, in Vann, where achievement was highest over the five-year period from 1975 to 1980, assignments were permanent, with the exception of the second grade. In the lowest-achieving study school, Madison, assignments were negotiated among the teachers, and constant arguments arose during the school year about the assignment of transfer-in students. This could also be due to their practice of giving the lowest-achieving classes to the least experienced teachers.

These practices point to the need for the training of teachers for permanent assignments so that yearly struggles to avoid the "ding-a-lings," as one teacher labeled the unwanted students, does not happen. Teachers could then be trained to develop the expertise to teach a certain type of learner, and students would feel wanted by the teachers to whom they are assigned. Furthermore, students whose standardized test scores exceeded their reading and mathematics placements could be pretested for the next level. Special treatment programs need analysis to avoid neglect of the average learner, and Title One scheduling needs more study.

The majority of the teachers in the study schools felt that they were able to accomplish high achievement in reading and mathematics because their discipline problems were minimal and the principal gave them unlimited support in this area. Without the assumption of this responsibility, these teachers would have displaced high achievement with discipline as a higher priority goal. Consequently, instead of directing their energies, talents and skills toward the elevation of achievement, they would have worked for an improvement in discipline. Further, these teachers did not depend on parents to help them to teach the children skill mastery in reading and mathematics. In fact, they considered the parents extremely handicapped in doing so. Even at Beltzhoover, where parents were encouraged to monitor teacher performance, the teachers felt that the parents had abdicated their parental obligations to the principal.

For instance, at Madison, schoolteachers were more occupied with disciplinary problems than instruction. The teachers tried to work out an alliance with parents to assist them in handling the difficult cases. However, the many chronic behavior problems at Madison further depleted the precious time available for instruction and totally consumed opportunities for extending the school day for students who were on a slow learning cycle. The data seem clear on this point. In poor and Black schools the principal must be aggressive in developing a system for dealing with discipline. He/she must take responsibility for the management of these problems and create more time for direct instruction. In addition, this action generates loyalty among the teachers and a spirit of group solidarity that leads to a consensus around high achievement as a group goal.

On the other hand, the data are not clear around high structure and its relationship to high achievement. Because Vann had the longest and most consistent record of high achievement, and was therefore highly structured, one can speculate that high structure, moderated by affection and consideration, is probably the best mode overall for poor and Black students. But, more research needs to be conducted on this relationship, because high structure may result in consistent performance over time (the environment is more controlled), but a flexible structure may result in the highest achievement at any given time because it permits more creativity. What is definite, however, is that loose structure can not produce high achievement in a poor and Black school. This fact forcefully speaks to the establishment of a strict discipline program that is firmly enforced in the poor and Black school in a considerate manner and demands a rigorous monitoring of teacher performance and compliance with the specified routines.

Only in Beltzhoover was the relationship of the principal and the parents a reciprocal relationship. In the other two schools, parents were clients who were expected to give the school support in exchange for the education of their children. At Vann, for instance, the role of parents was very limited and proscribed. And at Madison, parents were expected to help teachers with their discipline problems. In all three schools, the school principals dictated the roles of parents. However, at Beltzhoover that role was expansive, instructional and participatory.

Beltzhoover, the highest-achieving school during the school year from 1979 to 1980, had the most involved parent participation program. Parents were actually encouraged to sit in classes and observe and monitor teacher performance and student learning. The principal was a social activist who was actually sought after by the community for leadership in certain social and political areas. He served as a father figure for many of these families, and in many cases, parents surrendered their parental rights to him unequivocally. This benefit of community cohesion, coupled with the loyalty, solidarity and consensus among his faculty around high achievement as the highest priority goal, served to provide a foundation for the execution of an interesting form of hierarchical independence. However, this independence earned the principal the disapproval of the central office staff who called him a "loner," "not a team player," "independent," and "radical." This evaluation of his principalship prevented his consideration for promotion until his school became a subject of this study.

At Vann, the highest-achieving school over the five-year period from the school years of 1975 to 1980, the parents and the principal failed to develop the kind of community cohesion that characterized Beltzhoover. Some parents disliked the high structure and formal dress code established in the school, and others failed to control the behavior of their children in and out of school and protested the principal's handling of discipline from time to time. Parents desiring a more flexible environment sent their children to private, parochial and other public schools. In a few cases, these students actually transferred into lower-achieving schools. In one case the classification of the student changed when the student attended a private school. Consequently, the parent returned his child to Vann. To combat this division in the community the principal formed an organization called the School Family. This organization was composed of the school actors, the students and the parents of the achieving readers. It also allowed these parents to serve as buffers between the school and the opposing group.

At Madison, parents played the traditional PTA role: participating through this organization, becoming cluster parent representatives, and participating in Title One and Headstart parent groups, and teachers individually sought

170

out parents for disciplinary support. But in general parental involvement consisted of a small core of lunchroom aides organized around the lunchroom manager and the school principal. During the 1981 elections, this group attempted to mobilize community support for the candidate opposing the incumbent school board member for re-election. Their dismal failure revealed the extent of their representation of the actual parents of the school district. Without community and parent solidarity, and lacking loyalty and consensus among the faculty, and also encumbered by beliefs in teacher professionalism, collegiality and specialization, the principal was tightly coupled with central office for direction, supervision and support.

The data show a need for the mobilization of consensus among parents around high achievement as the highest priority goal. In addition, some effort must be made to incorporate them into a type of participatory scheme around the schools' program. The best situation is one of cohesion. Where this is impossible, the recruitment of a majority of the parents and community is basic. When schools fail in their basic task of instruction, the parents pick up the burden and bear the brunt. For example, at Madison, the data seemed to indicate that whatever learning occurred there during the study year was more the result of parental and home influence than school effects.

The data on these three schools can be summarized into the following:

(1) Beltzhoover treated parents as equals in a partnership; the other two treated them as clients who owed support in exchange for the education of the students.

(2) In the former, parents could monitor teacher performance, bring their observations to the principal and demand redress. In one of the other two, the principal prescribed parents roles. And in the remaining, their roles were defined by teachers.

(3) In the two highest-achieving schools, Beltzhoover and Vann, which were more alike, there was a mid-range consensus among the school actors around high achievement as the highest priority goal. In the other, there was low-range consensus around this goal.

(4) On other scales there was more consensus in the two more alike schools than in the third, where there was a difference in the conduct and views of new and veteran teachers.

(5) In the two highest-achieving study schools, the principals were authoritative, although the degree differed. In the third, the principal was guided by collegiality and specialization and was firmly based

171

in teacher professionalism and the adherence to standards.

(6) The two highest-achieving schools were loosely coupled with central office. Both principals were viewed as "renegades," "non-team players," "uncooperative," and "loners." The third principal was tightly coupled with the central office, running her school as best she knew how by the rules.

(7) In the two highest-achieving study schools, the principals assumed the responsibility for student discipline and parental conflict, generating loyalty among their teachers through the sense of obligation engendered by this action. In the third, an undercover war was created by the principal's failure to assume this responsibility, which was generally led by veteran teachers.

(8) In the two highest-achieving study schools, the principals monitored student progress and pacing, supervised teacher performance consistently and evaluated teachers promptly. In the third, the principal relied on her supervisory specialist for assistance in evaluation, and in-service and on external sources for help in supervision.

(9) In the two highest-achieving schools, the principals persuaded unsatisfactory personnel to transfer under the threat of the receipt of an unsatisfactory rating rather than undergo the long, tortuous, red tape process prescribed by the Board of Education and the Federation of Teachers (FOT). In the third, the principal was restricted by the presence of an FOT official on her faculty and forced to submit to that process.

(10) In the same manner, the third principal (at Madison) was constrained from using prep, special subject, social studies, science and ESEP periods for tutoring, remediation, reinforcement and re-teaching.

(11) This third school also had a higher faculty and student mobility and student absenteeism rate, a lower student population, a larger number of extra programs, more loosely structured classrooms, fewer poor students and a newer principal, compared to the other two schools. And because of its higher socio-economic status, investigators thought the achievement would be higher as an effect. This proved not to be the case. In fact, the data show a school in transition.

(12) The offices of the two highest-achieving schools were highly centralized and characterized by a business-like atmosphere. The third school's office had more of a central social meeting place aura.

It housed a soda pop machine inside the principal's office, through which teachers and staff trekked for purchases.

(13) Unattended student disciplinary referrals often played with messengers or student passers-by until the clerk noticed their behavior, and visitors often failed to notify the principal that they were in the school.

(14) Another difference was that the principals of the two highest-achieving schools spent a great deal of their work time interacting with students. The third principal spent her time with her own faculty and staff from central office and the university, specifically attending to the extra programs housed in her school.

(15) Teachers at this third school spent more time on discipline problems in their classrooms than did the teachers in the two highest-achieving schools. They were less cooperative with each other and more informal in their own behavior. Only in this third school did teachers fail to teach reading and mathematics every day, and only here did teachers interrupt each other's classes with consistent regularity for trivial reasons.

In addition, superintendents and boards of education need to consider several policy and/or administrative changes in order to test what will create and maintain high-achieving schools for Black and poor students. They should:

(1) Designate student achievement as one of the most important criteria on which teacher and principal performance will be judged.

(2) Lengthen the school day in schools where the population demands reinforcement, repetition and re-teaching and pay staff accordingly. This also entails improving student attendance.

(3) Require evidence that teachers can teach reading and mathematics before hiring, or have principals provide proof of these abilities during the probationary period, using student achievement as the basic criteria in cases where probationary teachers receive satisfactory marks or better.

(4) Provide probationary periods for principals and decentralize more authority at the building level for veterans; but monitor these principals' performances in elevating student achievement.

(5) Place research teams in schools that are high-achieving in the hope

of increasing the knowledge base.

(6) Recruit and hire more teachers and principals who believe that Black and poor students can learn and make this a requirement for working with Black and poor schools.

(7) Stringently monitor the selection and purchase of textbooks and educational materials for cultural bias and selected emphases for deviant populations, such as phonics, linguistics, word problems and ethnic history and culture.

(8) Monitor the proliferation of programs in schools that service Black and poor student populations. Where these programs are desirable, principals should be given assistant principals to deal with their administration and supervision.

The summary of findings from an ethnographic study of three high-achieving and predominantly African American elementary schools in the PPS: Beltzhoover, Madison and Vann. However, these were not the only high-achieving schools in Pittsburgh. There was also McKelver and Miller and Westwood. These schools had narrowed or eliminated the achievement gap, and each were schools that had not benefited from SIP programs. Instead, they were small self-decentralized school units that were loosely coupled with central office, and each had maverick principals who made a decision to change the routines in their schools without consulting their superiors. Miller was the most successful school from SIP. This was largely because the principal of the school, Henry Stephens, under Venson had followed SIP guidelines seriously.[51]

In 1979, the principal of Beltzhoover was Dr. Louis A Venson. At Madison Elementary there was Mrs. Vivian Williams; and, at Vann there was Mrs. Doris Brevard. Dr. Janet Bell headed another high-achieving school, Westwood. However, Venson and Brevard had high-achieving schools before 1979. Bell and Williams made their respective schools, Westwood and Madison, high-achieving schools after 1980.

In 1979, the high-achieving African American elementary school in the PPS was an anomaly and was not the result of ordinary organizational routines. It forced the system to explain the existence of low-achieving African American schools and raised questions about standard operating procedures and policies that allowed such schools to operate. Further, the research revealed routines that were very different from those in low-achieving schools.[52]

The principals of the high-achieving schools were moderately authoritarian. They implemented assessment routines, and monitoring and measuring routines, that provided continued feedback concerning goal achievement. And, in contrast to their counterparts in the school system, the principals of these high-achieving predominantly African American elementary schools institutionalized pacing routines that accelerated growth in order to keep students on grade level and on time in school.

Normally in 1979, most schools in the PPS measured their effectiveness by growth. A student was expected to grow ten months in ten months. If the students did this, the progress was considered good and the school effective. However, often students were a year or two behind. Consequently, a student who grew ten months in ten months, but who entered third grade with a 2.0 score in reading, was still a year behind when he or she entered fourth grade with a 3.0 score. Pacing routines helped this student to catch up. And to increase growth rates, routines institutionalized high expectations, increased time for instruction, and provided differential treatments for individual variation. It also emphasized conceptual development when pacing lagged.[53]

Because these principals were "on their own," so to speak, some practices greatly deviated from the school system norms. The use of teacher in-service time, and the stealing of class time from science, social studies and special subjects such as music, art and physical education for tutoring in reading and mathematics, are examples of these deviations. Another area of deviation was teacher evaluation.

In the high-achieving predominantly African American elementary schools studied, principals tended to mark teachers unsatisfactory when they were so. Moreover, these principals would often reject substitute teachers who were sent to their schools to replace teachers on leave. At the time, the practice in the PPS was to give unsatisfactory teachers two chances to make good before firing them. Therefore, a teacher who received an unsatisfactory mark from one principal could transfer to another school. If she or he did not receive consecutive unsatisfactory marks, she or he could remain teaching. However, principals in the high-achieving African American schools refused to take these unsatisfactory teachers. Needless to say, these principals were considered unfavorably by central office personnel, whose responsibilities it was to place these teachers.

Instruction in these schools was often highly structured. Here the term structure is defined by the presence of rules, regulations and directives and the dominance of routines for their execution that are enforced by a hierarchical authority. Classrooms in this study were classified as high, flexible and loose, according to the amount of structure observed in the organization and operation of their routines. Hence, teacher-student boundaries were clear. Study skill mastery instruction consisted of one-to-one teacher-student interactions and was sometimes called direct instruction.

But this was not practiced as stimulus-response behavior. In this plan, students were given information by lecture, or media, or demonstration or all three. Then students demonstrated their understanding by application, and teachers gave immediate feedback so that students could correct their mistakes. A variety of activities were pursued until students mastered the skill and/or concept. Differential treatments involved grouping students according to skill mastery, providing more difficult work for those who were more advanced and easier and more concentrated work for those who lagged behind. Students who lagged behind also received additional instruction in concept development. The assumption was made that they lagged behind because their understanding of the conceptual framework undergirding the skill to be learned was faulty. And, of course, all treatments were buttressed with homework.

Another element that was important to high-achieving schools was that principals were in charge of discipline, and, in general, they were firm overseers. They strictly monitored reading and mathematics achievement and teaching performances in their schools. They observed and visited classrooms daily, and teachers and students were confronted if noncompliance with school rules or routines was noted. Yet, neither dominance nor sheer authoritarianism was used to force compliance in these schools, even though many parents gave the principals the right to use corporal punishment on their children.

Routines that involved heavy monitoring, rewards, punishment and counseling were established for the resolution of disciplinary cases. Denial of attendance at student-preferred classes in special subjects, denial of privileges at lunchtime and dismissal, isolation, verbal harassment, and reprimands were all responses permitted at these schools. Jobs as monitors and school leaders, excursions to movies, participating and attending plays and other forms of entertainment and school parties were forms of rewards. Principals interacted heavily with students at dismissal, entry, recess and lunch times, mostly by counseling and advising. One major benefit of this activity was the opportunity afforded to the principals to communicate their high expectations to their students.

Teachers were also given help and assistance in the resolution of their instructional problems by the principal and by supervisors. Often principals in these high-achieving schools would use the expertise on their own faculties to assist teachers in need of assistance. Grade level meetings were held to discuss instructional and disciplinary problems, and teacher input was routinely solicited and used.

What became clear from this research was that the peripheral importance of teacher decision-making and parental involvement was key to high achievement. While teachers wanted to be informed and consulted about school issues, they did not want to administer the school. Of vital importance to them were decisions that affected their classrooms, such as the selection of materials and textbooks, the placement of children in groups, the handling of discipline and changes in scheduling. But in general, the teachers did not want to handle parental conflict or student discipline, order non-classroom supplies and equipment, requisition repairs, monitor the payrolls, supervise the clerks, custodians and lunch aides, or balance the school's budget. They felt the principal's main job was to make it possible for them to teach.

What's more, teachers and principals had accepted the liabilities of their students' parents. Some fulfilled their parental roles well. Some suffered from the exigencies of poverty. Others shared an apathy of hopelessness. Still others knew the overwhelming burden of single parenthood. Therefore, teachers expected little help from some parents and were overjoyed when they received it. But whether or not the parent was able or willing, their expectations for the students remained high. It simply didn't matter when the parent was chemically dependent, imprisoned or unconcerned with the students. The teachers and principals always stepped in to fill the gap.

Section 6.9   The Learning and Research Development Center

During the period between 1966 and 1992 the University of Pittsburgh was also engaged in school reform. Much research was taking place in the Learning and Research Development Center (LRDC). A report was prepared for PPS on August 29, 1975, discussing several programs. The report states that beginning in 1966 PPS and the LRDC had been engaged in a cooperative effort for developing, implementing and studying an individualized educational program in the Frick Developmental School. In 1969, the LRDC model was expanded to Homewood and Manchester Schools. And in 1971, Northview

Heights was added as the third demonstration school.

LRDC's goals were to develop, study, and evaluate components of adaptive educational environments for preschool and elementary students, and to integrate these components into the programs of public schools. It also had the task of exploring, designing and studying possible future educational alternatives and conducting fundamental and methodological research on the learning and developmental processes of children that were relevant to educational design. Accordingly, comparison schools were chosen: Belmar, Ft. Pitt and Murray. Beltzhoover, Madison and Vann were not. The report stated the following results:

> As far as achievement outcomes in the demonstration schools are concerned, the results of the fall and spring achievement testing, using the Metropolitan Readiness Test (MRT) and various levels of the Metropolitan Achievement Test (MAT), were not consistent at the three grade levels. The LRDC kindergarten students improved their scores on the readiness test and the first graders, as a consequence, were better prepared the next year, but by the end of the year, the first graders performed at approximately the same level as the comparison groups.[54]

In 1981, the LRDC received approximately $40,000.00 to evaluate the middle school program. And, in 1982 they received an additional $7,000.00 to assess the implementation of PRISM in the PPS. Further, in 1984 the LRDC received $24,000.00 to evaluate the research services at SHSTC and $7,000.00 to conduct a twelve-day staff development program to improve instructional skills. (At one time Lloyd Bond, an African American professor, worked inside the LRDC on test analysis. I remember he once gave a presentation on the items most frequently missed by African Americans on such tests as the Iowa Tests of Basic Skills (ITBS). His work was not widely disseminated, although he served on several PPS committees with me.)

The LRDC made many contributions to learning and cognition, but it never figured out how to eliminate the achievement gap. And, while the School of Education and the LRDC had close links, coordination and collaboration was not the rule. What's more, The Department of Black Community Education Research and Development (DBCERD) stood completely on the outside of all LRDC activity. Even when I conducted and reported my research on high-achieving schools there was little communication and collaboration between the two.

Carlos Brossard, former professor in the Department of Black Studies at the University of Pittsburgh, noted that the labs at LRDC began as a mechanism to improve school practices, but not students' essential school performances, or students' achievement or the achievement gap (specifically the Black/white achievement gap). He said:

> At best, these labs were to model ways to improve school practices by being a conduit to bringing the abstract psychological, educational research jargon and claims to life in what schools did. From 1969 to 1989 rarely was the specific focus on student achievement, although they used the overbroad language of teaching and learning without regard to specific thresholds, such as being on grade level.[55]

Brossard's comments bring clarity to this event. He believes that LRDC moved from research only (1966–1975), to school improvement work (1975–1990), and eventually to top experts teaching and learning through its involvement with public schools (1995).

Richard Wallace, former superintendent of the Pittsburgh Public Schools, embraced the LRDC and gave it direct contact with the PPS. William Cooley was then head of LRDC, and during his regime Wallace was very publicly enthusiastic about LRDC. Brossard believes that Wallace saw himself as a researcher. For instance, he noted that Wallace appointed Paul LeMahieu to handle analysis of school data for him and that LeMahieu always pushed Wallace on annual meeting panels at the American Educational Research Association (AERA) as a good example of a superintendent who knew and valued research and searched for ways to quickly get it in the schools. Beginning in 1982, Cooley's AERA presentations cited Wallace as a researcher that was bent on the use of educational research to improve schools. This practice of Cooley's continued through 1994.

Brossard also saw Lauren Resnick, the LRDC's lead mathematics researcher, as the chief beneficiary of this coalition. He noted:

> Since the Cooley/Wallace coalition, PPS became more accessible to the LRDC, for cause or no-cause. Essentially the Cooley/Wallace coalition paved the road for the rise of Resnick in the mathematics group at LRDC. That work gave her standing to deal with the National Governor's Review Commission on Mathematics, with the emerging standard's movement to modify the National Conference of Teachers of Mathematics (NCTM) Draft Standard's for mathematical literacy,

with the revised NCTM standards/high stakes testing movement and reform thrusts, with getting closer to pushing LRDC-style cognitive learning models and mathematical literacy research from 1970 to 1990 into schools, and with getting urban educational credentials and legitimization, without tackling race or Black children specifically.[56]

Brossard raises an issue that has always intrigued me. Why do researchers insist on universal claims when the case of African Americans is so specific? No other group has been held as examples of inferiority for so long as the African American group has been in research circles. The LRDC believes that neutral or good science would automatically be inclusive of Black students' needs. This justifies ignoring Black children with regard to specificity. Further, the cloak of universal validity precludes necessity or intrinsic interests to look at Black children with specificity, or as a special case or as a different cultural persona. This unstated super-integrationist model blunts any attention to Black-only research or perceived Black exclusivity in a research project. The presumptive inference is that, even if it is good research, it has limited generalizing qualities. More important, if one were good, by the dominant group standards, one would not even be looking at Black-only or Black specificity research. Either way, the dismissive/suppressive mechanisms click into high gear. The net result is that what a researcher describes as cavalier is in actuality continuous dismissal of Black school reform research.

Much currently revealed information now confirms Brossard's analysis of LRDC events ranging from 1981 to 2003. For instance, Debra Viadero notes in her article, "R.I. District Focuses on Research-Based Common Language" that Lauren Resnick founded the Institute for Learning in 1995 to act "as a liaison between researchers at the University of Pittsburgh's LRDC and practitioners in the field." This institute now works with dozens of school districts to synthesize twenty-five years of findings on how children learn and to distill them into nine teaching and learning principles. Viadero adds, "At bottom, the principles rest on a single belief: All children, when taught in such ways, can achieve at high levels." This sounds remarkably like the Effective Schools Model founded by Ronald R. Edmonds.

What's more, Viadero quotes Diane Lam, former superintendent of Providence, Rhode Island Public Schools as saying, "I came to the conclusion that unless we really focused on instructional leadership, we would not be successful." However, my 1983 research established this very thing with Beltzhoover, Madison and Vann—right in Pittsburgh where the LRDC is!

Unbelievably, the article says that the Institute for Learning also borrowed and adapted a tool from New York's District Two named the walk–through method. This is like the monitoring strategy in the Effective Schools Model, which was best utilized by J. Jerome Harris in District Thirteen. So, it's clear that Resnick is only rediscovering what Black practitioners of school reform and Black educators have known for the past twenty-five years or so.[57]

In August 2003, Lois Weiner, professor of elementary and secondary education at New Jersey City University, discussed the scholarship on Community School District Two (CSD 2) in New York City. Her abstract states the following:

> Data on achievement indicate a remarkable degree of social and racial stratification among CSD Two's schools and levels of achievement that closely correlate with race, ethnicity and poverty. In addition, when CSD Two's scores on state and city tests of mathematics are compared with results from CSD Twenty-five in Queens, a school district that serves a population demographically similar, the superiority of its functioning becomes questionable.[58]

The article goes on to explain why the design of research on CSD Two illustrates the perils to both research and policy when university–based researchers assume the role of "cheerleaders" promoting reforms they haven't aided in implementing and assisting.[59]

However, Lauren Resnick responded in an abstract that defended the close–working relationships between the researchers of the High Performance Learning Communities (HPLC) and the leaders of the CSD Two reform.[60] In it she described them as always open and acknowledged. She said, "The intent of the HPLC investigation was always to link scholars and practitioners in a new form of research and development in which scholars became problem–solving partners with practitioners."

There are important issues about how to profitably conduct such "problem-solving" research. These issues are worth substantial attention from the communities of researchers and practitioners, especially as collaborative research/practice partnerships proliferate. Serious studies of such partnerships that go well beyond the anecdotal attacks offered by Weiner are needed. Even Resnick's response acknowledges that she once more ignored the specific problems of urban schools with regard to race. For example, there was no discussion of the desegregation of Black student achievement. And her research mixed Hispanic populations with Chinese populations. Further, CSD Two was only 13.8 percent Black. Further, no school listed in the research from CSD Two was more than 30 percent Black. Resnick's work continues to avoid these facts.

Section 6.10   The Computer Room Takeover

Most of my informants argue that the advancement of African American interests at the University of Pittsburgh (Pitt) really started with the computer room takeover of January 15, 1969. Many stories about this event have circulated in the African American community. An analysis of common themes results in an account something like the following: Shortly after a small strike force of approximately six Black men invaded the Pitt main computer room, and with it, took hostage of important university files and data, they chained the front door. Other Black students joined them inside, and together they made several demands to which the administration agreed. The center was released and a meeting was held.

However, Jack Daniel, then chair of the Black Studies Department from 1969 to 1973, says that the university had considered increased recruitment of African Americans as students, faculty and administrators prior to that event. Curtiss Porter, former chair of the Department of Black Community Education Research and Development (DBCERD), from 1975 to 1978, stated that this impetus resulted from the assassination of Martin Luther King, Jr. in 1968. Julian Elloso Abuso seconds this in a case study dissertation, stating:

> [T]he assassination of Black civil rights leader Martin Luther King, Jr. in
> April 1968 created a spontaneous forceful reaction among the Black
> population. Black rebellions occurred in many cities across the country.
> Black students on predominantly white campuses suddenly formed
> themselves in a forceful collectivity, able to demand a relevant Black
> education, or Black studies, under their control.[61]

On May 10, 1968, the Black Action Society (BAS) was created at the University of Pittsburgh. According to Abuso, the students defined the organization as "the Black community on campus," and articulated its goals. They also submitted them to the administration in writing. In their list, they demanded that the university double Black student enrollment by September 1968, and that it continue to do so until Black student enrollment equaled twenty percent of the total student population. They also requested that the university inform them about existing programs affecting the Black community.[62]

Several informants and Abuso refer also to a speech given at Pitt by Stokely Carmichael, a leader of the Student Non-violent Coordinating Committee (SNCC) and originator of the Black Power ideology, as one of the impetuses for student activism during that time. The speech took place on March 2, 1967. Abuso reports that Curtiss Porter was particularly moved by the speech and that he admired Carmichael for "the way he marshaled his facts, the fervor and the beauty of his presentation, and in terms of his actual commitment."[63]

Other interviewees state that the computer room takeover led directly to the establishment of the Black Studies Department, the BAS, and other programs at Pitt. No matter what the impetus, the event clearly affected the community there. The names of the participants are listed on a plaque in the office of the department, although some students insist that they were not there. There were also other reasons why the participating students did not want to be known for being there. Some informants indicated that many of the students involved in the computer takeover did not want their names listed because of possible illegalities at the time. And some, who later became celebrated executives and professionals, did not want their youthful assault against the establishment advertised.

In addition to the hypothesis that the computer room takeover was the impetus for Black student activism on campus at Pitt, Carlos Brossard argues that outside influences, such as those coming from community activist, educator and PPS administrator Arthur (Art) Tuden, and the experience of the Black students at Pitt, contributed to the movement and the student takeover. He noted that "the institutional disconnect between what the non-Black Studies department at Pitt taught on Blacks, and what Black students felt and knew to be inadequate, spawned the consciousness for Black studies, even before the big Stokely speech."

Jack Daniel was the first director of the Black Studies department at Pitt, and Curtiss Porter was its first co-director. But Abuso refers to them as co-founders. Daniel negotiated the students' demands with Wesley Posvar, then president of Pitt, along with Ludwick (Luddy) Hayden, then interim director of Project A, and Eugene Davis, who served as project coordinator for the Malcolm, Martin, Marcus Scholars Program. Daniel was a traditional scholar and supportive of those requirements for scholarship and tenure, but not unsympathetic toward the changed Porter proposed.

Regardless, Brossard judges the tension high between the two men at the time. For instance, there was a struggle within the DBCERD when Daniel left his directorship. The members of the department chose Curtiss Porter to succeed him, but the University resisted. Fela Sowande, professor and musicologist at Pitt, was appointed by Dean Rosenberg, but eventually stepped down. Roland Smith was then recruited from Carnegie Mellon University, but never occupied the position. Next, Ann Jones, professor in the School of Social Work, was appointed acting director. However, the University later relented her appointment and appointed Porter chair when Jones supported his appointment.

Section 6.11 The Newly Formed Black Action Society

Another related struggle occurred when I joined the faculty in 1977. While some informants say that the Afro-American Cultural Society (AACS, was founded during the 1967–1968 school year,) was a body of both community and campus activists who made a number of demands that led to the formation of the DBCERD, the University Community Educational Programs (UCEP), and increases to the Black faculty and administrators, others say that at the time it was not the AACS, it was the newly formed BAS. The founding members of AACS, according to Luddy Hayden, were Curtiss Porter, Sala Udin, Gail Austin, Stanley Brown and Jake Milliones. One of the proven by-products of this group was the founding of the Pittsburgh Black Theatre Ensemble, when its members worked directly with August Wilson in the performance of his work.

No matter the argument over the impetus of the department, Joseph McCormick, second chairman of the BAS, confirmed that the BAS was founded in May of 1968 and that Porter and a number of Black undergraduate students were instrumental in its founding. He also noted that the first BAS chairman was Charles Morrow. And Porter states that the computer room takeover strengthened the BAS by giving it office space and university access. From research, I concluded that the AACS preceded BAS, but that BAS was the more aggressive of the two organizations and was reinforced as an organization by the demands ceded as a result of the computer room event. It also became the mobilizer and energizer of the movement, while AACS receded into the background and eventually disappeared.

Students and community activists from both groups fought to have the department and were in positions of leadership. Still, problematic was the issue of tenure. The university traditionally demanded certain requirements for tenure: the acquisition of a terminal degree, the production of publications, the rendering of service, and the teaching of classes. Some who had worked so long and hard for the department had not satisfied these conditions. However, Porter indicated that they had set out to establish alternatives to the traditional credential set.

I had not yet acquired my doctorate when I was hired in a tenure track position at Pitt. Porter explained that this is one instance that codified the nature of the struggle to change the meaning of tenure in a discipline whose foundations were not yet established. He posed these questions: "Should it count as service to engage one's professional development in the actual development of the discipline? Would it be considered an academic exercise to develop and demonstrate a working model of such a new discipline? Could tenure be accorded by a different set of standards that were as rigorously considered as the traditional and that, in fact, incorporated and transformed the traditional?" To prove his point, Porter cites Rob Penny, a tenured professor and street poet when hired, with no formal education beyond high school. He later became a friend and mentor to renowned playwright August Wilson. This struggle between the "credentialed" and the "non-credentialed" eventually fragmented the faculty and frustrated the chair.

Porter's ardent defense of the right of Black Studies to define itself, its mission and its procedures attracted enemies. This is no better illustrated than in the fight for his own tenure. Evidence seems to show that Porter's denial was political. While some members, Emmanuel Ladun Anise, Brenda Berrian, Carlos Brossard, Vernell Lillie and James Karioke, complied with the traditional tenure route, clearly Penny did not. Porter reports that his own dossier included elements of both traditional and transformed criteria, using his developmental work in building the discipline as his primary academic contribution. But according to Abuso, the vote on Porter was two to two at the college level, with one abstention. Nevertheless, his petition was denied by the very same dean who later gave support to the tenure and promotion of Penny, who served as chair from 1978 to 1985.

In fact, in 1981 Porter resigned over this controversy and because the university refused to appoint professors Lewis and Ntukoku. There were marches held in Porter's support, but he continued to be the "major resister." Porter defines the issues with great clarity. He said:

> The struggle related to the direction, which Black Studies as a discipline ought to take. This struggle, it was felt, would determine not only the direction of teaching

and learning practices within the department, but also the very existence of Black Studies at the university, and indeed, the viability of the DBCERD model, which engaged the academic curriculum in the life of the community and grounded its future growth in both the academically researched and the creatively felt needs of the local and Black community.

The issue of existence in the University of Pittsburgh's academic arena was therefore two-fold. This two-fold existence was sometimes good and sometimes bad. Some were firmly in the traditionalist camp, and others were in the academic activist group. Yet others struggled to do both. Porter stated:

I found myself in a dilemma, having adamantly requested that the two brothers (Lewis and Ntukoku) do something to meet at least the department's criteria, against which they argued. I was caught in the middle once too many times and resigned; the noble way out. Frankly, this work had taken its toll on my character, my family and my life on the whole. After thirteen years of having done some good and some bad, I was thoroughly done, spent. Nobody knows this and nobody has ever asked.

He further stated:

Remember the poem, "A Hero Ain't Nothin' But a San'wich?" Of course, there is a lot more to it. I made a lot of bad choices and a lot of good, but I was done. I made up my mind that this time I would stand down, no repeat of 1968, when I was encouraged, against my desire, to keep on pushing past the unwelcome signs posted all over Pitt. I had given up my direction toward creative writing and filmmaking to make this venture work. I could do no more. I'd lost my family and myself. That was enough.[64]

Some Porter supporters were unconvinced by his dedication to 'est', a training program founded by Werner Erhard, aka Jack Rosenberg, to help people to be, as Abuso describes Porter's views of the program as, a "transformation of consciousness process." Influenced by Barbara Ann Teer, founder of the National Black Theater in New York, Porter became convinced that 'est' could make a contribution to Black Studies.

I attended several sessions with Margaret Milliones, but could never see the relationship that Porter referred to. For me 'est' was a secularized version of Mark: 9, 10 and 11, especially its description as a progress through stages from survival, ignorance, awareness, catharsis, cathexis, to functionality. However, Porter argued that religion tended "to rope people into belief systems and take them out of the world instead of into the world with altered consciousness."[65] I saw 'est' as opposed to the dialectic, discouraging to dialogue, and somewhat anti-intellectual. Porter, on the other hand, saw it as an extension of the intellectual idea promoted by the Black People's Topographical Center, which generated data and demographics for a format, but failed to develop a logistic design, a delivery system and an ideology. He stated:

> 'est' continues today, though in greatly diminished proportions, as the Landmark Education Foundation. They continue to put their training and seminars with a hard core of believers, though they receive nowhere near the participation they enjoyed in the mid-70s and early 80s, before scandal rocked the house of 'est'. The 'est' movement is generally given credit for rocketing the "me generation" into notoriety. A basic tenet of it was the discovery through processes, copyrighted by Erhard, of changing the self to "God in My House." Thus it is easy to move to "me-ism" from there.

Porter tried to legitimize Black studies academically and to promote community activism. Upon Porter's departure, it was clear that he had held the elements together because there was a rupture soon after that began between the Africans from Africa and the Africans in the Diaspora.

Brossard describes this as a conflict between who was superlative and who was not, by mainstream standards. In 1976, Brossard shows that four traditionally credentialed Africans (Fela Sowonde, Emmanuel Ladun Anise, James Karioki and Tekie Fessehatzion), two traditionally credentialed African Americans (Jack Daniel and Vernell Lillie), five non-traditionally credentialed African Americans (Yusef Ali [Joe Lewis], Rob Penny, Robert [Bob] Johnson, Barbara Hayden, and Curtiss Porter), one non-traditionally credentialed Caribbean (Richard Blackett), and one non-traditionally credentialed African (Anugo Ntukoku) were on the department's staff. The tension between these groups undermined Porter's push to get out of the standardized university structure and make a new one that was community centered.

From 1977 to 1981, Brossard notes, three traditionally credentialed African Americans joined the faculty: Brenda Berrian, himself and myself. He also argues that two Africans, Anise and Karioki, dropped out of departmental business in time, the former actively by operating part-time and later full-time from the Department of Political Science, and the latter passively. He said, "The department was balkanized into competing interest groups, with the African segment working to destroy the organization." He also believes that I was blinded to most of these events due to my own interests: finishing my dissertation, ending long calendar commitments on the lecture circuit, and gearing up for courses. And he added that new faculty hired within that time fit the traditional tenure mode.[66]

The African tendency was to wander away from the problems of Mississippi and lean toward the solution of problems in Eritrea, Nigeria or Trinidad. As the department hired more and more Africans, the tension created by this practice rose. In addition, there was not enough money to fund research trips back and forth to African nations. Arguments dominated faculty meetings and problem solving became impossible. Add to this the differences between the nationalists and the integrationists, the former feeling that the department should have only Black faculty, and the belief by some that faculty members should marry only Black men and Black women, and the in-fighting increased.

Porter, however, views this condition differently. He sees the issue as being: those who supported the traditional requirements for tenure and promotion and those who supported the transformational requirements. He stated:

> The DBCERD model sought to accommodate these divergent tendencies and did to some measure of success; thus, the state of warfare between factions of the academy became the ordinary dialectic and discourse of a developing discipline. There ought to be room for divergence, and also for convergence, which was thought in this model to be the higher value.

Furthermore, Porter, himself a paragon of community activism, did not believe that the "prevailing traditional model allowed for academic activism; and to be sure, some who classified themselves as academic-activists were neither academic enough, nor activist enough to establish or represent the new standard." His vision was ahead of its time, perhaps. He, himself, noted that the 1999 Kellogg Foundation sponsored a study titled "Returning to Our Roots: A Learning Society," which was authored by the Kellogg Commission on the Future of State and Land Grant Universities. This commission included the presidents and chancellors of twenty-four major land grant schools and the executive director of the Kellogg commission. "A Learning Society" was defined as a study that was "socially inclusive" and ensured that "all of its members were part of the learning communities." Porter noted that this sounded a great deal like the academic activism that he had tried to promote thirty years before, specifically when the report stated that "the broader issues of "A Learning Society" include the importance of research and the creation of knowledge beneficial to society," and specified the university's role in the creation and dissemination of that knowledge and the importance of continuous education to society.

By the time I arrived the non-credentialed faculty at Pitt counted both Africans and African Americans. By then, most of us in social science had capitulated to the traditional academic requirements, although we extolled community activism as well. I acquired my doctorate in 1979. Disputes were not over that issue, but rather over how departmental funds were to be spent, what projects were to be supported and what goals and ends were to be pursued. Centered in education as I am, my goals then concerned the education of the vast majority of African American students concentrated in public schools and the courses and curricula we were designing for the Black Studies department. Students told me about professors who did not attend their classes, arrived late, and gave As to everyone in order to fill their classes. And constant criticism was directed to a Caribbean faculty member who was married to a white person. These divisive concerns inhibited the promotion of Porter's vision of the learning community. In essence, I saw Porter's vision besieged by this fragmentation.

Each faculty member in DBCERD had his or her own niche and pursued their own goals. The jewels of the department were the Kuntu Theater, then directed by Vernell Lillie, who also served as chair of the department from 1995 to 2000, and the Pittsburgh Childhood Environment Centers (PCEC), which was established by Barbara Hayden, who left Pitt in 1972. The Kuntu productions were professional ones and provided many opportunities for talented African Americans at Pitt. Lillie was the perfect mix of traditional academic and community activist. Abuso describes his work at Pitt as twofold. He saw drama as an instructional device, meaning that it is used as an aspect of academic curriculum, with a sub-form focusing on drama aesthetics, which occur on the stage or in a theater setting, and another sub-form focusing on typical and unusual curricular events, which manifest academic or social science approaches to Black studies. Abuso also described Lillie's activism as a strategy for ethnicization. He commented, "It requires modification of the content of drama, so that the Black experiences are given equal status to white ones. In turn, an indigenized drama, as objectified by the different cultural events, involves Black people in ethnic consciousness raising."[68]

Moreover, Kuntu supported the work of Rob Penny, noted playwright and mentor to August Wilson. Rob's plays were often produced on the stage. Porter, himself, describes Kuntu as the natural child of the Black Horizon Theatre (BHT), which was a traveling repertory theater that produced the plays of Imamu Baraka, Rob Penny and August Wilson, among others. Porter commented: "BHT was a theater in the vein of the Black aesthetic arts movement." However, even before Kuntu, the DBCERD housed Bob Johnson's Pittsburgh Black Theater Dance Company. Now here was a sparkling jewel. Bob Johnson, a New York-based choreographer, became another of those unorthodox Pitt faculty members. His training was on the stage and not in the academic setting, but he was wonderful in transforming ordinary Pitt students with dramatic interests into highly accomplished dancers, singers and dramatic performers at a level even higher than BHT could, and because he had been there and done the Broadway/New York/Chicago/L.A. theater thing, his productions were entirely professional.

The arts division of DBCERD most closely resembled the community activism concept that Porter idealized. He said, "Professor Johnson invited seasoned artists from the African Diaspora to perform, produce, direct and specifically lend their creativity and professionalism to the development of the aesthetic pursuits of DBCERD." And, artists like Bob Johnson, Rob Penny, August Wilson, Sonia Sanchez and Etheridge Knight produced a huge volume of Black aesthetic creativity for DBCERD, thus, further removing the DBCERD from the ordinary measuring rod for what Black Studies ought to be. Given the PCEC, BHT and later the PBIDC, DBCERD could be seen as walking the talk when it said that Black Studies ought to be a complete discipline that encompassed the mental, spiritual and physical virtues of the Black experience.

The Pittsburgh Childhood Environment Centers were established in Homewood and the Hill District in 1971. In its 1977 brochure, "Black Children Just Keep On Growing," Editor Madeleine Coleman said: "Although there is no formal affiliation, the CEC is in some ways related to the Black Studies Department of the University of Pittsburgh." As indicated in the background statement the idea for the preschool was encouraged by the Black Studies staff. The program director taught two courses in Early Education at the university, and these courses provided for student volunteers who assisted the preschool teachers.

Barbara Hayden, the director of PCEC, was considered the primary institutional builder of the DBCERD. Porter saw her efforts as the crown jewel of the department. He also noted that the PCEC "was as close as we came to establishing a legitimate counter institution that successfully encountered Black youth at an early age and educated them in ways far superior to what was then offered in public education and in many preschool models."

The curriculum that Barbara designed was for pre-K through second grade. Students emerging from the PCEC entered the public schools at an advanced level. Though in many cases those advances were reversed in short order by a system that was not as advanced in its content and techniques as was the PCEC. Her early childhood centers provided alternative educational sites for African American children in their communities. She had a prescribed curriculum and pedagogy based on the culture, history and life of African and African American people. And her ideas and vision later provided the guideline for independent and Afrocentric schools.

Madeleine Coleman writes that Childhood Environment Centers were founded upon three essential points: (1) Black children are competent; (2) the Black experience can be used as a basis for a full and rich curriculum; (3) teaching styles must be matched to the learning styles of the children and not vice-versa. The center's theoretical base was defined by a "flexible approach, with an emphasis on individual attention."

In other words, there was no one approach. But the program's theories on how the children learned were derived from practice. The basic premise being that children learn through a process of "self-discovery" and "experimentation, which is stimulated by presenting the child with a challenge or mystery." As the child solves the mystery, he discovers solutions that are effectively retained. This "flexible approach" interlocks varied child development approaches toward learning, i.e., cognitive growth and mastery, through external and internal stimulation, stage progression and skill mastery, and Piagetian and Montessorian principles and techniques. Coleman added, "the staff strongly believes that positive learning experiences may be derived from the child's [own] culture."[69]

In 1972, the DBCERD received a $50,000.00 Special Opportunity Grant (Model Cities Relatedness) from the State Commission on Academic Facilities of Pennsylvania to develop comprehensive facility plans for three community institutes. The objective of the study was to design new ways for the university to increase its enrollment of, and service to, minority students at an earlier and more meaningful level. E. Phillip McKain had explored these avenues in a 1970–1971 feasibility study of the Community Institute. Dr. Vernell A. Lillie, the project-planning director, submitted a voluminous final narrative report on January 17, 1973.[70] The purpose of the study was to develop comprehensive facility plans for the university to establish three community institutes in the Hill, Homewood and Manchester Districts of Pittsburgh, with programs in preschool through post-secondary education for minority youth and adults. The report answered the fundamental question of who was responsible for educating this population. It also described the organizational structure, program content, personnel needs, supportive services, formal relationships, transportation needs, physical facilities needs, community participation levels, operational and construction costs, and financial and human resources needs for the proposed community institutes.

DBCERD formed a planning partnership with the Pittsburgh Center for Educational Alternatives, a nonprofit tax-exempt community organization engaged in establishing educational alternatives for minority youth in order to ensure the development of an educational program designed by its consumers. In two biweekly planning sessions they engaged over eighty-one people, including parents, students, citizens, and professional educators, along with twenty paid consultants, to assist in the research, the evaluation and the design of the schools. The report presents an exhaustive and detailed curriculum organization, in-service training program, architectural plans and comprehensive school programs. However, it was abandoned when it was not funded further. Jerome Taylor also developed and institutionalized several early childhood programs in the Hill District around this time. And, I carried on this theme, unknowingly, with the Community Educational and Activity Centers (CEAC) from 1985 to 1987.

After being fired in Washington, D.C., two years lapsed between that time and the time I acquired a full-time job. James Turner, then the director of Africana Studies at Cornell University, offered me a contract, which I accepted. Not long after that Margaret Milliones called to tell me of the opening at Pitt in Black Studies. I told her that I could not let James down. He had been the only person on the planet willing to hire me. Margaret persisted by telling me that there were no Black people in Ithaca, that she was on the school board and there was this wonderful opportunity to help Black people, if the two of us were working together. I hesitated. Then she said, "James will understand. He is more interested in helping Black people than keeping you under contract." She was, of course, correct. I called James and he was delighted. He encouraged me to go. Not too long afterward, Curtiss Porter, the chairman of the Black Studies Department, called to offer me the position. Margaret Milliones was the link between the department and the public schools from her election to the school board and until her demise the year following my arrival. I tried to carry on that link. Often truth is stranger than fiction.

Since I had been superintendent of schools in D.C., I had relationships with some of the Black faculty in the School of Education. This included Ogle Duff, Anna Blevins Obong, Wilma Smith, William Thomas and James Kelly, who was the African American Dean of the School of Education from March 1, 1973, to June 30, 1985. Dr. Duff was the director of a federal assistance regional research center and conducted many workshops and professional development sessions in the PPS. Although DBCERD had many resources regarding African and African American history, life and culture, with the exception of Dr. Duff, the School of Education rarely tried, to my knowledge, to formalize any kind of collaborative activity for curriculum change or modification in its courses for the training of teachers. I served on many committees for the PPS during my tenure there, and I operated a funded proposal for the Creative Community Activity Centers that was not unlike the proposal developed by Lillie for the Pitt Black Studies Department in 1973. But mainly the DBCERD faculty was isolated from other faculties. For instance, I had to take the initiative to work with the School of Education faculty. I served as interim chair of the department from 1985 to 1986, but left in 1992.

Brenda Berrian came to Black Studies in 1976 with a doctorate from the Sorbonne. She is author of many books on African culture on the continent and in the Diaspora, and a distinguished literary figure in African studies. She often conducted workshops for English teachers in the PPS and was frequently recognized or consulted by the School of Education. She served as chair from 1990 to 1995.

Jerome Taylor, fondly called Jerry by his colleagues, was another link the DBCERD had with the School of Education. He had received many grants for early childhood services and parental education. And he later moved from the Education Department into the Black Studies Department. However, his service sites were outside of the university, and he was rarely at faculty meetings. Yet, he served on many PPS committees, as well, and was chair of the Equity Coalition.

Taylor operated his Values for Life Childcare Intervention Model, with an increasing demand for implementing this model nationwide. Florida is implementing it in two counties, with possibilities of a statewide adoption. In this model, Taylor and Kouyate use components of variance theory to understand the achievement gap between Black and white students on standardized tests.[71] They see student performance levels on given tests as composed of systemic and relevant variance, systemic and irrelevant variance, and error variance. Here, systemic and relevant variance would refer to that component of students' actual scores, ones that are attributable to students' real level of achievement. However, clearly equating actual with real level of achievement is indefensible, because remaining components of systemic and irrelevant variance and error variance also influence the actual score. Taylor and Kouyate sought to know which variables contribute to these various components.

They also sought to reduce the effects of variables like social stereotyping and internalized racism, through the implementation of programs that instill the values important to the parents they surveyed. The values for life are: learning orientation, self-confidence, self-persistence, self-esteem, self-reliance, love and respect, and interpersonal skills. In their study, the researchers found that values for life may have salutary effects on academic readiness and achievement outcomes. They see the challenge as that of protecting African American children from the negative effects of racism, while challenging them to academic, social and cultural standards that controvert racist claims.

Section 6.12   The University Community Educational Programs

The forerunner of University Community Educational Programs (UCEP) was started in the summer of 1968. It was called Project A and was funded by the Ford Foundation. This provides evidence for Daniel's statement that there had always been a comprehensive approach to what was needed at Pitt, long before Project A's staff included Luddy Hayden, then interim director, Curtiss Porter and Gail Austin, a new college graduate, and many other veteran community activists. Austin says of this project: "I had just graduated that April, and I was only one of the five Black students who graduated that year, fewer Black students than the University of Mississippi [graduated], if I remember my facts correctly." Project A was an attempt made by Pitt to address these students' demands. The following is Austin's recollection of UCEP's progression in that direction:

Under our leadership, we were asked to look at fifty Black applicants who were originally rejected for admission to Pitt for the incoming fall class. We called each student ourselves and told them that their applications had been reconsidered, and they were offered admission to the entering fall class, provided that they participated in a summer support program called Project A. All but two of the students came from Pittsburgh. One student was from Chicago, and the other was from New York City. I know that the Chicago student is now a successful entrepreneur, whose daughter is now thirty years old and also graduated from UCEP about eight years ago. The New York City student is now an attorney. I would say that at least fifty percent of the students graduated sooner or later. What is amazing about this whole process, now that I have been forced to recount it, is how young we were to have developed a summer program such as this in a short time, with no precedent for its development.[72]

Austin left Pitt briefly after that summer and lived in Philadelphia for a time. When she returned, she accepted a position with the Tri–M Program, which was the new name for Project A, and which was named after Martin Luther King, Jr., Malcolm X and Marcus Garvey. The admissions process was conducted in the Hill District, and it had been continued under the leadership of Dr. Donald H. Smith and Dr. Edward Barnes. Luddy Hayden was assistant director to Dr. Barnes. In his book, *Climbin' Up the Mountain Children*, Smith recalls his experience with UCEP:

My appointment as the highest-ranking Black administrator at Pitt was written about in the Sunday *New York Times*. Chancellor Wesley Posvar gave a welcoming reception, which many citizens of Pittsburgh attended, including the Archbishop, who was soon to be named Cardinal. But the warm welcome accorded by the university was countered by an unexpected event. Prior to moving to Pittsburgh I was invited by a group composed of some Black faculty, students and community people to talk about my plans for UCEP. I naively made the trip from Chicago, not realizing that the real purpose of the invitation was to discourage me from accepting the appointment.

Never before, or since, have I been subjected to such cruelty by my own people. For almost three hours I was grilled on my African consciousness, my skin color, my accomplishments and my reason for coming to Pittsburgh. One fellow got in my face and asked me what would I do if he pulled out a gun and told me to go back to Chicago. Though somewhat unnerved, I responded, "I'll answer that when you pull out the gun." He backed off. The torture session finally ended when a graduate student said, "enough." I was badly shaken, but came to Pittsburgh as planned. I later learned that Professor Norman Johnson of Carnegie Mellon University, who was part of the group, had applied for the job I was about to take. I couldn't tell Ed Barnes what happened. I don't remember if I ever did.[73]

Curtiss Porter noted that he thought Smith retired from the meeting with significant alliances in place. He said:

> The meeting itself was a strategic one to try to get the University to hear the voices of the recently organized BAS or AACS. And since Smith's appointment was already announced, our purpose was to get the student organization in on the cycle of influence, even if belatedly. At least we thought we would be accorded the respect of having been heard on the issue, though we knew it was largely decided. I do vaguely remember the report of someone from the community having made a threat. He probably should not have been there in the first place, but our Democratic ideals were way too open at that naïve stage of development.[74]

The graduate student leaders were all in support of Smith, Gail Austin, Luddy Hayden, Jake Milliones, E. Philip McKain and myself. Joseph McCormick also supported Smith's view of the "torrid meeting," but concluded, as did Porter, that the outcome was at least positive. Most informants thought Smith handled himself well and earned the community activist's support, so they showed surprise at his reaction and account. Porter further observed that Posvar was intent on hiring Smith and that hotter heads took that to be a loss of effort. "But cooler heads prevailed," noted Porter, "and rather than block such a candidacy the strategic decision was made to have an 'interview' with the candidate." He went on to note that:

> If the effort had centered on blocking the candidate that might have been a hindrance in the overall strategy; what if we failed? We would lose influence. What if it was a good person? We could lose a potential resource. How could we make it part of our growing influence in these matters? (hence the interview.) It was a compromise with reality, and another opportunity to make the university leadership deal with the Black Action Society as a factor.

And he added:

> Sure there were some nuts in the room, but overall it was a nicely conducted meeting given the times. Smith impressed a number of people as having

something on the ball, but I guess he felt under the gun, so to speak. Some of us, in fact, made sure that the coolness kept apace with the necessary strategic outcome of the meeting. The objective was to continue to grow the BAS's inclusion and influence in such matters on behalf of overall strategy and to increase the Black presence in a very concrete way, such as more Black faculty, more Black administrators, more Black students and a Black Studies program at Pitt.

Austin said that she did not remember Smith's leadership tenure. When she returned, she worked under Dr. Edward Barns, who she saw as a quiet, moderately–involved man who was happiest when doing research. Austin does not recall Barnes being comfortable with administrative responsibilities. Barnes served as director directly after Smith, with both Luddy Hayden and Robert Guthrie as his assistants. When Barnes left to work in D.C. for the Department of Education, Guthrie served as director.

During his tenure as director of UCEP, a few informants stated that Donald Smith seemed uninvolved in campus activities. Smith, on the other hand, reports that he attended almost every meeting of the BAS, gave them advice, and several times bailed them out of difficulties, for which their budget was threatened with withdrawal, and met often with and counseled individual students, including BAS leadership. Smith said, "opinions to the contrary are either based on faulty memory, deliberate revisionism, spin doctor approaches or the liar factor." He also notes that he was in D.C. on university business when the computer room takeover occurred. He, like others, had no knowledge of the impending event. While every informant did say that Smith supported the students, others marveled at how bitter Smith seems to be today and wonder why he has been unable to contextualize the event, given the historic, political and social atmosphere of those times.

Still others remarked on the encounters that occurred during the late sixties as "interesting and curious times." Austin chalks it all up to youth and inexperience, noting: "This was the age of Black Power, and we proceeded in a way that we thought was consistent with that philosophy. I do not think we would have behaved in the same way now. But I must admit we often proceeded like bulls in a china shop." She goes on to note:

I, myself, remember getting passed over for a position at Pitt.... It was a job for the newly created Black Admissions Director [position] and the job was given to a Black male because he was considered "more militant." I remember that the interview was uncomfortable [and that] it was chaired by Jack Daniel and included only Black males who had worked with me previously during our period of student activism. I imagine the interview was not too much different than Don Smith's. But unlike Don Smith, people knew me and knew I was a hard worker, and I had a history here. Don was relatively unknown by this body of people. For if they grilled me, I can only imagine what they may have done to Don. Fortunately, I am not bitter about it. In some way, it is almost funny. Given an opportunity to write an autobiography, I doubt if I would find the incident the slightest bit noteworthy.

The Tri-M program continued to grow with the selection of another cohort of students that were four times the size of the fifty students who comprised the first Project A and Tri-M group. This new Development Scholars Program, as it was called, was comprised of two hundred students; and the targeted population was broadened to include Native Americans, Chicanos and other Hispanic students. This experiment was short–lived, according to Austin, because most of the non-African American students ended up dropping out. Austin thinks this occurred because of geography and because Pittsburgh's Hispanic population at the time was small.

But she also describes an adult program that was added called New Careers. It was primarily initiated by the New Professionals Organization, which was a group of Black paraprofessionals who sought to address the problems facing paraprofessionals, especially in the disciplines of social work and, to a lesser degree, in public education. The program's primary goal was to help these students attain an undergraduate degree to augment their on-the-job training and experience.

Eventually UCEP became a part of the Academic Support Center (ASC) in August of 2002. Other units in ASC are the Math Assistance Center and the English Writing Workshop. The ASC is now currently located in the College of Arts and Sciences and has two large Department of Education Grants: Upward Bound and SSS. UCEP has also applied for a million-dollar grant for the Ronald McNair Program. If funded, it will have three TRIO grants, two of which have successfully operated for nearly thirty years. There is also a math/science research program called Quest, which Austin directs. Each year it admits twenty students from among the brightest of the entering freshman class. The students intern with a faculty mentor. And Austin is also now the associate director of the Academic Support Center, into which UCEP has been merged.

This review of UCEP points out the enormous contributions young students just out of college made to the educational enterprise at Pitt, in spite of their zeal and age. Their contributions were so enormously far-reaching that the positive outcomes of their efforts have outlived some of the participants.

CHAPTER 7

CHICAGO SCHOOL REFORM
1988–2002

Section 7.1 Chicago Public Schools and The 1988 Reformers

Chicago desired to improve the quality of instruction in order to elevate and accelerate student achievement, as measured by standardized test scores, but found it difficult. No matter what kinds of new programs or changes were introduced, nothing seemed to help. As a result, some educators fell back on old excuses such as poverty, family disruption, community disorganization, crime and violence.

Consequently, after the state legislature gave the power to operate the Chicago public schools (CPS) to the Mayor of the city of Chicago, Richard M. Daley, Jr. on July 1, 1995, everyone was surprised when the new CEO of the Chicago Public Schools, Paul Vallas the mayor's former budget manager, announced that children would be first and that there would be no excuses for low achievement in the CPS. To many African American researchers this was a true breath of fresh air.

Chicago experienced many years of reform by 1995. After the wars over desegregation from 1968 to 1978, thoughtful educators began to concentrate on student achievement or true reform. Even as early as 1982, Dr. Alice C. Blair, then deputy superintendent for education services, issued "A Discussion Paper for Improving General High Schools in Chicago," authored by an appointed task force committee of Ora B. McConner, Chairperson, Stephen H. Brown, Gerard J. Heing, Ellen Summerfield, Philip A. Viso and Ben Williams.

This discussion paper emanated from a mandate to improve secondary education in CPS, issued by, Ruth Love, the general superintendent. The report cited the following problems: social promotion, low achievement, decreased budget appropriations, instructional programs made ineffective by provisions mandated in the collective bargaining agreement, lack of uniform and clearly stated standards of achievement, poorly defined roles of department heads in the high school, varying levels of knowledge, skills and commitment of administrators and teachers for meeting the students' needs, inadequate support services for the secondary school at all administrative levels, and insufficient counseling services.[1]

Using Ronald R. Edmonds's work as a theoretical framework, the report offered the following recommendations: emphasize basic skills; stress high expectations for students' achievement; emphasize teachers' and principals' responsibility for high student achievement; and, offer systematic, sustained, substantive instructional programs.

Interestingly, another committee chaired by Gerard J. Heing, and including Maude H. Carson, Christine C. Loving, John T. Martin, James F. Moore, Robert A Saddler, Donald E. Sparks and Tee Gallay, recommended that students not reaching an 8.0 reading level by age fifteen-and-a-half would be programmed into the high school and placed in a core curriculum based upon the students' needs, and, taught by qualified teachers who should also hold a reading endorsement.[2]

By 1988, it was fairly clear that the problems with CPS were student achievement, student attendance and student dropout rates. Yet in December 1988 the Illinois Legislature adopted a school reform package (P.A. 85–1418) that changed not only the structure but also the governance of public education in Chicago.

Although Dorothy Shipps, Joe Kahne and Mark Smylie (1998), as well as G. Alfred Hess (1999),[3] argued that the goal was student achievement, the accent was on governance, not student achievement, nor accountability. What it did specify was the creation of 550 Local School Councils (LSCs), one for each and every school, consisting of six parents, two teachers and two community members, the principal and—at the high school, a student.

The Local School Councils was given several powers: (1) the authority to hire and fire principals, from whom all tenure rights were stripped, at the same time teachers retained theirs; (2) the control over state Chapter One funds, which were redirected to schools, avoiding central and district office interference; and (3) the right to determine and approve the School Improvement Plan (SIP). Completely ignoring the history of local school control in New York City and Washington, D.C., and its own Woodlawn Experimental School Project (WESP, 1967–1971), these Chicago community leaders, most of whom were white, proceeded with these governance theories, now instituted into law.

According to Hess, the 1988 legislation[4] mandated a reduction in central office staff, and removed from the central board the authority to appoint and control principals, while it limited its control over curriculum. In 1995, the state legislature amended the 1988 legislation with House Bill Number 206, giving control of CPS to the mayor and emphasizing central management and accountability. LSCs were maintained, but central office was replaced with a CEO, a Chief Education Officer, and a five-member Reform Board of Trustees, and the School Finance Authority (SFA) was suspended. According to Shipps, Kahne and Smylie "unprecedented fiscal flexibility" was given to the mayor and the board of trustees, removing all barriers to privatization and allowing the dismissal of employees within fourteen days if outsourcing removed their positions.[5]

But what was most important to the 1988 reformers, the law sent all increases in state Chapter One funds to the district, leaving the LSCs's share at 1994 levels. Teacher strikes were prohibited for eighteen months and certain items were stricken from the bargaining list in the school code so that individual schools were authorized to waive collective bargaining agreements if more than half of the faculty agreed.[6]

Vallas and Board of Trustees chairman Gery Chico, Mayor Daley's former chief of staff, began their assault against low achievement with aggressive accountability, taking on the neglected and woefully low-achieving city high schools. Vallas's plan had several major components: (1) a redesign plan for restructuring the high school; (2) the development of clear high standards; (3) the removal of principals; (4) the placement of schools on remediation, probation or reconstitution; (5) redirection of Chapter One monies to external partners, probation managers and other mentoring and monitoring personnel; and (6) an accountability system eliminating social promotion. Universities, agencies, corporations and organizations were invited to help CPS achieve its objectives.

Although the 1988 reformers denied it, they were opposed to accountability measures before the advent of the mayor's interventions when Argie Johnson was the general superintendent. During her short tenure

(1993–1995) Johnson attempted to implement her plans for the elevation and acceleration of student achievement in CPS. Johnson was the former deputy chancellor of New York City Public Schools and superintendent of District Thirteen in Brooklyn's Bedford-Stuyvesant neighborhood in New York City from 1988 to 1992. She also served under J. Jerome Harris, Community School District Thirteen superintendent from 1974 to 1987.

From 1979 to 1989, District Thirteen had shown more growth in student achievement through the effective schools's paradigm, using traditional and direct instruction, than the highly touted District Four had through choice and innovation.[7] Therefore, African American Education Researchers found it strange to read about District Four as the high-achieving district in David L. Kirp's "What School Choice Really Means" whereas District Thirteen's higher accomplishments were regulated to parentheses in the article.[8] Johnson was the first to stress student achievement as the system's highest priority since Ruth Love, general superintendent from 1981 until 1985. Moreover, Johnson proposed an accountability plan to assist low-achieving schools. The 1988 reformers jumped on her with a vengeance.

At one public hearing on her three-tiered plan for school improvement, LSC presidents—supported by groups like Designs for Change and Parents United for Responsible Education (PURE)—castigated her for top down decision-making and alleged the usurpation of LSC powers. Too many of these presidents, most of whom were African American and Hispanic, were overseeing the SIPs for schools where barely 10 percent of the student population could read! Some of these presidents were presiding over LSC units that were dysfunctional. These units could not carry on business because of a lack of a quorum, they had less than full membership because of resignations, and had parent representatives with non-parent status (the result of student departures or graduations) or they were allowing members to engage in illegal operations in schools.

Johnson's plan separated CPS schools into three tiers. Tier One schools were schools that were generally succeeding and needed minimum support. These were schools that had standardized test scores and other measures above the average, but included schools with scores below the average that had demonstrated progress during the previous four years. Tier Two schools were schools that had performed slightly below the average over the last four years and had shown no sign of improvement these schools needed moderate support. Tier Three schools were ones that had performed well below the average and had shown no sign of improvement or schools that had performed below average and had declined during the previous four years.

Johnson intended to use these tiers as guides for the distribution of resources targeted toward supporting school improvement plans. She made it clear, though, that while attention would be given to all schools, the top priority would be those in Tier Three. The principles upon which the three-tiered model were built revealed Johnson's effective schools's background. These principles were: all students can learn and are expected to learn to their full potential; the children of the urban poor can be educated for success in the twenty-first century; demographic characteristics describe children—they do not determine educational success; long-term improvement can only be brought about within each school by the staff, local school council and community of that school; the purpose of central administration is to help the schools succeed; and improvement is an inclusive process, with many of the best resources often found outside the school system.

Johnson suggested improvement strategies and a process for their implementation based off of these beliefs. However, the 1988 reformers judged this decision-making from the top down. Yet at that time in Chicago, Johnson was probably the only person who had elevated and accelerated student achievement in a school district.

Many of the 1988 reformers were university professors and administrators, foundation representatives and heads of private "watchdog" organizations. By 1999, their opposition had mellowed. In November of 1998, Marshall Field IV professor of urban education and a senior director of the Consortium on Chicago School Research (CCSR). Anthony Bryk clearly stated his disappointment with the newspaper's promotion of a false dichotomy between CCSR and Paul Vallas in a letter to the *Chicago Tribune*. Bryk, who was also a 1988 reformer and had a number of them in his advisory board and steering committee, said, "There was no 'CPS bashing' in the presentation of the key findings. There was, however, serious discussion about some important issues that still need to be addressed."[9]

Hess, who was a 1988 reformer, conducted a study at Northwestern University in 2002 on the implementation of the high school design plan. His first-year report presented these selected findings: (1) since 1996 high school reading achievement scores have been rising significantly, nearly recovering from a steep decline from 1990; (2) the Design for High Schools Program has begun to take the slack out of the high school system; (3) seven high schools were successfully reconstituted during the summer of 1997; in aggregate, about 30 percent of teachers were not rehired at their previous school and four of seven principals were replaced; (4) the content of subject matter being covered in classrooms in reconstituted schools appears to be well below the level expected, given course titles and grade level; (5) teacher resistance is associated with lower gains in student achievement; (6) low expectations of students is an issue in a number of schools, as reported by school leaders and faculty members; (7) Chicago teachers have a low opinion of their students' preparation for high school; (8) advisories are mostly in place but vary considerably from school to school, reflecting differences in teacher support; and (9) junior academies are the primary form of school restructuring.[10]

Mostly critical of Vallas's work, other 1988 reformers focused on three objectives: The development of new tests to replace the Iowa Tests of Basic Skills (ITBS) and the Tests of Academic Proficiency (TAP); the abolition of retention; and proving that the 1988 reforms were really the beginning of upward student achievement. The officers of Designs for Change and PURE were hopelessly opposed to anything proposed by Paul Vallas, no matter what it was. The leaders of both organizations were white.

An examination of the 1988 reformers' criticism of Vallas emphasized only the retention issue. Retention is only one of three consequences that occurs when a student does not "keep up" with the teacher's curriculum. The other two are social promotion or referral to special education. The latter is rapidly becoming the choice for African American males. To cancel out retention indicates a preference for the other two alternatives. Actually, none of these options work well for African American students. The realty is that, the three consequences are symptoms not causes.

The cause of failure is the pedagogy and the curriculum which teachers embrace in low-achieving schools serving students who live in low-income census zones characterized by crime and violence. Curriculum and instruction start with a whole lesson, usually prepared to achieve a learning objective;

although, in such schools, teachers often confuse the objective with the activity designed to achieve the objective.

The presentation of the lesson to the whole group is followed by modeling by the teacher, student demonstrations, some kind of guided practice and a measure. When the measure is given, the children fall out in a line of march from the student who made 100 and the one who missed them all. This is where the trouble begins. Teachers generally do not know what to do about human variation in learning. Consequently, they do not prepare activities for the accelerated to go on; the reinforced to get more practice; and those who need more time to learn to be re-taught. Missing this opportunity, the students fall farther and farther behind. At the end of the year, they fail or pass on without the knowledge to be successful at the next level, or they get referred to special education.

Another example of the struggle between the two sets of reformers is the argument which occurred in an issue of *Catalyst* (September 1999) between Paul Vallas and Linda Lenz over the dropout rate.[11] *Catalyst* argued that the dropout rate in Chicago was increasing due to the tendency of school personnel to push out students who were low-performing and not attending, but did not offer the counter argument that schools would lose money when they dropped students from their rolls. While school principals may have pursued this route to higher test scores, it didn't seem to make sense for school officials to encourage this practice. Moreover, principals who kept non-attending students on the rolls merely lied. Vallas insisted that the dropout rate was declining and used data from the regular high schools, excluding alternative schools, as the state did. Lenz used data from all of the schools.

Lenz has tried, since 1998, to be more balanced in her coverage of CPS, and her editorial board has broadened its membership to include fewer 1988 diehards. Every researcher understands the difficulty of producing accurate dropout data because: (1) delayed graduation beyond five years; (2) student mobility; (3) GED information. Lenz thought her position more valid, but she printed Vallas's letter of opposition in the next issue. When principals had been encouraged to drop students who had not been attending school (absent for forty days or more), the dropout rate had to increase. But the alternative would have been to lie about their enrollment, as had been done in previous years, and which provided the baseline data used to determine the rates.

By 1999, Vallas had gone to court to gain more power to change CPS from a pariah school district to one of excellence. He gained more power over principal selection and negotiated two successful contracts with the Chicago Teachers Union (CTU), although he acquired only small changes in the process for firing incompetent teachers.

Though the screaming has since stopped, this war between the 1988 and 1995 reformers consumed far too much energy those who should have been concentrating on how to eliminate the achievement gap between African American and white students. This unnecessary war between two groups who should have been allies diminished the chances for reform to work. However, since Mayor Daley fired Vallas and Chico in 2000, and appointed Arne Duncan as CEO, Duncan has brought the Consortium and the 1988 reformers inside the CPS as consultants and directors. Melissa Roderick is in charge of planning and John Q. Easton is back in charge of research. The Consortium has lost its critical voice of opposition. Even *Catalyst* has not challenged the Education Plan or the new data showing a decrease in the dropout rate. While, *Catalyst* still challenged the administration, the Consortium became an advocate.

Section 7.2 DePaul University

In his book, *Education for Renewal*, John Goodlad argues that the nation's schools of education should bring together three different groups of actors from three different settings: the schools, the arts and sciences and the schools, and colleges or departments of education. From 1992 until 1998 at DePaul University these three groups came together, but not in a coherent manner. There were disputes between some faculty from the College of Liberal Arts and Sciences (LA&S) and in the School of Education (SOE) about how these groups should work together. There was difficulty even in getting these two groups to agree on the teaching of mathematics and science. A favorite area of dispute was whether content is more important than methodology. These constant conflicts present many reasons why educating the poor, the excluded and minorities in this country defies improvement.

The conditions of CPS are often not understood by the SOE faculty responsible for preparing teachers. Too often, so-called research-based programs fail in public schools servicing students who live in low-income

210

census zones characterized by crime and violence because SOE and LA&S faculty are convinced that there are universal theories and practices which, though based on findings from samples which are predominantly white and middle class, can work with the poor, the excluded and minorities.

Yet, changes did occur at DePaul because the university worked hard to reach its diversity goals, although it still has a long way to go. The administration hired a special assistant to the president on diversity and an assistant executive vice president presides over professional development in cultural diversity. In addition, a committee on diversity was formed. It generated these observations:

> During our review of current hiring practices involving minorities, we interviewed several members of the DePaul community who had served on search committees. Several disturbing trends emerged. First, was the prevalence of a double standard, in which some issues were applied to or raised regarding minorities that were not with similarly-qualified majority candidates: age qualifications (regardless of credentials), theory driven research, teaching/research mix, personality, the value of life experiences, biased agenda-based teaching philosophies, or lack of them, ethnic self identification or authenticity, accent or dialect, rumors and the ubiquitous "fit." To elaborate, qualifications of minority candidates seem automatically suspect while those of majority candidates are assumed valid.

The recorder concluded:

> We must rethink what we propose as diversity. If, by diversity, we mean skin tone, with the underlying, unspoken assumption that we are all culturally the same, i.e., inhabitants of some amorphous white culture, then these concerns make sense. If, however, we mean by diversity, multiple cultural approaches, communicative and interactive styles and ways of being and seeing in the world, then our current practices fall short. The Diversity Initiatives Committee strongly supports this broader sense of diversity. As a university, we need to be more accepting of other ways of seeing and being. While one's cultural style may feel uncomfortable to another, all must own their discomfort and recognize that it signals their cultural preferences rather than some universal sense of best practices. Learning to interact in a variety of cultural styles would enhance our ability to work with our students and in the world.[13]

When I returned to Chicago armed with my own research on high-achieving predominantly African American public schools, I was neutralized by the champions of universal theories. Members of my own faculty ridiculed my work, saying that African American students were no different than any other. "A good teacher can teach any student," one tenured faculty member told me, "with the methods I teach. I think you are making too much of race." Some of my faculty members believed that race no longer was a problem and had been replaced by class issues. Others were permanently married to a certain pedagogy. One faculty member adamantly asserted, "I will never teach anything by rote and drill." How horrified he would have been visiting second-year veterinarian students studying anatomy. Additionally, CCSR's reports on quality of teaching showed teachers with low expectations and low standards. If new teachers are taught to discard what works with students who are poor and minority, they then meet failure and begin to lower standards and expectations. It becomes a reinforcing cycle of operations.

Faculty members in SOE pursued their intellectual theories and paradigms without regard to the situations in which they would be practiced. Guided by universals, they seldom examined particularist situations. For example, funding agencies both public and private reject proposals directed toward research in segregated environments, such as schools that are 100 percent African American or Latino. Faculty, then, submitted proposals that looked at mixed schools. Because the status of African Americans and Mexican Americans is particularistic, and not universal, many of these findings did not fit. Faculty tended to avoid race, not because they were racists, but because guidelines were deterrents.

When I was dean, most of the faculty members at SOE were against standardized testing for accountability purposes in public schools; yet, DePaul required all students to submit ACT or SAT scores for admission. Nor did anti-testing faculty consider the necessity for all students to take entry-level tests for employment, i.e., state licensure tests for barbers and beauticians. These are the true high-stakes tests, which minority applicants fail in large numbers.

DePaul University was founded by the Congregation of the Mission, whose founder was St. Vincent de Paul. These priests are called Vincentians, and they are committed to the evangelization of the poor and the alleviation of their misery. As a result of their mission, the university has a strong service expectation of its employees. Therefore, SOE has several outreach programs which support this mission. One of these is the Center for Urban Education (CUE).

The director of CUE, Barbara Radner, developed her own program with the Urban Teachers' Corps. She was one of the first people to train recruits from other career fields to teach. Her teachers had classes on Saturdays and worked in urban schools during the week. She made many attempts to involve faculty in this outreach work, taking them out of the ivory tower and into the public schools in low-income census zones characterized by crime and violence, but she was mostly unsuccessful. Later, her program consisted of those who were returning from the Peace Corps. And during the 2002–2003 school year she moved her operation to the more friendly School for New Learning (SNL), when the new SOE dean showed hostility toward outreach programs serving the poor.

SOE was part of LA&S prior to my appointment as dean. At that time, the dean of LA&S, who later became the executive vice president in charge of Academic Affairs, developed the Glenview School District Thirty-four Project, where DePaul trained teachers hired by District Thirty-four during a three-year period with the district's superintendent. An SOE faculty member directed this project. The Glenview Project involved only a few faculty members. District Thirt-four was located in Glenview, Illinois, a Chicago suburb, and CUE's schools were located in the middle of Chicago's notorious Robert Taylor Homes, or Cabrini Green, both large public housing projects. Unfortunately, although successful in attaining its objectives—one of which was providing District Thirty-four with qualified highly-trained teachers in the schools where they would teach–the project never was expanded and stayed a prototype of an excellent alternative route to certification.

As dean of SOE, I founded SAS, the School Achievement Structure, in an attempt to expand on the work done by CUE. After all, there were 550 CPS school units. SAS was based on my research in high-achieving predominantly African American schools, using Edmonds's theoretical framework for studying effective schools and Allison's Organizational Process Model (OPM).[14]

My research described ten routines that appeared in the high-achieving African American schools studied. These routines were: assessment, placement, pacing/acceleration, monitoring, measuring, discipline, instruction, evaluation, staff development and decision-making. Starting with ten schools, SAS eventually worked in sixty-three schools between 1994 and 2002. Like CUE, SAS worked in the schools in the least desirable residential areas and with the lowest achievement scores.[15]

Other outreach examples of DePaul University's SOE were the STEP Program and the DePaul Prep Program, both brainchildren of the former associate dean of SOE, Rafaela Weffer. These programs brought economically disadvantaged and culturally diverse CPS students and teachers to DePaul for Saturday and summer programs. STEP provided classes in language, mathematics and science to high school students on Saturdays during the regular school year. Graduates were placed in college programs at DePaul. DePaul Prep conducted a full six-week summer program for students in grades six and seven, stressing integrated curricula organized around units. DePaul Prep started as the McPrep Program, an educational collaboration initiated in 1994 involving Ronald McDonald Children's Charities, the DePaul University, School of Education and the Chicago Public Schools. Directed by Phedonia Johnson, former principal of Goldblatt Elementary School, which pioneered in both Direct Instruction and the Socratic method, the McPrep Program served a total of 101 CPS students who were to enter seventh grade at the start of the 1995–1996 school year.

Approximately 55 percent of the students were female, 70 percent were African American and 30 percent were Latino. Of these 101 students, eighty-six had participated in the 1994 program. Fifteen had moved out of Chicago and were ineligible for admission. The students were selected from low-achieving, low-income, inner city schools in Chicago. The nine cooperating schools were racially identifiable federal Chapter one schools; six were African American, and three were Latino. McPrep teachers and counselors were certified elementary school teachers from the cooperating schools. The general goal was to target inner city students before they entered high school and help them develop strong academic skills. The focus was on mathematics and science, through an emphasis on the scientific method.

The findings of the study conducted by William Evans and Phedonia Johnson concluded:

The average ITBS scores indicated that the McPrep students gained more than two years in reading achievement and one and a half years in math during the 1994–1995 school year. Relative to comparison group scores, the McPrep students' gains were sizable. The average scores on criterion-referenced tests reflected statistically significant gains on the part of the McPrep students. The case study results indicated that the McPrep students were becoming more motivated toward academic pursuits, were also developing socially and personally and were displaying better leadership skills. The self-assessment and student vision results provided evidence that the McPrep students were becoming more thoughtful with respect to their academic goals and objectives and that they were able to articulate the means by which they planned to attain their academic pursuits. In general, the results supported the notion that the children were making significant progress toward reaching the goals of the McPrep Program and revealed attitudinal changes with respect to academics and career goals.

During the 1997–1998 school year, CPS assumed funding for McPrep and the name was changed.

In 1999, DePaul Prep was administered by CUE. In the beginning, CUE placed no emphasis on reaching achievement standards as measured by standardized tests. CPS demanded none, and the universities applied no pressure. SAS changed that orientation. However, for each school SAS's goal was to reach the 50th percentile on the ITBS and TAP. In 1995, Paul Vallas invited the universities to serve as external partners to schools in which the Board of Reform Trustees had placed on remediation or probation. Schools on probation were assigned probation managers to oversee their compliance with SIPs. I was the only dean of an SOE to serve as a probation manager.

By 2003, SAS had been terminated, and STEP no longer existed. CUE had moved out of SOE and into SNL. The five-year plan for SOE indicated that its resources would be allocated to the creation of professional development schools around DePaul at Alcott, Prescott, Mayor and Lincoln Park high schools. Only one school presented tier two and three problems: Prescott.

SOE removed its presence from predominantly minority schools in low-income census zones. Except for a small $300,000.00 grant for a Gear-Up, the Vincentian spirit had departed from SOE. Clearly, this was a new DePaul. The old DePaul promoted the Vincentian mission of fighting poverty and promoting personalism. The new DePaul did not.

Section 7.3   The 1988 Reformers and The LSC

The 1988 reformers saw decentralization as the way to improve student achievement by concentrating decision-making in the hands of the community. In 1999, Hess wrote:

> The reform advocates who drafted the original bills agreed that change had to happen in each school at the school level; however, they recognized that the previous bureaucratic management system relied on top-down sanctions that could prevent things from happening, but could not cause good change to occur. The second premise was that if local schools were to be accountable for improving the outcomes of their students, they needed the ability and resources to make change happen.[16]

Unfortunately, this theory was conceived by people who were white and/or middle class. Therefore, few resources were allocated to train and educate people who were not. Without training, people do what they have always done, approximate the unknown experience to one that is known.

For most poor people living in public housing, for example, the closest experience to the LSC was the Democratic precinct order or the political patronage party. So, expectedly, in some schools in those areas where the people had no resources for their own uplift, LSCs became patronage outfits. These misfits were minimized in the CCSR report on LSCs, which they found to be productive and progressive. The report also identified serious problems among 10 to 15 percent of the LSCs. "Some of these councils cannot muster enough members to convene their meetings regularly; others are plagued by conflict; and a few have members who abuse their authority. Such councils fail to serve their schools and hinder improvement efforts. Although the proportion of schools where such activity is occurring is quite small, the lives of many children are still affected."[17]

There are about eighty of these schools, mostly African American and located in low-income census zones, and most of them are low-achieving and on probation. A few university faculty members whose children are enrolled in CPS serve on LSCs. Since their children generally attend magnet schools with test-in policies, they do not come into contact with dysfunctional LSCs. CUE, DePaul Prep, STEP and SAS had parent coordinators who worked directly with parents but only interfaced with the LSC occasionally. According to Catherine Gewertz, "when local school councils were new and excitement over the grassroots innovation was high, more than 17,000 people turned out to run for the 6,200 seats at 540 schools in the first election in 1989."[18]

In some schools, the principalship turned over each time an LSC election occurred, after which jobs were offered to friends or relatives of the new LSC members or their friends. In a few schools, the LSC members blatantly used their powers on behalf of their children as students in the schools, such as forcing grade changes, hiring relatives and using monies to create jobs for themselves and others. In one school, the LSC meeting evolved into a shouting match of profanity, forcing an adjournment and dismissal. The members argued over replacement of their own members. One group wanted to elect an alleged former drug addict and others refused to cooperate. A faction of the LSC had decided to pack the LSC with members who would vote for their candidate for the new principal. Yet Julie Woestehoff, the executive director of PURE, a nonprofit group that trains and advises LSC members, considered Vallas hostile to LSCs because he was concerned about these problems. Interestingly, she is also against testing and accountability.

Veteran principals experienced uncertainty also. In one school, one of the community representatives on the LSC held the principal hostage to protect her husband, who was an incompetent teacher in the school. This community representative obstructed every program, project or activity promoted by the principal until the principal agreed to some benefit for her husband. The principal was powerless to protest until an LSC election resulted in a more favorable majority. Prior to this event, nothing could be done, even when it was discovered that the community representative no longer lived in the district which she represented. The lawyer told concerned parents that they would need to conduct a bed check to determine the community representative's residence.

In another case, the principal, intent on pleasing the LSC and keeping his job, refused to behave as an instructional leader out of concern that this would agitate the teacher representatives on the LSC, and cost him their votes. This principal visited very few rooms, marked no one unsatisfactory, and issued no discipline warrants, suspensions or warning letters to incompetent, excessively absent and/or insubordinate teachers. The teachers did as they pleased. The CCSR issued a report showing that most LSCs were functioning properly and making a difference in instruction. However, the report did not reflect on how very bad the few dysfunctional were.[19]

The 1988 reformers thought that student achievement would happen as a by-product of parent/community intervention. Principals would be held responsible to the LSC, and thereby forced to act on behalf of the children and create a high-achieving school. This did happen in many schools. However, in too many schools located in low-income census zones characterized by crime and violence this did not happen. Isolated by poverty from resources and jobs, people were left to their own wits. In addition to the lack of resources for their own training, LSC members in these schools now had a principal with no tenure to oversee and monitor teachers who kept theirs. Moreover, two teachers served on the LSC to vote on the principal's contract. This contradiction negated the assumption made by the 1988 reformers that the LSC would force the principal to take actions to elevate achievement. While the principal could not fire teachers (she or he could only evaluate them as "unsatisfactory" after a long and tortuous process, only minimally changed by the Vallas administration), the teachers could theoretically fire him or her.

CCSR's report found that in at least 40 percent of the city's schools principals controlled the LSCs and were still in power. Charles Payne states in his report on the Comer Project:

> Parents have a numerical majority on the councils, but in fact parent members are probably the members who are least likely to come to meetings, if they come, they are the least likely to participate.... It is probably fair to say that in several respects, parents do not have the social capital, including the self-confidence, to take full advantage of the formal change in the arrangement of power.[20]

While Payne's assessment may be true, it does not describe the condition in too many schools at the very bottom of the city's schools rankings on achievement. In one such school, the principal wanted to hire a white assistant principal in a position funded by Title One Funds. A Black member of the LSC told the principal in private that if he did so, the LSC would abolish the position. When the principal said that this was illegal and that he would not participate in this action, the candidate withdrew because he did not want to be a center of controversy. The 1988 reformers viewed the Johnson and Vallas administrations as hostile to the LSCs. However, that has changed since the mayor appointed Arne Duncan as the chief educational officer.[21]

Yet the shortcomings of the 1988 reforms have never been widely acknowledged, while the successes have been frequently extolled. These shortcomings include: (1) the lack of regularly scheduled and consistent ongoing training of LSC members, and the failure to provide clerical help and information to LSC presidents; (2) the vulnerable position of tenureless contract principals who are expected to provide leadership over teachers who retained their tenure and who have voting positions on the LSC; (3) the adversarial condition which exists in so many LSCs, which provide governance for low-achieving predominantly African American schools between teachers and principals, and principals and LSC members; and (4) the problem of dysfunctional LSCs (cannot hold a meeting because there is no quorum) in low-achieving predominantly African American schools located in low-income census zones characterized by crime and/or violence.

Archon Fung, an assistant professor of public policy at Harvard University's John F. Kennedy School of Government, studied the function of LSCs as a tool of participatory democracy and thinks they are a "crucial avenue, especially in low-income neighborhoods," for the citizen engagement that he believes is necessary for school improvement. "But to function properly," he said, "the councils need a strong central administration. We're not talking about a command-and-control type of administration," said Mr. Fung, "I mean an administration that offers support, information-sharing, training and guidance."[22]

Section 7.4   The Chicago Teachers Union

It would take a principal approximately one year to follow the CTU contract's specifications for removing an unsatisfactory teacher. Even after that, the teacher could appeal to the state. Maribeth Vanderweele, in her 1994 book, *Reclaiming Our Schools*, describes the 1988 school reform:

> ...[W]hen one-third of elementary school principals say that no more than half their teachers have a good grasp of reading and language arts while seventy percent lack proper science skills, something is terribly wrong. Even if such statements are incorrect, as the teachers' union claims, the fact remains that the average age of a Chicago public school teacher in 1993 was [forty-seven] years old. No matter how competent, any teacher who has been away from higher education for twenty-five years or more would likely benefit from additional training. One type of training could be in the form of master teachers. To attract individuals with the proper credentials, these teachers could be offered higher salaries.... Since most principals who have arrived under reform are new, they should be supplied from the start with information on writing budgets and equipped with the proper leadership skills. As reform progressed, outside agencies and universities began to address this area of critical need. Some school districts have taken the issue further and already provide mandatory training academies for principals. This should be encouraged.[23]

When Vallas reconstituted seven high schools which had long histories of poor performance and low student achievement, every job in the school was advertised and applicants were interviewed for these released positions. As an interviewer on the teams for two high schools, I talked with veteran teachers who had taken no courses in their disciplines since graduation from college and too many who could not remember the last book read in their academic field.

One teacher grieved to the CTU about his interview, naming me as a violator of his rights. In the Illinois Educational Labor Relations Board, administrative law judge's recommended decision and order the following appears: [Most of which is testimony given by Gail Koffman, assistant to CTU's president for Field Services, without rebuttal.]

The CTU received reports that one interviewer, Barbara Sizemore, made racial comments. One teacher stated that Sizemore asked why he was not using more books written by African American authors. Sizemore also referred to materials that the teacher was using, including the *Washington Post*, as white supremacist material. Sizemore then stated in reply to the teacher's efforts to explain himself, that she was not supposed to argue with the interviewees. The union wanted to know the names of the interview team members to ascertain whether the same people conducted interviews at different schools, especially in light of the complaints about Sizemore. The union also wanted to know if the interview teams had members who had taken anti-union positions in the past. CTU also wanted to know if interview team members had been told to pick a percentage of teachers on racial lines....CTU wanted to know if all interviewers had been instructed to avoid arguments, or if this instruction had been limited to Sizemore. Koffman stated that "we wanted to know if everybody else was instructed not to argue or whether the Board knew that Barbara Sizemore was a hot potato or whatever you want to call it, and appointed her to the interview committees anyway.

My question to this teacher concerned the incorporation of culturally diverse material in the curriculum. When asked what he was using, he mentioned newspapers as primary sources. I questioned his use of the *Washington Post* for that purpose, reminding him that newspaper journalists were not historians.

To my astonishment, teachers are offended by any reference to the condition of African Americans in the real world of this capitalist democracy. They especially resent any reference to white supremacy or the imputation of Black inferiority in the curriculum or instruction. If the tenets of white supremacy are challenged in any way, the challenger becomes a racist. For example, one teacher called me racist because I challenged the generally accepted depiction of Jesus as white with blonde hair and blue eyes, a view which was later aired on the Discovery Channel as "Jesus: The Complete Story" during the Easter Weekend, 2001.[24]

A group of teacher resisters edit and publish a newspaper called *Substance* in an attempt to take over the CTU. They were opposed to the working relationship between CEO Paul Vallas and the officers of the CTU.

Each issue criticized and lambasted the union leadership, the mayor, Paul Vallas, Gery Chico and myself for supporting high standards, high expectations, and teacher and student accountability. Their platform is a return to the good 'ole days, when teachers were protected by the popular beliefs that they could not do anything for students who were Black, or poor, or spoke a language other than English.

Substance's platform is blame the principal, the students or their parents for the failure of the schools, anybody but teachers. Each issue advocates for teachers who can't teach, principals who can't administer or programs that don't work. Nor does the publication have a plan for improving schools's records in achievement. In its crusade against Paul Vallas and Gery Chico, they defamed anybody whom they viewed as supportive. For example, the following appeared in the June 1999 issue:

> Both Phillips and Harper were "reconstituted" two years ago by Paul Vallas
> with the help of a politically connected consultant from DePaul University, Barbara
> Sizemore. At that time, many of the teachers and principals of those schools were
> blamed for their low scores. Some were fired; all had to reapply for their jobs by
> interviewing with Sizemore's staff and the newly appointed politically connected
> principal. Now, after two years of continuous low test scores, we can only draw
> one or more conclusions: Vallas and Daley put the wrong politically connected
> principal in place at Harper and Phillips, Sizemore fired the wrong teachers and/or
> chose the wrong new teachers at these schools or it's the kids and not the staff and
> administration that are the key determinants of these school's test scores.[25]

I was involved in the interviewing at Phillips High School, although my staff was not; and neither they, nor I, were involved at Harper. At no time did I ever have the power to select or fire. My actions were only advisory. This article was written by two former high school teachers, one of whom published the Chicago Academic Standards Examinations (CASE) given at the end of the term to all high school students in protest of too much testing. He was fired from CPS for this violation and his trial was to commence in January of 2003.

However, several teachers from Curie High School refused to administer the CASE exams to their classes in January 2003. Substance proudly reported and announced in their December 5, 2002, issue that CPS would immediately suspend the controversial CASE. While, admittedly, CASE was not a good examination, it was no worse than some of the teacher-made final examinations given in the low-performing predominantly Black high schools. No announcements were made regarding that problem. CPS later reduced the damages in the $1.4 million-dollar suit to $500.00. Schmidt said that he would not accept the reduced damages and would appeal to the U.S. Court of Appeals for the Seventh Circuit.

Deborah Lynch, elected president of the Chicago Teachers Union (CTU), offered to take over low-achieving schools and improve achievement in them. However, she chose Success for All, which has minimum standards, for her model. Even so, she seems to be more thoughtful of the teachers' role in improving the quality of education and wants CTU to participate in the decision-making. Lynch believes that teachers are a part of the solution, not the problem and that "reform done with teachers will be better than reform done without teachers."[26] The Duncan administration generally has isolated teachers and community from decisions until they are made.

Lynch won 51 percent of her union's vote in May 2001 with the vigorous support of *Substance's* staff and supporters because of the resistance to accountability and testing. On the one hand, Lori Olszewski stated, "despite the divisions in the union, Lynch has been able to unite members around an effort to regain bargaining rights for teachers and other school employees that were taken away in the 1995 school reform law that gave Mayor Daley control of the schools and rights that teachers in the Chicago suburbs and across the nation regularly negotiate."[27]

On the other hand, Lynch, who is trying valiantly to take the union in the direction of creating good schools where all students could learn, does not yet have their complete support. She negotiated a contract with CPS that gave teachers a 4 percent raise for five years and smaller classes, but reduced health insurance fees. Her own board of delegates and her membership eventually handed her a defeat. Unfortunately, for Lynch, teachers' salaries are abominably low. In a nation where plumbers make more than teachers, it is easy to determine our regard for education. Teachers, especially those beset by huge college loans, are sick of this lowly status.

Section 7.5   The Changing of The Guards

Arne Duncan is reported to have formed a commission led by Samuel J. Meisels, the president of the Erikson Institute, a Chicago-based graduate school in child development, and Donald M. Stewart, the president and CEO of the Chicago Community Trust, to devise a system of assessments from preschool through high school that would be more immediately useful to teachers in the classroom to inform instruction. Duncan also established a new "accountability system recognizing schools for the gains they make with students and providing $10,000.00 cash awards to those that make the most progress, rather than just singling out low performing schools for intervention."[28] When a school where 91 percent of the Black students cannot read gets $10,000.00, this policy sends the wrong message to the African American community. Additionally, the policy tends to replace the concept of achievement with the concept of growth as its goal.

Too many teachers conduct boring sessions in their classes and blame the students and their parents for the high dropout rates and the low graduation counts in low-achieving, predominantly African American schools. There are too few examples of excited, enthusiastic teachers who struggle each day against the norms of their schools to make their material interesting to their students, and too many who think African American students are inferior. One English teacher conducting a discussion of Othello with her junior class failed to provide them with the prior knowledge necessary to understand the story. Deprived of any information about the Moors, the setting or the people of that time, the students brought their own understanding to the story, and Othello became another O.J. Simpson.

On the other hand, too many principals do not provide discipline routines that address the chronic need of teachers to have assistance with severe special education placements (Emotionally and Behaviorally Disordered or EBD4) and the peer pressure by Black males for low achievement in the academic and intellectual arenas. In many low-achieving African American high schools, the gangsta-thug mentality of Tupac Shakur and Notorious B.I.G. have dampened the pursuit of excellence, many educators romanticize these rappers and become apologists for their behavior.

Although *Substance* helped to elect Deborah Lynch, she seemed more thoughtful of the teachers' role in improving the quality of education and wanted CTU to participate in the decision-making. She believed that teachers were a part of the solution, not the problem and that "reform done with teachers will be better than reform done without teachers." Meanwhile, in general, the Duncan administration isolated teachers and community from decisions until they were made.

My observations led me to conclude that many schools are reform resistant. SAS's model determines the principal as instructional leader. With the help of the Principals' Center at DePaul University's SOE, directed by Margaret Harrigan, professional development was offered to the principals of SAS schools in order to change their leadership styles. Principals were mentored and mandated to sign agreements that they would change their behaviors to support teachers and provide time for them to improve the quality of their instruction. SAS argued that the teachers would never improve if the principal is not viewed as supportive, aggressive and accountable. Principals were asked to form an Instructional Leadership Team (ILT) composed of as many school actors as they could gather, including classroom teachers. Team-building training was given to develop consensus among the faculty and staff around problem solving because the lack of consensus and the adversarial relationship promoted by some LSC and union members often inhibited any kind of school improvement.

Payne refers to this condition as one of social demoralization. He states the following:

If we assume that we are implementing programs in environments where behavior is often irrational, even self-destructive, we would proceed differently. That might mean thinking in advance about mechanisms to prevent local decision-makers from exerting unhealthy influences, about mechanisms for insuring that appropriate in-building communication does in fact occur. It might mean that we would simply never have programs where teachers are "retrained" and then left to implement on their own. The military talks about having equipment "ruggedized" for the field; the issue is not whether the computer works, but whether it has been built to work under the actual conditions of combat, in extreme heat or extreme cold or in the middle of storm at sea. We could ask the same question of our programs. How can we ruggedize them so that whatever they offer of value can survive the actual conditions of inner city schools?"[29]

Feedback was given to professional development providers regarding teaching/learning conditions in SAS schools through impact visits that were made twice a year in all schools receiving this service. Every SAS school had an assigned coordinator who monitored compliance with the ten routines advocated by SAS: assessment, placement, pacing, monitoring, measuring, discipline, instruction, evaluation, professional development and decision-making, and provided professional development for teachers and worked with them to improve instruction in classrooms.

This coordinator also prepared for the impact visit. An impact visit involved a team of SAS coordinators, people who were assigned to work in a particular school every day except Friday, who observed classrooms in a school on a certain date known to those who were being observed. The visited knew exactly what the team would be seeking. After this visit a report was presented to the ILT of the school, citing the strengths and weaknesses and suggesting recommendations. Several weeks afterward, a follow-up visit was held to review the ways the school decided to address the weaknesses and how well the school had implemented the recommendations.

At one school, for instance, the teachers responded negatively to the observations presented to them by the visiting impact team. Their classes had been observed and they had been given a report of their observations. At the follow-up meeting the visiting team received the reactions and input on their report. The visited teachers were defensive and hostile. Finally, the visiting team told the teachers they had come to help and that if they considered themselves perfect and without need for assistance, then the team could leave. The visiting impact team tried to win the teachers over to their side, stating that the observations should be used to reflect on the practices that could be changed if they so wanted. After many assurances that the team had no intentions of incriminating anyone or causing job loss, the visited teachers softened their opposition.

Later, the impact team members were told that the union representative, who was also a member of the LSC, was opposed to the principal's plan to hire a first-grade teacher, and not one for the Alternative Instructional Room (AIR). This union representative was actively circulating a rumor to motivate others to be opposed to the principal in the LSC meeting to be held that afternoon. Whenever the matter was discussed with the principal, he reported that the week before she had told him that many teachers were complaining about the fumes from the painting which was going on in the school. When the principal investigated by talking with teachers individually, he found only one who was complaining. It is very clear that this teacher spent her time creating problems instead of solving them.

Correcting these problems is harder than most people think. The CTU does not demand that its members have enough time for professional development, nor do the taxpayers want to pay teachers for a longer school day or a longer school year so that there is time for them to plan and prepare interesting lessons or solve the many problems of serving students who must live with barriers to their progress—such as poverty, crime and violence. These schools are financed by the same formula as schools serving affluent children, and no staffing differences are made for need. Reconstituted schools lose teachers based on the same formula for magnet schools, where students must pass a test to enroll.

Special education presents a most egregious condition. All seven reconstituted high schools had an excess of 20 percent of their student populations placed in special education. According to the court order in *Corey H. v. CPS*, special education students are to be educated in the least restrictive environments. This means that a large number of students with learning disabilities, behavior disorders, emotional disturbances and various other handicapping conditions are placed in classrooms with teachers totally unprepared to meet their needs.

Teachers are assigned according to archaic formulae that does not account for the reconstituted condition. In one reconstituted high school, a regular education English teacher had more special education students in his class than could be legally placed in a self-contained special education class. CPS has abandoned terms such as "inclusion" or "mainstreaming" because they do not have enough money to provide the push-in team teaching model required for both.

According to a 2001 report by the Civil Rights Project at Harvard University, Black students are three times more likely than white students to be labeled "mentally retarded." Overall, Black students are less likely to leave special education and return to regular classrooms than white students. But is racism—overt or covert, intentional or inadvertent—wholly to blame?[30]

The category of intervention schools was abandoned by the Duncan administration. Yet Chicago has a number of selective high schools whereby admission demands certain test scores. Some principals are concerned about the way students are selected for magnet schools. They believe they overreach and create a disparate impact on non-selective schools. If a school accepts a large number of higher achievers from a region or area, this action depletes the pool of capable students for the general high schools in that area or region. Principals also complained about the recruitment of students by selected admissions after the enrollment deadlines. Moreover, principals in general high schools clamored for more certified teachers for the rising numbers of special education students in their schools.

The education plan for CPS, Every Child, Every School, was designed by the Duncan administration with the help of the Consortium of Chicago School Reform, and many participants from the community. It is constructed around eight goals, none of which address the real cause of the achievement gap, the imputation of Black inferiority, or racism. There is little indication of cultural pluralism in the plan. Low-achieving predominantly African American schools have more uncertified and new teachers than other schools. Additionally, they have a larger percentage of special education students.

On March 19, 2003, 42 percent of the freshman class of Austin High School was enrolled in special education. Moreover, CPS placed the Achievement Academies (poor performing eighth graders) into these general high schools, exacerbating an egregious problem. The low-achieving academies are placed in low-achieving high schools primarily because the latter have space. Yet these schools already have a multitude of problems to solve, presenting a further burden. This type of policy is not neutral. The effect is the creation of a two-tiered high school segregated system: one for those who can pass the test required for admission (usually the affluent and mostly white or Asian students) and one for those who cannot (usually the poor and mostly African American and Latino students).

To help these schools, they need more time for professional development, a longer school day for the teachers and a longer school year (mandatory summer school). While the plan acknowledges the need for the longer school year, there is no mention of the need for a longer school day. Instead, Chicago schools operate with the shortest school day in the state.[31] The administration and CPS did negotiate for a school day that would have been twenty minutes longer in the defeated teachers' contract for September 2003; but it also bargained for a shorter school year.

The goals of the education plan are: building instructional capacity, providing high quality teaching and leadership, establishing learning communities and professional development programs, maintaining support for student development and post-secondary training and education, making schools centers of communities in partnership with families, strengthening existing high school programs, providing expanded choice within neighborhoods, and establishing accountability to support improvement in all schools. All of these goals require a longer school day and a longer school year (including summer school and summer programs).

Two foci for effective instructional programs are discussed in the Educational Plan for the Chicago Public Schools: within classrooms and across classrooms. Within classrooms reflect emphases on standards-based instruction, instructional frameworks, instructional time, engaged learning, challenging assignments and assessment systems. However, there is no focus on discipline. People who have never taught in a low-achieving predominantly African American school talk about solving discipline problems by using Instructional Frameworks. Yet, teachers have more trouble engaging learning and providing challenging assignments precisely because they do not know what to do with unruly and disobedient students. Unless the administration and school provide support for teachers with these students, no engaged learning or challenging assignments will occur.

Under a safe and orderly environment the plan states: "The school environment supports the academic program by creating an environment of order and safety, strong positive behavioral expectations for students and support for teachers in addressing students' physical and socio-emotional health and other needs so that all students come to class ready to learn." I was unable to find in the document just how that was to occur.

The practice of the CPS is to make low-achieving predominantly African American schools abide by the same staffing patterns as high-achieving schools - to dump large numbers of special education students in the high schools, to send new and uncertified teachers to positions in these schools and to have the shortest day in the state for school. In addition, a principal who has disgruntled teachers or parents may find himself or herself out of a job; not because he or she has not performed well, but because the disgruntled teacher or the parent wants someone else.

Across classrooms, the Educational Plan lists a common vision, instructional program coherence, instructional pacing, developmentally appropriate practice, principle-driven professional development and family as partners. In order to accomplish these aims, Chicago will need to provide more certified teachers to the low-achieving predominantly African American schools. Teachers must know their content areas and their curriculum goals. Many teachers in the high schools are teaching in areas for which they are uncertified. There are too few special education teachers in schools where large numbers of students are placed in unrestricted environments without help.

The Educational Plan states that quality instruction requires that teachers have a research-based framework for how instruction should be organized in ways that promote student learning of the content areas by following the CPS reading framework, which emphasizes time on word knowledge, fluency, writing and comprehension. Yet no attention is given to teaching English grammar in a school system where approximately 50 percent of the students speak the African American English Vernacular (AAEV) and 40 percent speak Spanish. While word knowledge, fluency, writing and comprehension are critical to the development and maintenance of high reading skills, unless the students understand how English is constructed and used, the achievement gap will not be closed. Although writing is specified, there are no protocols for the teaching of English grammar, which many teachers do not know themselves. Comprehension demands an understanding of what is a sentence, what is a complete thought, what is a clause, thus, what is a complete and coherent paragraph.[32]

In 2002, Arne Duncan closed three low-achieving predominantly African American elementary schools: Dodge, on the west side, in the United Center, Terrell, in the State Street Corridor where public housing was disappearing, and Williams, near Dearborn Homes Public Housing on North State Street. I was asked to support these closings, which I did, although I thought the timing off. I preferred to make the announcement of the closings after the standardized test scores were released. My reason for supporting the closings was the opportunity for Dodge, which was the school with which I was most closely allied, to start over again. Indeed, Dodge's scores rose that year.

I was led to believe that a planning process would be designed wherein the community, teachers, administrators and university representatives could work together for the best interests of the students involved, but I had nothing in writing. I recommended that a core of the superior Dodge teachers be retained as the planning core for that school. Instead, DePaul University conducted a survey. The findings of this survey were never revealed to the advisory committee, which met several times, where they were told what was being done. In the end this committee proved to be nothing more than a rubber-stamp group. Some members told me that at two meetings no one from central office attended. Dodge is now a teachers training academy based on the Chicago Academy and New Leaders New Schools group and funded with federal and foundation monies.

CPS issued a press release that declared that Dodge and Williams would be schools of choice to which students from anywhere in the city could apply if there were spaces available and after all of the neighborhood students were accommodated. This leaves a dangerous loophole.

Because Dodge was closed, the area around the school was ripe for gentrification, because of the United Center. Many of the students may have moved from the neighborhood during the closing, or have since become used to the schools they are presently attending. This is especially true of students in the upper grades (seventh and eighth). In this case, the neighboring schools will be raided for their best students. Chicago's plan for school reform seems now to be: (1) the creation of schools for students who are selected either by recommendation or tests; and (2) the concentration of special education students in the other schools. This creates two tiers of schools. Those who attend the latter will get the least experienced teachers, the most uncertified teachers and the least competent teachers. They will also have fewer resources to address their chronic problems: poverty, family dysfunction and community organization.

In its editorial on the Dodge School, the *Chicago Tribune* said, "Obviously, this is a special case. It will be far too expensive to serve as a model for all the system's failing schools. If other schools are forced to close, they will not be able to count on private groups and federal grants to come to the rescue."[33] The editorial criticized the CTU for its opposition to the establishment of this elitist school, which could not be duplicated for the vast majority of failing schools. In her letter to the editor, Deborah Lynch said:

> A mindset exists that if we only had teachers from Ivy League universities and from second careers, if we only would contract out schools and programs to 'outside' groups, if we only would bring in university experts and consultants, our problems would be solved. This mindset is an insult and an affront to the front line teaching professionals working in our schools day after day after day.

Lynch does not seem opposed to outside consultants and university experts in general, since her plan was to work with the Success for All programs in several schools.

Drawing on the energy and opportunity generated by the 1988 Chicago School Reform Act, Michael Klonsky, a professor from the University of Illinois at Chicago (UIC), along with a community organizer, introduced the small-school concept to Chicago and began to mobilize educators who were interested in starting schools. Foundation support was secured to launch the Small Schools Workshop (SSW) at UIC. The goal of the workshop was to assist educators wanting to start small schools by supplying information, sharing technical assistance with teachers, and providing advocacy with top-level central office staffers to promote policy changes.

The Chicago Board of Education issued a resolution in 1996 supporting small schools as a preferred school reform model. The resolution described small schools as:

> Those with a small number of students, usually no more than 100–350 in elementary schools and 500 in high schools; a cohesive, self-selected faculty supported by like-minded parents; substantial autonomy as to curriculum, budget, organization, personnel and other matters; a coherent curriculum or pedagogical focus that provides a continuous educational experience across a range of grades; and an inclusive admissions policy that gives weight to student and parent commitment to the school mission.

Money to fund the small schools initiative in CPS was raised by Microsoft's founder, Bill Gates, and his wife Melinda. But, in fact, schools that had chosen small schools had not shown any more success than other reform models since 1995. In Hess and Cytrynbaum's report, "The Effort to Redesign Chicago High Schools: Effects on Schools and Achievement" the authors state the following:

> Small schools typically were organized with students physically co–located in a set of specific divisions, and their classes were taught by a faculty, which was mostly devoted to those students alone (though frequently these students took physical education and specialized courses like Art or Music with teachers not part of the small school faculty). Small schools were typically led by a teacher/director, and the faculty made significant organizational decisions, such as period of length and course requirements, which might vary from the pattern in the larger school or from other small schools. Some schools, such as Orr and Corliss, were organized into small units, with designated faculty by grade levels called "Houses."
> Houses were generally led by deans, who played more of a disciplinary role than an instructional leadership role.

In 1999–2000, there were four high schools on probation utilizing the small schools approach: DuSable, Harper, Manley and Robeson (though Manley was technically a career academy and Robeson also had a math and science academy). Seven of the nine external partners in 2000 saw an improvement in the number of students reading at the national norm in subsequent tests. This was over the number who had done so as freshmen. Only Northeastern Illinois University (NEIU) and the SSW did not have more tenth graders at the norm in 2000 than had scored at the norm as freshman in 1999. While the external partners made no gains that were large, compared to the increases from year to year, which resulted from more prepared students entering high school as freshman, they were more impressive gains made, especially in light of the fact that schools not receiving the assistance of the external partners generally had significantly fewer students at the norm on the tenth grade test in 2000.

The report went on to say that, "teachers were quite positive, in 2000, about the assistance being provided by most external partners." The UIC at Manley, and Campanile at Senn, received exceptionally high ratings by the faculties of those schools. While there was variation from school to school served by the external partners. When all the teachers served by an external partner and responding to the survey were combined, the positive responses far outweighed the negative responses for each of the external partners. The exception was SSW, which did not provide direct assistance to teachers in their classrooms, though it did arrange to provide that assistance through other sources.

In Wasley's study of small schools these schools were classified as historical, freestanding, schools within schools, and multischools. The small schools, which existed in Chicago at the elementary level for a long time, were historical. These small schools serve 350 students or fewer, are freestanding, and are not alternative or special education schools. The average elementary school in CPS serves students from census tracts with an average annual family income of $25,616.00. In contrast, historically small schools serve students from an average annual income of $32,367.00. Moreover, these historically small schools were located in neighborhoods that had lower crime rates in 1994, and a lower percentage of people on public aid in 1997. Twenty-six percent of historically small school student bodies consist of 30 percent or more white students, while only 13 percent or more of the schools in the system have student bodies composed of 30 percent or more white students. Moreover, more than 22 percent of small schools are magnet schools; in contrast, approximately 6 percent of the other public elementary schools in the system are academic magnets.

Students in Chicago's historically small schools also achieve at high levels. On average, 48 percent of students attending historically small schools scored at or above national norms in reading in 1997. This exceeded the system average in 1997 of 30 percent and approaches the ultimate goal of the system: to have 50 percent of its students reading at or above national norms. Surely this result is an effect of better prepared students from families with higher incomes in integrated schools, including magnets.

The report states that freestanding small schools are like conventional schools, in that they have their own space, budget and principal. There were fifty-three freestanding small schools in the CPS in 1997. Some freestanding schools share a building called a 'multiple with other freestanding schools. In any event, the freestanding school has its own unit number and principal.

Another type is the school within a school (SWS), where the small school is located within a larger school, called a host school. Schools within schools can be multischools, meaning a school building has been reconfigured into smaller schools. These small schools are organized in a variety of ways. In 1999, 52 percent of the SWSs served two or three grade levels and 24 percent of these schools served five grade levels. Of the twenty-five SWSs, only one served kindergarten through eighth grades, according to Wasley et al. By 2000, 65 percent of SWSs served tenth through twelfth grades at the high school level, 25 percent were full schools, and 10 percent served grades ninth through eleventh.

Small schools are organized around themes, grade levels and professions. High school SWSs seemed to exclude freshman for two major reasons: the process enabled the SWSs to recruit from the freshman class at their high school and the school was able to recruit students after they had successfully made the transition to the demands of high school. This condition had these advantages, but may have had others. By excluding freshmen, the class that contributes most of the discipline problems and the majority of its failures to the high school are excluded. However, during the time when eighth graders were not permitted in to the high school because of low scores on the standardized tests, the high scorers were also excluded.

The study provides this profile of small-school teachers and students. The new small schools in Chicago serve children of color, from predominantly African American schools at the high school level, and students from poorer families. The schools also cater to students who are achieving at levels below the average student in the system and students more likely found in poorly performing schools. Chicago's new small schools tend to attract more academically prepared students particularly when they are Schools Within Schools, which happen to be on probation. "These new" small schools had fewer special education students than the system average, employed School Within School teachers in their host schools and employed teachers who had worked outside the CPS system. Additionally, at the high school level, predominantly African American high schools and schools with higher student mobility rates tended to house Schools Within Schools.

I found it difficult to determine the number of small schools in the study from the tables provided, nor could I determine whether or not the small gifted and magnet schools were included in this information. A February 2002 memo from Matt Gladden, one of the authors stated the following:

> Analyses of historically small elementary schools did include magnet
> schools....Instead of excluding elementary magnet schools from the analysis, it
> was decided that I should control for their effects in the statistical analysis. Thus,
> a small magnet school would appear successful only if it performed better than the
> average magnet school in CPS, instead of an average elementary school. Also,
> student achievement and characteristics of neighborhoods in which the students
> lived and schools were located, were statistically controlled for in analyses of ITBS
> scores and retention rates. Since magnet schools were included in the analyses,
> your concern over there only being forty-five historically elementary schools in
> 1997 when you encountered close to sixty in your analyses of contemporary data
> may reemerge. In order to address this possible concern, I reviewed the
> September 1996 administrative data and discovered fifty-one elementary schools
> that serve 350 or less students that were also magnet or regular education schools.
> Alternative and special education schools were excluded from the analysis. Five
> of the fifty-one schools were newly opened small schools; one of the schools
> served predominantly special education students and was dropped from
> the sample and that left forty-five schools to be classified as historically small
> schools. This is consistent with the numbers reported in the study. At the high
> school level, selective high schools, selected through discussions were dropped
> from the analyses because these schools were qualitatively different from other
> high schools and insufficient numbers of selective schools exist to meaningfully
> control for their effect.

I located fifty-seven small elementary schools in the CPS (with student enrollments between 100 and 350). Twenty-three, or 40 percent, were not on the ISAT warning list for the State of Illinois. Of these, nearly one-third were gifted or magnets. Thirty-four, or 59 percent, of these schools landed on the warning list, although nearly one-fourth of them produced more than 35 percent of the student population at or above the national norm in reading on the ITBS, and four of them had 45 percent or more to meet or exceed the ISAT.

In 1997, the ITBS performance of host SWSs was 25.2 percent at or above the norm, for multischools it was 26.9 percent, for freestanding schools it was 20.1 percent, for historically small schools it was 48.1 percent, while the system average was at 29.1 percent. That same year TAP performance in high schools with host SWSs was at 15.7 percent, for multischools it was 9.7 percent, for freestanding schools it was 16.1 percent, and the system average was 18.8 percent. Clearly students in small schools tended to score slightly lower on the ITBS and TAP than students in other CPS schools.

This report goes on to confirm that significantly stronger mathematics students, stronger reading students, fewer special education students and more females were recruited by the SWSs than in the host schools. Yet, comparisons were constantly made between the two, as though the conditions were equal. While statistical methods may control for some factors, they do not control for the increase in disciplinary actions required in the classrooms of the schools where students differ in the controlled characteristics. When comparing the disparity across the students entering the SWSs with these students entering the host schools, the authors discovered that the SWSs located in high schools on academic probation were almost uniformly drawing more academically prepared students and fewer special education students. The difference between the percentage of special education students in SWSs versus their host schools was significantly greater in African American schools and significantly less in elementary schools that served a predominantly minority student body. These disparities tended to remain stable, or increase, between 1997 and 1999.

At the high school level 7.9 percent of the SWS students were in special education, compared with 14.6 percent for the host school students. By 1999, this difference had grown much larger: 8 percent for the SWSs and 27.6 percent for the host schools. While controls were made, the effect of the presence of large numbers of special education students in regular classrooms on the teaching and learning methods used there could not be controlled. The report goes on to say that the major reason for the increase in special education students at the high school level is the eighth grade retention policy, which excludes special education from retention, thereby causing their entry into high school, exceeded that of regular education students, who must comply.

In spite of these great differences between the student bodies of small

Schools Within Schools and their hosts, comparisons are made and the following conclusions claimed:

> When examining a range of indicators to assess student achievement the data from 1997 to 1999 suggest that students in small schools have better attendance rates; have significantly lower dropout rates; have higher GPAs; fail fewer courses; have stronger achievement test scores given that more students are taking the test and the test scores have not dropped; and that elementary SWSs are significantly less likely to have students repeat a grade than their host schools.

The authors summarized their findings in this way, "Small schools improved their reading and mathematics scores between 1997 and 1999 and tended to outperform their hosts in reading and showed mixed results in mathematics."

By comparing the SWSs with the host school, where there had already been an admission that the students were not the same, instead of comparing them with the historically small schools in the rest of the system, the authors set up a bias in the study. The real deal is revealed, however, in the study by the authors who wrote: "Although SWSs outperformed their host schools, SWSs performed significantly worse in both reading and mathematics by .78 grade equivalents and .87 grade equivalents respectively, than other high schools."

Claims of academic achievement in small schools are presently a hoax, much like year-round schools. Year-round schools certainly effectively use school space. However, they are no better at raising achievement than any other school. Will small schools close the achievement gap? Of course not. Everyone I've met has wanted to lower taxes or not pay any. It takes money to create effective small schools. As soon as Gates's money is spent, the idea will disappear. Then why are we pursuing this route?

We are doing so because the professional and business community has bought into it. The big foundations are willing to fund it. This is not unusual. We have walked this circle before. In his book, *The Education of Blacks in the South: 1860–1935*, James D. Anderson wrote:

The education of Blacks in the South reveals that various contending forces sought either to repress the development of Black education or to shape it in ways that contradicted Blacks' interests in intellectual development. The educational outcomes demonstrate that Blacks got some, but not much, of what they wanted. They entered emancipation with fairly definite ideas about how to integrate education into their broader struggle for freedom and prosperity, but they were largely unable to shape their future in accordance with their social vision.

These contending forces were the big philanthropists of the day: Robert C. Ogden, George Foster Peabody, William H. Baldwin, Jr., John D. Rockefeller, the Anna T. Jeanes Foundation and the Phelps-Stokes Fund. The philanthropists settled on General Samuel Chapman Armstrong's Tuskegee Model for the education of African Americans.

Will reform work in CPS? Certainly greater unity among the reformers needs to take place. The 1988 and 1995 reformers are communicating better and more often and seem willing to negotiate. The universities need to "ruggedize" their training programs for potential teachers for schools serving students in low-income census zones characterized by crime and violence. So that as new teachers they will still have high expectations for their students and demand that they meet high standards.

LA&S faculty members need to review the content of their subjects. Curricula frequently present distortions and omissions with regard to the content in order to support white supremacy disguised as Western civilization. This content needs review and reflection. Also, more attention should be paid to the development of the human spirit, one that is optimistic about the future, vigorous in overcoming obstacles and courageous about taking risks and trying new things. Although it pays to be smart, nothing overcomes depression, pessimism, doubt and defeat like the human spirit when it is properly nourished and cared for.

Reform will not work as long as the same old paradigms govern what is taught, how it is taught and why it is taught. As discussed in previous chapters, education has three functions: training, socialization and enlightenment. Training means teaching someone how to do something: how to read, how to drive a car, how to swim. Socialization means helping one internalize certain habits governing what one does, when one does it and where one does it. Enlightenment always explains why things are as they are. Minority poor children's education is long on training and socialization and short on enlightenment. They are taught, for the most part, to stay in their places and to believe they are inferior.

Race continues to be the most divisive element in this capitalist democracy. The very content which could eliminate the achievement gap between African Americans and whites is objectionable to defenders of Western civilization and the dominance of the English language. Carter G. Woodson had an interesting commentary on this kind of education:

> The Negro's mind has been brought under the control of his oppressor. The problem of holding the Negro down, therefore, is easily solved. When you control a man's thinking you do not have to worry about his actions. You do not have to tell him not to stand here or go yonder. He will find his "proper place" and will stay in it. You do not need to send him to the back door. He will go without being told. In fact, if there is no back door, he will cut one for his special benefit. His education makes it necessary.[35]

There is much research concerned with cultural diversity and its importance to the development of a global community. Jules Henry argues, that enlightenment, the process of testing the assumptions of a culture, usually leads to such questions as:

> Is our form of political economy the best and the only moral one? Does my life have meaning? Is goodness always rewarded? Is our form of marriage really the best? Are whites really the superior race? Is it right to be rich when others are poor? There is no enlightenment unless the conventional answers to these questions, and many others like them, are constantly examined, and there can be no education unless there is enlightenment. Any so-called educational endeavor that does not do this is doing no more than tooling up for conventional occupations.[36]

In summary, he says "common controversies in education revolve not so much around what students should know and how they should learn, but how stupid we can permit them to be without wrecking the country and the world." We exclude too many essentials for progressing in the real world from the schools's curriculum. We refuse to teach our students about living in a capitalist democracy. We emphasize the latter, and the students' obligations to its preservation, but we rarely tell them that it is the capitalist process that we value most and that this is what they will be asked to die for.

Preparing teachers to teach the excluded must challenge their belief systems, make them recognize and relinquish beliefs about the inferiority of others and their own superiority. Teaching the pariahs and low castes of a capitalist democracy is more than teaching content, although content is the most important construct. There is a spiritual and moral obligation here. There is the high-risk operation to be considered.

Universities are having trouble. If overcoming resistance to school reform is to be successful, universities must solve the following four problems by and through the teacher training curriculum: (1) lack of respect for the pariahs of the society; (2) the imputation of Black inferiority and the devotion to white supremacy; (3) mastery of the content in which the teacher will specialize; and (4) lack of resources in schools that serve the poor, as compared to those that serve the more affluent. To do this, university professors who train teachers will need more experience working in the public schools which service the pariahs. They must conduct more research in schools that are 90 percent to 100 percent minority and poor.

DePaul University was a good place for these changes to occur. Vincentian education seeks "to respond to the intellectual, spiritual, moral and affective needs of the students [it] educates, the heart as well as the head, blends the humanistic and the professional, the abstract and the practical; seeks to meet challenges, while maintaining a sense of the possible; is willing to adapt to the needs of the nontraditional students; places quality at the center of its educational activities where the instructor must not only be competent, but also be efficient, dedicated and reveal all of those virtues required of students; employs methods which enable the students to learn and enjoy learning; values all human dignity and life; seeks collaboration, partnerships and is focused on service to the poor" (Sullivan 1997.) But this type of education has not happened.

Can our society, as it is now composed, make reform work in the very lowest-achieving predominantly African American and Latino schools located in low-income census zones characterized by crime and violence? Are we ready to give up our commitment to white supremacy? Are we ready to spend the kind of money necessary to "ruggedize" our programs for success in these areas? Only the future can tell, but if the past is prologue, the outcome looks bleak.

We refuse to provide the resources necessary to produce the following: (1) a longer school day for planning, preparation and professional development; (2) certified and qualified teachers who know their subject's content and understand their students' needs in every classroom and every position; (3) a seat for every child; (4) an operational internet-connected computer for every child; (5) sufficient books, materials and supplies for every child; (6) a vehicle for the development of trust between all school actors; and (7) a curriculum that accommodates diversity and cultural pluralism and ends the reign of white supremacy and the imputation of Black inferiority.

Yet, Jennifer A. O'Day believes that a combination of bureaucratic and professional accountability will work.[37] While O'Day did a study of the Chicago Public School's implementation of bureaucratic accountability, such a study of Baltimore's professional accountability was noticeably absent. For her, bureaucratic accountability is top down and outcomes based. Professional accountability depends on effective teaching, which rests on professionals acquiring specialized knowledge and skills and being able to apply such knowledge and skills to the specific contexts in which they work. She does note the overall weakness of professionalism and professional accountability in U.S. education and the failure of professionalism in schools serving disenfranchised groups, especially schools in inner cities with large proportions of low-income students and students of color.

Chicago now plans to reward schools with cash bonuses for year-to-year improvement. Sixty schools (forty-eight elementary and twelve high schools) that showed the most improvement in last spring's test scores will each receive $10,000.00, funded through private donations. While this is still bureaucratic accountability, it might do more to facilitate the development of professionalism. Schools will be judged by their own growth records from year to year and classified as Schools of Excellence if 60 percent of the students in elementary school, and 50 percent of the students in high school, meet the standards. Schools of Distinction will exceed the standards by 40 percent in elementary schools and 30 percent in high schools. Schools of Merit will be those where 40 percent of the elementary and 30 percent of the high school students meet the standards. High schools where less than 15 percent of the students do not meet the standards, and elementary schools where less than 25 percent do not meet the standards, will be on probation. These represent very low expectations for these students, most of whom are African American. What's more, the trend of these new actions is to substitute growth for achievement. If students grow a year, in a year, in a particular school, for example, they will be recognized and counted in the statistic; yes, they might still be unable to read at the level required for success. What, therefore, is the message to African Americans when a school like the one in this example, "improves" in a year from 6 percent to 9 percent at or above the national norm in reading, receives a $10,000.00 reward? Ninety percent of the students in that school still cannot read!

The elimination of the achievement gap is reachable with enough money. This is unlikely, however, as long as schools are funded from property taxes. "Most of the resource inequality cannot be resolved at the state level," David Grissmer and Ann Flanagan, analysts for the Rand Corporation, have written. "States spending the least are southern and western states that also have a disproportionate share of the nation's minority and disadvantaged students. Yet the federal government does little to address this systemic inequality, and continues to contribute only about seven percent of the total spent on elementary and secondary schools." As long as people do not want to fund schools for other peoples's children, inequity will breed injustice and discontent.

CHAPTER 8

THE SCHOOL ACHIEVEMENT STRUCTURE AND THE STRUCTURED TEN ROUTINES

What the two perspectives, one Liberal and one Conservative, have in common is that they both offer the subordinate status of Blacks in relation to whites as a basic value, a paradigm, that, if challenged or changed, would activate both Liberals and Conservatives alike to seek to protect their status and reimpose subordination on Blacks. This paradigm is so powerful that it has the capacity to energize whites to invoke common interests and come together regardless of differences of political ideology or party.

—Ronald W. Walters, *White Nationalism, Black Interests: Conservative Public Policy and the Black Community*

Section 8.1 Thomas Kuhn

With the success of the Pittsburgh schools (Beltzhoover, Madison and Vann) still ringing in my ears, I returned to Chicago in 1992. As dean of the School of Education at DePaul University, I thought there should be a strong relationship between us and the Chicago Public Schools (CPS). With the approval of my provost and president, I established a school outreach program called the School Achievement Structure (SAS) at DePaul in order to help the Chicago Public Schools with its intent to improve the quality of education for all of the children in CPS. SAS initiated, implemented and institutionalized the Structured Ten Routines (STR), which emerged from the research conducted in three Pittsburgh Public Schools from 1979 through 1985 as reported in chapter three. STR addresses the massive underachievement of African American students in public schools. It rests on two theoretical models: effective schools correlates and Allison's Organizational Process Model (OPM).[1] These models arose from a belief that the school, the school system and the larger social order contribute to the problem.

Thomas Kuhn argued, "Normal science is the accumulation of achievements which provide scientists with a foundation for its further practice, definitions of legitimate problems and methods of a research field for future practitioners,"[2] he also insisted, "to be called a paradigm, these achievements must be sufficiently unprecedented to attract an enduring group of adherents away from competing modes of scientific activity and they must be sufficiently open ended to leave many problems for the redefined group to resolve."[3] Kuhn stated that paradigms gain status because they are more successful than their competitors are at solving a few problems which the community of scholars recognizes as acute. "Normal science," according to Kuhn, "does not aim to produce novelties of fact or theory even though new and unpredicted phenomena are frequently uncovered by it; moreover,

247

discovery commences with the awareness of anomaly or the recognition that nature has somehow violated the paradigm, inducing exploration of the unexpected event."[4] For Kuhn, this "exploration persists until the anomaly has become the expected, because of adjustments to the paradigm theory."

Kuhn further argued, "By ensuring that the paradigm will not be too easily surrendered, resistance guarantees that scientists will not be lightly distracted and that the anomalies that lead to paradigm change will penetrate existing knowledge to the core."[5] He insists that one theory is never forsaken unless another candidate was available. He writes, "…the act of judgment that leads scientists to reject a previously accepted theory is always based upon more than a comparison of that theory with the world. The decision to reject one paradigm is always simultaneously the decision to accept another, and the judgment leading to that decision involves the comparison of both paradigms with nature and with each other."[6]

Although there have always been schools with African American and/or poor students demonstrating high achievement as determined by standardized test scores, these have usually been the exception rather than the rule. As stated in a previous chapter, there have been five competing theories to explain the academic underachievement of African American students in the United States STR is based on the theory that the African American achievement gap results from inefficient, underfunded, and ineffective schools and school systems and a larger social order which values white supremacy and results in the imputation of Black inferiority.

Section 8.2   Ronald R. Edmonds's Effective Schools Model

The paradigm that best reflects this theory is the Effective Schools Model founded by Ronald R. Edmonds in the 1970s. In pursuit of his findings, I discovered racially isolated schools in Pittsburgh, Pennsylvania and Dallas, Texas where 90 percent or more of the African American students were scoring at or above the national norms in reading and mathematics on standardized tests, even though they lived in low-income census zones.

In Pittsburgh these schools were: Beltzhoover, Louis A Venson, Principal; Madison, Vivian Williams, Principal; McKelvy, Lawrence Nee, Principal; Vann,

Doris Brevard, Principal; and Westwood, Janet Bell, Principal. In Dallas there were: Charles Rice, Louise Smith, Principal; and Margolis Elementary and Maynard Jackson Middle School, Sherwin Allen, principal of both at different times. Also in Dallas, Texas, Lincoln High School proved to be the only high-achieving public majority African American high school located in a low-income census zone that I could find. The principal there, Napoleon Lewis, died in 1997.[7]

Dr. Napoleon Lewis believed that discipline had to be first in the all-Black high school located in a low-income census zone if academic achievement was to rise. His wife, Nell Lewis, recalled that:

> The auditorium was his classroom. Lincoln High School was known for its assemblies. Celebrations of excellence is what he liked to call them. Any and all achievements were celebrated in the auditorium with the choir, speakers, cheerleaders, and student leaders acknowledging the students' success. The most significant assembly was called The Ascension. It was held on the evening following the graduation of the seniors to elevate the junior class to senior class status. [There was] a candlelight ceremony featuring a leadership candle lighted by the graduating senior class president and presented to the junior class president, who held it for each arising junior symbolizing their assumption of leadership in the school. The auditorium was filled with parents who beamed with pride.

In this way, Dr. Lewis made his seniors accountable for the leadership (and discipline) of Lincoln High School.

But, discipline was a means to an end according to Nell Lewis. "Inspect what you expect" was one of Dr. Lewis's mottos. Teachers at their classroom doors and administrators monitoring the hall on every floor were the norm during the changing of classes. There were certain periods between which students could go to their lockers. When Dr. Lewis arrived at Lincoln High School, there were mostly Correlated Language Arts and Fundamentals of Mathematics classes. These were remedial courses for English and mathematics. There was only one section of English One, Two, Three, and Four. There was only one section of algebra: no calculus, trigonometry or physics. He was disturbed by this practice and questioned it.

The system provided that students who scored below the fortieth percentile on the standardized tests would have to enroll in these remedial courses. He asked how they could ever rise above the fortieth percentile if they had never been taught the regular curriculum. There was nothing to prohibit this from happening. The next year he eliminated all of the remedial courses, except for one class of each. The following year, all of them were eliminated. Additional mathematics courses were added, including calculus and trigonometry.

Dr. Lewis did not believe that Blacks were inferior. Teachers who did complained that students did not know the content of the standard curriculum. Dr. Lewis's response was "Teach them." He would not take no for an answer. Some twenty-seven teachers left the school in protest of the new requirements. Some filed grievances with Employee Relations. Dr. Lewis did not yield.[8]

Dr. Lewis developed his routines through his experience as the first principal of the new Howard D. Woodson Senior High School in Washington, D.C. In February of 1973, *Newsweek* magazine documented his administrative skill in the article, "Black Schools That Work," having served as assistant principal at several junior high schools, Dr. Lewis learned early that students would live up to the expectations of the administrators and staff. His own experience as a student taught him that Black boys are endangered in the school setting. He focused on their adjustment and involvement in an environment of academic and cultural excellence.

Nell Lewis admonishes us to note that cultural excellence is a vital part of the curriculum and instruction for the students because Dr. Lewis understood that knowledge of African American heritage and culture is essential to developing positive self-concepts, and that we must affirm ourselves in order to understand, appreciate and successfully pursue excellence in academics. When Dr. Lewis pursued this objective, adding cultural excellence to the curriculum and instruction was a daring idea that was unorthodox in public education. He had to request waivers to add courses, write curriculum for the courses, and justify their inclusion to the city and the Texas Education Agency. Moreover, mobilizing staff to integrate cultural pluralism throughout the curriculum was a challenge that required years of professional development and instructional planning and monitoring. Equally daring was the revamping of curriculum and instruction to eliminate the focus on remediation and offer students a wholesome standard curriculum and the appropriate instruction to ensure students' success.

Some of this risk taking was rewarded when the school's renowned Maurine F. Bailey Concert Choir was first invited to perform and compete in the International Youth and Music Festival in Vienna, Austria in 1983. They won second place in the world competition and received an invitation to return to Vienna in 1996 for the silver anniversary celebration of this festival. The choir is one of many performing groups that excel and bring many awards and achievements to the school.

Lincoln High School was selected as one of "Americas Best High Schools" in the April 1996 issue of *Redbook* magazine. It was one of sixty-three high schools in the nation recognized for overall excellence. *U.S. News & World Report* published a special report on outstanding American high schools in its January 18, 1999, issue. Lincoln was described as "a mix of hard work, racial pride and spiritualism that adds up to academic and cultural excellence." The Dallas Independent School District recognized Lincoln as one of its best. In the first two years of an accountability system based on ten academic excellence indicators, Lincoln ranked number one among the high schools, and staff members received awards of $1,000.00 for professional endeavors and $500.00 for support. They consistently maintained exemplary status on all measures during Lewis's tenure. The dropout rate fell from 6 percent to .09 percent. All of the school's graduating seniors took either the SAT or the ACT at least twice and passed the state-required test each year. Dr. Napoleon Lewis culminated his stellar career of fifty years in May 1997 and later succumbed to cancer.

Dr. Lewis more keenly than most, understood that educating African American students is largely a political decision. Because of this understanding, he assumed that there would be special challenges to ensure that his students had access to educational excellence. Students, parents, and teachers marveled at his talents and strengths in providing the administrative leadership for schools that motivate students to be the best that they can be, in spite of obstacles. At a time when inner city schools were targeted for discipline problems, low achievement, gangs and violence, Lincoln achieved against all odds. For this, Dr. Napoleon B. Lewis, affectionately called "Papa

Bear" by his students, is a legend in public education in America.

Following Edmonds, I described the processes, procedures and routines implemented in high-achieving predominantly African American schools like Lincoln. These schools were called outliers and anomalies, and frequently embarrassed responsible school officials who could not answer questions about the failure of large numbers of other predominantly African American schools where the majority of the students were low achieving. These anomalies mounted serious challenges to the other paradigms as well.

A strong supporter and advocate for the Effective Schools Model, J. Jerome Harris is best known for his ability to elevate and accelerate standardized test scores for African American youth in isolated schools and segregated communities. During his fourteen-year tenure as superintendent of Community School District Thirteen in Brooklyn, students' test scores rose continuously. Before his departure, all schools in District Thirteen, Bedford-Stuyvesant, were above the national average in both reading and math.

In 1988, Dr. Harris accepted the position of superintendent of Atlanta Public Schools in Atlanta, Georgia. About this commitment, he said:

> Atlanta was, in my mind, the school district where African American students would produce school achievement results above those of other major urban districts. I planned to produce, in four years, the same type of results I produced in District Thirteen. While I was familiar with the outcomes of the effective schools research conducted by Dr. Ronald Edmonds, the "Father" of the effective schools movement, I had not had an opportunity to institute the use of the five correlates of effective schooling on a district-wide basis. Likewise, I had not had an opportunity to meet him or to sit down with him, to question him and gain a better understanding of what I needed to do in order to bring about systemic change. Through the trials and tribulations commonly associated with change, and with the help of dedicated educators and community leaders who also believed in the ability of children, positive change was brought about in District Thirteen. I believed that the effective schools research coupled with fourteen years of experience as a successful change agent would provide the map for me to follow toward school district excellence in Atlanta.[9]

Harris went on to execute his commitment. He picked sixteen low-performing schools in Atlanta for special attention. According to Andy Miller, "It worked." Miller revealed that, "The central focus schools singled out because they historically had shown low student achievement were a major target of Dr. Harris's overall school improvement plan." All four central focus high schools showed improvements on TAP while the scores from middle schools were generally disappointing.

Even though Dr. Harris fulfilled his mission and raised test scores in Atlanta, the Board of Education felt he was too aggressive and abrasive. His style rubbed them the wrong way. They settled for comfort and low performance and let him go. Dr. Harris went on to serve as the state's monitor in Compton, California. In a rather tongue-in-cheek summation, Daniel de Vise commented that Harris "went to Compton to raise test scores. And test scores are rising. And suddenly, the grumpy dictator of Compton schools looks like a hero."[10]

Section 8.3   The Structured Ten Routines

The Structured Ten Routines (STR) were developed from the results of the Pittsburgh Study. The model is based on the assumption that the principal is the Instructional Leader, one of the basic correlates of Effective Schools Research. The vision of STR is to elevate and accelerate student achievement. The goal is to improve achievement in schools, as measured by standardized tests. The mission is to develop, implement and sustain leadership and instructional practices that elevate and accelerate student achievement. STR works with elementary and secondary schools, serving grades kindergarten through twelfth. Its focus is to elevate and accelerate student achievement in schools that are predominantly minority and that are characterized by poverty, crime and violence. So that 51 percent or more of the student body scores at or above the national, state and city norms on standardized tests in reading and mathematics. A requirement for school entry is the agreement of a majority of the school stakeholders to initiate, implement and institutionalize the STR.

Schools that adopt STR select an in-school coordinator, a full-time or part-time STR coordinator, and reading and mathematics consultants to come into the schools one or two days a week for twenty weeks each semester. On-site training is provided by STR during grade-level and departmental meetings and during the school's staff development time. STR has three stages of development: initiation, during which the vision and mission of the school are implemented, and the language of effective schools, the focus of the process, the disaggregating of data, the identification of strategies and the development of an action plan are established; implementation, during which the ten routines are put in place by modeling, mentoring and monitoring; and institutionalization, where the Ten Routines become standard operating procedures. The Ten Routines are as follows: (1) Assessment involves the disaggregating of student and school data and the creation of a five-week assessment routine. (2) Placement requires that students are placed in flexible, student-centered learning environments according to students' needs. (3) Pacing entails the delivery of instruction according to human variation in learning using grouping/regrouping instructional strategies and mandating the acceleration, reinforcement and re-teaching of curricula if necessary. (4) Monitoring supports the implementation of the routines and provides teachers with feedback to enhance instruction and student learning.(5) Measuring determines student mastery of established skills and concepts taught daily, dictates departmental or grade-level measures, and establishes and maintains timelines for administering the five-week assessments; (6) discipline promotes and maintains a positive school environment and establishes, posts and ensures understanding of school rules and enforcement of reasonable consequences for their violations. (7) Instruction maintains high expectations for student and teacher achievement and performance, integrates the students' cultures, lives and histories into every lesson, promotes high standards for rigorous subject content and enforces teacher professionalism and conduct. (8) Evaluation occurs for all school actors and programs on a regular basis to determine the impact on student achievement.(9) Staff Development restructures the school to facilitate common grade-level and/or departmental meetings, establishes a calendar for weekly staff development activities and provides time for professional development. (10) Decision-making involves all components of the school community in the decision-making and problem solving process, establishes an Instructional Leadership Team (ILT) to enhance decision-making and problem-solving and builds a spirit of consensus among the school actors around student achievement as the highest priority and goal.

Section 8.4   Chicago Schools and The School Achievement Structure

During the 1993–1994 school year, the Principals' Center, directed by Dr. Margaret Harrigan, former principal and administrator in the CPS, opened in the School of Education (SOE) at DePaul University. At the same time, the School Achievement Structure (SAS) was established and Dr. Kymara Chase became the director. The twelve schools in SAS were: Michele Clark Middle School, Marietta Beverly, Principal, Josie Letcher, Coordinator; Lucy Flower Vocational High School, Dorothy Williams, Principal, Artyce Palmer, Coordinator; Goldblatt Elementary, Lillian Nash, Principal, Dr. Corene Casselle, Coordinator; Gregory Elementary, Sherye Garmony-Miller, Principal, Delores Saulsberry, Julienne Mallory, Coordinators; Charles Evans Hughes Elementary, Audrey Cooper-Stanton, Principal, Delores Saulsberry and Julienne Mallory, Coordinators; Juarez High School, Jose Rodriguez, Principal, Gloria Cortes, Coordinator; Mayo Elementary School, Dr. Ida Cross and Frederick McNeal, Principals, Julienne Mallory and Josie Letcher, Coordinators; McCorkle Elementary, Dr. Jerry Johnson, Principal, Dr. Corene Casselle, Coordinator; Phillips High School, Juanita Tucker, Principal, Margo Crawford, Coordinator; Sbarbaro Elementary, (now Ashe), Dr. Velma Wilson, Principal, Josie Letcher, Coordinator; Spencer Elementary, Dr. Sandra A. Givens, Principal, Kymara Chase and Ollie McLemore, Coordinators; and Tilden High School, Dr. Hazel Steward, Principal, Earl Jeffrey, Coordinator.

The first year did not start until January 1994, due to Chicago Public Schools's budget problems. Each school paid for the services for SAS with Chapter One or the Creating A New Approach to Learning (CANAL) funds; therefore, no services could be provided until the budget was loaded, which was late in October. Hiring did not commence until December. In addition, there was difficulty recruiting school coordinators for the high schools because high school teachers received additional pay for extracurricular activities and the school coordinators's pay was not competitive.

Moreover, due to the late start in the first year, elementary schools did not receive adequate staff development to stimulate change. Schools did struggle with these limitations. At the end of that year, Goldblatt and McCorkle, which had adopted Direct Instruction, left SAS to pursue that route with the University of Oregon. Sbarbaro Elementary also left to work with another university. In the 1994–1995 school year, Mayo Elementary left and Price Elementary joined, Dr. Carl Lawson, principal, Josie Letcher, coordinator. The next year, (1995–1996), Juarez High School left to pursue another route for advancement and Calumet High School entered. Its principal was Tam Boston Hill. This was followed by Near North Career Metro High School, whose principal was Faye Grays. Two schools graduated that year, Clark Middle and Charles Evans Hughes Elementary. Both schools had learned enough to elevate and accelerate student achievement independently, and the SAS family agreed with that assessment. Hughes, demonstrated dramatic leaps in achievement the first year.

From 1994 until 2002, SAS served forty-nine elementary schools and fourteen high schools. SAS is a process. It does not present a packaged program for teachers and principals to follow. It facilitates the initiation, implementation and institutionalization of the Structured Ten Routines (STR) described above and required for accelerated student achievement. The principal as Instructional Leader is the model for SAS. STR helps the principal to inspire, motivate and facilitate the change in behavior required for the transition from a low-achieving school to a high-achieving school.

The first step is the selection of a School Coordinator. This person facilitates the creation and building of the school's instructional leadership team (ILT) which promotes consensus and team building. The School Coordinator observes classrooms, monitors the implementation of STR, models strategies for accelerated learning, provides professional development, solicits resources for the school, helps to distribute resources and assists the ILT in problem solving and planning. One day a week, the school coordinator has professional development meetings at DePaul University, undergoing debriefing and problem solving.

The ILT is the prime vehicle for change in the school. It meets on a weekly basis, and reports and makes recommendations to the principal, who also meets with the group regularly. The ILT also monitors, as does the principal. But only the principal evaluates. Monitoring has several purposes, among which are: determining what resources are necessary, identifying staff development needs and providing mentoring for teachers with identifiable instructional problems.

Central to the SAS process are the Structured Ten Routines: Assessment, Placement, Pacing/Acceleration, Measuring, Monitoring, Discipline, Instruction, Evaluation, Staff Development and Decision-making. Each school selects strategies compatible with the students' needs in that particular school. These needs are determined during the assessment routine. From these needs the faculty makes curriculum choices. Therefore, no packaged program is given. SAS/STR works with whatever standards and curriculum the school has chosen.

In order to be successful with STR the principal, faculty, staff and parents need: (1) to believe that all students can learn and be successful on the traditional measures used by society to determine who has access to higher learning and better paying occupations (SAT, ACT, LSAT, MCAT, GRE); (2) to understand that the obstacles of poverty, family instability and community disorganization can be overcome by the human spirit and will; (3) to know the needs of the students and to value their culture, language and heritage; and (4) to entertain high expectations for the students, the faculty, the principal and the parents. If these beliefs and understandings are held by a majority of the school's staff the decision-makers and movers a strong and active ILT will develop and implementation of STR will occur. No school achieves without strong leadership. If teachers and principals refuse to change the behaviors that reaped low achievement in the past, the outcomes will remain the same.

SAS/STR has been successful in the elementary schools and moderately successful in the high schools. Unlike Success for All (SFA) and other New American Schools Comprehensive School Reform models, SAS/STR schools are not at the minimum until 50 percent or more of the students are at or above the national norms, or meet or exceed the state standards. Of the forty-nine elementary schools, only two have reached that standard in reading as measured by the Iowa Tests of Basic Skills (ITBS). At Kellman Corporate Community School, 72.1 percent scored at or above the national norm in reading, and at Crane Elementary, 51.1 percent scored at or above the national norm in reading. Four have reached it in mathematics. At Dyett Middle School, 50.6 percent scored at or above the norm; Kellman, 68.8 percent; Mayo, 54.9 percent; and McCorkle, 53.3 percent. Seven elementary schools gained twenty points or more in the number of students at or above the national norms in reading: Brown, 23.9; Crane, 33.1; Kellman Corp., 46.2; Mayo, 23.7; McCorkle, 29.3; Overton, 31.5; and Spalding, 24.4. Sixteen elementary schools gained 20 percentage points or more in the number of students at or above the national norms in mathematics: Ashe, 22; Brown, 31; Crane, 27; Dyett, 33.9; Faraday, 21.6; Fuller, 21.6; Hughes, 21.4; Kellman, 29.3; Libby, 24.3; Mayo, 40; McCorkle, 48.3; Overton, 41.6; Paderewski, 20.8; Sherwood, 20.6; Spalding, 40.1; and Spencer, 26.5.

Of the fourteen high schools, as of 2004, two were closed: Near North Metro High and Martin Luther King, Jr. Senior High. The latter reopened as a test-in magnet high school in September 2002 with only a freshman class. In 2002, high school students took only the Prairie State Achievement Examination (PSAE) in the eleventh grade. No longer did freshmen and sophomores take the Tests for Academic Proficiency (TAP). Collins, Crane and Westinghouse, which had been removed from probation because of elevation of TAP scores, fell back into that category again when using the PSAE. Ten SAS high schools were on probation from 2002 to 2003: Austin, Calumet, Collins, Crane, Englewood, Marshall, Phillips, Spaulding, Tilden and Westinghouse. Two former SAS high schools that were not on probation were Lucy Flower Vocational High School, which had been changed to a magnet, and Benito Juarez.

In 2002, Chicago had the shortest school day in the state of Illinois. In the high schools, this is a severe limitation. The state demands 300 minutes of instruction daily. Most high schools are right on the money. If the students take more than four minutes in passing from class to class, they are below the state requirement. There is no time for teachers to plan together (as in vertical teaming), prepare lessons, have professional development, build teams or develop consensus around student achievement as the highest priority. Low-achieving schools continue to attract the newest, the most uncertified and the least competent teachers, and they receive the least amount of resources. In Chicago, the staffing pattern for the lowest-achieving high schools is the same as the highest-achieving magnet. To add insult to injury, the lowest-achieving high schools receive the highest percentage of special education students with the fewest and least certified teachers to meet the demand of inclusion.

SAS high schools have a larger percentage of special education students than other high schools. In the city, 15 percent of the students are in special education. In SAS high schools for the 2002–2003 school year the high schools have the following: Carver Military had 23.4 percent of its student body in special education in 2002 and 22 percent in 2003; Collins had 19.2 percent in 2002 and 20 percent in 2003; Crane Technical had 19.3 percent in 2002 and 20 percent in 2003; Englewood had 24.6 percent in 2002 and 27.3 percent in 2003; Marshall had 18.8 percent in 2002 and 20.46 percent in 2003; Tilden had 22.9 percent in 2002 and 20.2 percent in 2003; Westinghouse had 6.7 percent in 2002 and 8 percent in 2003; and Austin had 24.4 percent in 2002 and 42 percent in 2003.

Gradually, the city is building a two-tiered system, one for middle-class and affluent students who can pass tests and another for those who cannot and those in special education.

Section 8.5 Abolishing and Reorganizing

In August 1995, Gery Chico, president of the new School Reform Board of Trustees for CPS and Paul Vallas, CEO, abolished the eleven subdistricts and reorganized CPS into six regions, each composed of approximately 100 schools. Two former SAS principals were appointed to the position of regional education officer, Hazel B. Steward and Sherye Garmony-Miller. Both promoted the effective schools model. Dr. Steward was appointed to Region Three,[11] which at that time had the largest number of schools on the state's warning list. Most of these schools were placed on academic probation later by the CEO. During the 1996–1997 school year, Dr. Steward organized her own program for the initiation, implementation and institutionalization of STR.

Region Three was bounded on the east by Lake Michigan, and on the west by the city limits. Its northern boundary was 400 North Madison Street and southern boundary 2200 South. The region encompassed the Westside of Chicago, where the most economically depressed residents are plagued by high unemployment, intense poverty, substandard housing, abandoned buildings, absentee landlords and vacant lots. In 1968, this area was hardest hit by the riots following the assassination of Martin Luther King, Jr. These communities have never fully recovered. Moreover, the communities which constitute the West side (of Chicago) are characterized by gangs, gang and domestic violence, drugs, teen pregnancy, drugs and alcohol abuse. In spite of these demographic data, Dr. Steward brought academic success to many schools through her leadership in Region Three.

During Dr. Steward's tenure, 1995-2001, Region Three served eighty-seven schools and ten Child Parent Centers and was located in two Empowerment Zones, which include U.S. Census Zones 26, 27, 29, 30, 31 and 33, all low–income areas prone to crime and violence. In the 1999–2000 school year there were 55,000 children in the Region Three schools in grades kindergarten through twelve. More than 95 percent of the students were eligible for free or reduced lunch.

In 1995, thirty-four schools in Region Three were on academic probation; in addition, forty-one were on the state's Academic Watch List. In total, there were 148 CPS schools on the list. A school was placed on probation when less than 15 percent (and later 20 percent) of its students scored at or above the national norms on the ITBS in the elementary schools or the TAP in high schools. Schools were placed on the state's Academic Watch List when they failed to make progress over three years on the Illinois Goal Assessment Program (IGAP) and when less than 50 percent of their students had an average score at or above the state's average on all subtests. No other region had as many schools on probation and/or on the Watch List as did Region Three.

Having previously served as principal of Tilden High School, Dr. Steward took her extremely competent team with her when she assumed her new responsibilities. Dr. Steward used both corporate and educational research to buttress her "team" philosophy. Utilizing a "team" concept as an integral part of her planning process, her first task was to assist the Region Three staff in developing such a philosophy. Each team member brought special talents, and their combined experience as professionals in educating children totaled more than 200 years. The original team had expertise in mathematics, science, social studies, language arts, special education, elementary education, bilingual education and counseling. They cross-trained each other in these skills. Dr. Steward called them her A+ Team. The Region Three motto was, "Everyone does Everything."

Region Three's mission was to provide support, resources, direction and leadership to the schools, to assist them in establishing teaching and learning goals consistent with CPS and the State of Illinois's academic standards; and to help schools achieve those goals by providing a comprehensive professional development plan.

The Region Three Education Plan, completed in September 1995, was designed and intended to increase student achievement; reduce the dropout rate; improve student attendance; maximize resources provided by the Region; foster a safe and secure school and community environment; encourage parental and community partnerships; promote professional development collaboration; and facilitate school leadership. The Region Three Achievement Structure (R3AS) used as its framework the STR. The Region Three staff was trained in STR, its process and its philosophy. During the first year of operation (1995–1996) twenty-two schools agreed to work with the Region on a purely voluntary basis to improve instruction and school achievement.

There is much evidence in education research that indicates that the average growth rate is .75 years of growth for .75 years of instruction. The year-one test data for the R3AS schools was phenomenal. In many cases the growth rate doubled, and in several it tripled, according to grade equivalency expectations in terms of months of growth compared to months of instruction. However, it was found that growth in the percentage of students at or above national norms was not evident. This perceived discrepancy occurred because there was an increase in the number of students in the lower two quartiles, who were raising their scores within the quartile range or even going from quartile one to quartile two. Yet the percentage of students at or above the national norms did not show an increase, because students are not considered to be at the national norm until they have moved into the third quartile or are above the top of the second quartile. This success yielded an increase in the number of participating schools from twenty-two to thirty-five for the 1996–1997 school year, and to forty-five during the 1998–1999 school year.

Professional development was conducted by Region Three principals, teachers, career service personnel, educational support staff, the A+ Team, and outside consultants. The "trainer of trainers" model was used, which places monitoring and implementation responsibilities into the hands of the principal and the school staff. This work was very demanding on the A+ Team, so it was important for the team to receive continual renewal for the uplift of their spirits. In Region Three rarely were the leader and the team builder the same person. It was important that leaders understood that they could not conduct the workshops and build the team at the same time, because it would seem that the leader was not a part of the team.

During the 1996–1997 school year Region Three conducted a two-tiered program. The Phase II schools received their initial training in the R3AS process to improve student achievement, while Phase I schools focused on surmounting challenges not resolved in the first year. The A+ Team facilitated two separate series of workshops to accommodate the schools, one series of workshops for high schools and three series of workshops for elementary schools. The school site visits to help school staff monitor the program continued, and the schools continued to improve.

Funds came from Title One discretionary sources, Comprehensive School Reform allocations, foundations and grants. Initially, three schools participated: Emmet, Spencer and Ellington elementary schools. Of these, Spencer was the largest, and sent twenty-two teachers to the first training session of the Sesame Program at the University of Chicago, which gave training for elementary and high school mathematics teachers so that they were equipped to teach mathematics at a higher level while earning a mathematics endorsement from the state at Illinois. One of the reasons that STR was chosen was its compatibility with any instructional program.

In addition to the staff development provided by R3AS during the regular school year, each summer there was a focus on the Assessment Routine for schools near the cut-off point for both the probation and the state's Watch List. Teachers and administrators needed to know the outcomes of the previous year's ITBS, TAP and IGAP. Schools also needed to find ways to assist teachers who were having difficulty in teaching specific skills, especially reading and mathematics. Both of the highest-scoring SAS schools, Kellman Corporate Community School and grades seventh and eighth at Crane Technical High School, were in Region Three.

Region Three decreased the number of schools on probation from thirty-two to seventeen, from 29.4 percent to 21.7 percent of the citywide total, during 1995 to 1999. During the 1998–1999 school year, twenty-six CPS schools were removed from probation. Included in this number were ten schools from Region Three, including the first 100 percent African American high school, Collins. Unfortunately, Collins's principal, Clement Smith, retired in January, 1999. The faculty and the Region thought that the assistant principal, Learna Baker-Brewer, would be selected because she had been the spearhead behind Collins's move off probation. Instead, two teachers opposed to her tenure convinced the Local School Council to choose another person. Ms. Baker-Brewer transferred. Several excellent teachers followed her to Tilden, and turmoil reigned at Collins for the entire school year. Finally, the CEO had to remove the contract principal and place an interim principal in the school. By that time the damage had been done. Collins was back on probation.

Turmoil reigned at Collins under the new principal selected by the LSC. Teachers protested the new regime in letter writing campaigns to the Chief Educational Officer and the CEO. The new principal, although an exceedingly bright former assistant principal and educator, could not pull the teacher's together. She was eventually replaced and the school was subsequently subjected to intervention, a process where a team of administrators and subject specialists are assigned to the school to bring about change in order to elevate and accelerate student achievement. This took place during the 2001–2002 school year. The trouble with the intervention process was that: (1) it removed the principal from the day-to-day operations of the school because she was mandated to observe every teacher five times before the school year ended; (2) the Intervention team leader was in charge of day-to-day operations; yet, there was nothing in the union contract to support her authority over teachers; (3) responsibility for discipline routines were ambiguous; and (4) no extra time was allocated to the schedule, nor was the length of the teachers' day increased. Intervention was abandoned as a failure when Arne Duncan became CEO in 2001.

During each academic year from 1995 to 1999, Region Three either matched or exceeded the citywide gains in reading. The greatest growth differential noted during this period was during the 1998–1999 academic year, where Region Three elementary schools demonstrated growth of 3.4 percent to the city's 1.8 percent in third through eighth grade for students at or above the national norms. The most significant growth occurred during the 1997–1998 school year. Both the city and Region Three posted an increase of approximately 4 percent growth in third through eighth grade for students at or above the national norms. In mathematics, Region Three schools outperformed the city, with the exception of the 1996–1997 school year. However, during this year Region Three elementary schools showed an average 4 percent growth in the percentage of third through eighth graders at or above the national norm in mathematics on the ITBS. The largest differential between the city and Region Three occurred during the 1998–1999 academic year when Region Three elementary schools posted an average growth of approximately 6.5 percent to the city's 4.9 percent.

During academic year 1995–1996, both the city and Region Three experienced a decline in the percentage of high school students at or above national norms in reading. Citywide, students slipped by approximately 3 percent and Region Three by less than 1 percent. The greatest yearly growth differential occurred during the 1998–1999 academic year, for Region Three high schools which posted an average growth of 10 percent to the city's 4 percent on ninth and eleventh grade students' scores at or above the national norms in reading. As in the reading scores, both the city and Region Three experienced a decline in the percentage of ninth and eleventh grade students at or above the national norms in mathematics. The city slipped by approximately 4 percent and Region Three slipped by approximately 3 percent. The greatest yearly growth differential occurred during the 1998–1999 academic year. Region Three high schools posted an average growth of 14 percent to the city's 11 percent in ninth and eleventh grade students at or above the national norms in mathematics.

Thirty–five schools that had been consistently involved in R3AS and other Region Three academic improvement programs exceeded the entire Region by almost 1.5 percentage points in reading growth and the CPS by 4.5 percentage points in reading growth. Similar results are evident for mathematics. The group of schools that continuously participated in Region Three's professional development programs surpassed the Region's growth by 2.5 percentage points in reading and 3.5 percentage points in mathematics.

Dr. Hazel B. Steward retired from CPS in July 2001. She left a rich legacy to her successor, Marietta Skyles. In July 2002, Arne Duncan, the newly appointed CEO, abolished the six regions and created twenty–four Instructional Areas. Region Three was subdivided into four sections, each with its own Area Instructional Officer (AIO).

Section 8.6 Corporate Community School of America

The Corporate Community School of America (CCSA), later named the Joseph Kellman Corporate Community School, was founded in 1988 by Joseph Kellman, chairman and CEO of Globe Group, along with Vernon R. Loucks, Jr., Chairman and CEO of Baxter International. The school was founded in an effort to create a partnership between schools and corporate funding to improve education for children. The principal of Kellman in 1999 was Dr. Rollie Outlaw Jones,[13] an energetic, highly qualified committed educator with a vision of excellence and a mission of change, who later became the AIO in Area Eight.

Kellman operated a year-round academic calendar, an eleven-month school year and a seven-hour school day. Students were selected based on a lottery from the Lawndale area, and kindergarten through sixth grade progress was reported through a narrative format, as opposed to letter grades. Seventh and eighth graders received letter grades, which were transferable to high school. This had been the procedure for CCSA since its opening. Talks of negotiation with CPS started in 1991 when Ted Kimbrough was superintendent and concluded under Superintendent Argie Johnson in 1994.

In the spring of 1994, prior to the merger with CPS, Dr. Louis Gatta, Educational Consultant Associate, administered the ITBS to grades three through eight. Dr. Gatta concluded that the generally weak 1994 results, when carefully analyzed, showed that "students were capable of higher achievement levels." But he said, to achieve better results the school needed to substantially improve its instructional monitoring system, teacher development programs, and instructional programs for language arts, mathematics, social studies and science. In the fall of 1994, Kellman Corporate Community School opened as a Chicago public school and continued with the seven-hour academic program and eleven-month school year. Children continued to come from the Lawndale area, as well as from the Garfield Park and Austin areas.

In order to ascertain the academic ability of the students in grades three through eight, the ITBS was administered in October 1994. The results were quite discouraging. The vision of the founders was not evident in the test scores. Twenty-two percent of the students scored at or above the national norm in reading and 24 percent of the students scored at or above the national norm in mathematics. The results of this test correlated closely with the results produced by Dr. Gatta, and the staff agreed that the school needed to improve its instructional program, instructional monitoring and teacher professional development.

In order to address the documented deficit, Kellman teachers, staff and the principal decided to focus on the instructional program. During the 1994–1995 school year, they viewed the number of programs that they hoped would increase student achievement in reading and mathematics. One of the specific programs in which there was much interest was SAS.

During the summer of 1995, the Kellman staff attended the SAS workshop, which focused on the Ten Routines, site-based management, the Instructional Leadership Team (ILT), and the in-house coordinator. As a staff, Kellman felt the SAS program would help to improve their achievement in reading and mathematics. They were assured that adherence to the Ten Routines would enhance student achievement through analysis of skills, reinforcement, grouping/regrouping, measuring growth, alternative learning environment, lessons that would elicit student participation, ongoing monitoring/evaluation and improvement of teachers' competencies.

In the fall of 1996, Kellman opened as an SAS school. In order to prepare for this new program and school year, skill charts were developed in reading, mathematics and writing for all grade levels. Skill charts were also developed for social studies and science in fourth and seventh grades. The item analysis for the ITBS was utilized to develop the charts. Every classroom received skill charts consisting of thirty to forty skills that had to be mastered prior to standardized testing.

An SAS Planning Team was formed. Each member of the team was responsible for at least two of the routines. The core planning team also met with the SAS coordinator who was in the school three or four times a week as a site resource and/or support person. The core planning team, along with the coordinator, developed the initial program design that was the blueprint for the Kellman SAS Program. The ten routines remained the driving force behind the blueprint design and they were implemented across the curriculum. This process was facilitated in each routine.

Assessment data for all students were given to teachers in July and the ITBS student analysis report was individual and by class. These data were used to assess areas needing remediation. During August staff development, Kellman staff reviewed data or made plans for student placement and finalized the instructional program. The Illinois Student Achievement Test (ISAT, which replaced IGAP), results were shared as soon as they were made available to the school. The results were used to make decisions concerning student remediation needs for ISAT test mastery. All students in grades four through eight had a section in the school agenda book, which contained a personal skills chart. They were responsible for the maintenance of their own charts. Teachers and students reviewed progress made as well as areas needing remediation and enrichment.

Every five weeks the teachers sent home a progress report. School-wide reading and mathematics diagnostic assessment tests (Stanford) were administered in September. The results from these tests were used for grouping and regrouping in the classroom. School-wide reading and mathematics assessment tests were administered every five weeks to assess students' progress. Copies of charted results were given to the principal.

Students were initially grouped according to the ITBS results in reading and mathematics. They were regrouped by mastery of skills. Students with non-mastered skills/concepts were given additional time for skill focus, which included: (1) individualized tutoring before and after school; and (2) tutoring by teaching assistants and high school/college student tutors who provided additional help during the school day. Prior to the school's opening, the special education teacher developed special education students' schedules and Individual Educational Plans (IEPs). The classroom teacher adjusted the special education student's classroom instruction to reflect the IEP. In September, ISAT test results were used to address further placement in mastered and non-mastered skill areas.

SAS charts were completed prior to the first day of class; showing mastered and non-mastered skills, individualized student charts monitored by the students; and SAS room charts with timelines to identify skills/concepts to be learned in the 1998–1999 school year. During the first week of school this routine was reviewed with all Kellman students. Individualized student charts were reviewed. Emphasis was placed on the need for students to master all non-mastered skills by January 31, prior to ISAT testing. Planned student enrichment activities were in place to further enhance the skills/concepts mastered.

The principal, assistant principal and SAS Leadership Team were responsible for overall monitoring of the SAS Program. The chairpersons of each routine were assigned for the school year. The SAS Leadership Team's responsibility was to monitor progress on the implementation of these routines. The administration evaluated teacher performance in the following areas: charts, pacing, assessment, and instruction. Bi-weekly update meetings were held to assess progress in each routine and also to address concerns.

The school's staff determined the tools that were used during the school year for kindergarten through eighth grade to address ITBS, IGAP and Chicago framework/standards skills concepts in need of remediation. Test Best, IGAP Coach (reading, mathematics, science, social studies), IGAP Review, and IGAP Writing (paragraph, essay) were all considered. "Scoring High on the ITBS Test," "Taking the Terror out of ITBS," CRTs, Bridging the GAP SRA Comprehension/Math for fifth week assessments, "Specific Skill Kit," "Math the Write Way" and "Teacher Made Tests" were used. Each classroom teacher established his or her own test banks. Kellman staff reviewed and updated these test banks yearly.

Kellman's school-wide discipline rules and consequences for violation were reviewed and established for the school year. Classroom rules, rewards and consequences had been established for grades kindergarten through eight. Large school-wide rules and consequences were posted in the hallways and the cafeteria. The administration met with students in the primary grades kindergarten through third, and intermediate/upper grades to review: school-wide discipline, student agenda books, bus discipline, SAS routines, instructional programs, classroom management procedures, school uniform and/or appropriate dress and the student contract.

An all-parents meeting was held at the beginning of the school year. At this meeting the following were discussed: rules and policies, parent involvement programs, the Malcolm X Satellite College Program at Kellman, preparation of children for ITBS and IGAP (ISAT) testing, effective use of agenda books, school fees, staff and responsibilities, ITBS and IGAP(ISAT) test results, instructional programs, IASA parent programs, school uniforms and/or appropriate dress, uniform discipline code, student contracts and the SAS program.

The discipline rules were posted in the hallways and were sent home to parents the first week of school. An in-school suspension program was established. Students assigned to in-school suspension reported to the assistant principal. Chronic violators were identified and measures implemented to address misbehavior. A review of classroom management procedures was completed prior to the opening of school. All classroom teachers completed the skill chart information. All charts were in place prior to the first day of school.

Instructional materials and supplies for the school year were distributed to teachers on staff development day in August. Teacher preparation schedules were developed, duplicated and distributed to teachers by the second week of school. Skill groups and skill charts were established in classrooms for grouping and regrouping for the first to the fifth week. Procedures for instruction were reviewed during the March/April workshops. They included how to develop instructional tests; how to develop and maintain a good classroom climate; how to develop and maintain good classroom discipline; how to deal with chronically misbehaving children, how to utilize materials and plan lessons with African American cultural experiences; and how to monitor and maintain skill charts and folders. During the August 1998 staff development days, instructional time was also allotted.

The school-wide curriculum program was enhanced with the addition of: school-wide phonics; an integrated computer curriculum program (satellite and internet); departmental instruction for sixth through eighth graders; foreign language instruction; music instruction (individualized and band); Junior Achievement and high school/college tutors; Mercantile Exchange Experiences for sixth through eighth graders; Hands on Science with Columbia College; Intensive Writing Program; competitive activities such as Academic Olympics, Spelling Bee, Science Fair; Bank at School Program; and Junior Great Books program.

The effectiveness of Kellman's instructional program was the focus of half-day staff development workshops. They reviewed their instructional programs, added new ones and terminated others. Evaluation criteria for the instructional program were reviewed and established for the school year.

A Kellman School survey was developed by the leadership team. The staff completed the survey in May. Staff development workshops—led by teachers and consultants—for areas of need were established. Staff development days were on Fridays from 12:45 to 2:30 P.M. Staff development survey sheets were developed for the 1998–1999 school year to assess the effectiveness and usefulness of workshops.

With the 1998–1999 SAS Leadership Team in place, the principal and team worked to prepare staff during the half-day in-services for the school year. Parents and Local School Council members were included in the decision-making. Decisions were made and supported by the staff at Kellman. The principal had the final word on all deliberations, made the final decision and followed through on their implementation.

Kellman continued to elevate and accelerate its students' academic achievement and the staff has received recognition for their growth in reading and mathematics scores for the past several years. Kellman was the first SAS school to reach the 50th percentile in reading and mathematics. Their growth has been continuous since September 1994. Their goal is to reach the ninetieth percentile.

In 1995, only 25.9 percent of Kellman's students scored at or above the national norm in reading on the ITBS, rising to 51.3 percent in 1999 and to 72.1 percent in 2001. In mathematics, the rise was from 39.5 percent in 1995 to 68.8 percent in 2001. In its study, "Left Behind: Student Achievement in Chicago's Public Schools" the Civic Committee of the Commercial Club of Chicago described the schools in Area Eight:

In Area Eight, there are two schools, Irving and Kellman, whose 2002 ISAT results meet or exceed Illinois's 40 percent target for 2002 in all demographic groups in both reading and mathematics. Two schools, Dvorak and Jensen, meet the state target in reading, but will need to make six to seven point gains in mathematics in 2003. One additional school, Plamondon, meets the state target in mathematics, but needs to make two to three point gains in reading in 2003 to comply with Adequate Yearly Progress (AYP) requirements. On the other end of the performance spectrum, 15 of 25 schools will need to make seven to nine point gains in reading to meet AYP requirements. And, 19 of 25 schools will need to make similar gains in mathematics to meet No Child Left Behind (NCLB) expectations. Gains of between one and six points will need to be made by six schools in reading and by three schools in mathematics.

Even though Dr. Jones had proven that she knew how to create and sustain a high–achieving, predominantly African American school that served low-income students, she must comply with the system's programs and mandates.

Section 8.7   Tests of Achievement and Proficiency
Crane and Melver Scott

The principal of Crane Technical High School is an energetic, insightful, determined educator named Melver Scott. On the Tests of Achievement and Proficiency (TAP), administered in CPS every spring, Crane has progressed from 8.5 percent at or above the national norms in reading comprehension for grades nine and eleven combined in 1991 to 41 percent in 2002. When Crane Tech High School joined the SAS, its student population of 1,305 was comprised of 98.6 percent Blacks, 1 percent Hispanics and .04 percent whites. Located in the western part of Chicago, 94.6 percent of these students were from low-income families. The student dropout rate at Crane during that year, 1996–1997, was cited at 31 percent by the 1997 school report card.

Making changes at Crane required interaction and coordination across offices, programs and disciplines. Collaborative work across programs and disciplines helped the departments better coordinate and integrate the provisions needed to assist Crane's students in preparing for the TAP.

Under the principal's leadership and the guidance of the Instructional Leadership Team, a school profile based on students' test analyses was set up. An item analysis was provided each department. Timelines were constructed and skills/concepts mastery were aligned with state goals and CPS objectives. Departmental examinations were developed and given each quarter. Students who were at or above grade levels were identified and the grouping process began.

When Crane was without a coordinator during the first semester of the 1998–1999 school year, the assistant principal, Dr. Loretta Lawrence, took charge of the implementation of this routine with Dr. Christina Stringfellow. Testing schedules and test preparation materials were set and selected and

271

personnel appointed for coordination of them until a coordinator was made available. In the end, Crane was fortunate to have Phedonia Johnson, the former director of project CANAL, as a part–time coordinator. Ms. Johnson was also the former principal of Goldblatt Elementary, which had made progress using both Birect instruction and the Socratic Method. Additionally, Ms. Johnson served as the first director of the enormously successful DePaul Prep Program when it was funded by McDonalds and called McPrep. She is presently the National Director of One Church One School.

Methods of grouping were researched and evaluated. Strengths and weaknesses of students and teachers were determined. A placement that would effectively meet the needs of all students was selected and operationalized. Grouping with flexibility was established and students were given information about charting their own mastery of skills and concepts.

Careful consideration was given to the placement of special education students in regular education classes, to achieve the least restrictive environment. Students were placed by graduation needs, course needs and the number of students in the class. Individual Education Plan (IEP) needs were incorporated into this matrix. Administrators monitored information about the special education students to make sure they were available to the programmer so that large numbers of these students were not placed in any one regular class. IEPs were reviewed to determine whether or not students could take the TAP and what modifications needed to be made for the students who took it.

A pacing schedule was developed. Levels of mastery were determined and students who did not achieve mastery were identified. Instructional plans to assist students who needed additional help were constructed, including team teaching, tutoring and computerized instruction. Ms. Johnson gave seminars on pacing and acceleration, and modeled the teaching behavior which facilitated this objective and mentored teachers who failed to adopt such options. Her reports reflected this concern. In one, she planned a modeling activity for a teacher who stayed in his seat the entire period of observation. She noted that teachers did not, on the whole, assign projects to independent learners or use them in cooperative learning group endeavors. Mr. Scott also noted these teachers and recommended professional development for them to SAS.

A monitoring team was created and established and a monitoring schedule was implemented. Staff development for understanding the purpose of monitoring was conducted. Instant and constant feedback was given to faculty and staff. The principal, his administrative team and his teachers monitored the implementation of STR at Crane. Each member submitted a report of his or her monitoring to Dr. Lawrence and their summaries were thoroughly discussed in the ILT meetings.

Standardized test data were analyzed and provided to all faculty. Pre-test sample data were given; skills/concepts were incorporated in lesson plans and tested for mastery. A well-organized system of administering and grading the five-week assessments was in place at Crane and was overseen by the ILT. Reports of these tests were discussed in both the ILT and the departmental meetings. When teachers were found not to be using the same tests for the same subjects, creating all sorts of problems with validity and reliability, the principal and the ILT considered the use of Kinney & Associates or Abacus to generate tests for all students in a course such as English I. Professional development sessions were held around the construction of five-week assessments to preserve their reliability and validity.

Staff and students were orientated on school rules and the consequences if violated. Parents were notified of school rules and procedures by meetings and by U.S. mail. School-wide assemblies were held to orientate students and staff. Mentoring, peer intervention, student council and Safe Foundation programs were scheduled and conducted. Rewards and incentives were provided to reinforce positive activities. Severe and excessive problems were referred early.

The principal at Crane was very concerned about discipline and attendance at the high school, and constantly sought ways to improve them. Since freshmen disproportionately were involved in school rule violations, their problems were often the topic of discussion at both ILT and departmental meetings. Staff tried to identify attendance problems upon entry. At one ILT meeting, a faculty member recommended that students with attendance problems be assigned to an advisory and given special attention from a division teacher who was aware of their needs and from a counselor who could tend to their problems.

This advisory was held every day for seventeen minutes of the twenty-seven minute division. Every student at Crane had an advisory. On Monday and Friday the focus was on character development and self-esteem. On Tuesday, it was on mathematics. On Wednesday and Thursday the emphasis was on reading and language arts. Two or three adults were present in every advisory. Although a majority of the teachers supported them, others felt overwhelmed. Administrators, SAS coordinators and department chairs all assisted these teachers.

Another ILT member proposed that these students meet once a month with a group of high school seniors who could help them to develop habits of good attendance and punctuality. Hall sweeps occurred on a regular basis. So did parental involvement. At one point, when the deposit of garbage and refuse increased in the halls, the principal determined that hall walkers had increased. During the hall sweeps, the transgressors were collected and given brooms to clean the halls they had previously been walking, instead of attending class. While this approach is no doubt controversial, it did decrease the hall walkers at Crane.

Curriculum materials were selected to develop lessons that matched students' needs for mastering prioritized skills and concepts. Teachers' procedures were demonstrated as well as students' procedures. Professional development was scheduled and conducted on instructional techniques. Adequate teaching materials and supplies were made available and distributed. Lesson plans included relevant African American history, culture and life in each lesson and aligned outcomes and state goals. An abundance of supplementary and auxiliary materials were available in the library.

Data were compared and analyzed from TAP. Pacing charts and timelines were reviewed. Professional development activities were considered. Ongoing teacher conferences were held. Teacher evaluation was clearly explained and student achievement was an important criterion in that evaluation. Five-week assessments were always evaluated to determine what had been learned from what had been taught during that time period. Close attention was paid to pacing and acceleration, since there was an intense desire to move the students out of the bottom quartile and into the second or third quartile, and to move those from the second and third quartiles into the third and fourth quartiles. The effectiveness of programs was determined by the students' success on all tests. Only the principal could evaluate teachers.

Needs were surveyed school–wide, departmentally and individually. These needs were ranked and prioritized. A school calendar was established. Internal strengths of departments and individuals were identified and explored. Experiences were provided to meet the needs of staff, students, parents and community. SAS brought in strong experts in each field in addition to the coordinators and the supervisor.

An Instructional Leadership Team (ILT) was formed, composed of representatives of all school actors. Problems were identified; solutions were posed; information was shared. In addition, suggestions and strategies for teaching were designed. Among the topics discussed during the 1998–1999 school year were the following: staff development; Impact Visit, the review of STR; responsibilities of ILT members; five-week assessments; assignments to committees for STR routines (there was a committee for each routine); housekeeping; beautification; small group tutoring; and English, math and reading progress reports.

Melver Scott's leadership of this enterprise has proved successful over the years, from this imminent beginning. Persistent in his efforts to elevate achievement, Mr. Scott has pursued his goals through STR.

Section 8.8 Spencer Mathematics and Science Academy

Spencer Mathematics and Science Academy is an elementary school located in what is known in Chicago as the Austin community. According to its former principal, Dr. Sandra A. Givens, it was once a thriving middle-class neighborhood. Now it is a community of predominantly single-parent households, fraught with drugs and gang violence and teeming with children needing to be loved.

The school consists of two large buildings, one built near the turn of the century, featuring an addition built some sixty years later, and another building on the west side of the campus built in 1970 as a temporary structure with nineteen classrooms. The two buildings house more than 1,350 children in grades pre-K–eighth. Each day about 125 staff members, including assistant principals, counselors, teachers, teacher's assistants, engineers, business managers, clerks, security officers, janitors and lunchroom staff, and fifteen to twenty parent volunteers, join forces to teach the multitude of students.

In 1991, when Dr. Givens became the principal, Spencer was a troubled school setting. The principal had been removed and the LSC was sharply divided. Parents had lost confidence in the school. Dr. Givens was the consummate counselor, having served as the administrator of guidance and counseling for 900 elementary and high school counselors in the CPS. To tap this gift further, Vallas chose her to head the Teacher Evaluation Unit in his Office of Accountability.

To bring order and discipline to her school, Givens executed many strategies and activities, such as: (1) instituting an open door policy for staff and parents; (2) conducting an open dialogue with the LSC on a regular basis; (3) visiting each classroom, since there was no PA system in either building; (4) meeting with staff individually on a regular basis; (5) responding to the concerns of the Principal Professional Advisory Committee (PPAC); (6) planning and implementing the Open House and Report Card Pick Up event, raffling turkeys to encourage participation; (7) providing pizza parties for students with the highest percent attendance at Report Card Pick-up; (8) holding holiday luncheons and giving gifts to parent volunteers; (9) supporting PTA dinners and meetings; (10) encouraging teachers to attend Christmas celebrations for the purpose of developing a "family atmosphere;" (11) meeting with parents individually and addressed their concerns; and (12) planning a summer retreat on Cooperative Learning.

During the 1992–1993 school year, a uniform policy was instituted. This, together with the activities and strategies described above, improved the discipline in this large and previously troubled school. Givens then set her sights on the academic arena.

At one of my workshops at CANAL, Dr. Givens heard about SAS and joined. The LSC voted unanimously to initiate the Ten Routines during the 1993–1994 school year. After a two-week SAS training workshop in the summer of 1993, a leadership team was organized, consisting of an equal number of "for" and "against" staff members.

Kay Lovelace Taylor, then of the Detroit Public Schools, and later to be assistant superintendent of Philadelphia Public Schools and professor at Temple University, conducted the workshop on team building that summer. Spencer's participants felt that the SAS training afforded them an excellent insight into the process and allowed teachers who needed reassurance to work together and to develop relationships with others with whom they had not bonded in the two years of Givens's tenure.

In September 1993, members of the Leadership Team in-serviced the total staff on the SAS process. Student test data was disaggregated. Common planning time was scheduled for each grade level. The curriculum was aligned and pacing charts were developed. Each staff member was mandated to belong to one of the teams addressing the Ten Routines. Leadership members served as chairpersons. Teachers who were not performing and needed assistance were identified as "focused teachers." Kymara Chase was the first coordinator for SAS at Spencer. During the 1992–1995 school year, Spencer was on the move.

Using the item analysis from the 1993–1994 ITBS, teachers disaggregated data, classified the items, identified the skills that were mastered by the students and made profile charts of each student, as well as each subject matter taught in the class. Quarterly reading and math tests were established. Tests for the end-of-the-year assessment to assist with placement were ordered and administered.

Students transferring into Spencer were administered the same placement test prior to classroom placement. A coordinated system of grouping students with similar strengths and weaknesses within the grade level was implemented. Pacing schedules were revised to meet the needs of individual students and classrooms (monthly outlays). Strategies to elevate students to grade level, including acceleration of instruction, were utilized. A complete school-wide calendar for 1994–1995 was constructed.

Individual skill and concepts to be taught at each grade level were collaboratively determined before the school year began (learning outcomes of the SIP). Long-range planning of instruction-pacing schedules were established. Pacing schedules to meet the needs of individual students and classrooms were revised. Strategies to elevate and accelerate student academic achievement were implemented.

A monitoring team and schedule were established. The team observed, assessed and discussed strengths and weaknesses with the focused teachers to promote change and improvement. The team held weekly meetings to discuss common problems.

Quarterly whole-school testing results with item analyses were returned to classroom teachers for charting of skill mastery. Teacher made assessments of skill mastery at individual grade levels at regular intervals, administered, then charted.

A behavior management program was implemented. School-wide discipline procedures were revised. An in-school suspension room was opened. A computerized discipline system was established. A hall monitor (parent volunteer) hotsheet procedure was developed for disruptive students. A positive self-image mentoring program was implemented for students with special needs. Activities were developed that were to be completed while students were assigned to the in-school suspension room.

Common time grade level preparation periods were allowed every day. A Math Specialist was added to improve mathematics instruction. A Curriculum Specialist was created to coordinate instruction. A teacher resource center was created. Science and social studies concepts were correlated to streamline instruction. A textbook committee was established to review textbooks purchases. Skills taught at each grade level were reviewed to establish correlated and accelerated instruction.

Outside evaluation of instruction, process and classroom management were reported to all pertinent staff. Teachers, teacher's assistants and other personnel were regularly evaluated for job performance, with remediation plans developed for focused individuals. Programs were semiannually evaluated for effectiveness and continued need.

A year-long schedule for staff development opportunities was established. Plans for a yearly retreat were established. Staff development needs were semiannually surveyed. In addition, staff development activities were planned and implemented for staff while students were engaged in alternative activities.

A steering committee was established to coordinate ideas and activities for SAS. All staff members were asked to serve on at least one committee. Grade levels met twice a week to voice concerns and make suggestions, and grade level chairs met twice a month to voice concerns and make suggestions. A PPAC reflective of all teaching personnel was established. Parent volunteers met monthly to voice concerns and offer suggestions about school matters. After receiving recommendations from the above groups, the principal, with the support of the LSC, implemented the decisions made.

At the end of the 1994–1995 school year, Spencer's principal and staff were very excited about their accomplishments. However, when the state's Watch List was published, Spencer appeared on it. The magic number then was 50 percent; that is 50 percent of the students in any given school were required to meet state goals. Spencer was at 49.3 percent on the Illinois Grade Assessment Program (IGAP), up from 38 percent the previous year. Progress proved hard to achieve because Spencer was such a large school. In fact, supporters of the Small Schools Initiative (SSI) predicted that Spencer would not achieve its goal.

On October 18, 1995, SAS conducted an Impact Visit at Spencer. The Impact Visit involves a number of SAS coordinators observing in every classroom to determine compliance with the Ten Routines. Spencer had a higher percentage of strengths than it did weaknesses. Immediately, the principal and staff increased the activities and strategies for each routine. Classrooms were monitored on a daily basis. Although some of the teachers were committed to their responsibilities, others required constant monitoring for effective implementation of the routines.

The role of the principal was massive, with fifty-two classroom teachers, twenty-three ancillary personnel, and thirty-three educational support personnel, conducting a six-hour school day with 1,200 students. To provide assistance, the LSC approved the hiring of a second assistant principal. A school-within-a-school was established for the sixth, seventh, and eighth grades. The new assistant principal was responsible for monitoring these grades on a regular basis. The other assistant principal was assigned to grades three, four and five, while a lead teacher continued her responsibilities as the administrator of the primary building of pre-kindergarten, kindergarten and grades one and two. This arrangement provided the principal an opportunity to spend more time with the focused teachers, with the assistance of the SAS coordinator.

The 1995–1996 school year ended successfully. Spencer was removed from the state's Watch List. Sixty-one percent of Spencer's students reached or exceeded state goals, as tested by IGAP. In addition, though CPS had placed many schools on probation and remediation based on the results from the ITBS, Spencer escaped by a narrow margin. The cutoff score was 15 percent at or above the norm, and Spencer had 15.4 percent. Of course, this was not something to brag about, but it was important for them to stay off probation.

Many new strategies and activities were added to the Ten Routines at Spencer. Morale increased and the collaborative spirit usually attributed to small schools was manifest there. By 1999, Spencer had risen from 15.4 percent at or above the state norm in reading to 24.6 percent, and from 20.6 percent at or above the state norm in mathematics to 41.1 percent.

The principal left the school in 2000 to become director of Teacher Evaluation in the Office of Accountability. A new principal was chosen by the LSC. By 2002, Spencer had risen to 29.8 percent in reading and 36.8 percent in mathematics. In 1998, before changing the state tests, 45 percent of Spencer's third graders met or exceeded the state goals in reading, compared to 10 percent in 1994 and 82 percent exceeded state goals in mathematics in 1998, compared to 21 percent in 1994. All grades improved on the IGAP, but not as well as the third graders in reading. This tremendous improvement in the third grade boosted spirits and encouraged teachers and staff to continue their hard work. Most schools plummet in achievement after principals move; yet, Spencer seems to be staying on an upward trajectory.

Kymara Chase conducted a case study of Spencer Elementary School during the years 1996 to 1999 to determine whether or not the delivery of instruction using the Ten Routines was effective at the school and whether or not the Ten Routines were institutionalized. Chase concluded that student achievement did increase during the first three years of using the ten routines.

The ITBS scores increased overall, according to the Chicago Board of Education's 1999 report from the Office of Accountability website, from 11.8 percent at or above the norm in reading in 1993 to 24.4 percent in 1999, and from 8.5 percent in Mathematics in 1993 to 41.1 percent in 1999. On the IGAP, improvement was best in third grade, as noted above, remained about the same in the sixth grade, and was worst in the eighth grade, where there was a decline from 57 percent meeting or exceeding the state goals to 47 percent; although, this was a rise from a low of 36 percent in 1996.

Chase also found that eight of the Ten Routines were institutionalized, while discipline and instruction remained in the implementation stage. This study showed that large schools can improve, with more resources, time and staff.

Section 8.9   External Partners

According to Hess and Cytrynbaum[14] "the decision to involve outside contractors to provide assistance to schools on probation, through the institution of probation managers and external partners in both elementary and high schools, was a significant break with the past when outside forces were not welcomed into Chicago's schools." Although STR/SAS entered prior to this breakthrough and involved more than schools on probation, this welcome of outsiders was appreciated. The new Duncan administration is also appreciative of outsiders, but more prejudiced toward the University of Chicago in its major decision-making and much more secretive about its negotiations and tends toward white and rich partners.

Hess and Cytrynbaum found nine external partners serving the thirty-three high schools on some form of probation in 2000. Four of these partners, Accountability, Center for Urban Education, SAS, and Northeastern Illinois University, served twenty-seven schools.

"External partners were charged with improving the instruction of faculties in lower performing high schools. One measure of the success of this effort is whether the number of students reading at the national norms increased among the students in high schools in which they worked," noted Hess and Cytrynbaum. They found that seven of the nine external partners achieved improvement in 2000, but that was "on a per school basis, SAS had the largest gain, an average increase of about eleven students." In addition, they noted that "external partners received much lower ratings for helping to create collaboration between various school leaders and the teachers, with many receiving almost as many negative responses as positive ones. However, Northeastern Illinois University, SAS and Campanile received twice as many positive responses as negative ones."

On May 20, 2001, Dr. Edward T. Klunk, Deputy Officer, North High School Cluster in the Office of High School Development, reported the following to his superiors:

We have all been exposed to the elements of a comprehensive school improvement process. This process is most often viewed as a set of tasks rather than a "way of doing business." There are many models out there to

281

establish a "way of doing business." Principals must be encouraged to select an existing model, or the school must develop their own approach that is inclusive of what research has shown to be effective. Research indicates that for an approach to be effective there are five essential imperatives that principals must practice, leading to authentic and long-lasting change: (1) eliciting the school's values, beliefs and mission; (2) developing best practice, knowledge and commitment; (3) shaping a collaborative vision and goals for the school; (4) developing plans to accomplish school goals; (5) enabling and monitoring the school's action plans. This information is not new and many models are being used in some of our high schools quite effectively. For example, I have observed "The School Achievement Structure," developed by Barbara Sizemore at DePaul University, used very effectively by Crane and Westinghouse. Schools on probation that are supported by university partners have used other models effectively. The issue is that all high schools need a model process for continuous instructional improvement that in the school culture becomes a "way of doing business."[15]

In spite of SAS's successes, it does not rank high on the present administration's list of external partners. The preferences have been noted above. Because this present administration is so secretive, principals do not know what monies they can get or when they can get them. Much of the discretionary money usually allotted to LSCs and schools are now vested in reading specialists and offices for eighteen new Area Instructional Officers. Principals and LSCs are now forever searching their meager budgets for sources of income for funding their many needs. When the CEO says a school has a million dollars, this sounds like a lot. But if that school has advancing gang problems, excessive numbers of special education students, not enough certified teachers, and parents unable or unwilling to help, it is not a lot of money. As long as CPS continues to have one standard staffing pattern it will not meet its goal of No Child Left Behind. A school like Collins High School in the CPS cannot be staffed the same way as Whitney Young Magnet.

No model which emphasizes African American progress can expect the same respect or inclusion as Success for All (SFA). SAS petitioned to join the New American Schools. We were rejected. Yet, the U.S. Department of Education accepts SFA as the accrediting agency for comprehensive school reform models. The School Achievement Structure has higher standards than Success for All, and higher success rates with low-performing predominantly African American high schools. Yet, the imputation of Black inferiority carries on.

CHAPTER 9

ELIMINATING THE ACHIEVEMENT GAP

Section 9.1 White Superiority and Black Inferiority

If the achievement gap between African Americans and whites is to close, more attention must be given to the impact of white supremacy and Black inferiority on the lives of the students. In her article, "Disparate Measures"[1] Lisa Fine asks: "Is racism to blame?" But the question is rhetorical and no answer is given. The author goes on in the next sentence to say "researchers say socioeconomic factors contribute to a student's increased likelihood of needing special education." If poverty, atypical family structures and poor neighborhoods cause the achievement gap, between Blacks and whites then why is there an achievement gap between middl-class and affluent whites and African Americans?

The purpose of this book has been: (1) to stress the importance of the imputation of Black inferiority and white superiority on the achievement gap between Blacks and whites; (2) to seek more research on the impact of white supremacy and the imputation of Black inferiority on the achievement of Black students and any difference in resource distribution, certified teachers, time in school and condition of facilities between schools that are predominantly Black and those that are predominantly white; and (3) to encourage a spirit of struggle against the value of white superiority and its counterpart, Black inferiority.

The residential and school segregation of Black students in the United States caused by white flight is evidence that whites do not want to live or go to school with Blacks. Why? Research rarely attempts to answer this question. Consequently, strategies and approaches for eliminating the achievement gap deal with symptoms rather than causes. If employed teachers and administrators feel that Black students are inferior and cannot learn, they will have low expectations, but moreover they will feel that it is futile to invest a lot of energy into teaching and administration.

Because white supremacy is the overriding value which dominates the social order of Black people, few question it or look for it in research. Researchers, in fact try to hide it, avoid it, and ridicule it—anything but study it. Derek Bok, in an article for more research to discover the causes of this gap, mentioned a few who study this question. He stated, "No one yet knows the precise reasons for [African American] underperformance." But, the Princeton University sociologist, Douglas S. Massey, and his former colleagues at the University of Pennsylvania were making progress, as described in their book, *The Source of the River*. Bok stated that Massey surveyed the experiences of almost 4000 students entering twenty-eight selective colleges in 1999 and discovered little evidence to support the theory, supported by Signithia Fordham, that Black student culture and peer pressure actively discouraged academic success. In Massey's study the Black and Hispanic freshmen were "more likely than white students to have had friends who thought that good grades were important and began college studying harder than their white and Asian classmates." Bok writes that Massey found significant support "for the hypothesis advanced by Claude M. Steele, a Stanford University professor argues that minority students often labor under the suspicion that they are intellectually inferior." Bok opposed remedial programs which confirm minority students' fears of being perceived as intellectually inferior. It is this constant inference of inferiority that affects achievement.

It is hard to find a visibly Black person who has not experienced being seen as inferior in one way or another. Examples of this abound, such as the case where the white woman refused to get on the elevator with a man because he was Black, and she thought he might be a suspected rapist or thief. Black guest speakers are confused with waiters and other menial help; John Hope Franklin, distinguished African American historian and keynote speaker, was once asked by one of the white conference participants to take her coat. Jim Tilmon, an African American airline pilot and CBS television weatherman was once asked to check a passenger's baggage. When a white Boston man who killed his wife accused a Black man of doing it, the police arrested one. Then there was the South Carolina white woman who drove her car into a lake, killing her children, and blamed it on a Black man.

The support speech for segregation and Jim Crow given by Trent Lott of Mississippi, former Majority Senate Leader, at Strom Thurmond's 100th birthday party is another testimonial to the prevalence of white supremacy in American social practice. In addition, the revelation of Thurmond's Black daughter after his death confirms the blatant hypocrisy of white superiority. While Carrie Butler, the mother of Thurmond's daughter, Essie Mae Washington-Williams, was only sixteen at a time in U.S. history when she had no standing or status in the social order of South Carolina, her relationship with Thurmond, who was twenty-two, was not considered statutory rape but an affair by the national media. Moreover, Washington-Williams illustrates the degree of accommodation Black people exhibit, as, in spite of Thurmond's aggressive defense of white supremacy and the oppression of Black people, his "mixed race" daughter was in chronic denial, and as such she became the supreme accommodationist.

Section 9.2   A Distorted System

The curriculum of America's education system is filled with distortions, omissions and false statements regarding the African and the African American. The whole issue of slavery has been muted, while emphasis on the Holocaust has been pronounced. The front page of the *Chicago Tribune* posted a story titled, "Nightmare World" it describes the holocaust survivors with Alzheimer's who suffer flashbacks of old horrors, and tells how nursing homes are learning how to help them. At the same time no such efforts go on in nursing homes serving Black survivors of lynching and the terrorism of Jim Crow,[2] which forced them to run away from Mississippi and the South.

As mentioned before, there are generally five causes for the achievement gap presently found in research. Favored research explanations are: socioeconomic (poverty, parental involvement), cultural (child rearing, peer pressure, acting white), and school related (tracking, low standards, low expectations, social promotions, uncertified teachers, uncommitted principals). Those not favored are genetic (hereditary low intelligence or Black inferiority) and societal (white supremacy and a curriculum promoting its interests).

Having failed to identify the problem adequately, researchers have trouble finding solutions. Siegfried Engelmann argued in his article, "The Dalmatian and Its Spots: Why Research-Based Recommendations Fail Logic 101" that "at least part of the problem educators have in establishing effective instruction has to do with the illogical recommendations that researchers make."

Research has found few answers to the riddle of the achievement gap. Moreover, there are many differences in the findings. The National Reading Panel produced findings that were criticized by other reading experts. In addition to this, studies of African American students are rarely funded. Ellen Condliffe Lagemann stated that "no two schools train teachers in exactly the same way. No two schools prepare researchers in the same fashion," and believes "this lack of common standards and norms seriously weakens our field." She argues that "the field of education does not have a widely shared criteria to distinguish good from bad teaching or good from bad research."

More descriptive of the problems is a letter written by Vinita Moch Ricks, professor at Harold Washington College, to G. Alfred Hess, director and research lecturer at the Center for Urban School Policy at Northwestern University in Evanston, Illinois, dated October 11, 2000. In her letter she stated that researchers were often unwilling to modify theories that were held about schools and pushed the ethnographers to accept these analyses as the only plausible explanations for the events in complex environments. She felt that research was compromised when researchers focused on validating what they thought they already knew. My complaint is this, researchers do not investigate the impact of the myths of white superiority on the achievement gap.

In spite of this research, CPS makes only small dents in the huge achievement gap among its Asian, white, Hispanic and African American students. A recently published book by Anthony S. Bryk and Barbara Schneider,[3] *Trust in Schools: A Core Resource for Improvement*, resurrects the school reform wars of the 1990s. Bryk is the director of the Consortium for the Study of Chicago School Reform at the University of Chicago and a supporter of the 1988 reformers, whose goal was the redistribution of power in governance. The book has two purposes: to establish relational trust as a concept pertinent to school reform and to defend the 1988 reform act and movement.

Because the Consortium and the University of Chicago play such an important role in the changes occurring in CPS under the watch of CEO Arne Duncan and Mayor Daley their research is of great importance to the African American and Hispanic students who dominate the school system and whose low achievement precipitates most school reform measures.

At the same time that efforts are made to improve achievement, Chicago is undergoing gentrification in areas along the lakefront, joining the Loop with Hyde Park, where the University of Chicago is located; along the Dan Ryan (Interstate 94 South) where the Robert R. Taylor public housing structure was dismantled; and around the United Center that Michael Jordan built. To lure the middleclass back to Chicago, test-in schools (magnets) have been established near or in these areas. An example is the Martin Luther King, Jr. College Preparatory High School, designed to be the premier performing arts high school of Chicago, but abandoned for that purpose because it became 100 percent African American and poor.

Bryk and Schneider claim to have selected twelve CPS elementary schools according to criteria which would have given them a sample representative of the entire school system; and of these twelve, they selected three as case studies. It is unclear as to what criteria were used for this purpose. But of the three, the 100 percent African American school happens to have a white principal. In the study there are three kinds of trusts mentioned: organic trust, which is predicated on the more or less unquestioning beliefs of individuals in the moral authority of a particular social institution; contractual trust, which is a material and instrumental form of social relations that defines basic actions to be taken by the parties involved; and relational trust, which views the social exchanges of schooling as organized around a distinct set of role relationships, i.e. teachers with students, teachers with other teachers, teachers with parents and teachers with their school principal. While Bryk and Schneider see relational trust as particularly suitable to school reform, they neglected to describe and account for the contractual trust that exists between the principal and the Local School Council (LSC) and between the school principal and the Chicago Teachers Union and CPS. The LSC is a legislative body. Its members are elected. Sometimes parents agree with the actions of the LSC. Sometimes they do not. Bryk and Schneider considered the LSC and parents as one. Teachers and the Union were considered one; yet the effect of the Union's contract on the teacher's role was not discussed. The Chicago Teachers Union does not appear in the index. As a result, neither the Union nor the LSC was considered as an entity, so there was no discussion of relational trust between the teachers and the LSC, the principal and the LSC or the parents and the LSC; nor was there any discussion of relational trust between the teachers and the Union, the principal and the Union or the parents and the Union.

Relational trust is said to diminish whenever individuals perceive that others are not behaving in ways that can be understood as consistent with their expectations about the other's role and/or obligations. Bryk and Schneider wrote: "[M]oreover, fulfillment of obligations entails not only 'doing the right thing,' but also doing it in a respectful way and for what are perceived to be the right reasons."[4]

Bryk and Schneider present relational trust as a three–level theory, beginning with the intrapersonal, set within the interpersonal, and finally rooted in the organizational. This theoretical framework resurrected Getzel, Lipham and Campbell's General Model of the Major Dimensions of Behavior in a social system, which had nomothetic (institutional), idiographic (individual), and cultural dimensions.[5] In this system, role is the most important analytic unit of the institution and is defined by role expectations, is an institutional given, is more or less flexible, is complementary and is varying in scope. For Bryk and Schneider, the expectations were studied through four lenses: respect, competence, personal regard for others and integrity.

Strangely, in a school system where racial conflicts occur frequently, this study downplayed these conflicts in its discussions.[6] In this study racial conflicts were more prevalent in predominantly African American schools, although the text reads: "In previous analyses of these data, racial conflicts were found to be more prevalent in schools that enrolled several different racial-ethnic groups and where no one group dominated."[7]

Additionally, in the Chicago Public Schools, large numbers of African American students, especially males, are referred and placed in Special Education. However, Special Education was not in the index, nor was it mentioned as a trust problem. This was surprising. The anticipated conclusion of the study is the following:

> In theory the base level of trust at any given point conditions a school's capacity
> to undertake new reform initiatives. This effect should be especially strong for
> complex reforms that require mutual support and coordinated work among school

professionals and sometimes parents as well. Our theory also suggests that the underlying social processes of school change entail a recursive dynamic. Small wins at school improvement help expand relational trust, thereby creating an enlarged capacity to undertake more complex changes in the future. Assuming these subsequent efforts also are successful, such efforts should further enlarge the social resources of the school community for subsequent rounds of work. In short, school improvement and social resource development are processes that occur over extended periods and in a real sense, feed each other.[8]

In other words, does high academic achievement produce relational trust between teachers and parents, parents and teachers, teachers and the principal, and teachers and teachers or vice versa?

Interestingly, Bryk and Schneider found that teacher background variables contributed only modestly to explaining changes in school productivity. These were a teacher's educational background and a teacher's professional background. There was no information on certification. In many predominantly African American schools, teachers are not teaching in their certified areas. Also, no information was available on the amount of knowledge teachers had in the teaching of reading and/or mathematics. In at least one predominantly African American elementary school where I observed, there wasn't one teacher who had had more than one course in the teaching of reading.

Like all educational research the important question to pose is: Does this most recent work present a possible solution to the academic achievement gap between white and African American students? A solution may be found, but only if the basis of the lack of trust is uncovered. Do teachers believe in white superiority and Black inferiority? Are there financial and personnel resources available for change? What about policies which are in place to uphold white superiority and its infamous counterpart? Students who are plagued with problems of race, poverty, family dysfunction, community disorganization or apathy cannot receive the services they need with the same staffing formula as schools that are magnets and whose students test into the school. Moreover, neither can communities of learners be established nor relational-trust exist where teachers are not certified to teach the students assigned to them. Time is needed to nurture and to expand trust. Yet, CPS has the shortest school day in Illinois. However, there were and are attempts being made to extend the school year.

While this research on trust looks at African American schools, it avoids looking at white supremacy. Proposals are rejected if they do not investigate universals. A universal concept is one that works theoretically anywhere. This was the problem with whole language. Whole language works better with children who already speak standard English or know English alphabet and words. Although the research on small schools does not show an acceleration or elevation of scores on standardized tests in reading, they are being touted as the answer to the problem of the achievement gap.

Now when states are forced to make drastic cuts to meet balanced budgets, there will be no money for reducing the size of schools or classes, or lengthening school days or years. Without an increase in time, professional development and meeting among teachers, preparation and planning become idealistic thoughts. As long as teachers can transfer in and out of low-achieving schools at will, competent, respected, caring teachers will be drafted by the high-achieving schools in order to fill their vacancies. Vacancies in low-achieving schools will be filled with inexperienced, less competent and less caring teachers. Union contracts make it difficult to terminate such teachers.

There is another way to look at the case study of the Holiday Elementary School in *Trust in Schools*. An equally important outcome of the Bryk and Schneider research was the portrait of a white principal who could deliver relational trust in a 100 percent African American school in a public housing district. In this situation, however, the LSC was dysfunctional. For example, the researchers said "Dr. Goldman made a sharp distinction between parent involvement and parent input. In his view, direct involvement was more like interference, while input, in the form of recommendations or suggestions was appropriate and desirable." In another place they noted:

> The crushing poverty and limited education of parents at Holiday created a severe imbalance in their power relationship with teachers. Even though parents held a majority representation on the local school council, they had little capacity either individually or as a group to affect directly what the school did about their children's education. In this regard, parents remained largely dependent on the good intentions of school staff. The Holiday School faculty acknowledged this parental vulnerability and acted vigorously to relieve it.[9]

So, what we have is a group of parents without the education, experience or capacity to affect the lives of their children. The principal exploited this vulnerability by relegating their participation from the local democracy intent of the 1988 legislation to his own advantage. The parents deferred their rights to the principal and the teachers in the face of this impotence, very similar to the action of parents at the Beltzhoover School in Pittsburgh in the 1980s. No information was given about the student achievement in *Trust in Schools* case studies.

No information was given about the student achievement in these case studies. However, at Holiday Elementary School and Nathaniel Dett Elementary School 18.5 percent of the students scored at or above the national norm in reading in 1994, 13.3 percent in 1995; 15.8 percent in 1996; and 21.2 percent in 1997; in mathematics, 18.7 percent in 1994; 23 percent in 1995; 17.7 percent in 1996; and 31.4 percent in 1997. Dett does show a 3.7 percent gain over the four years in reading, and a 12.7 percent gain in mathematics. But these gains do not appear to be any better than those accumulated at Beethoven, Drake and Hearst which serve similar public housing students or at Dvorak, Emmet, Kellman and Lawndale which serve poor predominantly African American students. Bryk and Schneider agree that instructional changes must be implemented if the elevation and acceleration of student achievement is to occur.

In my experience, the Structured Ten Routines, an Effective Schools Model, accommodates both the development of relational and contractual trust and the initiation, implementation and institutionalization of instructional routines. The decision-making routine calls for the establishment of an Instructional Leadership Team (ILT) which includes all school actors in decision-making. Also, principals and administrators are asked to include an LSC member. The job of the ILT is to develop and nurture consensus around high achievement as the highest priority goal in the school and to generate a learning community through collegial and collective activities. The generation of trust, however, is much more difficult because it depends on a change in values, not just in behavior. The Trust in Schools study does not consider this problem.

The Consortium on Chicago School Research (CCSR), led by Bryk, also produced many studies on the school reform effort in Chicago. Their studies of retention showed that the Chicago effort had raised achievement overall, but had not helped the students most in need. When the mayor declared an end to social promotion in 1996, the purpose was to help students to progress in mastering standardized tests. I refuse to call them high stakes test because the high stakes tests are those that determine who eats: entry level job tests, state licensure tests and tests used for admission to higher education. We should not confuse the two.

CCSR, under the leadership of Melissa Roderick, who also served as a consultant to CPS at the same time, examined how successful retained students were in raising their test scores to the promotion standard during their retained year. Nagaoka and Roderick found that retained students struggled in their second time trying to meet the promotional standards. Even with an extra chance to pass the tests in January, "less than 60 percent of retained third and sixth graders in 1998 and 1999 were able to raise their test scores to the promotional cutoff. "Close to 20 percent of retained third and sixth graders were placed in special education within two years of the retention decision."

Nagaoka and Roderick found little evidence that retained third grade students did better than their low-achieving counterparts who were socially promoted. For third grade, the researchers concluded that retention did not proffer any sustained academic benefits, nor did it have any substantial negative effects. Retained sixth graders had lower achievement growth than their low-achieving counterparts who were socially promoted, with that effect, remaining two years after the initial promotion or retention decision. Nagaoka and Roderick explained that their statistical model, which controlled for selection effects, suggested that achievement growth of retained sixth graders was six percent lower than that of their low-achieving counterparts who were socially promoted. Students placed in special education after retention continued to struggle two years later.

Nagaoka and Roderick were quick to show that social promotion was no better a solution to the problem of low achievement and inadequate progress toward it than retention. They found that "low-achieving students in all our groups started school substantially behind their classmates and had already fallen further behind before the promotional gate grade. Neither promotion nor retention led to a significant closing of this achievement gap after the gate grade for those low-achieving students who had test scores close to the cutoff."

Their study, as do most studies, avoids exploring the impact of the myths of white superiority and Black inferiority on the achievement gap. African American students were disproportionately retained. The two reasons considered were: minority students might be affected differentially if they had lower test scores; and minority students, with even the same level of school achievement, may be affected differentially if they have fewer resources and supports upon which to draw. The researchers opted for lower test scores. There is absolutely no thought about the impact of lower expectations or the absence of aggressive effective methodology due to teachers' and/or administrators' belief in Black inferiority, even though they found that "retained students were placed in special education at nearly five times the rate of the average third grader and nearly seven times the rate of the average sixth grader." This is also the result of the failure of research to look for causes at the classroom level.

An interesting turn of events took place with the CCSR study of retained eighth-grade students' achievement. Instead of looking for whether or not retention helped or harmed eighth graders in improving achievement, Elaine Allensworth examined the relationship of retention to dropout rates. The report acknowledges that achievement improved substantially with the postpolicy eighth-grade cohorts. It states:

> By the 1998 cohort, achievement was more than one–half of a standard deviation higher than it was in prepolicy cohorts, among included students. In other words, the test score of an included student who was at the 50th percentile in the 1998 cohort would have been at the 70th percentile in the 1992 cohort. Achievement was also much higher among students whose scores were excluded from test reporting, even though a much larger percentage of these students were tested and were used in calculating the averages for excluded students, postpolicy.

Allensworth also found that overall dropout rates did not rise with implementation of the policy. So what a lay person can draw from these two studies with regard to achievement: (1) intervention must occur before third grade; (2) retention does not help in the sixth grade if achievement does not occur by the third grade; and (3) retention seems to work in eighth grade. However, CCSR did not give it that spin.

To be sure, for those who started teaching in the 1940s and the 1950s, this research did not come as news. In the 1960s, the non-graded elementary school, known in Chicago as Continuous Development, attempted to deal with human incommensurability and eliminate retention and double promotion, both widely used at the time. Individual instruction and grouping were also promoted during those years. For over fifty years we have known the limitations of retention without high quality teaching, sufficient resources and enough school time. In the 1940s we looked to smaller classes, enough schools and teachers, books and supplies and a curriculum free of white superiority and remedial subjects. We thought desegregation would bring these to fruition.

No lesson demonstrates the mobilization of white superiority interests better than desegregation. In the fiftieth year of the *Brown v. Board of Education* decision, desegregation has failed and the courts are declaring the segregated society already integrated, in spite of the reality. Brown led us down a dangerous path, which began when we agreed to say that anything all Black was all bad. Brown failed to attack the imputation of white superiority, leaving the all-white school as good.

While the Supreme Court's decision said that "[T]he basis of segregation and 'separate-but-equal' rests upon a concept of the inherent inferiority of the colored race," the problem of the imputed inherent superiority of the white race went untouched. Segregation is a symptom of this very worrisome problem. White superiority masquerades as colorblind when whiteness is the only color it sees.

As a result, those who were responsible for educating Black students in segregated schools felt that Black students were inferior and could not learn. Expectations were low and a sense of futility triumphed, diminishing the energy invested into teaching and administration. The *Chicago Tribune* reported on November 7, 2003, that CPS submitted a new integration proposal in federal court, focusing on fair funding, rather than desegregation. It included a promise to create financial reports that would show if it spent as much on racially isolated neighborhood schools as it did on its elite magnet schools. Such statistics paint a brighter picture than the situation warrants. Spending the same does not bring equity. The reported lower figure for Hispanics was due to overcrowding, while the higher figure for African Americans was due to over representation in Special Education. As usual, the problem of the racial myths remained invisible; often racial interests are hidden in policies which are considered benign. The Federal Judge agreed to a two-year plan that could end the Chicago Public Schools's twenty-four-year-old desegregation agreement.

This retreat on the commitment to desegregation has occurred in the midst of the conservative movement's war in support of white superiority and against civil rights. The Republican Party, in control of the U.S. presidency and both Houses of Congress, is now the refuge for those committed to white Supremacy. An example of this occurred in the 2002 elections. Roy Barnes, democratic governor of the state of Georgia, and Max Cleland, former democratic senator from Georgia, along with Tom Murphy, who served Georgia in the House of Representatives for forty-two years, (twenty-eight of them as Speaker), were defeated by rural whites in an election because the three of them supported the removal of the image of the Confederate Flag from the state flag. Everyone knows that the Confederate Flag is the banner of white Supremacy, the heritage that its supporters want to maintain. No one is willing to play this race card, however, and so we stand in chronic denial.

In the African Americans's struggle for survival and autonomy we have walked in a complete circle. After the Civil War was the first Reconstruction period (1865–1877), after which there was the first Jim Crow period, where the violation of African Americans's citizenship rights was legal, oppressive and overt. After Jim Crow there was the second Reconstruction period, which started with *Brown* and ended with *Bakke v. The University of California at Davis (1954–1977)*. We are now in Jim Crow, where the violation of African Americans's socioeconomic rights is extra-legal, closeted and covert. Yet, instead of waging an outright assault against this white supremacy, we accommodate it.

We allowed desegregation policies that reinforced the claim that 80 percent white and 20 percent Black was a good measurement of a school's racial makeup, even when these desegregation policies identified tipping points when there were too many Blacks in a school, making whites uncomfortable. We allowed the Court to say that separate educational facilities were not considered inherently unequal. So, instead of destroying the imputation of white superiority, Brown reinforced it. Following were policies sure to fail, firing of Black principals and teachers, busing of Black children into hostile white neighborhoods, and flight of whites from the cities to avoid living with, and certainly going to school with, Black children. At the same time that we were agreeing to the proposition that anything all Black was bad, we had our own excellent Black colleges, churches, universities, organizations and institutions.

Charlotte-Mecklenburg, North Carolina was once touted as the most successful desegregated school district in the U.S. But on January 21, 2003, Greg Winter wrote that dozens of Charlotte schools had basically colored in the months since the appeals court lifted the desegregation order. In 1997, white parents in Charlotte filed suits, contending that their children were being discriminated against because they could not go to schools of their choice. A federal appeals court ruled in their favor in 2001, lifting the district's ban. The Supreme Court declined to hear the case in 2003, making 2004 the first in three decades in which the Charlotte school system did not use race (the Black race only) to help determine where its children went to school. Race was still used to place white Children in white schools.

Adam Cohen summarized these issues in his article "The Supreme Struggle" which appeared in the *New York Times*. He argued that "Brown rebuked centuries of government-sanctioned black inferiority and began to give real force to the post-Civil War amendments to the Constitution, passed to lift up the freed slaves, and overturned *Plessy v. Ferguson*, the court's most infamous 1896 ruling endorsing separate but equal accommodations for the races." Cohen deplores the court's order "with all deliberate speed." The court did issue an immediate order to "recalcitrant Mississippi school officials to desegregate at once" in 1969 and busing orders to Charlotte-Mecklenberg, which started the white backlash in support of white supremacy.

Under Chief Justice William H. Rehnquist, Cohen says that "the court made it far easier for school districts to skirt desegregation orders already in place." This leniency gave school systems the nod to resegregate. Then the Court "dismantled the Kansas City, Missouri's program to attract white suburban and private school students willingly to heavily black city schools." Cohen concludes his article with this pathetic statement: "After [fifty] years, the real lesson of *Brown* may be that to achieve racially-integrated schools, we need less blind optimism—and more appreciation for how much hard work remains to be done." Such a statement belittles the lifetime of work done by Gary Orfield and others. At some time, Adam Cohen must come to the realization that there can be no integrated society as long as whites retain their undeserved privileges and advantages due to the myth of white superiority and the value of white supremacy. Frustrated by desegregation's failure to provide a remedy for high quality Black education, Blacks turned to decentralization as a means to that end.

Section 9.3   Centralization and Decentralization

Centralization and decentralization can be understood as shifts in organizational routines generated by various competing groups and is designed to seek three goals: representativeness (responsiveness), politically neutral competence (accountability, administrative efficiency and managerial effectiveness) and executive leadership (ability to acquire and use knowledge and information). Centralization is the concentration of administration at a single center, which is also the locus of power and authority. Decentralization is the delegation of authority to lower levels of a governing hierarchy and/or the devolution of power to lower dimensions of the structure of the organization or the state. Both decentralization and centralization have been chosen at one time or another by groups seeking more power to govern. The decentralization that started with community control was such an effort. Black and Hispanic communities wanted control over the policy-making mechanisms of public schools that affected the life chances of their children. Although there have been many efforts to decentralize school systems, recentralization seems to be in vogue now, in Chicago and New York City, and now Pittsburgh's mayor wants to do so.

In its decentralization effort, the 1988 Illinois legislation made the principalship much more vulnerable in Chicago than prior to its enactment. The LSCs that were created had the power to hire and fire the principal and to decide how discretionary monies would be spent. In many 100 percent African American schools, LSC members sought to do just that. When members turn over on the LSC, and such turnovers are frequent at times, the LSC changes. A principal can lose all of his or her support in one year. The sole desire of oncoming members may be to extend the job to someone they know and support, regardless of the respect, competence, and personal regard of the incumbent. Principals then take risks when they put the interests of students above the LSC. When a principal loses his or her contract, that principal is through with the CPS because he or she has no tenure in the system, even as a teacher if he or she has been one. Principals then move at the margins of the system. Their power is illusory, unless they have six votes for four years. However, under the law teachers retained their tenure in the system, and they had two votes on the LSC. In essence, they are in a position to exert great control over other members. In fact, this is exactly what happened during the 1996–1997 school year at Collins High School. In both the CPS and the PPS principals who took risks to place the interests of their students above all other interests were punished in some way. Usually, the system denied them any kind of promotion or acclamation.

In 1995, the state of Illinois gave power over the CPS to the mayor of Chicago, Richard M. Daley. Since the mayor's takeover, the powers of the LSCs have eroded and been usurped by the central office. In 2004 CPS had trouble recruiting enough candidates for LSCs. Lori Olszewski reported that, "the Duncan administration has embarked on policies that have eliminated councils altogether in some schools and shifted the powers of others back to the central office." Olszewski thinks that the biggest blow to the LSCs resulted from the policy that took away the council's power to hire principals or approve budgets at probationary schools. In 2004, eighty-two councils lost that power because their schools were placed on probation. Tougher standards will likely increase that number during the 2004–2005 school year.

In both New York City and Chicago, the mayor took over the city schools. New York City's mayor has taken a lot of criticism for his stand on social promotion. I have delineated my position on social promotion. The February 9, 2004, editorial in the *New York Times*, "Grading the Mayor on Schools," objected to Mayor Bloom's proposed plan to fail as many as 15,000 children each year in third grade. It reported:

> Centralization seems to have isolated the administration from reasonable criticism. This is clearly the case of the student disciplinary process, which was once housed in the thirty-two district offices that were swept clean of staff in the consolidation plan. Under the old system, schools knew within forty-eight hours whether or not

they could proceed in suspending a student who had proved violent. Since the fall, when the disciplinary program shifted to a half-dozen regional locations, it has taken as long as three weeks to complete the suspensions, leaving violent children walking the same school halls as the people they had attacked. Now the Bloom administration is scrambling to reinvent a disciplinary structure that actually worked pretty well before consolidation.

Clearly, the mayor of Pittsburgh wants to take over. The report from the Pittsburgh Mayor's Commission on Public Education recommends that the responsibility for the schools be vested in the mayor to ensure that the schools are accountable to the city as a whole. In addition, the board of education should be chosen by the mayor from a pool of candidates provided by a nominating commission whose members reflect the racial, geographic, professional and economic diversity of the city.

The Pittsburgh NAACP opposes the idea of the appointed school board. At their news conference on January 22, 2004, the organization described a lack of trust in the mayor, among many residents of the city of Pittsburgh in general and the African American community in particular. The news release stated, "The current mayor was openly involved in fundraising activities of persons who were most destructive to the students and taxpayers of Pittsburgh by their behaviors, actions and policies. Many of these actions and policies are contrary to the spirit of some of the recommendations of this report, such as the closing of excess building facilities."

The NAACP Pittsburgh branch also opposed the dissolution of the elected school board, whose history was given in an earlier chapter. The organization argues that the present superintendent, John Thompson, "Inherited a $40 million dollar deficit, which he turned into a $82 million surplus, while the City of Pittsburgh has a $60 million deficit, facing the possibility of bankruptcy or takeover by the Commonwealth of Pennsylvania." Why should the board of education turn over its business to the city?

While we have changed once again from decentralization to recentralization, decentralization is still recommended in the form of vouchers, home schooling and charter schools. In this way the power to choose is handed over to parents. The U.S. Congress recently approved a bill funding vouchers for public school students in Washington D.C., on January 22, 2004. The D.C. law offers $13 million in vouchers worth up to $7,500.00. *The Wall Street Journal* in its editorial, "Free at Last" (January 23, 2004) declares this "[A] victory for civil rights as it is for education reform"

This is a bill forced on the people of a colony, the District of Columbia, without their vote; under Article Eight, the U.S. Congress rules D.C. Its local government and board of education are fictional entities because the U.S. Congress and the president can veto any legislation they pass. The citizens of the District should have been given the right to vote on whether or not they wanted to have a voucher program. But because they vote for only one of the congressmen who sit on the four committees in the House and the Senate which rule the District, they have no influence.

Section 9.4   Charter Schools and The Madhubuti Legacy

Charter schools may hold out hope to African Americans if there are enough of us willing to do the hard work necessary for the accumulation of capital and the formation of business acumen. Haki and Safisha Madhubuti, also known as Don and Carol Lee, have for over thirty years maintained a private African-centered school on Chicago's South side called the New Concept School. In 1998 they opened Betty Shabazz International Charter School in their building at Seventy-eighth & Ellis. This is a K–eight school.

In 2002, 50.5 percent of their students reached or exceeded the national norms on the ITBS in reading, and 46.5 percent of their students reached or exceeded the national norms on the ITBS in Mathematics. The school has never been on probation. Of the fourteen charter schools for which scores are available, it ranked fourth in reading and sixth in mathematics in 2002. It is 100 percent African American and predominantly poor.

Safisha Madhubuti is the chairperson on the Board of Directors and greatly influences the school. She is an associate professor at Northwestern University in Evanston, Illinois, and has written widely on reading and culture in the education of African American students. For one year, Madhubuti was the teacher of record for a regular freshmen English class at Fenger Higher School in Chicago. Her study "Is October Brown Chinese?" has been published in the *American Educational Research Journal.* The abstract describes this

304

study as an analysis of the "quality of intellectual reasoning of a class of high school students with standardized reading scores in the bottom quartile. The analysis situates the intellectual work on one day of instruction in terms of the history of the activity system out of which the dispositions of these students were constructed over time." It deconstructs the historical dimensions of the cultural practices these students learned to acquire. Madhubuti uses a framework of cultural-historical activity theory, examining her knowledge base as a teacher and researcher to coach and scaffold a radically different intellectual culture among students who were underachieving.

In spite of these initiatives, we are no closer to the elimination of the achievement gap in public schools. In fact, those who know how to do it and have done so have risked their careers and receive no respect. This includes: J. Jerome Harris, former Distict Thirteen superintendent of New York City, and former superintendent of the Atlanta Public Schools; Sherwin Allen, former superintendent of Benton Harbor, Michigan Public Schools; Napoleon Lewis, former regional superintendent of schools in Washington D.C. and former principal of Lincoln High School in Dallas, now deceased; Doris Brevard, principal of Vann Elementary School in Pittsburgh; and Louis Venson, former director of the School Improvement Program in the Pittsburgh public schools. All were punished in some way for taking these risks. In the CPS and in PPS, those whose schools were low-achieving, but well disciplined, were rewarded; keeping the African quiet is more important than educating him. This, in and of itself, is a manifestation of the imputation of Black inferiority.

Section 9.5   Affirmative Action

The aggregated assault against affirmative action has been a long persistent attack. Now called reverse discrimination, the chances for its use as an effective remedy against white privilege, which rest on the basis of claims to white superiority, languish. The large African American middle class that now exists can be attributed to affirmative action programs of the 1970s and 1980s. I would never have been chosen dean of the School of Education at DePaul University had not an African American been provost, and another assistant provost. University positions are typically awarded according to kinship, friendship and political networks. Because whites have long dominated the selection process, Blacks need not apply. Even when Blacks have better qualifications and experiences, whites get the jobs because they "fit in."

Cheryl I. Harris, in her seminal piece, "Whiteness as Property" in the *Harvard Law Review* (June 1993), she wrote the following:

> The Supreme Court's rejection of affirmative action programs on the grounds that race-conscious remedial measures are unconstitutional under the Equal Protection Clause of the Fourteenth Amendment—the very constitutional measure designed to guarantee equality for blacks—is based on the Court's chronic refusal to dismantle the institutional protection of benefits for whites that have been based on white supremacy and maintained at the expense of blacks. As a result, the parameters of appropriate remedies are not dictated by the scope of the injury to the subjugated, but by the extent of the infringement on settled expectations of whites. These limits to remediation are grounded in the perception that the existing order, based on white privilege, is not only just there, but also is a property interest worthy of protection. Thus under this assumption, it is not only the interests of individual whites who challenge affirmative action that are protected; the interests of whites as whites are enshrined and institutionalized as a property interest that accords them a higher status than any individual claim to relief.

In addition to our failure to confront the imputation of white superiority as one of the highest values of our culture, we refuse to deal with the ambiguity of race. The United Nation's Education, Scientific and Cultural Organization (UNESCO) states in its report, "The Race Concept: Results of an Inquiry" that:

> The concept of race is unanimously regarded by anthropologists as a classificatory device providing a zoological frame within which the various groups of mankind may be arranged and by means of which studies of evolutionary processes can be facilitated. In its anthropological sense, the word "race" should be reserved for groups of mankind possessing well-developed and primarily heritable physical differences from other groups. Many populations can be so classified but, because of the complexity of human history, there are also many populations,

which cannot easily be fitted into a racial classification.

In the United States this definition is applied without the caveat. For example, race here usually means classification on the basis of skin color, hair type and head, eye, nose, lip size and shape. Berry and Blassingame noted, "Fugitive slaves, for example, were frequently described as having straight hair and complexion so nearly white that a stranger would suppose there was no Negro blood in him, or as having light sandy hair, blue eyes, ruddy complexion; he is so nearly white as to easily pass for a white man." They concluded that race was determined by visibility and reputation.

Du Bois stated that race was defined by a group of contradictory forces, illogical facts and irreconcilable tendencies. We simply have no scientific criteria for the determination of race. It is simply an artifact used to claim white supremacy by declaring others inferior.

Conservatives stand as the last vanguard for the promotion of white supremacy, a stand which is rarely articulated, but is regularly practiced. While conservatives claim they want to restrict and limit government spending, this is only rhetoric because they expand subsidies (welfare to corporations) and decrease their own taxes (ability to move corporations offshore). Conservatives believe in the free market as the solution to all of democracy's inequity problems. Yet, capitalism is an amoral economic model which has as its goal to make a profit "by any means necessary." Without regulation, it will sell the public mad cow-diseased meat, cars with gas tanks that explode, recreational vehicles that overturn at certain rates of speed and food supplements that kill. Corporations have gone wild is the result.

Equity has been lost because of the apathy and despondency in the African American community. Now, instead of equity the focus is on cultural diversity. Other minorities who have never suffered from the legacy of slavery have become preferred. In many fields, Asians are this minority. And even though many immigrants are not the descendants of slaves, if they are Black in skin color they automatically enter the same inferior caste. This causes much discontent. How many Hispanics who are Black are treated as though they are African Americans? How many should be counted as Black?

The impact of race on affirmative action is also obscured by tests, that is, the real high stakes tests. Tests are judged as objective measures, but serve to segregate students by race because they do not account for the impact of the belief in Black inferiority on learning. Nor do they account for the history of poor instruction, poor support and inadequate service to Black students in schools.

Magnet schools and all test-in schools magnify the impact of white superiority and supremacy and the benefits enjoyed because of them. This starts in elementary and secondary schools through our system of tracking, which has often been modified, but never abandoned. In his front page article, "Test Questions: Boosting Minorities in Gifted Program Poses Dilemmas" in the *Wall Street Journal*, Daniel Goldman states that gifted programs emerged nationwide in the 1970s to give talented elementary school students extra challenges.

I have described my own children's experiences with these programs in Chicago, Evanston and Pittsburgh. In some areas, the programs were promoted by white parents trying to circumvent court-ordered desegregation, according to Goldman. He wrote, "Districts typically identified students as gifted who scored in the top 5 percent or 130 or above on traditional intelligence tests measuring verbal and math skills. Whites tend to outscore minorities on these tests, which made gifted programs overwhelmingly white." He went on to say that in the 1990s the Clinton administration began pushing to desegregate gifted education, particularly in the South. Some states reached agreements with the government to adjust their standards. Other states adapted without federal action.

By changing the standards of gifted education, though, said Goldman, traditionalists say school districts seeking classroom equity are undermining academic excellence. Some minority students identified as gifted are actually struggling in regular classes, raising questions about whether the new criteria accurately gauges academic ability. Goldman cites Greenville County, South Carolina's response of creating super-gifted programs that are almost entirely white. Black students must be taught that whites are not superior people and that the barriers to passing tests can be overcome, but not without struggle against the real cause of the problems.

Section 9.6 Responsibility

The present argument about African Americans centers around responsibility. Who is responsible for the plight of Black people? Conservatives say it is our own fault. We do not promote education in our families. Our gangs kill each other over drugs. Fathers do not wed mothers, who bear children to live in single parent households. Teachers in public schools complain that the students do not want to learn, are not properly motivated by their parents, and do not appreciate education. Social scientists like Signithia Fordham and John Ogbu argue that Black children "are unduly influenced by the peer group and see excellence in education as a 'white' thing." Others, like Stephen and Abigail Thernstrom see the Black family as the problem, articulating the position of Daniel Patrick Moynihan's thesis of 1965. For them, the solution to the problems of African Americans lies in our assumption of moral responsibility and academic excellence. Much research needs to be done here. For example, do middle-class Black families oppose education and tell their children not to study or pursue education excellence? If so, what percent?

What this excludes is the context within which the assumption of moral responsibility and academic excellence takes place. African Americans have been in this position before during the 1920s, 30s and 40s. Two generations of African Americans grew up in families where the old folks and parents encouraged their children to be "better than white folks" and to "work hard in school, or whatever the endeavor, so that you will uphold the race and progress." Academic excellence was regarded as an important value. Moral responsibility required men to marry women whom they impregnated. Although there were many of what have come to be called "shotgun weddings," these moves were widely enforced. But moral responsibility and academic excellence were no match for Jim Crow, white superiority and Black inferiority. I remember a Black man who had a doctorate in chemistry who was working in the U.S. Post Office in Terre Haute because of the Black codes in 1937. Here we are in 2004, and Black people who hold doctorates cannot find tenure track positions at universities in the animal science and genetics disciplines because of kinship, friendship and political networks. What kind of encouragement is this for moral responsibility and academic excellence?

Gradually, jobs paying salaries adequate to support a family above the poverty level vanished from the Black community in the central cities, the overwhelming effects of poverty crushed spirits and limited horizons. Drugs flowed into the overcrowded public housing areas, luring young, restless men with no job opportunities and few educational avenues to its underworld business. Guns became available as police and politicians took payoffs and open-air drug markets were allowed to flourish.

In the Black community on the west side of Evanston, community residents intent upon keeping drugs out of their community repeatedly reported activities to the police regarding crack houses and drug sales, without response. Nothing was done about this problem until 2000, when a man was killed in an altercation in the crack house. After it was closed, confiscated and resold, the police disappeared. In 2004, the drug market is beginning again. The government's drug policies are pathetic. The policies protect neither the people who are not involved in the business, nor the innocent from the bullets flying in the trade.

When Africans were enslaved they were criminalized. Charsee Lawrence-McIntyre writes about this in her book, *Criminalizing a Race: Free Blacks During Slavery*. She argues that the Europeans did not originally enslave Africans because they were Black: "The English enslaved, killed, maimed, imprisoned and exported to colonies the Irish, Welsh, and English poor, then the Native Americans. They later mistreated African Americans in the same inhuman manner. This European subjugation requires cultural domination, which, because of race, has become a worldwide system of white supremacy." McIntyre concluded that:

> Two results occurred from the overall maltreatment of African Americans. The designating of the entire group as "outsider deviants" ensured that a disproportionate African American population would always be present in American prisons, and this reality has remained since the inception of that institution in 1790. More important, the accusing and punishing of African Americans of more criminality (for whatever reasons) than European Americans for 200 years has reinforced the perception in most whites minds that any and all Blacks represent criminals or potential ones. Equally destructive is the development in most African American minds that the criminal justice system has been and is geared to victimize any member of this group. What has occurred in fact is the criminalizing of the entire race.

After the first Reconstruction period, the Black codes, which deprived Blacks of their newly won rights, were passed, and sharecropping became the only means of survival. Sharecropping reduced Blacks to slavery again. During the second Reconstruction period, affirmative action made accessible jobs which had never been available before. Then, during Jim Crow, these jobs dried up. Affirmative action came under attack and reverse discrimination became the new race card played by whites. Drugs became the new sharecropping experience. More African American men are in prison now then ever before. This has also become a way to deprive them of their voting rights.

In "The State of the Dream 2004 United for a Fair Economy" report, Muhammad, Davis, Wright and Lui noted that there was at least thirteen states in which there were more African American men in prison than in college. As studies from the Sentencing Project, the National Center on Institutionals and Alternatives, and many others have documented, the unconscionable rate of Black incarceration is the product of persistent racism in the criminal justice system.

We know these differences are due to white supremacy. Yet we equivocate regarding our responses. We let the John McWhorters go unanswered. Marable Manning describes, In *Losing the Race: Self–Sabotage in Black America*, as self-hating. In it, McWhorter argues that affirmative action cripples African American students by contributing to a spirit of Black "anti-intellectualism" and a "deep reaching inferiority complex" that there is no greater threat to the social progress America has made over the last three decades than the dramatic increase of incarceration for African American men in 2000. He makes this statement: "In my years of teaching, I have never had a student disappear without explanation or turn in a test that made me wonder how she could have attended class and done so badly, who was not African American."

Like many, for McWhorter there are no bad white students. I taught in colleges for twenty years and I cannot make this same statement. But then, I taught in colleges where there were poor white students also. McWhorter is an associate professor of linguistics at the University of California at Berkeley and a senior fellow at the Manhattan Institute. McWhorter accommodates white supremacy.

Who accounts for poor public schools, which most Blacks attend? But more importantly, until the No Child Left Behind legislation, neither the U.S. government, nor anyone else was even interested in whether Black children learned to read. NCLB set adequate yearly progress standards for all children which must be met within certain time frames. Before then, there was never any argument about teaching to the test, because only white children were being taught to it! The problem is that NCLB is unfunded and states cannot comply with its mandates for fully certified teachers, summer school, tutoring and school choice.

Just as Jim Crow abrogated the rights assured by the Fourteenth and Fifteenth Amendments to the U.S. Constitution and violated the Civil Rights Law of 1875, which was later declared unconstitutional and in complete defiance of the Fourteenth Amendment, so does Jim Crow abrogate the rights assured under the Fourteenth Amendment, the Civil Rights Laws of 1964 and the Fifteenth Amendment. The whole purpose of white superiority and white supremacy is to maintain as permanent the privileges that accrue to whiteness.

We do have five levers of power: God, knowledge, money, votes and guns. We simply do not use any of them for our own best interests. We are too busy accommodating. Now, we have been here before too. The argument between Booker T. Washington and W. E. B. Du Bois reflected the two sides of the issue: accommodation and agitation. If culture is the sum total of artifacts any group accumulates in its struggle for survival and autonomy, then in that struggle our group, the colored, the Negro, the Black African American group, has acculturated on some things (hair and clothes, for instance), remained traditional on others (church and food), and has become bicultural on others (language). The loss of cultural artifacts, which helped us overcome Jim Crow, have increased divisiveness, stimulated differences and created deep chasms in the community. Our churches are dominated by male leadership, but female congregations. Men only come to church to lead. Our music is divisive, stressing violence, anger and hate. To too many of our young, our women have become "h*s" and "b***hes" and our men "playas" and "pimps." Models of the behavior emulating struggle is scarce. Just as we take our stands against the preservation and prominence of the Confederate Flag in our lives, so we should use every lever of power to combat white privilege wherever we see it. Since we know what the levers of power are, we must devise strategies for the use of God, knowledge, money, votes and guns to our best advantages.

We do not use either God or knowledge to our benefit. We take our dictates from the establishment that protects white privileges. Our God is generally white, although the Bible is pretty clear about how the Messiah looked. And although Clinton berated Sister Souljah in order to garner redneck votes, she was exactly right about our misuse of guns. We should not turn them on ourselves. They are to protect us, as Malcolm X argued. Our money should never support businesses or organizations that support white privilege in hiring or issuing contracts. We should support our own organizations and institutions and build our own businesses. We should support our own politicians. We should always vote in large numbers in order to make a difference. Because so many African Americans voted, Harold Washington was elected mayor of the city of Chicago.

People constantly tell me that the days of protest and marching are over. If they are, who is telling this to the anti-abortionists who are carefully conducting their reign of terror? If these days are over, when will the anti-gay folks be told? If votes do not count, who has told this to the religious right, who happen to be a minority in this country? If people do not use the levels of power available to them, then what can they expect to happen? Frederick Douglass informed us many years ago that power concedes nothing without a demand. It never did and never will.

Because Blacks are a minority, neither party has been faithful to the commitment of Black equality. The candidates of both parties have used the race card of white supremacy to capture white voters, although the Republican strategy has also been aggressive: Jesse Helms with his praying hands, George H. Bush with Willie Horton and George W. Bush with Bob Jones. Clinton, of course, used Sister Souljah and Howard Dean, and the Confederate Flag–ornamented truck drivers. But, the secret is that there is only one party in the United States, the Capitalist Party of the U.S., and it has two branches, the Democrats and the Republicans. No wonder people switch around at will. African Americans must choose individuals who represent their interests, whether they are Black or not. Black people usually vote Democratic only because this party is perceived as the party of the poor, the downtrodden and the disadvantaged. Yet, it too is a party of the white and privileged. So, to it Blacks must make the demand. Muhammad, Davis, Lui and Wright remind us in their report of the following:

313

The typical black family had 60 percent as much income as a white family in 1968, but 58 percent as much as in 2002. In 2001, the typical black household had a net worth of just $19,000.00 (including home equity), compared with $121,000.00 for whites. blacks had 16 percent of the median wealth of whites, up from 5 percent in 1989. While white homeownership has jumped from 65 percent to 75 percent of families since 1970, black homeownership has only risen from 42 percent to 48 percent. A Chicago study revealed that blacks with incomes of $90,000.00 a year were denied mortgages which whites with incomes of $37,000.00 received. A black high school graduate working full time from age twenty-five through age sixty-four would earn $300,000.00 less on average than their white counterpart during their working years. A black college graduate would earn $500,000.00 less.

Making the demand is not going to be easy, but it must be done. Those of us in the university have an obligation to teach African American history, literature and culture to our students. Only knowledge of the African American experience will prepare African Americans for a lifelong struggle against the perils of white privilege and the unequal playing field it creates. This loss of knowledge about our people as a result of desegregation has made a profound difference in activism and has formed the new Black conservative class represented by John McWhorter, Shelby Steele, Thomas Sowell and Walter Williams. The most dangerous of these, of course, is Clarence Thomas.

Not to deprecate the conservatives' positions completely, I must acknowledge that Blacks must assume responsibility for struggle. Blaming white privilege is no excuse for this abdication. Sooner or later, we must use the levers of power to improve our chances, as we have always done in the past. But, next time we should take on the problem full frontal. Attack white supremacy at its roots, not at its symptoms. I do not think I can say it better than Manning Marable:

The main pillars of structural racism throughout American history have been prejudice, power and privilege. By "prejudice" I mean a deep and unquestioned belief in the natural superiority of white people over nonwhites. In his 1920 essay, *The Souls of Black Folk*, W.E.B. DuBois described white supremacy as the belief "that every great soul the world ever saw was a white man's soul; that every great deed the world ever did was a white man's deed; that every great dream the world ever saw was a white man's dream." A belief in the purity of whiteness demands—and is dependent on—the denigration of blackness.[10]

The struggle for reparations, the teaching of African American history, life and culture, the exposure of white benefit and advantage, all unmask the roots of white privilege. For that alone, it is worth the energy to pursue these strategies. White privilege must be identified, unmasked and removed. Otherwise, we will not have learned the lessons from the past.

Never in the history of the African's journey in America have the majority of voters been willing to pay for the education of the indigent and poor. Unless the money is spent on the affluent, it cannot be passed into law. Teachers, administrators and parents complain about the failure of the poor to live up to their parental obligations and use poverty, family dysfunction and community disorganization as excuses for poor student performance on standardized tests. Yet, there is a profound and persistent unwillingness to address these issues with resources.

Teachers are expected to be more altruistic than the general population, working for wages lower than those received by sanitation workers, bus drivers and plumbers, whose vocations do not require expensive college degrees. Schools are expected to make up for the poverty deficits in the same time and with fewer resources than schools whose students do not suffer from such deprivation. Very little is done to help schools where concentrations of students assigned to special education exist. More often than not, these students are not provided with the services that they need because there are insufficient certified teachers in those areas. Yet, these schools have the same standards with which they must comply.

Section 9.7 The Cyclical Cycle

In the first part of this book I tried to reveal my beliefs and through the revelation of my life's story, values. I know that Blacks were not inferior to whites because my own experience belied such convictions. It was clear to me through my own endeavors as a teacher and an administrator that Black children could be taught and could achieve highly. I learned that instruction required teachers who knew their own content and how to impart that understanding to learners. I knew that the university could not prepare you to be a teacher. The university can only give you content. Most university professors have never taught a poor Black child anything, nor have they ever been near a predominantly Black school, much less one serving public housing in a big city like Chicago. There is no public housing anywhere like that that exists in Chicago. If there is no mentor in the public school to help the novice teacher, that teacher will succumb to whatever the school's cultural norms are. In some large public schools in Chicago, until Arne Duncan and Chief Education Officer Barbara Eason-Watkins installed the reading specialists, there was no one who knew how to teach reading.

I chose the Effective Schools Model as the paradigm through which I studied the high-achieving predominantly African American school. I tried to describe those schools in Pittsburgh practicing this model. I brought this seasoned model to Chicago and used it to work as an external partner. Here in Chicago, as in Pittsburgh, there has been much resistance to the high-achieving predominantly African American school. Very little recognition is given to Black principals who so achieve; promotion generally goes to others. I tried to show how we constructed and implemented a model, the Structured Ten Routines, to increase achievement and eliminate the achievement gap.

Chicago is interested in creating schools for the affluent middle class, which Mayor Daley is luring back into the city to increase its tax base. Gated communities have been formed to close off streets to neighboring public housing residents. Magnet schools have been formed all over the city for these future residents. And public housing is being dismantled and those residents sent to the South suburbs, where middle-class Blacks sought refuge from high-priced homes in the city.

There is a consistent denial of racism in this country, and research showing the inequities of local, state, federal and corporate policies does not make a difference in this. In her article, "Tackling the Myth of Black Students' Intellectual Inferiority" Theresa Perry claims "...[T]he ideology of African-American inferiority is more robust today, in terms of its impact on students, than it was in the pre-Civil Rights Era, when unequal educational opportunity was an uncontested reality."[11] Camille Z. Charles and Douglas S. Massey conducted research that found "American-identified Black and Latino students are more likely than their counterparts with the strongest racial identities to stereotype their groups as tending to be lazy, unintelligent, hard to get along with, to give up easily and to discriminate against others." The researchers thought that many of these traits were tied to achievement and "suggest that American-identified Blacks and Latinos may be more concerned with confirming negative group stereotypes and, therefore, their poor academic performance is the result of stereotype threat,"[12] which had been previously studied by Claude Steele.

Almost daily the media details white opinions about being Black. Rarely is there concern about Black opinions about being white. In 2003, Illinois out-going governor, George Ryan, commuted the sentences of all death row prisoners because the justice system of Illinois is so corrupt and because the Illinois legislature took no steps to reform the system after the commission, which the governor set up to study it, presented its findings and recommendations. Ryan placed a moratorium on the death penalty in 2000 after thirteen death row inmates were exonerated.[13] The overwhelming majority of these death row inmates were Black and Latino. While the *Tribune* emphasized the flaws in the justice system affecting the death penalty in Illinois, national television stressed the majority's opposition to the governor's action. Ever since I have been in this world, Black men and women have been treated unjustly by the justice system. This is a direct carryover from Jim Crow (1877–1965).

On January 6, 2003, Mamie Till-Mobley died in her home at the age of eighty-one. She was the mother of Emmett Till, the young Black who was brutally beaten and killed by two white men in Money, Mississippi, where he had gone to visit relatives in 1955. His murderers were acquitted by an all-white jury, even after they bragged about killing him. Mrs. Till-Mobley, determined to let the world know about this terrorism in the South, which the nation wanted to whitewash as it does racism now, had an open casket service for her son, deliberately showing his bloated face, broken nose and ripped-out eye.

In a *Chicago Tribune* article Mary Schmich stated, "It was a sight to make you gag, gasp, gawk, jerk your eyes away."[14] Yet, although the author decried ignorance of racism's effects and lamented the omission of racism from United States' history, she also said, "...[A]nd yet it's not 1955. That's significant too. To equate race relations today with race relations then is to ignore today's truths. The truth that disadvantage today is often more a function of class than of color. The truth that the South has progressed racially, perhaps more than the rest of the country. The truth that the rest of the country was never as racially innocent as it still wants to believe." What Schmich could not know, since she is white is this: Blackness only exists as a social construct in relation to something else. That "something else" became known as whiteness. Blackness as a category relegates other identities—ethnicity, sexual orientation, gender, class affiliation, religious traditions, kinship affiliations—to a secondary, or even nonexistent status. I am not discriminated against because I am poor. I am not poor. I am discriminated against because I am Black and female. My son is discriminated against because he is Black. We fight racism within the university system, so that ignorance cannot be the reason, as Schmich claims. A better answer for Schmich comes from Manning Marable:

> Racist perceptions of Blacks have given energy to policies and practices (such as racial exclusion in housing, impoverished schooling and stingy social welfare programs) that have facilitated the growth of egregious, crime-spawning conditions that millions of Americans face in urban slums and rural backwaters across the nation. Thus, it is not the objective reality of difference between "races" that produces disparities and social inequality between groups; it is structural racism that reproduces "races."[15]

Truly, to most black people Trent Lott, the senator from Mississippi who lauded Strom Thurmond, represents the silent majority of American whites. Marable, expressed it this way:

> This American version of apartheid, reinforced through terror and lynching, produced among the great majority of whites an unquestioned conviction in the inhumanity of blackness. As Gaston put it, "the values and beliefs of the white supremacy culture...included the belief that black people, not individually, but as a race, were genetically inferior to white people and that this genetic deficiency was responsible for the fact that black people were: less intelligent than white people; more prone to crime than white people; diseased; unclean; untruthful; unreliable; immoral; violent; sexually promiscuous; and sexually threatening, through their men, to white women."

School reform as we know it now in Chicago, Pittsburgh or Washington, D.C. will not work because the main problem is the education of African American and Latino children. As long as these school reform measures fail to attack the main pillars of structural racism, African Americans will not be successful. So as long as Black people tolerate the least qualified teachers, the fewest resources, the worst facilities, inadequate supplies and books, a curriculum that denies the existence of Black people, their heritage and history, school reform will fail. To reveal the depth of the myth of Black inferiority, note the attitude of the Mayor of the City of Chicago, Richard J. Daley, who is in charge of the Chicago Public Schools: Mayor Daley said that he was not disturbed that unusually large percentages of poor minority students in Illinois have teachers without even minors in their subjects because teachers shouldn't have to be "specialists" in everything they teach. He said, "They are educators. They have college degrees. Some have master's degrees. So I have to have all specialists and I can't move you around? You cannot do something else in the classroom? Let's be realistic. We have to be more flexible."[17]

Of course, this reflection is for minority and poor children trapped in these schools, not for white middle-class people whom the mayor is trying to lure back to the schools. What is there left for the CEO, Arne Duncan, to do when the boss feels this way? Now we are back where we started. Instead of blatant, overt, brutal, terroristic Jim Crow, we now have muted, subversive, undercover Jim Crow couched in the forms of universals, color–blind rhetoric, nonviolence, assimilation and accommodation language and the ubiquitous "forgive the past" approaches. Nothing is done to atone for past injustices or to remedy the present injustices. You can hear it in the mayor's tone. This is what I hear: Give these minority poor kids any teacher we can find.

Dorothy Shipps argued that "reform is a long, steady process of improving our empirical knowledge about the changes required to meet the needs of disadvantaged children. The other situates urban schools in big city politics and focuses on the civic capacity necessary to generate and sustain change."

Shipps studies school reform in Chicago through urban regime theory emphasizing local actors, coalition building, resources and power. Civic capacity means the formation of reform coalitions and the forging of connections with the governing regime. She sees three reform types: changing pedagogy, curriculum, instruction and the culture of the school; altering the power relations among adults working in and concerned with schools; and shifting the incentives and rewards for both adults and children from the professional and bureaucratic expectations that dominate government-run schools to the economic and survival consequences of markets.

She names four types of regimes: performance, necessitating a change in pedagogy and the culture of the schools; empowerment, requiring some kind of decentralization for better and more innovative decisions; market, demanding a restructuring of schooling the image of the marketplace; and employment, that buffering the existing system for political interference, resisting change and stabilizing the system.

Chicago has flirted with all these regimes. Noting its problems with the empowerment regime, Shipps said, "Over the ensuing decade, a series of studies repeatedly found that schools with mixed Latino and Black populations were the most likely to have LSCs that functioned poorly and had the lowest levels of student achievement." She described the Chicago Annenberg Challenge as the impetus for a performance regime that says it failed because it could not secure teacher or union support. She concluded that some kinds of civic capacity are easier to develop than others and noted the following:

> The Chicago example clarifies that narrow, materially invested coalitions have resource and maintenance advantages over broad–based and cross–sector coalitions for reform with a broader social purpose. But, ironically, if the Chicago example is reflected elsewhere—and a rash of big-city mayoral takeovers suggests that it might be—the narrower coalition is less likely to develop a reform agenda aimed at improving pedagogy and school culture to the advantage of the low–income students of color who are most in need.

Of greater importance for African Americans might be this conclusion:

> More disconcertingly, Chicago's large and relatively well-organized Black community has been left out of all three reform coalitions. Because blacks controlled the schools when the first reform was proposed, critics were provided with an excuse to ignore their concerns. Blacks seemed synonymous with the employment regime that had to be dismantled. Yet black educators had held

320

their positions of leadership for only a few years and were hardly entrenched by 1987. The tension between the hope of better educating tomorrow's black and Latino students and the wish to safeguard the solid middle-class careers of Black teachers and administrators was, for the Black educators, a fundamental conflict unrecognized by the coalition. As a result, the majority of black educators resisted participation. Even the few black corporate executives in the coalition described divided loyalties in response to the 1988 empowerment change…these complicating factors help to explain why there is no evidence that the black-white performance gap has closed, despite fifteen years of reform, and why children of low–income blacks have been disproportionately sanctioned under the latest regime. Eschewing participation in any reform coalition clearly registers disapproval, but it also reduces influence on the reform agenda and may help to ensure that the cycle of coalition building and reform starts all over again.

There has not been any substantive changes in the political reality described by Shipps. Blacks are still on the sidelines. In fact, any attempt to start a dialogue on strategies for change reap responses characterized by intentions to retire, transfer out of the system, or leave. Presently, the voice of parents is articulated by a white woman, the teachers' spokesperson is a white woman, the Chief Education Officer is a white man, the mayor is a white man. The only Black with any kind of power is the Chief Educational Officer. In May 2004, the head of the Chicago Principals Association was a Black woman, whose office was being challenged. I attended a research forum sponsored by CCSR on April 6, 2004, and of the nearly 100 people present, there were only eight African Americans.

Again, hardly a dent has been made in my efforts to mute white supremacy and its counterpart Black inferiority. When I was born Blacks were at the bottom of the socioeconomic ladder, and Blacks are still at the bottom. We have truly been walking in circles.

Afterword

One of the greatest puzzles in the history of education is how providing high educational outcomes for students is seen as some kind of problem of student capacity, a problem of discovering new ways to teach, or a problem of cultural deficiencies, in the face of the experiences of educators for whom none of these things is problematic. The very students, who are diagnosed and identified as deficient, excel academically in the hands of good teachers. There are many many examples of this. Yet, educational planners seem to not know about powerful schools and powerful teachers.

The practice of teaching and schooling is always situated inside a political and economically charged environment. Any honest look at schooling will show that contests for power spill over into the design and operation of schools, affecting equality of opportunities. It seems much easier to look at teaching methods and student "deficiencies" than to look at the power and ideological struggles that shape educational opportunities.

Dr. Barbara Sizemore was involved in the struggle for academic and cultural excellence, successfully, for many decades. Few educators can match her record of excellence in teaching, research, theory building, institution building, and political activism.

Dr. Barbara Sizemore's contributions to education, and to African liberation, are nothing short of colossal. She was a superior educational leader whose mere presence invoked awe and respect. Her revered status and authority came from a lifetime career of extraordinary successes, within a wide variety of educational and socialization challenges. As examples, a few of the most visible of these challenges include being an advisor to several low-income predominately African schools, which reached high levels of achievement in Pittsburgh. Two of these schools were the Robert L. Vann Elementary School, led by Ms. Doris Brevard, and the Madison Elementary

School, led by Ms. Vivian Williams. Both schools were at the very top in achievement in Pittsburgh, with Vann leading the district for nearly twenty years.

Some educators and media people refer to schools like these as "miracles," and attribute their successes to "charismatic" leaders. Yet, as with so many other things in her life, Dr. Sizemore's work showed that such assessments were simpleminded and superficial, trivializing the hard work and the genius of the educators who produced high achievement outcomes. Such observers failed to understand the deep structure of school success. On the other hand, Dr. Sizemore spent her lifetime in study, teaching, research and activism, which led to the evolution of original understanding of the causes of school successes and failures.

How do we explain such school successes like those mentioned above, in the face of the pessimistic forecasts for the students by so many educators and others? Dr. Sizemore wrote a classic short description and analysis of one powerful pathway to success in an article, "The Algebra of the High Achieving African American School." With great clarity, she distilled the essence or principles associated with some of the successful approaches to teaching and school leadership, capturing the wisdom of it all. One manifestation of this clarity is the highly successful School Achievement Structure approach, created by Dr. Sizemore, rooted in her research-based "Ten Routines" for successful schools. It is because of such insights and practices in teaching and learning and school operations, as Dr. Sizemore's that we can show that excellence in teaching and school leadership can be taught. It is a pity that this point still has to be made at this stage of educational development in the United States. Children, regardless of their status, respond to teaching excellence. To accept this fact is to establish a very different expectation for teacher and school leader education than the low-level custodial goals that so many educators project for poor ethnic minority children.

Dr. Sizemore's main body of work was rescue work, in that it was work to overcome the devastation of structured oppression of African people, and other oppressed groups. This devastated state had come to be regarded as normal, setting the stage for institutionalized lowered expectations for the students, and poor pedagogical practices. Dr. Sizemore's work also overcame these things as well as the evolved cultural expectations of oppressor nations, which did not have free public education for the masses in their own histories, free public education for the masses, with traditions of excellence. How then could these oppressor societies expect or want those who they dominated to achieve excellence?

On the other hand, both publicly supported education and expectations of excellence were a common part of many African societies, though the awareness and the memories of this were destroyed, even among African people themselves. Instead, we have the Hollywood stereotyped version of African people, the missionary and the entrepreneurs stereotyped versions of the Africans to be exploited. Few outsiders have been able to understand the sophisticated structures of African societies, or to acknowledge and accept these structures, when they had vested interests in African exploitation. African structures are almost universally misunderstood, misinterpreted, or falsified. Popular images of Africans as "savages," "pagans," "uncivilized," and worse, were the extreme and false products of ignorance and the rationalization of the self interest of those who sought to dominate and to exploit Africans and their resources. We tolerate such low expectations for African achievement now, and indeed, low expectations for the achievement of children in general today, mainly because of the general public mindset that has been created by academic and mass media falsehood and propaganda.

Dr. Barbara Sizemore understood all of this and more. She was the rarest of treasures, with great intellect, impeccable character, the highest level of professional scholarship, the deepest theoretical analysis, absolute fearlessness as an advocate, unconditional commitment to her people, and to our children. Moreover, she was a proven institution builder, a tireless sentinel, and a fierce moral and professional critic of any and all who were responsible for the education of African children.

Therefore, this book, *Walking in Circles*, is a priceless and welcome window on the views by a master "from the bridge." We benefit here from the lifetime experiences of this warrior scholar, who "took no prisoners," who loved the truth, her people and humanity.

American education today is in a mess, in general, with international comparisons that rank its schools near the bottom of the "industrial world."

Within that, the best that can be said for most African children is that, far from being in liberating institutions, their schools are a great weight on them. Even given the "savage inequalities," that have been documented by Jonathan Kozol and others, enormous resources are spent in the public schools, with meager benefits to the students. In too many cases, the more children absorb the "lessons" of the school, the more disabled they become. This has been true for more than 400 years since Columbus, even with the cessation of legal slavery and segregation. Where are the places where the masses of African children are taught so that they achieve academic and cultural excellence? Sadly, for African children in other parts of the European world, conditions are much the same. It does not have to be this way.

Because of America's global power, the mess here is being exported all over the African world, and elsewhere. IQ testing, theories of "cultural deprivation," "culture of poverty," scripted instruction, low-level "vocational" curricula and the absence of or suppression of African cultural studies, are only some examples. Where are the centers of excellence and critical consciousness anywhere in the world for the masses of African people that are supported by foreign "aid," philanthropy, and missions? Quite simply, they do not exist, nor are they in the purposes, plans, or even in the imagination of those who have taken the lead in creating the current structures. "Experts," "specialists," and "advisors" are everywhere, but success is not. Why?

Aside from the mis-education and the mal-education of African children, there are really at least two common types of education for all students, one for the classes and one for the masses. Education for the upper classes mainly produces rulers, competitors, and often exploiters. It is education for power, money and rule by the elite. On the other hand, education for the masses is for minimum competency skills and compliance, making exploitation of the masses effortless, and their survival a struggle. Leaving the rhetoric of some supposed local and global mission of the powerful to spread "democracy" and "civilization" aside, only a cursory look at the evolution of public education in urban centers in the United States is needed to see the tradition of deplorable general conditions in schools that serve our children.

There is virtually no community influence or control over school experiences. Privatized, standardized, minimum competency, schemes are rampant and growing in low-income ethnic minority areas. This of course is built on the industrial or business models of standardization and mass production of instruction, invalid assessment devices, and worse, the scripting of the teaching/learning process itself. These things are rooted in plans for Africans that date back to the think tanks at Lake Mohonk, New York, and Capon Springs, West Virginia, led by political, educational, and industrial elites. This means that low standards and expectations are structured.

Savage inequalities in school resources still exist, in "integrated" schools just as they did in "segregated" schools. In many ways the situation is worse than in the days of official segregation, since many students are actually segregated inside "integrated" schools through tracking and special education disproportion. Because of the above, our children have become commodities in schemes where private profiteers win, whether children achieve or not, since the same services will be purchased, regardless. Increasingly, therefore, educational "leaders" function as managers, whose main creativity is to shop in the supermarket of school reform "programs." This entire emerging system is still largely the product of alien think tanks, whose real goals are to reproduce the class structure and preserve the wealth of the powerful, while masking these intentions under the rhetoric of "leaving no child behind."

Mechanisms of legitimacy, such as accreditation and licensing, are caught up in the jet stream of this seismic change in the structure of schooling that seems to have occurred without the awareness of parents, communities, or even the professional communities. Certainly, there seems to be no general awareness of what is really happening, and there is no real sense of urgency about our failures to reach all of our children.

It is in this context that our warrior Dr. Sizemore moved as a powerful warrior leader in our struggle. Dr. Sizemore was like the great educators that I knew as a child. Even under the bitter conditions of segregation, I was blessed with teachers who loved their students, who accepted no nonsense from them, who conveyed a vision of high possibilities, and who demanded excellence. They saw themselves as members of proud communities? They knew the evil and devastation of American apartheid, and that it robbed them of opportunities and resources to which they are entitled. They were well aware of the devastation that this evil system wrought. They prayed and fought for its end. Their goal was to get their fair share of the resources, to have control over the education processes for their children, and to have a legitimate curriculum, including a strong cultural education.

The educators that I knew never doubted their abilities to teach, or our children's abilities to learn. Their focus was on overcoming our economic and political obstacles. Sadly, many of those warrior educators in the Sizemore tradition have been worn down, or they have been eliminated from the schools altogether.

The mess that we are in now is not only largely separate and unequal; it is also filled with negative assaults on our children and our communities, through academics and through the mass media. Actual surveys of elite educators and psychologists have shown that "Bell Curve" thinking, far from being the whimsy of a few misguided or malevolent scholars, is the norm! New versions of invalid recycled arguments and explanations continue to blame our children and our communities for the failures of a destructive education system that we do not control. "Low mental abilities" and "bad cultural values" are the two dominant hypotheses that drive current popular education reform and educational leadership today, not just "back then." *The Bell Curve* and *No Excuses* are the most recent examples of domestic sources, while *IQ and the Wealth of Nations* and the *Culture Matters* are the most recent international versions prepared mainly for the African continent. These recent texts are merely the capstones of pyramids of propaganda and pseudo-science in the service of hegemony. Even the educators who do not consciously subscribe to these notions, or the few who actively disavow them are now often pessimistic and puzzled about what to do to get African children to achieve excellence. Few today have any knowledge of the wide variety of educators who consistently produce excellence, or the traditions of those who have in the past. They do not know that these educators have always been here, from slavery to the present. Therefore, they doubt the children just as they doubt themselves.

Nothing in place currently will rescue the masses of our children. Educational "reform" is uninformed, tepid, and misguided. Dr. Barbara Sizemore's co-authored work with Dr. Nancy Arnez, "An Abashing Anomaly," reflects genius in capturing the core of the matters. Simply put, how is it possible to explain that some educators are highly successful with African children, poor or wealthy, while others who work with the same children are ranked as failures. That is the question which, if faced, will force change in the debate about what to do and who can do it. Who can teach teachers and lead? Who can accredit schools and teacher education? Who can govern schools? It is clear to me that only successful educators should lead.

It is here again that Dr. Sizemore displays her range and versatility as a scholar, theoretician and philosopher. She shows here a keen understanding of the economic and political context within which our school structures are located. She stares straight into the intent, content, and camouflage of the greed driven exploiters and unmasks them. Just as the "prison industrial complex" now feeds on social dysfunction, and seems to have a vested interest in its continuation, schools are the new grounds for "privatization." In the "business" of education, deals are made, mega deals using the inner cities as the "cash cow."

Walking in Circles is a challenge, charging that real purpose and commitment to educate our children has been lacking. It challenges all of us to fight for our dream to have our children be critically conscious, and a challenge to our action agenda. The "moonwalk" is a dance where one actually walks backwards while appearing to go forward. *Walking in Circles* evokes the same image, the image of those who are always in motion but do not make progress. In the case of African people, it tells us that "desegregation," "integration," "school restructuring" and "reform," etc., have left us in the same position, or worse than we were in before. The real issue is that neither segregation, desegregation, integration nor any of the proposed structural changes in education are grounded in a fundamental knowledge of or respect for African people, and in the genuine intent to produce excellence.

Carter Godwin Woodson told us that credentials alone might not lead to the liberation of our people, and the education process itself could be, and indeed was, a tool of oppression. Dr. Sizemore lived long enough, and was close enough to the schools to see that change is not necessarily progress. *Walking in Circles* is a bold charge that no real rescue process has really been in place, and none is one in place now. We actually have new forms of "segregation" in our schools, since there are vast differences between the educational opportunities that are available to the masses of our children and to that of the mainstream, no matter what the slogans, and no matter that the budgets are increased.

For African people to be ignorant of African excellent intellectual and socialization traditions on the continent, during slavery, and during segregation, leaves us vulnerable to stereotypes and propaganda. We begin to believe that minimum competency is good. It means that many of us have lost trust in ourselves, and have transferred that trust to those who are not trustworthy, even to those who doubt and/or despise us as a people, and some who are our mortal enemies.

We must know ourselves. We must know white supremacy intent and actions, structures and ideas. We must know about current successes, and about those who do not fail to produce them.

Yes, Dr. Sizemore was uniquely qualified to make the valid points that she has made here. The authenticity and validity of *Walking in Circles* are rooted in Dr. Sizemore's own history as a master educator, of demonstrating how to be successful. Having produced so much in so many different arenas and with so many targets, we can truthfully say that it is her works that have spoken. Let her or she who has produced greater success mount any challenge to her wisdom.

I owe a great personal debt to my beloved sister Barbara. We collaborated on many important projects, such as co-editing "Saving the African American Child" for the National Alliance of Black School Educators. We teamed as the chief advisors for the "Every Child Can Succeed" television series and book, produced by the Agency for Instructional Technology. We traveled together, studied together, fought for causes together. Because of these and many other experiences, I learned much from her and was always highly inspired by and drew courage from her model.

Walking in Circles is one more gift of her genius. Will we listen this time?

Asa G. Hilliard III-Baffour Amankwatia II, Ph.D.

Endnotes

Endnotes for Chapter 1 The Roots of My Biases

1. Robert M. Taylor, Jr. Errol Wayne Stevens, Mary Ann Ponder and Paul Brockman. *Indiana: A New Historical Guide.* (Indiana Historical Society, 1990).
2. Geneology for the Stewart family was compiled by the Stewart/Norton families
3. Herbert W. Laffoon Sr. 2002. Genealogy for the Alexander and Laffoon Families
4. John W. Lyda. 1953. *The Negro In The History of Indiana.*
5. Taylor et al, op. cit.
6. Geneology for the Alexander and Laffoon families was compiled by Herbert W. Laffoon, Jr. Los Angeles, California.

Endnotes for Chapter 2 The Details of My Education

1. Jane D. Shackelford. *The Child's Story of the Negro.* Washington: Associated Publishers, 1956.
2. John Wesley Lyda, Sr. *The History of the Negro in Indiana.*

Endnotes for Chapter 3 Making a Living

1. Barbara A. Sizemore and Kymara Chase. "I Dig Your Thing, But It Ain't in My Bag," *Notre Dame Journal of Education,* 1970.
2. On March 19, 2003, the *Chicago Tribune* reported that Lindblom College Preparatory High School, once the pride of the South Side and one of the city's best public high schools, experienced a budget

slashing and subsequently experienced violence during the previous week. Applications to the preparatory had dropped by ten percent over the previous year, and reports of turmoil had circulated off-campus, as well. Edward Klunk, Deputy Chief Officer in the district's office of high school development and one of its most Perceptive administrator's, is quoted as saying that it is not just problems within the school that have affected enrollment, but that the dangers of the West Englewood neighborhood, where it is located, have also affected the school.

3.   One of the troubling legacies of *Brown v. Board of Education* was the failure of the educational system to take on white supremacy, which was the cause of all evils. One of the Supreme Courts later "Findings of Fact" from this decision stated that "Segregation of white and colored children in public school has a detrimental effect upon the colored children. The impact is greater when it has the sanction of the law; for the policy of separating the races is usually interpreted as denoting the inferiority of the Negro group. A sense of inferiority affects the motivation of a child to learn. Segregation with the sanction of the law, therefore, has a tendency to retard the educational and mental development of Negro children and to deprive them of some of the benefits they would have received in a racially integrated school system." This meant that African Americans would need to accept anything that was all-Black as negative and anything that was all-white as positive. Hence, nothing that held white supremacy in place was challenged. See James T. Patterson, *Brown v. Board of Education: A Civil Rights Milestone and Its Troubled Legacy* (New York: Oxford UP, n.d.)

Endnotes for Chapter 4 Being a School Leader

1.   Christopher Chandler, "South Side Principal Denies Uprising is Afoot," the *Chicago Sun Times*, (31 March 1966): 66. See also Bill Van Alstine, "School Staff Hits Ben," the *Chicago Defender*, (21 March 1966): 1; Sam Washington, "Forrestville: Turmoil Brews in School" the *Chicago Defender*, (3 Dec. 1966): 1; Christopher Chandler., "The Embattled

Principal: Schools of The Inner City Wage Historic Struggle," the *Chicago Sun Times*, (12 Oct. 1966): 70.

2. Gerald Butler, "*A Case Study in Urban Teacher Education: The Center for Inner City Studies, 1966–1971*," diss., (U of Massachusetts, April 1971), 11.

3. Donald Hugh Smith. *Climbin' Up the Mountain Children: The Journey of an African American Educator.* (New York, NY: Falu Foundation Press, 2002.)

4. Donald H. Smith and Nancy L. Arnez. "Inner City Studies: Graduate Training for Teachers of the Disadvantaged" *Journal of Teacher Education*, 1969.

5. Douglas B. Reeves. "High Performance in High Poverty Schools: 90/90/90 and Beyond, 2002."

6. Bernard C. Watson. *Negro Colored Black: Chasing the American Dream.* (Philadelphia, Pa: JDC Books, 1997.)

7. John Hall Fish. *Black Power/White Control: The Struggle of the Woodlawn Organization in Chicago.* (Princeton, N.J.: Princeton University Press, 1973.)

8. Hugh J. Scott, *The Black Superintendent: Messiah or Scapegoat?* (D.C.: Howard UP, 1980) 163.

9. *Ibid*, 164.

10. *Ibid*, 67.

11. *Ibid*, 169–170.

12. Task Force I. "Saving the African American Child". (Washington, D.C.: National Alliance of Black School Educators, 1984.)

13. Task Force I. "Saving the African American Child," (Washington, D.C. National Alliance of Black School Educators, 1984.)

14. *Ibid*, 35–36.

15. *Ibid*, 37.

16. Donald H. Smith, *Climbin' Up the Mountain Children*, 189.

17. *Ibid*, 192.

18. Barbara A. Sizemore," Sexism and the Black Male," *The Black Scholar* 4:6, (March/April 1973): 2–11.

19. Task Force II. Demonstration Schools/Communities Initiative. Submitted to the National Alliance of Black School Educators, 2000.

20. Task Force III. Demonstration Schools/Communities Initiative. Submitted to the National Alliance of Black School Educators, 2000.

21. My speech at the annual meeting of the African Heritage Studies Association (April 1975) did not help me one bit. In it, I outlined what I thought to be the gentrification plan for D.C. See also Barbara Sizemore, "Education: Is Accommodation Enough?" *The Journal of Negro Education* 54 (summer 1975): 239–245.

22. Several of the board requests were denied by Congress and all federal grant proposals had been submitted in a timely fashion. A record of these submissions can be found in Nancy L. Arnaz's "The Besieged Superintendent: A Case Study of School Superintendent-School Relations in Washington, D.C., 1973–1975" (Lanham, MD: UP of America, 1981) 550–559.

23. John Rawls, A Theory of Justice (Cambridge, MA: Harvard UP, 1971).

24. Stephen E. Colter, "Rallies for Sizemore Continue, Support Grows," *The Washington Post*, (1 July 1975): Frontpage. See also "Some Lessons in the Sizemore Case," editorial, (30 July 1975): A14; "The Sizemore Hearings and the Schools," editorial, (4 Aug. 1975): A16; Martha M. Hamilton, "Sizemore Group Stages Walkout," *The Washington Post*, (12 Aug. 1975): C1; Annette Gilliam, "Barbara Sizemore," *Essence*, (March 1975): 21.

25. James S. Coleman, et al. "Equality of Educational Opportunity" (D.C.: U.S. Department of Health, Education & Welfare, Education GPO, 1966.)

Endnotes for Chapter 5 The Search for a New Paradigm

1. Among others see Faustine C. Jones, *A Traditional Model of Educational Excellence: Dunbar High School of Little Rock*, Arkansas (D.C.: Howard UP, 1981); Thomas Sowell, *Black Education Myths and Tragedies* (New York: David McKay, 1972) 283–286; Mary Gibson Hundley, *The Dunbar Story: 1870–1955* (New York: Vantage, 1965); Barbara A. Sizemore, "The Effective African American Elementary School." *Schooling in Social Context: Qualitative Studies*, eds. George

W. Noblit and William T. Pink (Norwood, N.J.: Abex, 1987) 175–202; Barbara A. Sizemore, "The Madison School: A Turnaround Case." *The Journal of Negro Education* 57:3 (1988): 243–266, rpt. *Going to School: The African American Experience*, ed. Kofi Lomotey (Albany: State U of New York P, 1990); Barbara A. Sizemore, "The Algebra of African American Achievement," *Effective Schools: Critical Issues in the Education of Black Children*, ed. Robert Smith (D.C.: National Alliance of Black School Educators, Charles D. Moody Institute, 1989) 123–150, rpt. *Every Child Can Succeed: Readings for School Improvement*, eds. Alan Backler and Sybil Eakin (Bloomington, IN: Agency for Instructional Technology, 1993) 105–122.

2.   James S. Coleman, et al., *Equality of Educational Opportunity* (D.C.: U.S. Department of Health, Education & Welfare, Education GPO, 1966); see also Kenneth B. Clark, *The Dark Ghetto* (New York: Harper, 1965) 111–153; Patricia Cayo Sexton, *Education & Income* (New York: Viking, 1961); Patricia Cayo Sexton, Testing Measurements and Afro–Americans, *The Journal of Afro-American Issues* 3:1 (1975); Thomas F. Pettigrew, *A Profile of the Negro American* (New York: D. Van Nostrand, 1964) 100–135; Gerald David Jaynes and Robin M. Williams Jr., eds. *A Common Destiny: Blacks and American Society* (D.C.: National Academy, 1989) 346–361; Elaine M. Allensworth and Shazia Rafiullah Miller, "Declining High School Enrollment: An Exploration of Causes," Consortium on Chicago School Research: Prestigious Colleges Ignore the Inadequate Intellectual Achievement of Black Students, *The Chronicle of Higher Education* B11–B12 (13 Sept. 2002); Catherine Gewertz, "More Chicago Pupils Flunk Grade," *Education Week* 22:6 (9 Oct. 2002).

3.   Arthur R. Jensen, "How Much Can We Boost IQ and Scholastic Achievement?" *Harvard Educational Review* 39 (1969): 1–123. See also Richard J. Herrnstein and Charles Murray, *The Bell Curve: Intelligence and Class Structure in America* (New York: Free P, 1994).

4.   Frank Reissman, *The Culturally Deprived Child* (New York: Harper & Row, 1962). See also Charles A. Valentine, *Culture and Poverty* (Chicago: U of Chicago P, 1968); Martin Deutch, "Facilitating Development in the Preschool Child," *Social and Psychological*

Perspectives in the Disadvantaged Child: Studies of the Social Environment and the Learning Press, ed. Martin Deutsch & Assoc. (New York: Basic Books, 1967) 61–62; Signithia Fordham, "Racelessness as a Factor in Black Students' School Success: Pragmatic Strategy or Pyrrhic Victory?" *Harvard Education Review* 58:1 (1988): 54–84; Signithia Fordham, "Peer Proofing Academic Competition among Black Adolescents," *Empowerment through Multicultural Education*, ed. Christine Sleeter (Albany, NY: State U of New York P, 1991).

5.   David P. Moynihan, *The Negro Family: The Case for National Action*. (D.C.: GPO, 1965); see also Edward C. Banfield, *The Unheavenly Child* (New York: Little, Brown & Co., 1970); Stephen S. Baratz and Joan C. Baratz, "Early Childhood Intervention: The Social Science Basis of Institutional Racism," *As the Twig is Bent*, eds. Robert H. Anderson and Harold G. Shane (New York: Houghton, 1971) 34–52; Peter Sacks, *Standardized Minds* (Cambridge, MA: Perseus, 1999) 158–162; Gerald W. Bracey, "The 12th Bracey Report on the Condition of Public Education," *Phi Delta Kapan* (Oct. 2002): 146–149.

6.   Ronald R. Edmonds, "Some Schools Work and More Can," *Social Policy* (March/April 1979) 28–32. See also: Barbara A. Sizemore, "Push Politics and the Education of America's Youth," *Phi Delta Kappan*, (Jan. 1979): 364–369; Donald H. Smith, "The Black Revolution and Education" *Black Self Concept*, ed. James A. Banks and Jean D. Grambs (New York: McGraw–Hill, 1971) 46–52; Henry M. Levin, "What Difference Do Schools Make?" *Saturday Review* (20 Jan. 1968): 57–58; John I. Goodlad, "Can Our Schools Get Better?" *Phi Delta Kappan* (Jan 1979): 342–346; Barbara A. Sizemore, "The Pitfalls and Promises of Effective Schools Research," *The Journal of Negro Education* 54:3 (summer 1985): 269–288. Pamela Bullard and Barbara O. Taylor, *Keepers of the Dream: The Triumph of Effective Schools* (Chicago: Excelsior! 1994); Barbara O. Taylor, "The Effective Schools Process: Alive and Well," *Phi Delta Kappan* (Jan. 2002): 375–378; Judith K. March and Karen H. Peters, "Effective Schools: Curriculum Development and Instructional Design in the Effective Schools Process," *Phi Delta Kappan* (Jan. 2002): 379–381; Janet

H. Chrispeels, "Effective Schools: The California Center for Effective Schools: The Oxnard School District Partnership," *Phi Delta Kappan* (Jan. 2002): 382–385; Gloria Ladson-Billings, The Dreamkeepers: Successful Teachers of African American Children (San Francisco: Jossey-Bass, 1994).

7. John U. Ogbu, *The Next Generation* (New York: Academic P, 1974). See also Sara Lawrence Lightfoot and Jean J. Carew, *Beyond Bias* (Cambridge: Harvard UP, 1979); Asa G. Hilliard III, *SBA: The Reawakening of the African Mind* (Gainesville, FL: Makare, 1997) 33–67; Jonathon Kozol, *Savage Inequalities: Children in America's Schools* (New York: Harper, 1991); Jonathon Kozol, *Amazing Grace: The Lives of Children and the Conscience of a Nation* (New York: Harper, 1995); Maribeth Vander Weele, *Reclaiming Our Schools* (Chicago: Loyola UP, 1988).

8. Richard Kluger, *Simple Justice* (New York: Random, 1977).

9. Richard Kluger, "Desegregation in the 1970s: A Candid Discussion," *The Journal of Negro Education* 47:1 (winter 1978). See also Robert G. Newby, *Desegregation: Its Inequities and Paradoxes: Toward an Equitable and Just Educational Policy for Afro-Americans*, ms., (Wayne State U, Detroit, 1979); Robert G. Newby, "Just Schools: A Special Report Commemorating the 25th Anniversary of the Brown Decision," *Southern Exposure* 7:1 (summer 1979); Everett Abney, *A Survey of Black Public School Principals Employed in Florida During the 1964–1965 School Term* (Coral Gables, FL: U of Miami, 1976); Nancy H. St. John, *School Desegregation: Outcomes for Children* (New York: Wiley, 1975); Jacquelyn J. Jackson and Larry C. Harris, "You May be Normal When You Come Here, But You Won't be Normal When You Leave, or Herman the Pushout," *Black Scholar* 8 (1977): 2–11; Ira Simmons, "The Whitening of Central," *Louisville Times* (21 Dec. 1976); Derrick Bell Jr., *Shades of Brown* (New York: Teacher's College P, 1980); Derrick Bell Jr., *And We are Not Saved: The Elusive Quest for Racial Justice* (New York: Basic Books, 1987); Theodore Cross, *Black Power Imperative* (New York: Faulkner P, 1984) 606–611; Taylor Branch, *Parting the Waters: America in the King Years*, 1954–1963 (New York: Simon & Schuster, 1988) 51–52,

154–158, 230; Gary Orfield, "The Growth of Segregation in America's Schools," *Equity and Excellence* 27:1 (1994): 5–8; Cheryl Harris, "Whiteness as Property," *Harvard Law Review* 106 (1993): 1707–1791; Catherine Prendergast, "The Economy of Literacy: How the Supreme Court Stalled the Civil Rights Movement," *Harvard Educational Review* 72:2 (summer 2002): 206–227.

10. Ronald R. Edmonds and John R. Frederiksen, ts., "Search for Effective Schools: The Identification and Analysis of City Schools That are Instructionally Effective for Poor Children," (New York: Office of Educational Evaluation, n.d.) 4, 8–14, 16–18. See also R.R. Edmonds, *Testimony before the House of Representatives Subcommittee on Elementary, Secondary and Vocational Education*, (D.C., 27 Oct. 1981.)

11. Barbara A. Sizemore, Carlos A. Brossard and Birney Harrigan, *An Abashing Anomaly: The High Achieving Predominantly Black Elementary School #G-80-0006G* (D.C.: The National Institute of Education, 1983).

12. Hope Landrine and Elizabeth A. Klonoff. "African American Acculturation: Deconstructing Race and Reviving Culture". (Thousand Oaks, CA: Sage, 1996.)

13. *Ibid*, 11.

14. Cheryl Harris, op. cit., and Catherine Predergast, op. cit.

15. Barbara A. Sizemore, "Educational Research on Desegregation: Significance for the Black Community," *The Journal of Negro Education* 47:1 (winter, 1978): 59–68. See also Nancy L. Arnez, "Implementation of Desegregation as a Discriminatory Process/Genocidal Alternative," 47:1 (winter 1978): 28–45; Charles V. Willie, *The Sociology of Urban Education* (D.C.: Lexington, 1978) 59–76; David A. Bennett, "Integrate City and Suburban Students," *The American School Board Journal* 176:5 (May 1989): 21–24; Gary Orfield, Sara Schley, Diane Glass and Sean Reardon, "The Growth of Segregation in American Schools: Changing Patterns of Separation and Poverty Since 1968," *Equity & Excellence in Education: The University of Massachusetts School of Education Journal* 27:1 (April 1994): 5–9; Gary Orfield, Jennifer Arenson, Tara Jackson, Christine

Bohrer, Dawn Gavin, Emily Kalejs, and many volunteers for the
Harvard Project on School Desegregation, "Summary of City
Suburban Desegregation: Parent and Student Perspectives in
Metropolitan Boston," *Equity & Excellence in Education: The
University of Massachusetts School of Education Journal* 31:3 (Dec.
1998): 6–12; Paul Ruffins, "Whatever Happened to Integration?" *Black
Issues in Higher Education* 15:23 (7 Jan. 1999): 18–20; Stephen
Caldas, Roslin Growe and Carl A. Bankston III, "African American
Reaction to Lafayette Parish School Desegregation Order: From
Delight to Disenchantment," *The Journal of Negro Education* 71:1-2
(winter/spring 2002): 43–59.

16.   Sizemore, *The Ruptured Diamond: The Politics of the
Decentralization of the District of Columbia Public Schools* (D.C.: UP
of America, 1981) 16–17, 43–49. See also Equal Educational
Opportunity–part 13. "Quality and Control of Urban Schools."
Hearings before the Select Committee on Equal Educational
Opportunity (D.C. U.S. Senate, 92nd Congress, First Session: GPO,
27–29 Aug. 1971) 5844–5912; Marilyn Gittell, "Community Control
of Education," *Politics of Education*, ed. Marilyn Gittell and Allan G.
Hevesi (New York: Praeger, 1967); Henry M. Levin, ed., *Community
Control of Public Schools* (D.C.: The Brookings Institute, 1970);
George R. LaNoue and Bruce L.P. Smith, *The Politics of
Decentralization* (New York: D.C. Heath & Co., 1973); Naomi Levine,
Ocean Hill-Brownsville: A Case History of Schools in Crises (New
York: Popular Library, 1967); Arthur D. Little Inc., *Urban Education:
Eight Experiments in Community Control*, Report to the Office of
Economic Opportunity (D.C.: GPO, 13 Oct., 1969); Preston Wilcox,
"The Thrust Toward Community Control of the Schools in Black
Communities," *Racial Crises in American Education*, ed. Robert L.
Green (Chicago: Follett, 1969) 299–318; James G. Cibulka, "School
Decentralization in Chicago," *Education and Urban Society* 7 (Aug.
1975): 422; Charles E. Wilson, "201 Steps Toward Community
Control," *Schools Against Children*, ed. Annette
T. Rubinstein (New York: Monthly Review Press, 1970) 211–227; Alan
A. Altshuler, *Community Control* (New York: Pegasus, 1970); Henry

Hampton, Steve Fayer and Sarah Flynn, eds., *Voices of Freedom: An Oral History of the Civil Rights Movement from the 1950s through the 1980s* (New York: Bantam, 1990) 485–510.

17. Sizemore, *The Ruptured Diamond*, 47. See also Reginald Stuart, "Community Boards have Few Powers," *Race Relations Reporter* 2:8 (3 May 1971): 10–11; Hampton & Fayer, op. cit. 508–509.

18. Consortium on Chicago School Research, University of Chicago (1997), *Charting Reform: LSCs-Local Leadership at Work.* See also Illinois P.A. 85–1418 (Dec. 1988).

19. William Snider, "Power of Parents Put to the Test in Chicago Reform Experiment," *Education Week* (21 Nov. 1990): 14–15. See also Joyce Young, "Questions before the Boards," *New York Daily News* (5 Feb. 1989): 1–3.

20. Paul E. Peterson, *The Politics of School Reform, 1870–1940. (Chicago:* University of Chicago Press, 1985.)

21. Paul E. Peterson, *The Politics of School Reform: 1870–1940* (Chicago: U of Chicago P, 1985) 19. See also David Tyack, *The One Best System: A History of American Education* (Cambridge: Harvard UP, 1974) 127; Joanne Wasserman, "Grade Time for Education Chief," *New York Daily News* (26 Feb. 1989): 5.

22. Coleman, op. cit., 325. ; Marshall S. Smith, "Equality of Opportunity, the Basic Findings Reconsidered," *On Equality of Educational Opportunity*, ed. Frederick Mosteller and Daniel P. Moynihan (New York: Basic, 1972) 230–243.

23. Coleman, op. cit., 22.

24. Moynihan, David P. *The Negro Family: The Case for National Action.* D.C.: GPO, 1965.

25. Jonathon Kozol, *Death at an Early Age: The Destruction of the Hearts and Minds of Negro Children in the Boston Public Schools,* (New York: Houghton, 1967); Jonathon Kozol, *Savage Inequalities* (New York: Harper, 1991); Jonathon Kozol, *Amazing Grace* (New York: Harper, 1995); John Holt, *The Underachieving School* (New York: Pitman, 1969); Charles Silberman, *Crises in the Classroom* (New York: Random, 1970); Diana T. Slaughter, "Alienation of the Afro American Children," *Cultural Pluralism*, ed. Edgar G. Epps (New York:

McCutcheon, 1974) 144–169; James Herndon, *The Way it Spozed to Be* (New York: Bantam, 1965); Herbert R. Kohl, *Thirty-six Children* (New York: New American Library/World, 1967); Bel Kaufman, *Up the Down Staircase* (New York: Prentice–Hall, 1964).

26. David Rogers, 110 *Livingston Street: Politics and Bureaucracy in the New York City Schools* (New York: Random, 1968) 169–192, 197, 215, 273, 284–285, 331. See also Samuel Bowles and Henry M. Levin, "The Determinants of Scholastic Achievement: An Appraisal of Some Recent Evidence," *Journal of Human Resources* (1968): 3–24; Samuel Bowles and Herbert Gintis, *Schooling in Capitalist America* (New York: Basic, 1976); Robert Schwartz, Thomas Pettigrow and Marshall Smith, "Fake Panaceas for Ghetto Education," *New Republic* (23 Sept. 1967): 16–19; Roger R. Wooch, ed., *Education and the Urban Crises* (Scranton, PA: International Textbook, 1970) 218; Rosalind Rossi, "Who Can Fix Schools First?" *Chicago Sun Times* (7 May 2002): 1; Lori Olszewski, "True or False: Teachers are Part of the Solution, Not the Problem, in School Reform?" *The Chicago Tribune Magazine* (18 Aug. 2002): 10–18, Deborah Lynch, "Letter to the Editor," *Chicago Tribune* (2 Jan. 2003).

27. George Weber, as cited by Ronald R. Edmonds, "A Discussion of the Literature and Issues Related to Effective Schooling." Ronald R. Edmonds, "Some Schools Work and More Can."

28. George Weber, "Inner City Children Can be Taught to Read: Four Successful Schools," *Occasional Paper 18* (D.C.: Council for Basic Education, 1971).

29. William Brookover, et al., *Elementary School Climate and School Achievement*, National Institute of Education G No. 74–0020 (D.C. Department of Health, Education and Welfare, 1978).

30. George Weber, as cited by Ronald R. Edmonds, "A Discussion of the Literature and Issues Related to Effective Schooling," 20.

31. Ronald R. Edmonds, "Some Schools Work and More Can," op. cit., 32.

32. William B. Brookover and Lawrence W. Lezotte, ts., "Changes in Student Achievement," A study from a project carried out at the College of Education (1977) 57–58.

33.   *Ibid,* 60.

34.   Ronald R. Edmonds, "School Factors Influencing Reading Achievement: A Case Study of Two Inner City Schools". *State of New York Office of Educational Performance Review,* March 1974.

35.   Ronald R. Edmonds, "School Factors Influencing Reading Achievement: A Case Study of Two Inner City Schools," *State of New York Office of Educational Performance Review* (March 1974). See also Educational Leadership 37:1 (Oct. 1979) 24–28.

36.   Brookover, William B. and Lezotte, Lawrence W. "Changes in School Characteristics Coincident with Changes in School Achievement" *Occasional Paper* 17: ed.

37.   Bruce R. Joyce, Richard H. Hersh, and Michael McKibben. "The Structure of School Improvement." (White Plains, NY: Longman, 1983.)

38.   MacKenzie, Donald E. "Research for School Improvement: An Appraisal of Some Recent Trends," *Educational Researcher,* April 1983.

39.   Donald E. MacKenzie, "Research for School Improvement: An Appraisal of Some Recent Trends," *Educational Researcher* 12 (April 1983): 8.

40.   Ronald R. Edmonds, "Some Schools Work and More Can," op. cit., 32.

41.   Dan C. Lortie, *Schoolteacher* (Chicago: U of Chicago P, 1975). See also Willard Waller, *The Sociology of Teaching* (New York: Wiley, 1967).

42.   Brookover and Schneider, op. cit., 83–93. See also Brookover et al., op. cit., 301–318.

43.   Dan C. Lortie. *Schoolteacher.* (Chicago: U of Chicago P., 1975.)

44.   Brookover et al., *School Social Systems and Student Achievement: Schools Can Make A Difference* (New York: Praeger, 1979).

45.   Sara Lawrence Lightfoot and Jean J. Carew, op. cit., 146.

46.   Eleanor B. Leacock. *Teaching and Learning in Inner City Schools.* (New York: Basic, 1969.)

47.   Eleanor B. Leacock, *Teaching and Learning in Inner City Schools* (New York: Basic, 1969).

48.   Dan C. Lortie, 23.

49.   *Ibid*, 219.

50.   Pamela Bullard and Barbara O. Taylor, *Keepers of the Dream: The Triumph of Effective Schools* (Chicago: Excelsior! 1994) 253.

51.   Jerry Leiter, "Perceived Teacher Autonomy and the Meaning of Organizational Control," *Sociology Quarterly* 22 (spring 1981) 236.

52.   *Ibid*, 234.

53.   Ogbu, *The Next Generation*, 142–143.

54.   *Ibid*, 144.

55.   *Ibid*, 257.

56.   Dan C. Lortie, *Schoolteacher*, 219.

57.   John C. Ogbu, *Minority Education and Caste* (New York: Academic P, 1978).

58.   *Ibid*.

59.   *Ibid*, 212.

60.   *Ibid*, 133–145.

61.   Susan Goldsmith, "Rich Black and Flunking," *East Bay Express* (21 May 2003). See also John U. Ogbu and Astrid Davis, *Black American Students in an Affluent Suburb: A Study of Academic Disengagement* (Mahwah, N.J.: Lawrence Erllbaum, 2003)

62.   Susan, Goldsmith. "Rich Black and Flunking," East Bay Express, 21 May 2003.

63.   John H. McWhorter. *Losing Race: Self-Sabotage in Black America.* (New York: Free P. 2000.)

64.   Shelby Steele. *The Content of Our Character.* (New York: St. Martin, 1990.)

65.   Goldsmith, "Rich Black and Flunking," 8.

66.   Karla, Scoon Reid. "Meager Effort Said to Fuel Racial Gap". *Education Week,* (12 March 2003.)

67.   Carole E. Joffe. "Friendly Intruders." (Berkeley: U of California P., 1977)

68.   Jerome Taylor. "The Black Family: Toward a Theory of Viability," presented to the African American Heritage Studies Association (Pittsburgh: U of Pittsburgh, April 1979).

69.   Chester I. Barnard, The Function of the Executive (Cambridge:

Harvard UP, 1938) 19.

70.   Barbara A. Sizemore, Brossard, Carlos A. and Harrigan, Birney. "An
        Abashing Anomaly: The High Achieving Predominantly Black
        Elementary School." Grant No. G–80–0006. D.C.: National Institute
of
        Education, January 1983.

71.   Sizemore, et al., *An Abashing Anomaly.*

72.   Robert E. Klitgaard and George R. Hall, *A Statistical Search for
        Unusually Effective Schools* (Santa Monica, CA: Rand, 1973).

73.   This interpretation evolved from personal discussions with Carlos A.
        Brossard.

74.   Brian Rowan, Steven T. Brossart, and David C. Dwyer, "Research on
        Effective Schools: A Cautionary Note". *Educational Researcher*, April
        1983.

75.   Brian Rowan, et al., op. cit., 24–31.

76.   Brian Rowan, "Shamanistic Rituals in Effective Schools," *Issues in
        Education* (summer 1984): 76–87. Shamanism is a religion that
        embraces a belief in powerful spirits who can be influenced by
        Shamans—medicine men acting as holy priests and doctors who
        work with the supernatural. Rowan's intent is to relegate research on
        effective schools to what he deems an inferior symbolic universe.

77.   *Ibid*, 80.

78.   Stewart C. Purkey and Marshall S. Smith, "Effective Schools Review."
        Elementary School Journal, March 1983.

79.   *Ibid.*

80.   *Ibid*, 430.

81.   *Ibid*, 435.

82.   *Ibid*, 439.

83.   *Ibid*, 442.

84.   *Ibid*, 444.

85.   *Ibid*, 446.

86.   *Ibid.*

87.   Gary Orfield. *Metropolitan School Desegregation: Impacts on
        Metropolitan Society.* (New York: Peter Lang, 2001.)

88.   John A. Powell, "Living and Learning: Linking Housing and

Education," *In Pursuit of a Dream Deferred*, ed. John A. Powell (New York: Peter Rand, 2001) 16.

89.   Richard Kluger, *Simple Justice* (New York: Random, 1975) 782.

90.   Powell, op. cit., 18.

91.   Powell, *Ibid*, 29.

92.   Powell, *Ibid*, 35.

93.   Douglas B. Reeves, *High Performance in High Poverty Schools: 90/90/90 and Beyond* (dreeves@MakingStandardsWork.com, 2002).

94.   John O. Simpson, "Beating the Odds," *American School Board Journal*
190 (Jan. 2003).

95.   Janet H. Crispeels, "The California Center for Effective Schools: The Oxnard School District Partnership, *Phi Delta Kappan* 83:5 (Jan 2002) 382. See also Charles Teddlie and Sam Stringfield, *Schools Do Make A Difference: Lessons Learned from a Ten-Year Study of School Effects* (New York: Teachers College P, 1989).

96.   Daniel U. Levine and Lawrence W. Lezotte, "Unusually Effective Schools: A Review and Analysis of Research and Practice" (Madison, WI: The National Center for Effective Schools Research and Development, 1990.)

97.   Daniel U. Levine and Lawrence W. Lezotte, *Unusually Effective Schools: A Review and Analysis of Research and Practice* (Madison, WI: The National Center for Effective Schools Research and Development, 1990) 71.

98.   Daniel U. Levine and Rayna F. Levine, *Society and Education*, 9th ed. (Boston: Allyn and Bacon, 1996) 443.

99.   Donald M. Thomas and William Bainbridge. "All Children Can Learn: Facts and Fallacies," *Phi Delta Kappan,* May 2001.

100.   M. Donald Thomas and William Bainbridge, "All Children Can Learn: Facts and Fallacies," *Phi Delta Kappan* 92:9 (May 2001): 660–662.

101.   Barbara O. Taylor, "The Effective Schools Process: Alive and Well." *Phi Delta Kappan,* January 2002.

102.   Barbara O. Taylor, "The Effective Schools Process: Alive and Well," *Phi Delta Kappan* 83:5 (Jan. 2002): 375–378.

103.   Judith K. March and Karen H. Peters, January 2002. "Curriculum

Development and Instructional Design in the Effective Schools Process". *Phi Delta Kappan.*

104. Judith K. March and Karen H. Peters, "Curriculum Development and Instructional Design in the Effective Schools Process," *Phi Delta Kappan* 83:5 (Jan. 2002): 379–381.

105. Peter Schmidt. "Affirmative Action Survives and So Does the Debate: The Supreme Court Upholds Race-Conscious Admissions in Principle, But Not Always as Practiced," *The Chronicle of Higher Education* (4 July 2003): 52.

106. Richard J. Herrnstein and Charles A. Murray, *The Bell Curve: Intelligence and Class Structure in American Life.* New York: Free Press, (1994.)

Endnotes for Chapter 6 The Pittsburgh Administration

1. Sizemore *Centralization and Decentralization. Encyclopedia of School Administration and Supervision*, edited by Richard A. Gorton, Gail T. Schneider and James C. Fisher. NY: Oryx Press, 1988, 50–51.

2. Sizemore *Centralization and Decentralization. Encyclopedia of School Administration and Supervision*, edited by Richard A. Gorton, Gail T. Schneider and James C. Fisher. (NY: Oryx Press, 1988), 50-51.

3. *Ibid*, p. 51.

4. Sizemore, B.A *The Ruptured Diamond: The Politics of the Decentralization of the District of Columbia Schools.* Lanham, MD: University Press of America, 1981, p. 17.

5. Sizemore, "The Limits of the Black Superintendency: A Review of the Literature," *Journal of Educational Equity and Leadership* 6:3 (fall 1956) 180–208.

6. Sizemore "The Limits of the Black Superintendency: A Review of the Literature." *Journal of Educational Equity and Leadership.* 6:3, (Fall, 1956), 180-208.

7. Board of Education Minutes, February 24, 1959, p. 138. Board of Education Minutes, May 20, 1958. Edmunds, Arthur J., *Daybreakers.* (Pittsburgh: Urban League of Pittsburgh), p. 127–130.

8. Board of Education Minutes, January 26, 1971.

9.   Constance A. Cunningham, "Homer S. Brown: First Black Political Leader in Pittsburgh," *The Journal of Negro History*, 64:4, (Winter, 1981-1982), 304–317

10.   *Ibid*, 307.

11.   Paul Francis Black. *A Historical Study of the Structures and Major Functions of the Pittsburgh Board of Public Education*. Pittsburgh, (Pa: University of Pittsburgh, 1972), 211–217.

12.   *Ibid.*, 229.

13.   *Ibid.* See also Peter Schrag. "Pittsburgh: The Virtues of Candor," *Saturday Review*, (November 19, 1966), 83–84.

14.   Board of Education Minutes, February 26, 1963, 141.

15.   Board of Education Minutes, October 22, 1963, 452.

16.   *Black*, op.cit, 229.

17.   Board of Education Minutes, June 23, 1964

18.   Board of Education Minutes, February 25, 1964, March 23, 1965, May 24, 1966.

19.   The great high school concept was a proposal to build five large new high schools by which pupils who were segregated at that point in time would be desegregated by reassignment to these great high schools.

20.   *Black*, P.E., op. cit., 230–231.

21.   *Ibid*, 231.

22.   Board of Education Minutes, May 16, 1968.

23.   *Black*, P.E. op cit., 232.

24.   *Black*, P.E. op. cit,.233.

25.   The Public Schools and the Public Report of the Select Commission to Study the Pittsburgh School Board. (Pittsburgh, Pa: 1969), 33–34.

26.   Interviews with Louis A . Venson, April, 1979; October, 2002.

27.   Jake Milliones, Jerome Taylor and Louis A. Venson, personal interview (Pittsburgh) 19 June 1981, 29 Sept. 1986.

28.   *Chronology of Desegregation Efforts* 1968-1980. Mimeographed sheet published by the Pittsburgh Public Schools, (Pittsburgh, Pa., 1981.)

29.   *Ibid.*

30. *Pittsburgh Press*, Monday, January 30, 1978,

31. Edwina Rankin. "City School Leadership Stressed." *Pittsburgh Press*, April 1, 1979.

32. Barbara Gubanic. "State Oks City School Desegregation Plan." *Pittsburgh Post-Gazette*, (Saturday, November 20, 1982.)

33. *Black*, P.E. op. cit., 249–250

34. Board of Education Minutes, November, 1972.

35. Board of Education Minutes, October 21, 1975

36. Board of Education Minutes, November 17, 1975

37. "The New Board President." Editorial. *Pittsburgh Press*, (Wednesday, December 7, 1983).

38. Dan Donovan. Milliones Demands Accountability in Education. *Pittsburgh Press*, (Monday, December 15, 1986.) Front page.

39. Caren Marcus. "Integrationists' School Triumph Counters Trend." *Pittsburgh Press*, (November 23, 1979.) "Three School Integration Backers Win." *Pittsburgh Press*, (Wednesday, November 7, 1979.)

40. Susan Mannella. "Rivals for City School Board Support Each Other's Challengers." *Pittsburgh Post Gazette*, (Thursday, April 30, 1981.) Diane Powell. Jake Milliones: The People's Choice. *The Pittsburgh Courier*, (June 13, 1981.)

41. Alvin Rosensweet. "Engel edges out Milliones to head school board." *Pittsburgh Post Gazette*, (Tuesday, December 8, 1981.)

42. Barbara Gubanic. "Milliones Wins top School Board Post." *Pittsburgh Post Gazette*, (Tuesday, December 6, 1983.)

43. The External Review Teams Report to the Pittsburgh Board of Education. Final Report of the External Review of the Pittsburgh Public School District, January 25, 1989. Mimeographed. Pierce Hammond, Floretta Dukes McKenzie, Miles Myers, Rita Walters and Beatrice Ward.

44. Sizemore, "The Madison School: A Turnaround Case." *The Journal of Negro Education*, 57:3, (Summer, 1988), 243–266; *The Effective African American School in Schooling in Social Context: Qualitative Studies*, edited by George W. Nobllit and William T. Pink (Norwood, N.J.: Ablex Publishing Company, 1987), 175–202.

45. "The Final Report of the External Review," vii.

46. Bill Zlatos, "City Schools Opening Multicultural Center to Help Stem Racism," *Pittsburgh Press*, (2 May 1989): Frontpage.

47. Barbara A. Sizemore, Carlos A. Brossard and Birney Harrigan. *An Abashing Anomaly: The High Achieving Predominantly Black Elementary School.* Funded by the National Institute of Education Under Grant application No. 9–001721, (Pittsburgh, Pennsylvania: University of Pittsburgh, January, 1983.)

48. "Ocean Hill School Closing in Peace." No byline. *The New York Times*, (Wednesday, June 25, 1969.), p.49. Charlayne Hunter. "Unrest on Rise in Harlem School Complex," *The New York Times*, (Tuesday, March 23, 1971), p. 39.

49. Karl Weick. "Educational Organizations as Loosely Coupled Systems." *Administrative Science Quarterly*, (1976), 21, 1–19.

50. David R. Olson, "What is Worth Knowing?" *School Review* 82:1 (Nov. 1973) 35.

51. Renee Henderson. "Vann, Madison Exceed National Testing Norms." *New Pittsburgh Courier*, (October 4, 1986.)

52. Sizemore, Carlos A. Brossard and Birney Harrigan. *An Abashing Anomaly: The High Achieving Predominantly African American Elementary School.* Unpublished Report. (University of Pittsburgh, Department of Black Community, Education Research and Development, January, 1983.)

53. Sizemore, "The Effective Elementary School," 185.

54. "Evaluation of the LRDC Individualized Programs in the Pittsburgh Public Schools," Prepared for the Pittsburgh Public Schools by the LRDC (Pittsburgh: U of Pittsburh, 29 Aug. 1975)

55. Carlos Brossard, personal interview via e–mail, 29 June, 2003.

56. *Ibid.*

57. Debra Viadero, "R.I. Focuses on Research-Based Common Language," *Education Week* 22, (2 April 2003): 20–21.

58. Lois Weiner, "Research or 'Cheerleading'? Scholarship on Community School District 2," *Education Analysis Archives*, (New York, 22 Aug. 2003) <http://epaa.asu.edu/epaa/v11n27/>.

59. Larry Cuban, "Researcher Advising Policymakers: A Word to the Wise." *Educational Psychologist* 23:3 (1998) 287–293.

60. Lauren B. Resnick, "Reforms, Research and Variability: A Reply to Lois Weiner," *Education Policy Archives*, (New York, 22 Aug. 2003) <http://epaa.asu.edu/epaa/v11n28>.

61. Julian Elloso Abuso, "Symbols and Strategies in Black Studies: A Case Study," diss., (U of Pittsburgh, 1983). 54–55.

62. *Ibid*, 57, 60.

63. *Ibid*, 52.

64. Curtiss Porter, personal interview via e-mail, May 2003.

65. Curtiss Porter, op. cit.

66. Carlos Brossard, op. cit.

67. Julian Elloso Abuso, op. cit., 148.

68. Ibid, 178.

69. Madeleine Coleman, "Black Children Just Keep on Growing," *Black Child Development Institute* (D.C.: 1977) 87.

70. Vernell A. Little, "Final Narrative Report," (University of Pittsburgh, 17 Jan. 1973.)

71. Jerome Taylor and Malick Kouyate, "Achievement Gap Between Black and White Students: Theoretical Analysis with Recommendations for Remedy," *Handbook of Racial and Ethnic Minority Psychology*, eds. Guillermo Bernal, Joseph E. Trimble, A. Kathleen Burlaw, and Frederick T. L. Leong (Sage, 2003): 327–355.

72. Gail Austin, personal interview via e-mail, 18 Feb. 2003.

73. Donald H. Smith, *Climbin' Up the Mountain Children*, op. cit., 98–99.

74. Curtiss Porter, op. cit.

Endnotes for Chapter 7 Chicago School Reform 1988-2002

1. Alice Blair, et, al. *A Discussion Paper for Improving General High Schools in Chicago. Chicago, Ill.: Chicago Public Schools.* Reported also in Barbara A. Sizemore, *Imputation of Black Inferiority: Does It Contribute to the Achievement Gap? In Surmounting All Odds: Education, Opportunity and Society in the New Millennium*, edited by Ronald D. Henderson and Carol Camp Yeakey, (Greenwich, Conn: Information Age Publishers, 2002.)

2. *Ibid.*

3. G. Alfred Hess. "Understanding Achievement (and other) Changes Under Chicago School Reform." *Educational Evaluation and Policy Analysis*, (Spring, 21:1, 67–83, 1999.)

4. G. Alfred Hess. *School Restructuring Chicago Style*. Newbury Park, CA: Corwin Press, 1991.

5. Kahne Shipps and Smylie, op. cit.

6. *Ibid.*

7. J. Jerome Harris. "A District-wide Application of the Effective Schools' Research." *The Journal of Negro Education*, 57:3, (Summer, 1988.)

8. David L. Kirp. "What School Choice Really Means." *Atlantic Monthly*, (November 1992), 124.

9. Anthony Bryk. Letter to the Editor. *The Chicago Tribune*. (November, 1998.)

10. G. Alfred Hess. Summary Section of Interim Report on Various Aspects of the Design for High Schools filed with the Chicago Public Schools, (October, 1998.)

11. Catalyst, (September, 1999). See also Greg Hinz. "New Student Dropout Report Shakes Up Biz." *Crain's Chicago Business*, (March 19, 2001), Frontpage.

12. John Goodlad. *Educational for Renewal: Better Teachers, Better Schools*. (San Francisco, CA: Jossey-Bass publishers), 1–29.

13. Barbara A. Sizemore, *The Imputation of Black Inferiority: Does It Contribute to the Achievement Gap? In Surmounting All Odds: Education, Opportunity and Societyin the New Millennium*, edited by Ronald D. Henderson and Carol Camp Yeakey, (Greenwich, Conn.:Information Age Publishers, 2003).

14. Ronald R. Edmonds. "Some Schools Work and More Can." *Social Policy*, 9, 28-32, (1979). See also Ronald R. Edmonds and John R. Fredericksen. *Search for Effective Schools: The Identification and Analysis of City Schools That are Instructively Effective for Poor Children*. ERIC, #ED 179 396. Ronald R. Edmonds. *A Discussion of the Literature and Issues Related to Effective Schooling*. Unpublished manuscript. (Cambridge, MA: Harvard University, 1979). Graham T. Allison. *The Essence of Decision Making: Explaining the Cuban*

Missile Crisis. (Boston, MA: Little, Brown & Co., 1971.)

15. Barbara A. Sizemore, Carlos A. Brossard and Birney Harrigan. *An Abashing Anomaly: The High Achieving Predominantly African American Public School.* Washington, D.C. National Institute of Education. Grant #G-80-0006, (January, 1983). Barbara A. Sizemore. *The Effective African American Elementary School in Schooling in Social Context: Qualitative Studies* edited by George W. Noblit and William T. Pink. Norwood, N.J.: Ablex Publishing col, 175-202, 1987. Barbara A. Sizemore' "The Madison School: A Turnaround Case." *The Journal of Negro Education,* Vol. 57:3, (Summer, 1988), 243-266. Reprinted in *Going to School* edited by Kofey Lomotey, Barbara A. Sizemore. *The Algebra of African American Achievement in Effective Schools: Critical Issues in the Education of Black Children.* (Washington, D.C.: National Alliance of Black School Educators. Charles D. Moody Institute, 123–150, 1989). Reprinted with update in Every Child Can Succeed.: Readings for School Improvement. (Bloomington, Indiana: Agency for Instructional Technology, 105-1222, 1993).

16. G. Alfred Hess, op. cit, 1991

17. Anthony Bryk. *Charting Reform: LSCs—Local Leadership at Work.* (Chicago, Ill.: Consortium on Chicago School Research, University of Chicago, 1997).

18. Catherine Gewertz. "Chicago Ponders How to Balance Governing Power." *Education Week,* (April 24, 2002), Frontpage.

19. Anthony Bryk, *Charting Reform,*op.cit.

20. Charles Payne. *I Don't Want Your Nasty Pot of Gold: Urban School Climate and Public Policy.* A Report on an Evaluation of the Comer Project. (Evanston, Ill.: Institute for Policy Research. 1997).

21. *Education Week,* 21:32, (April 24, 2002).

22. Gewertz, op. cit., p. 27

23. Maribeth Vander Weele. *Reclaiming Our Schools.* Chicago, Ill.:Loyola University Press, 1988.

24. Brad R. Braxton. "Guess who's coming to dinner? The black Jesus \ and Easter." *The Chicago Tribune,* (April 14, 2001). Section 1,p.19. Steve Johnson. "Jesus' Documentary Offers a Wealth of Facts." *The*

Chicago Tribune. (April 15, 2001). Section 5, p.4. See also William Mosley. *What Color Was Jesus?* (Chicago, Ill.: African American Images, 1987).

25. Tom Sharp and George N. Schmidt. "How Chicago Cheats." Substance, 24:10, (June 14, 1999).

26. Lori Olszewski. "True or False: Teachers are Part of the Solution, Not the Problem in School Reform." *Chicago Tribune Magazine*, (August 18, 2002), p. 10. See also Rosalind Rossi. "Who Can Fix Schools First?" *Chicago Sun-Times, Metro,* p. 9.

27. Lori Olszewski. "True or False: Teachers are Part of the Solution, Not the Problem in School Reform." *The Chicago Tribune Magazine*, (August 18, 2002), p.11–12.

28. Lynn Olson. "Chicago Panel to Devise Curriculum-Based Tests to Guide Teaching." *Education Week*, (January 8, 2003), p. 7

29. Payne, op. cit.

30. Lisa Fine. "Disparate Measures." *Education Week*, (June 19, 2002), p.30.

31. Diane Rado. "School Day Falls Short in Poorer Districts." *The Chicago Tribune.* (Sunday, September 29, 2002), Frontpage.

32. *Every Child, Every School: An Education Plan for the Chicago Public Schools*, (Chicago, Ill.: Chicago Public Schools, September, 2002).

33. Editorial, *The Chicago Tribune*, (December 26, 2002), p. 26.

34. Letter to the Editor, Deborah Lynch. "Teachers are important part of solution in schools." *The Chicago Tribune*, (January 2, 2003), p. 16.

35. Carter G. Woodson. *The Miseducation of the Negro.* (Washington, D.C.: The Associated Press, 1932).

36. Jules Henry. *Is Education Possible? Are We Qualified to Enlighten Dissenters? In Public Controls for Nonpublic Schools* edited by Donald A. Erickson. (Chicago, Ill.: University of Chicago Press, 1969), 83-102.

37. Jennifer A. O'Day. "Complexity, Accountability and School Improvement." *Harvard Educational Review.* 72:3, (Fall, 2002), 293–329.

38. Lori Olszewski. "Improving Schools Get Bonus." *The Chicago Tribune*, (Wednesday, October 30, 2002), Frontpage.

39.   *Ibid*, p. 15.

40.   James P. Pinkerton. "A Grand Compromise. Saving American Education Requires Ending the Reliance of Rublic Schools on Local Property Tax Bases. The State of the Union." *Atlantic Monthly*, (January/February 2003), 115.

Endnotes for Chapter Eight The School Achievement Structure and the Structured Ten Routines

1.   Graham T. Allison. *The Essence of Decision: Explaining the Cuban Missile Crisis.* (Boston: Little, Brown, 1971).

2.   Thomas Kuhn. *The Structure of Scientific Revolutions.* Second Edition, 2:2, (Chicago, Ill: University of Chicago Press, 1962), p. 24.

3.   *Ibid*, p. 10.

4.   *Ibid*, p.52.

5.   *Ibid*, p. 65.

6.   *Ibid*, p. 77.

7.   Dan McGraw. "Inspired Students." *U.S. News & world Report*, (January 18, 1999), 68–70.

8.   Nell Lewis. "You Get What You Expect To Receive." Unpublished paper, (Dallas, Texas, 1999).

9.   Nell Lewis. "You Get What You Expect To Receive." Unpublished paper, Dallas, Texas, 1999.

10.   Daniel de Vise. "Harris: Hero or Villain?" *Compton Press Telegram*, (October 2,1995). A1.

11.   Hazel B. Steward. "School Reform in Region Three-CPS, written for a proposed book on School Reform." Unpublished. (Chicago, 1999).

12.   Steward, op. cit. "There has been a recent change in this trend as portions of the West Side, specifically the near West Side, have become gentrified. The building of the New United center, home of the Chicago Bulls and the Black Hawks has caused an economic revitalization of the area evidenced by a housing boom Abandoned building are being razed and once vacant property is now being developed. Unfortunately, the new six-figure housing in a community where the average per capital income $6057 is out of the economic

range of the current residents."

13. Rollie Outlaw Jones. "School Achievement Structure." Unpublished paper. (Chicago : School Achievement Structure, 1999).

14. G. Alfred Hess and Solomon Cytrynbaum. "The Effort to Redesign Chicago High Schools." (Evanston, Ill.: Northwestern University, School of Education and Social Policy. Center for Urban School Policy, 2000).

15. Edward T. Klunk. Memo To Wilfredo Ortiz. School Visit Reports High School Cluster North. (May 20, 2001).

Endnotes for Chapter 9 Eliminating the Achievement Gap

1. Lisa Fine. "Disparate Measures." *Education Week*, (June, 19, 2002), p.30.

2. Tom McCann. "Nightmare World." *The Chicago Tribune*, (January 24, 2003), Frontpage.

3. Anthony S. Bryk and Barbara Schneider. *Trust in Schools: A Core Resource for Improvement.* A Volume in the American Sociological Association's Rose Series in Sociology. (New York, N.Y.: Russell Sage Foundation,2002).

4. *Ibid*, p. 21.

5. Jacob W. Getzels, James M. Lipham and Roald F. Campbell. *Educational Administration As a Social Process: Theory, Research, Practice.* (New York, N.Y. Harper & Row Publishers, 1968).

6. Bryk and Schneider, pp. 112–113.

7. *Ibid*, p.99.

8. *Ibid*, pp. 101–102.

9. *Ibid*, p. 84.

10. Marable, op. cit.,321.

11. Thelma Perry, "Tackling the Myth of Black Students' Intellectual Inferiority," *The Chronicle of Higher Education*, (January 10, 2003), B10-12.

12. Camille Z. Charles and Douglas S. Massey. "How Stereotypes Sabotage Minority Students," *The Chronicle of Higher Education*, (January 10, 2003), B10–11.

13. Maurice Possley and Steve Mills, "Clemency for All" *The Chicago Tribune*, (January 12, 2003), *Frontpage*.

14. Mary Schmich, "Emmett Till Photo Won't Let Us Ignore Evil," *The Chicago Tribune*, (January 12, 2003), Section 4, page 1.

15. Manning Marable. *The Great Wells of Democracy. The Meaning of Race in American Life*. (New York, N.Y.: Basic Civitas Books, 2002), 12.

16. Marable, op. cit., 43. Quote from Paul Gaston, "My University Under Attack: The Anti-Affirmative Action Brigade Comes to Virginia," Southern Changes, 21:2, (Summer 1999), p. 10.

17. Fran Spielman and Rosalind Rossi. "Daley Unmoved By School Critique." *The Chicago Sun-Times*, (Thursday, January 9, 2003), 12.

Index

A

B

C

U

V

W

December 17, 1927–July 24, 2004

Barbara Ann Sizemore was a devoted mother, author, educator, public speaker, and scholar. She worked diligently to bring equal access and educational opportunities to black children and underserved people of all ethnicities. Barbara's foundational philosophy was that "All children can learn." As a result of this principle, she worked vigorously to close the achievement gap between black and white students. The success she achieved in this vein will continually serve as a beacon to educators everywhere.

In her youth, Barbara inherited her commitment to education from her mother (Delila Mae Alexander Stewart,) and her provocative personality from her father (Sylvester Walter Laffoon.) She attended Northwestern University in Evanston Illinois, earning both her BA (1947) and MA (1954) from the prestigious school. While at Northwestern, she pledged Delta Sigma Theta and later became the founding member of the Evanston North Shore Alumni Chapter. In 1979, she earned a Ph.D. from the University of Chicago in Educational Administration.

Barbara was a teacher and administrator with the Chicago Public Schools from 1947 to 1972; the first African American woman to be appointed Superintendent of a major city school system (Superintendent of Schools for Washington, D.C. from 1973–1975); Professor and Interim Chair of The Department of Black Community, Research and Education at the University of Pittsburgh from 1977 to 1992 (Professor Emeritus, 1992); and Dean of the School of Education at DePaul University, Chicago, Illinois from 1992 to 1998 (Professor Emeritus, 1998).

In Pittsburgh, she worked to desegregate the Pittsburgh Public Schools. She was also an instrumental member of Pittsburghers Against Apartheid, an organization that struggled to end apartheid in South Africa. In 1992, she returned to her home, Chicago, where she began her tenure as the Dean of the School of Education at DePaul University. At DePaul she founded the School Achievement Structure, an organization that utilized the "Structured Ten Routines,™" a model that accelerates achievement and educational excellence in under-achieving schools and districts. Barbara lectured to thousands of educators and organizations about this model and other educational issues.

She has received numerous awards and recognitions including: Northwestern University Merit Award, 1974; U.S. National Commission for UNESCO, 1974–1977; United Nations Association of Pittsburgh Human Rights Award, 1985; Presidential Award from the National Council of Black Studies for Community Service, Promotion of Black Studies and Scholarship, 1991; Racial Justice Award, YWCA, 1995; Detroit Public Schools Distinguished Educator Award, 1997; Sigma Gamma Rho Pearl Award, 1997; Phi Delta Kappa, Distinguished Educator Award, 1998; Charles D. Moody Service Award, National Alliance of Black School Educators, 1999; Harold Delaney Educational Leadership Award, American Association of Higher Education, 1999, New Jersey Association of Parent Coordinators Award, 2000 and most recently History Makers 2003 to name a few. She holds four honorary doctorate degrees from Delaware State College at Dover, Delaware, 1974; Central State University, Xenia, Ohio, 1974; Baltimore College of the Bible, Baltimore, Maryland, 1975; and Niagara University, Niagara, New York, 1994.

Barbara was a well-recognized scholar and author of *The Ruptured Diamond: The Politics of the Decentralization of the District of Columbia Public Schools*, she has also penned over twenty chapters in books and twenty articles in journals.

Yet, the honors and awards do not tell the whole story. Barbara was a tireless truth-teller and an exceptional speaker who spent much of her time studying and teaching. She would often remind us of what Fredrick Douglass said, "Without a struggle, there can be no progress," therefore she would read veraciously to be armed for the struggle to right injustices against civil and human rights. Always energetic and vivacious she did not tarry in this work even through her recent personal trial. She was a strong, independent, loving, and giving woman. She was generous with all that she had and touched many lives with her caring soul in ways that extended far beyond her professional accomplishments.